HOW TO OBTAIN YOUR U.S. IMMIGRATION VISA
FOR A PERMAMENT STAY.

The Immigrant Visa Or Green Card Kit.

Immigration Manual Volume 2

By
Benji O. Anosike, B.B.A., M.A., Ph.D

Library of Congress Cataloging-in-Publication Data

Anosike, Benji O.
    Immigration manual / by Benji O. Anosike.
        p. cm.
    Includes bibliographical references and index.
    Contents: v. 1. How to obtain your U.S. immigration visa for a temporary stay : the
nonimmigrant visa kit -- v. 2. How to obtain your U.S. immigration visa for a permanent
stay : the immigrant visa or green card kit.
    ISBN 0-932704-52-2 (v. 1) -- ISBN 0-932704-53-0 (v. 2)
    1. Emigration and immigration law--United States--Popular works. 2. Visas--United
States--Popular works. I. Title.

KF4819.6.A562 2003
342.73'082--dc21

2002041610

Printed in the United States of America
ISBN: 0-932704 –53-0

Library of Congress Catalog Number:

Published by:

Do-It-Yourself Legal Publishers
60 Park Place
Newark, NJ 07102

Acknowledgments

Our profound thanks and gratitude go to the following persons and organizations: Colorado's C. James Cooper, Jr., the immigration legal practitioner and authority, the author of *The American Immigration Tapes*, and its *Form Book*, whose illustrated printed forms (and other information) are extensively reproduced in this manual (particularly in its Volume 1) for illustrative purposes; immigration lawyer and author Dan P. Danilov of Seattle, Washington, and his publisher, *Self-Counsel Press, Inc.*, from whose book, *"Immigrating To The U.S."*, a limited number of select forms are reproduced for our own illustrative purposes; lawyer and author of *The Green-Card Book*, Richard Madison of New York city, from whose publication we reproduced a few select forms or tables for their great value as illustrative tools. Others whose works proved particularly fitting, relevant and useful for the purpose of this manual and specialized readership for which it is intended, include Christopher C. Henry's *How To Win The U.S. Immigration Game* (The O'Brien Press, Dublin 6, Ireland); and the two ACLU books, David Carliner's *The Rights of Aliens* (Avon Books, 1977), and David Carliner, et al's *The Rights of Aliens and Refugees* (Southern Illinois University Press: 1990); and *The Federal Immigration Laws and Regulations*, 1998 Edition, published by West Group, and many, many others, too numerous to mention herein.

All have, in one way or the other, and by your deed, pioneering works and/or research in the field – and by your ever unselfish readiness to share and to disseminate the fruits thereof – made the present undertaking both more purposeful and easier for the present author and his publisher.

The Publisher's Disclaimer

✳ *Praise For* ✳

The Previous Edition of *"How To Obtain Your U.S. Immigration Visa."*
Here are what the **EXPERTS** say:

"...refreshing to encounter so much information about visa (laws and procedures) ... step-by-step procedures are clear and forthright ... such good research (with sample forms and illustrated sheets) that the result is a very valuable book, and because of the dearth of latest information on immigration laws, this volume(s) will be a useful addition to any library or individual seeking immigration information."
—— **Vic A. Kassery,** Asst. Exec. Editor
Patrician (Radio/TV) Productions, N.Y.

"Whether prospective immigrants to the U.S. decide to hire a lawyer or do it themselves, it will help if they thoroughly understand the immigration process. This manual (provides such information) ... The steps to be taken to obtain an immigrant (or non-immigrant) visa, are outlined, including the procedures to obtain labor certification ... A useful public library book." —— American Library Association's **The Booklist.**

"Information-packed guide which emphasizes both a practical understanding of how visa laws operate and how one may be obtained without a lawyer's advice ... a lot of information ... and many technical explanations of how visa standards are applied to individuals and families."
—— The Midwest Book Review's **The Bookwatch**
(Book was the "Reviewer's Choice" selection of the month)

"Anosike's book is full of many positive elements ... useful contents, and index."
—— **Matindale-Hubbell's Legal Publishing Preview.**

"This (2003 edition) two-volume manual is extremely useful in showing the step-by-step process for foreign nationals to qualify for a grant of entry visa into the U.S. Full descriptions are given to each kind of visa by which one can gain entry into this country... possible problem areas are brought to light ... The author even takes the reader inside the U.S. immigration office to see how things work there. A handy and unique reference."
—— American Library Association's **The Booklist.**

TABLE OF CONTENTS

Chapter 4
KEY PROBLEM AREAS FOR ALIENS SEEKING A GREEN CARD ON THE BASIS OF HAVING A FAMILY-RELATIONSHIP WITH A U.S. CITIZEN OR IMMIGRANT VISAHOLDER

Chapter 5
THE IMMIGRANT VISA QUOTA SYSTEM: HOW IT WORKS, AND THE WAITING PERIOD INVOLVED

Chapter 6
GETTING YOUR IMMIGRANT VISA (The Green Card) BASED ON YOUR BEING MARRIED TO A U.S. CITIZEN OR PERMANENT RESIDENT ALIEN

Chapter 7
THE K-I VISA: SPECIAL ENTRY VISA FOR FINANCE(E)S ENGAGED TO MARR BY A U.S. CITIZEN

Chapter 8
GFTTING YOUR IMMIGRANT VISA BASED ON BEING A CHILD OF A U.S. CITIZEN OR PERMANENT RESIDENT: FILING AS A PARENT FOR A SON OR DAUGHTER

Chapter 9
GETTING YOUR IMMIGRANT VISA (The Green Card) BASED ON BEING A PARENT OF A U.S. CITIZEN: FILING AS A CHILD FOR YOUR FATHER OR MOTHER

Chapter 10
GETTING YOUR IMMIGRANT VISA (The Green Card) BASED ON BEING A BROTHER OR SISTER OR A U.S. CITIZEN

Chapter 11
GETTING AN IMMIGRANT VISA (The Green Card) BASED ON ADOPTION OF A NON-ORPHAN ALIEN CHILD

Chapter 12
GETTING AN IMMIGRANT VISA (The Green Card) BASED ON ADOPTION OF AN ORPHAN ALIEN CHILD

Chapter 13
GETTING YOUR IMMIGRANT VISA (The Green Card) BASED ON HAVING
EMPLOYMENT OR JOB SKILLS: THE FIRST PREFERENCE PRIORITY   WORKERS

Chapter 14
GETTING YOUR IMMIGRANT VISA (The Green Card) BASED ON HAVING EMPLOYMENT
OR JOB SKILLS: SECOND PREFERENCE OR 'EXCEPTIONAL ABILITY' PROFESSIONAL

Chapter 15
GETTING YOUR IMMIGRANT VISA (The Green Card) BASED ON HAVING
EMPLOYMENT OR JOB SKILLS: THE SKILLED OR UNSKILLED WORKERS ALIEN

Chapter 16
GETTING YOUR IMMIGRANT VISA (The Green Card) BASED ON
HAVING EMPLOYMENT OR SKILLS: SPECIAL IMMIGRANTS

Chapter 21
THAT VISA INTERVIEW

Chapter 22
ENTERING THE UNITED STATES: THE PROCESS OF GETTING ACTUALLY "ADMITTED" INTO THE COUNTRY AFTER YOU'VE GOT YOUR VISA IN HAND

Chapter 23
ALIEN LABOR CERTIFICATION: THE PROCEDURES FOR OBTAINING A CERTIFICATE

Chapter 24
LEGAL GROUNDS FOR INADMISSIBILITY OF ALIENS TO THE UNITED STATES

Chapter 25
INSIDE THE U.S. IMMIGRATION OFFICES: HOW THEY WORK, HOW TO GET THE BEST RESULTS IN YOUR VISA PROCESSING

APPENDICES

FOREWORD:
THE PUBLISHER'S MESSAGE

*Of all the mighty nations in the East or in the West
This glorious Yankee nation is the greatest and the
best;
We have room for all creation and our banner is
unfurled,
Here's a general invitation to the people of the world.
Come along, come along, make no delay.
Come from every nation, come from every way.....*

So reads a passage from a 19th Century American Ballad

To All Our Readers:

The subject matter of immigration to the United States of America – the governing laws, the ways and means, and procedures by which persons may officially gain entry into, or stay in the United States – has always been a "hot", deeply felt subject for America, in deed the world, for as long as the United States has existed as a nation. In the interest of brevity, suffice it to say, simply, that the United States can legitimately lay claim to its historical reputation as a "nation of immigrants" – a nation whose citizens are overwhelmingly the sons and daughters and descendents of persons who came to United States from other lands. With the subject of immigration, one at once finds the one subject about which there's so common an experience shared by all of us AMERICANS; hence the great emotions and ambivalence with which this matter has been treated historically in America!

It requires no great intellect, therefore, for one to see that *a working knowledge of, or at least some familiarity with, the matter of who gets to be selected for admission into the country, or excluded or expelled from it, and how and why, is an issue that is of crucial interest and importance to a great many American citizens and residents, as well as foreign nationals the world over.*

What this Manual Will Do for you

HOW TO OBTAIN YOUR U.S. IMMIGRATION VISA WITHOUT A LAWYER, is primarily concerned with one fundamental but limited aspect of the immigration issue: 'the knots and bolts' of securing a U.S. entry visa; exposition of the officially prescribed requirements and procedures by which the foreign national may qualify for a visa under the laws and regulations of the immigration authorities; and the actual preparation and assembling of such requirements and its filing with the immigration authorities who grant the visa. *In brief, with a working knowledge or mastery of the contents of this manual, YOU (any foreign national) will know what and what requirements and qualifications you need to have in order to be eligible for a grant of entry permit into the United States, or to stay in the country if already admitted; and, even more important, you will, solely by YOURSELF and without any "expert" assistance, be able to undertake all the filing procedures necessary for you to apply for and obtain the type of entry visa, immigrant or non-immigrant, which you desire and qualify*

---

*Quoted from *"The Rights of Aliens.* The Basic ACLU Guide to An Alien's Rights, by David Carliner (Avon Books: 1977). p.25

for. And, if you are a U.S. citizen or a permanent resident already, you will be able to determine whether or not you qualify to bring your family members to the U.S., and how to actually do so; and if you are an official of a corporation or business or institution, you will be able to master the process by which you can hire a foreign national to work for you in a vital capacity.

One fundamental premise underlies this manual: Whatever else may be said to be involved in obtaining an entry visa by which an alien can become lawfully admitted into (or to remain in) the United States, the process itself is, at its most basic level, primarily a clerical and ministerial operation, requiring no complex "legal" procedures or expertise or any specialized technical theories or knowledge of law, or one which calls for a lawyer or other such professional. Rather, all it calls for is merely a simple knowledge of the types of documentations or other evidence you need present to establish your eligibility for a given class of visa, and the ability to write up or gather such documentations for the benefit of the immigration authorities.

The National Scope – And Purpose – of This Manual

HOW TO OBTAIN YOUR U.S. IMMIGRATION VISA aims, first and foremost, at providing at "street level" to the people directly affected – namely, the aliens and foreign nationals, themselves, who seek or desire entry into or to stay in the United States – the practical tools and knowledge with which they can, themselves, seek their objectives, and in a relatively inexpensive, affordable and accessible way open to the ordinary man and woman all the world over. Similarly, the handbook is aimed at providing vital knowledge of the basics involved for the benefit of the immigration-related non-specialists engaged in various religious, civic and community organizations, voluntary agencies, non-profit organizations and other recognized public interest groups across the United States who counsel and assist aliens with various immigration-related needs and problems inside and outside the United States.

The book is published in two (2) volumes for purposes of simplicity of exposition and greater ease of comprehension of the material contents. Volume 1 deals with the procedures of obtaining the *temporary* type of U.S. visa – The NON-IMMIGRANT visa; and Volume 2, deals with the procedures of obtaining the *permanent* type of U.S. visa – The IMMIGRANT visa or Green Card.

Long-standing Recognition OF Need for a Guidebook of this Kind

This manual could not be more timely or its contents more relevant or needed for our present historical times. Even as we speak (and, even as you, the reader, probably goes through the contents herein!), the world increasingly promises to get still smaller and smaller. It's simply inevitable! With astronomical technological changes continuing – and destined – to occur all over the world and rapidly transforming the world into one "inter-related global environment," and with the historic revolutionary upheavals which have been occurring in the recent history of Asia, Eastern Europe, even in Africa and other parts of the world, which promise to sweep away (or at least chip away at) the major historical differences and barriers between social, economic and political systems among peoples and nations of the world, one thing is almost certain, namely: *the attraction and the attractiveness of the United States as the "land of opportunity" and the "last beacon of hope" for those in search of political freedom or economic betterment throughout the world, is all two likely to increase, not decrease.* The sounds and signs are all around us, and every bit of world event and evidence around the world suggest that America of the present and immediate future, is likely to see not less, but a lot more discussions and concerns centering around such immigration-related historic anxieties as the "influx" of "illegal aliens," the need for "defense of American borders" or the "amnesty program", and the issue of the "undocumented aliens", the "boat people," "refugees", and so on and so forth. This manual, it is hoped and intended, will help America – and the citizens of the world – to better understand and cope with such matters or developments, and in a more responsible and rational manner.

In deed, immigration administrators and workers, policy makers, volunteer agencies and operatives, and even legal practitioners who work in the area of immigration matters, have long seemingly recognized the crying need for a <u>practical</u> manual such as this book and hungered for one. And many of them, frustrated and unable to find such practical guide books or programs for use in their day-to-day work or encounters with their immigrant clients, have from time to time bemoaned the unavailability or inaccessibility of such practical materials.

Thus, as far back as 1986, C. James Cooper, Jr., a Denver Colorado immigration attorney who is one of the few and earliest among the crop of legal practitioners and experts in the field of U.S. immigration, draws a powerful but vivid portrait of the kind of reality in America's immigration world which now underlies the rationale for the publication of the present manual. Cooper sums it all up this way:

> "I have felt for a long time that there has been a need for an immigration program that would give people a better understanding about our immigration laws and policies. There are very few, if any public sources for this information.
>
> Public libraries, generally, do not.... Even if they do, it is difficult to find information on some of the "dos and don'ts" of immigration. The (U.S.) Immigration Service is very helpful in giving you the necessary immigration forms; however, they cannot legally give you advice. I have had many clients who relied on advice from well intended friends and relatives which was either misleading or misunderstood.....
>
> Qualified immigration attorneys (lawyers) are a good source of information ... However, in many cases you may only need one consultation to clarify some problem area or to get an assessment on whether you have a good chance of getting what you want or whether you should anticipate some problems....
>
> There are many things you can do by yourself without the need for any legal assistance....(and a handbook of the type will hopefully)..... guide you through some of these areas by giving you practical points on what has worked in the past and to prepare you for any potential problems.
>
> For those areas which could cause problems (from what you may discover from the knowledge you gather from your reading of the handbook), it may be worthy your time and expense to consult an attorney at least once .... As a result, you will have a better understanding about your situation and can then decide if you want to proceed (by yourself) after the consultation.
>
> (Indeed, even) if you decide you'd (rather) use the services of an attorney to prepare your entire case, [still you can benefit by reading such as guidebook, for]..... the more information you have about our immigration system, the better are your chances for getting a visa. ***Experience shows us that the most successful people are those who have the best information. I assure you, as an attorney with many years (over 40 years) of experience, that clients who have understood the immigration system and knew what to expect, were usually successful.*** This is due in large part, because such clients knew what to anticipate, and, as a result, were easily able to contribute relevant information...they were more relaxed and confident in any contacts they had with either (the) immigration or the Consulates"*

Translated, the central point is: whichever route you, the alien, intend to go, whether, on the one hand, you will choose to file for the American entry or residency visa yourself and completely pursue it by yourself; or, on the other hand, you will choose to engage the services of an immigration lawyer to do it for you in part or in whole, having this practical handbook in hand would still be to your invaluable advantage and helpfulness as a visa seeker, and might even spell the critical difference between your successfully obtaining one and your not

---

*Quoted from "AMERICAN IMMIGRATION TAPES" (Text), Allterra Visas. Ltd., 1986 pp. 1-2. Passage is quoted in such extensive detail as it makes the present publisher's intended point so well.

obtaining one!!

The New World of Terrorism & The New Age of U.S. Immigration Policy of The Post-September 11ᵗʰ 2001 Era!

In deed, even as this book is readied or goes to press, one recent, humongous, world-changing event that literally exploded on the world scene in the United States, has, in and of itself, single-handedly made the need for this manual even far more particularly timely and necessary both for the U.S. visa-seeker (present and future) and the U.S. immigration professionals and authorities: the catastrophe of September 11ᵗʰ 2001 and the epoch-making crashing of airplanes into the U.S. Pentagon and the famed World Trade Center twin towers in New York. Since that event, American authorities of all level – and its general public – have since learned, needless to say to their utter regrets and chagrin, that almost all of the highjackers involved in the deadly act, were foreign nationals, and that most of them had entered the country on temporary visas that had been readily and easily granted them by U.S. embassy and consulate officials largely with little or no screening or controls, or any follow-up checks after they have entered the country.

One fundamental reality is crystal clear already: namely, that in light of the heightened anxiety in America about foreigners in the wake of the event of September 11ᵗʰ 2001, and the general outcry among the nation's policy makers and politicians about the U.S. immigration system that is said to be "lax" and "riddled with loopholes," the immigration procedures of the U.S. will likely see many changes and tightening up in the

immediate future. They'll likely be, however, mainly in the area of greater screening, scrutiny and control of the visa granting requirement and procedures, and the monitoring of visa holders and non-U.S. citizens once they are in the country. *Whatever the nature and parameters of the future immigration policy, however, in the end simply having a copy of HOW TO OBTAIN YOUR U.S. IMMIGRATION VISA in hand, and making certain to understand and master the contents and procedures outlined therein, will still go a long way in aiding the reader to better understand the types of immigration issues that are likely to arise, anyway and how to address and handle them properly and successfully.*

Here's The Fundamental Essence and Message of This Book

In point of fact, the point of HOW TO OBTAIN YOUR U.S. IMMIGRATION VISA, should not be mistaken or misunderstood. We emphasize that the cardinal aim of this manual is neither to debunk the actual or potential usefulness of ever employing the services of a competent immigration lawyer or other professionals in all circumstances, nor to advocate solely a do-it-yourself approach by the alien or the non-professional in all circumstances. Rather, *the objective position of the manual is that, if equipped with a basic understanding of its workings and process, the non-lawyer and non-specialist could do just as good a job as, perhaps even a better job (and definitely a less expensive one!) than the average lawyer in applying for or securing the average U.S. visa. And it is specifically contended that this is so especially with respect to the more usual, routine types of cases which, as a rule, are generally clerical and straightforward, hardly involving any complex or technical issues of law or policy.*

Thank you all again   Do-It-Yourself Legal Publishers

Newark N.J

9/11 (2001)!

POSTSCRIPT

THE NEW IMMIGRATION ERA OF POST-SEPTEMBER 11TH 2001! A NOTE ABOUT THE PROBABLE FUTURE WAY OF DOING IMMIGRATION BUSINESS IN AMERICA

A. "LAX" U.S. IMMIGRATION SYSTEM PRIOR TO SEPTEMBER 11TH 2001?

True to its historical reputation as the "land of opportunity" and the "last beacon of hope" for people in search of political freedom or economic betterment throughout the world, American has always been known, far and wide, by friends, as well as by foes, as a free, pluralistic and open society readily welcoming of and receptive to foreign persons and foreign ideas alike. *In deed, America's diversity, its free market economy and free-wheeling brand of democracy, are held to be the unique quality that makes America a nation distinctly different from all other countries in the modern world.*

Unfortunately, however, most likely these American realities and qualities about America would soon change. They are likely to change in terms, particularly, of the way in which America views the foreigner, especially the foreign person seeking entry into the United States, or who is already within the country. Simply summed up, the world-changing catastrophe of the now infamous September 11th 2001 crashing of airplanes into the U.S. Pentagon and the famed New York's World Trade Center twin towers by persons who turned out to be foreigners who entered the country largely on easily obtained temporary visas, has provoked such a heightened anxiety among Americans about foreigners and about the nation's immigration system and procedures. The general outcry has emerged across America among the nation's policy makers and politicians that the American immigration system is too "lax" and "riddled with loopholes," in that, it is commonly claimed, it failed to ferret out the vicious foreign highjackers. Given this prevailing mood all across the country, *one thing certainly seems rather crystal clear already, even this early, namely: the immigration procedures of the United States will almost certainly see many changes and tightening up in the near future.*

B. THE PROBABLE CHANGES OF THE FUTURE

What, exactly, is the specific nature or the parameters of the changes that will probably come about? That remains to be seen for now (as of this writing). This much can be said with some degree of certainty, however: the changes will likely be primarily in the area of a greater screening and tightening up of the requirements and procedures of the visa granting system for visa applicants, and of the monitoring of visa holders and non-U.S. citizens who enter or stay in the country.

The new immigration law and system will probably center around immigration-control measures such as the following:

• a moratorium on issuing student visas

• establishment of an "exit lane" control – a measure which systematically matches entries by foreign students and visitors into the U.S. with corresponding exits, thereby being able to identify those who have overstayed their visas

• greater vigilance and tracking measures on foreign students and foreigners to detect those of them who have overstayed their student, tourist, visitors or temporary work visas

• creation of electronic databank on foreign students which will be accessible to U.S. law enforcement authorities

• placing vital control information on ALL visa applicants and holders on database, such as the National Crime Information Center, used by federal and local law enforcement officials, and making such information accessible to all agencies with a need to know, including the airlines

• sharing of F.B.I. crime records with the U.S. Consulates and Embassies overseas

• legal authority by federal agents to detain immigrants (non U.S. citizens) on mere suspicious of being a terrorist or having a terrorist background or intention.

• devotion of more personnel and more senior staff to the visa reviewing process by U.S. embassies and the INS

• requiring American universities and employers to keep the INS informed when a visa holder is no longer attending classes or no longer working, and when the foreign student's immigration status changes.

• instituting a mandatory waiting period in the processing of temporary visas – some 20 to 30 days – to allow the immigration staff time to check an applicant's name against lists and to run it by the foreigner's hometown authorities.

• requiring every person to apply for a visa in his country of origin as that is where his or her local authorities will be familiar with his/her past history and record

• tighter security restrictions and stricter scrutiny at crossings along the nation's international borders (Mexico, Canada, and the like), including running background checks on foreigners; and

• tighter enforcement of immigration laws and crackdown on illegal immigration and illegal aliens by the INS.

C. BUT HERE'S THE GOOD NEWS FOR ALIENS

BUT HERE'S THE OTHER SIDE OF THE STORY, THE "GOOD NEWS" PART FOR YOU, THE FOREIGN VISA-SEEKER: nothing in the kinds of measures and reforms envisaged remotely suggest that America will not still remain a "nation of immigrants" that it has always been, regardless, a nation that still welcomes and takes in foreigners, and probably in the same huge numbers as previously. Only that, this time, it will be more scrutinizing and more verifying of their backgrounds in doing so. In other words, for a foreign person, the new visa processing and granting procedures may cause a little more inconvenience than before, or take a little more time. But, in the end, if you are a qualified visa applicant (or resident alien), any way, if you have no criminal background or evil intent on America, then you still have nothing to worry about as a foreigner. You'll still get your visa to come to America, just as well, and you'll still be welcomed into America just as well; the same as you would have BEFORE the infamous September 11th 2001 event! *In a word, only for the "bad guys" have the rules of the immigration game for getting an American visa or for getting admitted into or living in America really changed, in the final analysis.*

Just months before the awesome September 11th 2001 event, America city planners and governments were busy outbidding each other to attract immigrants. They offered grants and various "immigrant-friendly" incentive programs and packages to lure immigrants to their localities to help revive their economies and, as one report put it. "help restock urban neighborhood populations that shrank as the middle-class moved to the suburbs." (See a New York Times newspaper headline of May 30th 2001 below). Don't suppose that this sort of trend is necessarily going to be all dead just because of September 11!

To Fill Gaps, Cities Seek Foreigners

HEAD COUNT

Moving In From Abroad

The top 25 metropolitan areas by net international migration from 1990 to 1999 as a percentage of estimated 1999 population.

RANK	METROPOLITAN AREA	NET INTERNATIONAL MIGRATION	AS PERCENTAGE OF 1999 POPULATION	1999 POPULATION
1	Miami	337,174	15.5%	2,175,634
2	New York	974,599	11.2%	8,712,600
3	Los Angeles-Long Beach	902,097	9.7%	9,329,989
4	Orange County, Calif.	233,168	8.4%	2,760,948
5	San Diego	164,016	5.8%	2,820,844
6	Oakland, Calif.	135,027	5.7%	2,348,723
7	Houston	209,859	5.2%	4,010,969
8	Washington, D.C.	240,117	5.1%	4,739,999
9	Chicago	366,607	4.6%	8,008,507
10	Dallas	132,574	4.0%	3,280,310
11	Riverside-San Bernardino, Calif.	119,038	3.7%	3,200,587
12	Seattle-Bellevue-Everett	79,353	3.4%	2,334,934
13	Nassau-Suffolk, N.Y.	70,812	2.6%	2,688,904
14	Boston*	137,313	2.5%	5,423,689
15	Atlanta	82,580	2.1%	3,857,097
16	Denver	41,029	2.1%	1,978,991
17	Phoenix-Mesa	62,280	2.1%	3,013,696
18	Tampa-St. Petersburg-Clearwater, Fla.	42,826	1.9%	2,278,169
19	Philadelphia	91,672	1.9%	4,949,867
20	Minneapolis-St. Paul	45,981	1.6%	2,872,109
21	Detroit	68,449	1.5%	4,474,614
22	Baltimore	32,727	1.3%	2,491,254
23	St. Louis	25,310	1.0%	2,591,456
24	Cleveland-Lorain-Elyria	17,247	0.8%	2,221,181
25	Pittsburgh	8,935	0.4%	2,331,336

*Not the Boston primary metropolitan statistical area, but a group of counties that generally corresponds to the Boston area.

Source: Center for Social and Urban Research at the University of Pittsburgh, from Census Bureau estimates

BY THE NUMBERS

Legal Immigration

800,000

600000,

400,000

200,000

0

'79   '85   '90   '94

In addition to these immigrants, 2.7 million illegal aliens have become legal permanent residents under a 1986 law.

Source: Immigration and Naturalization Service

The New York Times

INTRODUCTION: HOW TO USE THIS MANUAL

DO YOU HAVE THE RIGHT VOLUME OF THIS BOOK?

This book on U.S. immigration laws and visa procedures is organized, by deliberate and purposeful design, in two volumes. *Volume 1, How to Obtain Your U.S. Immigration Visa for a Temporary Stay: The Non-Immigrant Visa Kit,* deals with the rules and procedures for obtaining the **temporary** types of visa (see Section B.2 of Chapter 2). While Volume 2, *How To Obtain Your U.S. Immigration Visa for a Permanent Stay:* The *Immigration Visa or Green Card Kit,* deals with the same material but as it related to obtaining the **permanent** type of visa, the visa more commonly known to immigrants and visa-seeker as the "Green Card" (See Section B.1 of Chapter 2, and Chapter 3).

This is done for a simple reason: to make the book more manageable for the reader, and to make the contents better organized and more comprehensible for the benefit of the reader.

FIRST, KNOW THE RIGHT VISA YOU QUALIFY FOR OR SHOULD SEEK

Get this right into your head, if ever you are to be successful in the end in this business: the basic rule is that you first determine the type of visa for which you qualify, and that visa – and only that – is the visa you then apply for. As a rule, if all that you did wrong is to apply for the wrong visa, in the first place, or to apply for a visa in the wrong visa category, (say, a student visa when you should have applied for a visitors, or an immigrant visa when you should have gone for a non-immigrant visa), you've just about guaranteed to lose out from the very start just for that single error alone!

Here's what you do in simple terms:

- First, determine whether you should apply for (whether you seemingly have the required qualifications for) a non-immigrant (temporary) type of visa, or for an immigrant (permanent) type. Go to Chapter 2 for the answer to this all-important question.
- Next, if you think you most likely qualify for a temporary visa and can possibly meet the requirements for one, then the book you need is Volume 1 of this manual. But if you're best suited for a permanent visa, you should go to Volume 2.
- In each of the two Volumes, the book is organized into separate chapters with each chapter devoted to a specific green card (in Volume 2), or a specific non-immigrant visa category (in Volume 1). For the Volume you pick, you may then zero in on the chapter which fits your specific situation and read those ones. And once you find that you meet substantially all the qualifications necessary for the particular visa of your choice - and will be able to document and prove it to the U.S. immigration authorities – you may then commence the application procedures outlined in the appropriate chapters, accordingly.
- If you find you do not meet all or most of the requirements for the first visa choice you made, you may consider "going back to the drawing board" – check another kind of visa or category; you may better have the requirements for that. Or, if all else fails for the moment, rather than rush into making an application for the wrong kind of visa and possibly lose all chances of getting a U.S. visa in the future, you may consider just cooling it for now. Go back, perhaps, and consider how you can possibly change the present conditions in your life so that you can meet the prescribed requirements over time to be able to get that green card or other temporary visa you want.

CHART 2.

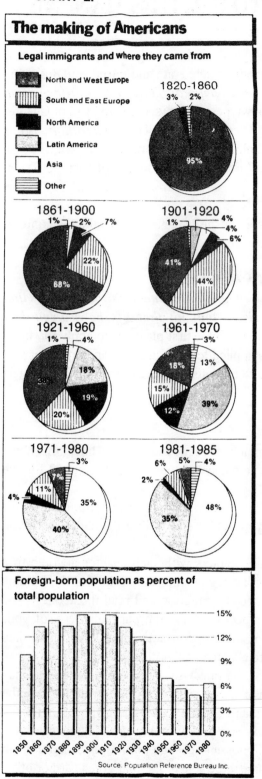

The making of Americans

Legend immigrants and where they came from

- North and West Europe
- South and East Europe
- North America
- Latin America
- Asia
- Other

1820-1860
3% 2%
95%

1861-1900
1% 2% 7%
22%
68%

1901-1920
1% 4% 4% 6%
41% 44%

1921-1960
1% 4%
18%
19%
20%

1961-1970
3%
18% 13%
15%
12% 39%

1971-1980
3%
7%
11%
4%
35%
40%

1981-1985
6% 5% 4%
2%
35% 48%

Foreign-born population as percent of total population

15%
12%
9%
6%
3%
0%

1850 1860 1870 1880 1890 1900 1910 1920 1930 1940 1950 1960 1970 1980

Source: Population Reference Bureau Inc.

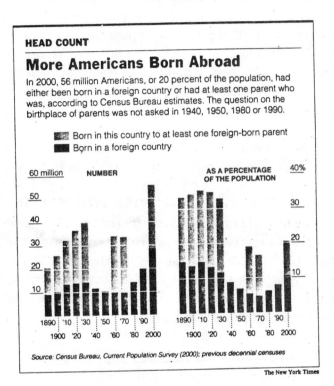

HEAD COUNT

More Americans Born Abroad

In 2000, 56 million Americans, or 20 percent of the population, had either been born in a foreign country or had at least one parent who was, according to Census Bureau estimates. The question on the birthplace of parents was not asked in 1940, 1950, 1980 or 1990.

- Born in this country to at least one foreign-born parent
- Born in a foreign country

60 million NUMBER   AS A PERCENTAGE OF THE POPULATION 40%
50   30
40   20
30
20   10
10

1890 '10 '30 '50 '70 '90 2000
1900 '20 '40 '60 '80

1890 '10 '30 '50 '70 '90 2000
1900 '20 '40 '60 '80

Source: Census Bureau, Current Population Survey (2000); previous decennial censuses

The New York Times

As cited in The New York Times,
Sunday, April 10, 1988 p.E5.

THE NEW YORK TIMES **METROPOLITAN** *SUNDAY, MARCH 11, 1990*

Alien Students Learn More Education Is the Key

By MARVINE HOWE

It was Rap Day at John Dewey High School last week, and most of the workshops focused on sex and drugs. But in room 343, it was standing room only as students, teachers and professionals discussed the really hot topic of the times — the rights of illegal immigrant children.

Lawyers and other experts emphasized to the students that New York City's public schools are open to all young people, whether or not they are in the country legally. They also passed out Board of Education leaflets welcoming "undocumented and documented immigrants" in six languages.

"But if I can't get a job, why should I get an education?" an Asian teenager asked, expressing the frustration of many undocumented students. For illegal teen-agers, the 1986 Immigration Reform and Control Act has been both an opportunity and an obstacle. The act offered illegal aliens a brief amnesty in which to become legal, but also created stiff penalties for employers who hire illegals.

"Hope," responded Kathleen Jarvis, who heads the Advocates for Children's Immigrant Student Rights Project. "Eventually that law is going to change, so get your foot in the door and acquire a skill the United States needs."

Train Parents and Staff

Although figures vary widely for New York City's undocumented population, Columbia University's Center for Social Sciences conservatively estimated that after the expiration of the amnesty in May 1988, 250,000 undocumented aliens remained in the country, including 46,000 children.

The visit to John Dewey, in the Coney Island section of Brooklyn, was part of a program to help immigrant schoolchildren cope with the new system, and part of a day of discussions at the school. It was organized by the City Bar Association in New York and Advocates for Children, a nonprofit organization. They train school staff and parents, run seminars for students, and operate a telephone help line.

About 40 students signed up for the workshop. At least 80 showed up.

"There's a great need to reach out to immigrant schoolchildren who are afraid to ask for help," said Laurie Milder, director of the Bar Association's Community Outreach Law Program. She said about 60 immigration lawyers have volunteered their time.

Can They Get Financial Aid?

More than 1,000 of John Dewey's 3,000 students are foreign-born, and Ms. Milder and the other speakers faced a barrage of questions.

Are illegals entitled to go to college? Can they get financial aid? How can an illegal student get a green

During Rap Day at John Dewey High School lawyers and other experts tried to assuage some students' fears that being undocumented immigrants would prevent them from getting jobs. Kathleen Jarvis, of the Advocates for Children's Immigrant Student Rights Project, was at right.

The New York Times/Vic DeLucia

Many youths are surprised to find that they can go to college.

card — permanent resident status? If an illegal student gives birth to a child here, can the mother stay in the country?

Ms. Jarvis told them that the 17 colleges of the City University of New York are open to undocumented students and do not require a student to show a Social Security number. Later she described the case of a 17-year-old star athlete in a Brooklyn high school who had been offered athletic scholarships by 13 universities. But, because she was an illegal immigrant, from the West Indies, and all the schools insisted on having a Social Security number, she had to go to CUNY.

Undocumented students used to pay nonresident tuition, double that of residents, in the city's colleges, but now they are eligible for the residents' rate.

Undocumented students are not yet eligible for Federal or state financial aid, Ms. Jarvis said. "But we advise you to take one or two courses because you'll hear about scholarships; it's like the lottery, you've got to be in it to win it."

Robert Washington, an immigration lawyer and former teacher, told the audience that while the amnesty period was over, there were other ways to become legal. Sponsorship by a close relative or acquisition of skills listed by the Labor Department as needed in the United States. Such categories include priest, minister or religious worker, physical therapist or someone of outstanding scientific or artistic ability.

An immigration judge would probably let the undocumented mother of an American-born baby stay "because the policy has been to keep families together as a general rule," Mr. Washington said.

Ms. Jarvis later described the case of a pregnant illegal teen-ager who was thrown out of her home and moved to a shelter. Lawyers said she was entitled to some welfare benefits "because she was carrying a U.S. citizen child," Ms. Jarvis said.

After the session ended — with a burst of applause — Enid Margolies, assistant principal, gathered a dozen students to prolong the discussion.

"Now maybe there's a chance for me to continue my studies," a Haitian boy of 14 said excitedly, explaining that he had not known City University accepted undocumented students. His parents had left him with an aunt, who is a United States resident, and she was willing to adopt him but her husband was reluctant.

A Cuban boy of 17, who came here more than four years ago, asked how to get a green card "so I can study and go into the Navy."

For specific problems, the students were told to call the Immigrant Students Legal Rights Helpline at (718) 729-8866.

In the past, most calls came from school counselors, but now it is mainly students who want to go to college, Ms. Jarvis said. Since undocumented students are generally afraid to disclose their identity, they are promised confidentiality and asked only their first name, age, country of origin and school.

Chapter 1
A Brief History Of American Immigration Laws & Trend: An Overview

A. A NATION OF IMMIGRANTS

The United States of America has often been described as 'truly a nation of immigrants'. As its now generally well-known history reveals, the United States was founded by immigrants – that is, by people who were not originally from the nation. And consequently, the subject of immigration and immigration laws, have always been central to the hearts and minds of the people in the United States. The vast majority of Americans (U.S. citizens) today are descendants of parents, grandparents or great-grand-parents who themselves came to the U.S. from other lands.

B. THE BEGINNINGS OF REGULATION OF IMMIGRATION

In terms of the country's immigration history, the motivating force which compelled the original wave of immigrants (other than, of course, the slave population and indentured servants) to leave their countries to settle in the United States, was to escape deprivation and persecution in their home countries. The new continent, once discovered by people from other lands (mostly from Europe), did not take long before it become a magnet to people from different countries, as they flocked to America primarily to escape negative forces in their home countries, and as a special "land of opportunity" – a place to start a new life and to make personal sacrifices in return for political, religious, and economic freedom and betterment.

Consequently, for the first 150 years of the founding of the United States, leading us to the end of the 19th century, there was basically no structured immigration policy for the United States; there was no control or limitation on the free-flow of people into and out of the country. However, starting from 1882, all that changed.

By 1882, brought on by the Gold Rush of 1849 in California, some 300,000 Chinese laborers (among others) had found their way to America from across the Pacific Ocean, contracted for labor primarily because of their very low cheap wages. The Chinese were highly valued for the cheap labor they provided for the nation's growing innumerable construction jobs, such as the construction of the Union Pacific Railroad, but were not granted the right to become citizens. Rather, because they were distinctly different from Americans in their skin color, culture, habits and looks, they were indiscriminately subjected to widespread racial discrimination and hatred by Americans. It culminated in the passage of the first restrictive immigration law in the history of the United States – the Chinese Exclusion Act of 1882, which completely banned non-citizen Chinese from immigrating to the United States.

Since the Chinese Exclusion Act of 1882, the United States immigration policy has developed and been modified periodically to meet the changing needs or desires of the nation. A series of immigration laws have been enacted, designed to place restriction on immigration and to control the type and number of people who may enter or stay in that country.

C. HIGHLIGHTS IN U.S. LEGISLATIVE IMMIGRATION HISTORY

The following are some of the major highlights in the legislative and legal history of immigration to the United States.

1798 – the Alien Act: This gave the President authority to expel aliens who he considered to be dangerous to the peace and security of the nation. Was terminated two years later, however.

1808 – U.S. Constitution, Article 1, Section 9: Constitutional amendment banned the importation of slaves.

1875 – Qualitative restrictions on immigration: Congress designated categories of aliens (communists, prostitutes, mental and physical incompetents) who were prohibited from entering the United States.

1882 – Chinese Exclusion Act: The increasing importation of low-wage Chinese labor resulted in growing public antagonism and racial hated. The law banned the future immigration of Chinese laborers into the United States and excluded them from citizenship, and remained in effect until 1943.

1892 – Amendment to the Chinese Exclusion Act: Required registration of Chinese laborers living in United States and authorized deportation if after one year they could not produce a certificate of registration.

1907 – Immigration Act: Restricted entry of immigrants over 16 years of age who were unable to read who came from central and eastern Europe, and permitted no immigration at all to the U.S. from the Asiatic Barred zone which included Orientals like China, Japan, India, Indochina, Iran, Arabia, etc. *This law marked the beginning of a great change in American immigration policy.*

1921 – First Quota law: After World War 1, with America facing economic depression and unemployment, the immigrant to America became the public scapegoat for the hard times and the mood of the country was such that Congress established the first numerical restrictions on immigration limiting the number of aliens of each nationality who were permitted into the United States to 3% of the foreign-born persons of that nationality living in American during the 1910 census, and allowing a total of approximately 350,000 to immigrate annually. (Aliens residing for one year in an independent country of the Western Hemisphere prior to admission to the United States, were exempt from the quota.)

1924 – National Origins Act: The 1921 law, which had been enacted as a temporary measure, was made permanent by this statute. For the first time, Congress established permanent numerical restrictions on immigration of aliens to the United States from all parts of the world, except the Western Hemisphere, under a ceiling of 150,000 per year, with national quotas based on the ethnic composition of the United States in the 1920 census. Prospective immigrants were required to obtain a sponsor in the United States and a visa from an American consulate abroad. Further restrictions were placed on Asian immigration, particularly prohibiting the immigration of all aliens who were ineligible for U.S. citizenship.

The object of the law was expressed to be "to arrest a trend toward a change in the fundamental composition of the American stock" – that is, not simply to limit immigration of certain aliens (e.g. those from southern and eastern Europe), but to favor certain kinds of immigrants (e.g. western Europeans) and keep out others completely (e.g.

Asians were completely excluded).

1940 - Alien Registration Act: All aliens in the United States were required to register and be fingerprinted. **The** exclusion and deportation of criminal and subversive groups was expanded.

1943 – Repeal of the Chinese Exclusion Act of 1882: Residents of China were now permitted to immigrate to the United States.

1945 – War Brides Act: With the end of World War II, the American immigration door was again to open – but this time, not so wide, and only for some carefully selected groups of aliens. By this law, Congress meant to facilitate the union and immigration of 118,000 alien spouses and children of members of the U.S. armed forces who had fought and married or fathered children overseas.

1948 – Displaced Persons Act: This legislation provided for the admission of 400,000 refugees from Germany, Italy, and Austria to the United States. These were mostly persons who had been displaced during the war from other countries (Poland, Romania, Hungary, the Baltic, Ukraine and Yugoslavia) and had been placed in refugee camps in these countries.

1952 – Immigration and Nationality Act (commonly called the MacCarran-Walter Act): This is the Basic immigration law of the United States, as we know it, although frequently amended. This legislation provides for family reunification, protection of the domestic labor force and the immigration of persons with needed skills. This law consolidated and codified under a single statute, all laws relating to immigration to the United States. It provided by national origins a quota system, and unrestricted numerical immigration to the U.S. from Western Hemisphere countries.

1953 – Refugee Relief Act: When the communist Iron Curtain fell on eastern Europe, by this law an additional 214,000 refugees from communist countries were admitted to the United States.

1965 – Immigration and Nationality Act Amendments: The racially-biased national origins quota system was repealed by this legislation. Basically, these amendments introduced two basic ways of becoming an American immigrant – by family relationship to an American citizen or immigrant, and by the employment and skills needs of the U.S. Thus, a new, eight-category *"preference system"* was instituted to reunite family relationships and admit aliens with talents or job skills on a "first come, first served" basis in each category. The new law provided an annual limitation of 170,000 for immigrants from Eastern Hemisphere (Asia, Europe and Africa), and applicants from this group were subject to a preference system, and had a quota limit of 20,000 per country; immigrants from North and South America, on the other hand, had a quota limit of 120,000 and applicants were not subject to the preference system. Spouses and children of U.S. citizens and parents of citizens over 21 were exempt from numerical ceilings. Requirements for labor certifications were instituted to control the admission of skilled or unskilled foreign workers. As a separate category, an annual admission of 10,000 refugees was authorized. *With this law a new phenomenon began to emerge in the U.S. immigration system: application of admissions policies without regard to national and racial origins.*

Not too long after these amendments were enacted, the impact of the new immigration policy began to be felt even worldwide. In the United States, for example, skilled workers, who had a higher "preference" under the law than unskilled workers, immigrated more easily and in greater numbers to the United States, and highly trained professionals (doctors, lawyers, engineers, scientists, accountants, nurses, teachers, etc) departed their home countries for the United States in large numbers, and caused a "brain drain" in their home countries around the developed and developing countries.

1976 – The Immigration and Nationality Act Amendments of 1976: The aim of this law was to eliminate the inequities in the existing law between Eastern and Western Hemisphere. Hence, it extended the eight-category 'preference system' to all Western Hemisphere countries, together with 20,000 per country limited according to eight-category preference system which gave priority to persons having:
Close family ties with family relatives already in the United State; (b) Labor skills in short supply in the United States; (c) Refugee status.

However, additional numbers of refugees could be brought into the United States above the numerical limitations by approval of the Attorney General, as in the case of Indo-China refugees.

1978 Law - the 95th Congress made sweeping changes in immigration legislation, and these became effective in October 1978. The separate immigration quotas for Eastern and Western Hemispheres were eliminated and replaced by a worldwide numerical limitation of 290,000 persons annually. Children of one U.S. and one non–U.S. parent are now able to retain U.S. citizenship without ever living in the United States, and naturalization is now made possible for anyone who is 50 years of age and has been a legal permanent resident for 20 years. The British colony of Hong Kong was allowed a yearly quota of 5,000 immigrants into the U.S. Changes were also made in the regulations governing the adoption of foreign children and the status of refugees.

1980 – New Refugee Act: This was basically in reaction by Congress to the flood of refugees to the U.S., from two areas of the world: the Indochina with the end of the Vietnam War, and Cuba with the declaration of Fidel Castro in 1980 that the Port of Mariel was open to anyone who wanted to leave. The law basically removed the preferential treatment of refugees from the Communist countries and redefined a refugee more literally as being simply someone who fears persecution in his or her home country based on religious or political beliefs, race, national origin, or ethnic affiliation. (Later, by the immigration Act of 1990 – see below – the refugee policy of the U.S. was further expanded; a refugee was now defined to include a person fleeing war or natural disasters, such as earthquakes, flood, etc).

Congress eliminated the seventh preference and allotted 6% of this numerical allocation of worldwide visa numbers to the second preference. Distinctions in the definitions of "refugee" and "asylum" provide for new procedures for those people to become permanent residents in the United States. A limit of 50,000 refugees was authorized by Congress to enter the United States in 1980, 1981, and 1982. The annual worldwide limitation on visa numbers for immigrants to the United States was reduced to 270,000 persons.

1986 – Immigration Reform and Control Act of 1986: The law, more commonly known as the Amnesty Law, opened the U.S immigration still wider: it legalized the legal status of aliens who were already in the United States without legal status since January 1982, while at the same time trying to control the future influx of illegal aliens into the nation. The law established the following measures:

(a) Civil and criminal sanctions/penalties imposed against all employers who knowingly hire illegal aliens.
(b) Illegal aliens who resided in the U.S. prior to January 1, 1981 were granted amnesty and allowed to apply for legalization of their status as permanent residents in the U.S; and
(c) Spouses of U.S. Citizens and Permanent Alien Residents were accorded "conditional" Resident Status, and

after 24 months of obtaining the immigrant visa, must apply to the INS for permanent resident status if the marriage is bona fide and not terminated by divorce. Changes were made in the law to prevent fraudulent marriages by aliens in order to acquire immigration benefits.

1990 – The Immigration Act of 1990: This is probably the most comprehensive overhaul of the U.S. immigration law by Congress since 1965. The law provided a huge increase in the number of aliens that could enter the country annually (700,000 in each of the years 1992 to 1994, and 675,000 from 1995 onwards). *But, even more importantly, the law solidified a policy shift in the nation's basic U.S. immigration objective:* the thrust of the policy would be to emphasize attracting persons who possess certain desirable or preferred occupational skills or economic resources. To be sure, the law still maintains the traditional immigration policy of providing for the unification of families and close relatives of U.S. citizens, and, though to a lesser extent, of permanent resident aliens. But the primary, dominant emphasis was to attract aliens who have the education, occupational skills or money to contribute to and to enhance the economic growth and well-being of the U.S. Thus, the law, now for the first time ever, established a specific category of permanent visa meant for millionaire entrepreneurs and investors who establish or invest in new job creating enterprises. And, as anticipated, the new law has been hugely successful in the area of attracting doctors, lawyers, engineers, scientists, accountants, nurses, teachers, inventors and other such highly skilled professionals to the United States.

1996 - The Illegal Immigration Reform and Immigrant Responsibility Act (IIRAIRA): The law, designed primarily to stem the flow of illegal immigration to the U.S., contains some of the toughest provisions ever enacted by Congress in immigration matters. For example, under this law, immigrants living in the United States who have been long-term law abiding citizens of the nation, may still be subject to deportation, and an immigrant's dependents such as his or her spouses and children, who may have inadvertently exceeded or violated his or her visa status, is readily deportable.

Chapter 2

All The Different Types Of Visas By Which One Can Gain Entry Into The U.S: The Immigrant & Non-Immigrant Visas

A. WHAT IS A VISA?

A visa is, in a word, a document issued to an alien person (i.e., a foreign person or non-national of the U.S.) by the responsible U.S. government agency, which authorizes the alien person to lawfully enter the United States. This authorization would usually be stamped in your (the alien's) passport by an America consul (a U. S. government officer) in a U.S. Embassy abroad, or an immigration agency official within the United States. This formality merely conforms with the common procedure in international law.

Under the international law which applies, as well, to virtually every country in the world, in order to lawfully enter the United States from another country (with the possible exception of Canada and certain "exempted" countries which are, by special arrangement, exempt from this rule)*, every person must, in addition to having a passport from his/her own home country, be granted a "visa" from an American Embassy or Consulate – that is, a U.S. government's (written) permission – allowing him to enter the U.S. If you enter the United States with a valid visa – with the proper permission – you are called a "legal" alien by the U.S. immigration authorities. On the other hand, if you were to enter the country without a valid visa – without the proper documents showing the required government permission – you are called an "illegal" alien or "undocumented alien," and would face a lot of difficulties at the hands of the U.S. government authorities in trying to live and function in the United States.

Under the immigration laws and regulations of the United States, the term "ALIEN" is used to denote "any person not a citizen or a national of the United States." In other words, every person applying for entry to the United States – unless he or she is a U.S. citizen or a national – is an "alien" under the parlance of the U.S. immigration authorities.

B. THE TWO MAJOR BROAD GROUPS OF U.S. VISAS

In the broadest term, there are TWO kinds of visas that an alien person can receive from the U.S. Embassy or Consulate in order to gain admission into (or to remain in) the United States: either an IMMIGRANT type of visa, or a NON-IMMIGRANT type of visa.

*See pp 14–15 for a list of such countries

1. The Immigrant Type of Visa

The IMMIGRANT type of visa is the visa for the alien who is intent on entering the United States for permanent stay or residence there. With this kind of visa, you are given an unlimited amount of time; the legal right to live and work permanently in the country. There is only ONE kind of immigrant visa (also called "permanent residency visa" or the "green card"), and it is the type of visa which, once obtained, has no other classification or conditions attached to it.

There are two or three basic ways by which to secure a "green card" (the name by which the immigrant visa is popularly known): through having a family relationship to a U.S. citizen such as being married to a U.S. citizen, or through having an employment relationship or labor certification for an employment in the United States (see Chapter 3 for the full details). However, for our purposes here in this chapter, what is important for you to know, is that regardless of the avenue by which you obtain a green card, *all Green Cards are exactly the same in terms of the rights and privileges they confer on the holder of the card; they confer upon you an unlimited right to work and live in the U.S. for as long as you wish, whether permanently or otherwise.* One other major distinction which applies between the immigrant type of visa and the non-immigrant type, is that the number of immigrant visas issued by the U.S. government each year, is limited by a quota, while the number of non-immigrant visas issued in the various categories, is unlimited by law or any quota.

TYPES OF U.S. VISAS AVAILABLE

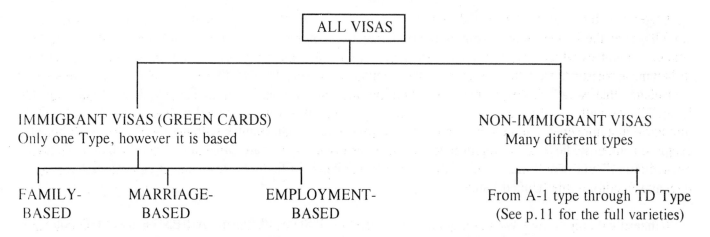

ALL VISAS

IMMIGRANT VISAS (GREEN CARDS)
Only one Type, however it is based

NON-IMMIGRANT VISAS
Many different types

FAMILY-BASED MARRIAGE-BASED EMPLOYMENT-BASED

From A-1 type through TD Type
(See p.11 for the full varieties)

2. The Non-Immigrant Type of Visa

The NON-IMMIGRANT type of visa, on the other hand, is the visa for the alien who is intent on entering and staying in the U.S. for a temporary period of time and for limited purposes (such as to visit or to do business or study, and the like). With this kind of visa, you are given the legal right to stay in the U.S. for a temporary period of time with limited rights.

Unlike the immigrant visa, which has only one classification, there are, however, many different types and classes of Non-immigrant visas and each type has its own set of qualifications and rights and conditions in terms of the duration of the visa and the rights and privileges to which the card holder is entitled, or the activities he/she may or may not lawfully engage in. On the average, unlike the immigrant visas, which can take months or even years to obtain because of the quota requirements, non-immigrant visas can usually be obtained very quickly.

C. THE DIFFERENT TYPES OR CLASSES OF NON-IMMIGRANT VISA AVAILABLE

There are, in all, about 56 different "classes" (types) into which the non-immigrant visa category is divided. (See Figure 2 - 1 below).

As previously stated, there are a variety of types of non-immigrant visas for the reason that each type is issued for a specific and different purpose. Consequently, when you are issued a non-immigrant visa of a specific kind or the other, the government, assuming simply that you will perform the applicable specific activity while you are in the United States, will merely issue you a specialized visa authorizing that particular activity (paying a visit, or undertaking a course of study, for example), and no other activity. Furthermore, in contrast to an immigrant type of visa, which is in all instances absolutely <u>permanent</u> in character, all non immigrant visas have one major thing in common: they are all <u>temporary</u> in character, granted only for a specific period of time deemed reasonable to have completed the authorized activities for which that type of visa is granted. As an alien involved in a visa application or processing for a nonimmigrant type of visa with a U.S. Embassy (or Consulate), you will often hear the Embassy officials refer to such classifications in shorthand by a symbol composed of a letter followed by a number.

The following chart provides a summary of all the nonimmigrant U.S. visa classifications or types that are available.

Figure 2-1

VISA CLASSIFICATION SYMBOL	CLASS (TYPE) OF NON-IMMIGRANT VISA	MAXIMUM ADMISSION PERIOD
A-1	High foreign government officials, such as ambassadors, public ministers, consular officers or career diplomats, and their immediate family members	Duration of status
A-2	Other foreign government officials or employees and their immediate families	Duration of their status
A-3	Personal attendants, servants or employees of A-1 or A-2 visa holders, and their immediate families	1 year
B-1	Temporary Visitors for business	6 months
B-2	Temporary Visitors for pleasure or tourism	6 months
C-1	Alien travelers in immediate and continuous transit through the U.S.	Not more than 29 days

C-2	Alien traveler in transit to or from the United Nations Headquarters	Duration of status in transit to U. N.
D-1	Crewmen (sea or air) remaining with vessel or aircraft	Time carrier is in port not to exceed 29 days from arrival
D-2	Crewmen (sea or air) discharged from vessel or aircraft arrival	Not to exceed 29 days from
E-1	Treaty trader, his spouse or children, if accompanying of following to join him	2 years
E-2	Treaty investor, his spouse or children accompanying or following to join him	Duration of status
F-1	A student coming to pursue a full course of study at a qualified institution	Duration of status
F-2	The Spouse or minor child(ren) of the F-1 alien	Same as in F-1
G-1	Designated principal resident representative of a foreign government coming to the U.S. to work for an international organization and his/her staff members and immediate families	Duration of status
G-2	Other representatives of foreign governments coming to the U.S to work for an international organization, and their immediate families	Duration of status
G-3	Representatives of foreign governments and their immediate families who would ordinarily qualify for G-1 or G-2 visas except that their governments are not members of an international organization	Duration of status
G-4	Officers of employees of international organizations and their immediate families	Duration of status
G-5	Attendants, servants and personal employees of G-1 through G-4 visa holders, and their immediate families	1 year
H-1B	Alien temporary worker of some distinguished merit or ability coming to perform exceptional service or services requiring such qualities, and/or to work in a specialty occupation requiring at least a bachelor's degree or its equivalent in on-the-job experience.	2 years with possible 1 year extension up to 5 years
H-2A	Temporary agricultural workers coming to the U.S to fill positions for which a temporary labor shortage of American workers had been recognized and declared by the U.S Department of Agriculture	2 years
H-2B	Temporary workers of various kinds coming to the U.S. to perform temporary jobs of skilled or unskilled labor for which there is a shortage of available qualified American workers	2 years
H-3	Temporary trainee worker coming as "Industrial Trainee"	Length of program
H-4	Spouses or minor children of H-1B, H-2A, H-2B or H-3 visa holders	Duration of H-1B, H-2A, or H-2B or H-3 alien
I	Bona fide representative of foreign press, radio, film, or other information media, coming solely to engage in such vocation, and his spouse or minor child(ren) if accompanying or following to join him	1 year
J-1	So-called "Exchange Visitor": a bona fide student, scholar, trainee, teacher, professor, research assistant, specialist, leader in a specialized field of knowledge or skill, or similar person, coming to participate in a program designated	

	by the U.S. Secretary of State for the purpose of pursuing such activity.	Duration of status
J-2	Spouse and minor children of J-1 alien, if accompanying or following to join him.	Same at J-1 alien
K-1	Alien fiancées and fiancés of U.S. citizens coming to the U.S. for the purpose of getting married.	90 days
K-2	Children of K-1 aliens	Same as K-1 alien
L-1	Intra-company transferees who work as managers, executives or persons with specialized knowledge.	1 year interval extendable to 3 years.
L-2	Spouses and minor children accompanying or following to join L-1 alien	Same as for L-1 above
M-1	Vocational or other nonacademic students	Duration of status, but generally 1 year
M-2	Immediate family members of an M-1 visa holder	Same as for M-1 alien.
N	Children of certain special immigrants	Varied
'NATO alien'-1	Principal permanent representatives of member states to North Atlantic Treaty Organization or NATO, including subsidiary bodies who are resident in the U.S., and resident official staff members, secretaries general, assistant secretaries general, and executive secretaries of NATO, other permanent NATO officials of similar rank, or their immediate families.	Duration of status
NATO-2	Other representatives to NATO member states, including any subsidiary bodies, its advisers and technical experts of delegations, members of Immediate Articles 3, 4 UST 1796 families; dependents of members of armed forces entering in accordance with the Status-of-Forces Agreement or in accordance with the Protocol on Status of International Military Headquarters; members of such a force, it issued	Duration of status
NATO-3	Officials clerical staff accompanying representatives of NATO member states, including any subsidiary bodies, or their immediate families	Duration of status
NATO-4	Official of NATO, other than those who can be classified as NATO-1, or their immediate families	Duration of status
NATO-5	NATO "expert," or member of a civilian component, other than officials who can be classified as NATO-1, accompanying or attached to a force under the NATO, and their dependants.	1 year
NATO-6	Members of civilian components accompanying forces entering in accordance with provisions of the NATO Status-of-Forces Agreement; members of civilian components attached to or employed by allied headquarters under the Protocol on Status of International Military Headquarters set up pursuant to the North Atlantic Treaty, and their dependents	1 year
NATO-7	Attendants, servants or personal employees of aliens of NATO-1 through NATO-6 classes, or their immediate families	1 year
O-1	Aliens of extraordinary ability in the sciences, arts, education, business or athletics	2 years with possible 1 year extensions up to 5 years.

O-2	Accompanying aliens of O-1	Same as O-1 alien
O-3	Spouses or children of O-1 or O-2 visa holders	Same as O-1 alien
P-1	Internationally recognized athletes and entertainers	Duration of program
P-2	Artists or entertainers in reciprocal exchange programs	Duration of program
P-3	Artists and entertainers coming to the U.S. to give culturally unique performances in a group	Duration of program
P-4	Spouses or children of P-1, P-2 or P-3 visa holders	Same as for P-1, P-2, or P-3 alien
Q-1	Participants in international cultural exchange programs	Duration of program
Q-2	Immediate family members of Q-1 visa holders	Same as or Q-1 alien.
R-1	Ministers and other aliens in religious occupation	2 years
R-2	Spouses or children of R-1 visa holders	Same as R-1 alien
S-1	Certain aliens supplying critical information relating to a criminal organization or enterprise	Duration of need or status
S-2	Certain aliens supplying critical information relating to terrorism	Duration of need or status
S-3	Immediate family members of S-1 or S-2 visa holders	Same of S-1 alien
TN	NAFTA professionals	1 year
TD	Spouses or children of NAFTA professionals	Same as TN alien

D. A FEW SPECIAL CASES WHEN ALIENS MAY BE EXEMPTED FROM HAVING A VISA FOR ENTRY INTO THE U.S.

In other chapters of this manual, we shall outline in great detail the applicable qualifications and requirements needed, as well as the procedures, for applying for and obtaining each of the various types of visas outlined in Section B and/or C above. However, for your immediate information, you should note that under a relatively new agreement between the U.S. government and some 21 countries or so, there are situations when citizens of a few select countries are allowed to come to the United States without first obtaining a visa, providing the interested person meets certain minimal conditions.

THE VISA WAIVER PROGRAM

Under a special program called the VISA WAIVER PILOT PROGRAM which was started by the U.S. Department of States (DOS) in 1989, applicants for U.S. visas from certain approved countries (see list below) who are clearly temporary visitors requiring a tourist visa, are allowed to enter the U.S. as tourists without having or using visa. All that they require are a passport from their home country and a round-trip ticket. And, upon their arrival at a U.S. port of entry, the U.S. Immigration and Naturalization Service will readily admit them without any questions.

1. Countries Which Are Covered In the Visa Exemption Program

As a matter of U.S. policy, countries included or includable in the Visa Waiver Program usually demonstrate certain basic common characteristics: they would generally have a low rate of refusals of tourist visa applications, and would have evidence of very few violations of the U.S. immigration laws, particularly with regard to over-staying their visa and working illegally in United States.

As of this writing, following countries are included among the countries whose citizens and passport holders are exempt from having a visa in order to enter the United States:

Andorra	Great Britain	Luxembourg
Argentina	(United Kingdom)	Monaco
Austria	Holland	New Zealand
Australia	(Netherlands)	Norway
Belgium	Iceland	San Marino
Brunei	Ireland	Slovenia
Denmark	Italy	Spain
Finland	Japan	Sweden
France	Liechtenstein	Switzerland
Germany		

NOTE: Under the Visa Waiver Program, the U.S. Department of State, which is the policy administrator of the program, is authorized to expand or to decrease the number of countries eligible for the program from time to time. Furthermore, as a rule, visa application rules and procedures may change from time to time, and at times visa application procedures may differ from one U.S. consulate to the next. Hence, it is always wise – and hereby strongly advised – that you check with your U.S. consulate to be sure that your country is currently included among the list of visa exempt countries before you set out on your travel.

2. The Minimum Conditions Required

To be eligible to come to the U.S. without first obtaining a visa under the visa waiver program, you only need to meet the following conditions:
- You (the person seeking entry into the U.S.), have to be planning to come to the United States for a duration not more than 90 days;
- there are no reasons, or "grounds of exclusion" (usually meaning criminal convictions), why you should not be admitted to the United States;
- you will be flying on a *participating* airline (check to see if an airline is participating before you pay for your ticket);
- you will be able to show a round ticket at the time of your departure out of your country and arrival in a U.S. port of entry as evidence that you are simply visiting and will return to your country not later than 90 days.

THE NEW YORK TIMES, SUNDAY,
FEBRUARY 24, 1980

SPOTLIGHT

He Gets Visas for the Famous

By SUSAN HELLER ANDERSON

LONDON — Well-heeled, well-educated and wanting a piece of America, hundreds of thousands of foreign business executives, professionals, skilled workers and heavy investors emigrate annually to the United States. In contrast to the impoverished or persecuted refugees who have historically flocked to American shores, they sport Savile Row suits and Vuitton luggage.

On hand to help them through the complicated entry process is a fast-growing group of legal professionals — the immigration lawyers. More than 1,200 attorneys are engaged solely in this specialty, which until five years ago was all but ignored in law schools.

One immigration lawyer is Richard D. Fraade of Beverly Hills and — since early this year — London. Attorney for some of the world's most prominent would-be Americans, Mr. Fraade is believed to be the first of the lawyers to open an office in London, the scene of much immigration activity. The United States Embassy's visa office on Grosvenor Square is the world's busiest and expects to issue a million visas in fiscal 1980, a 30 percent increase over 1979.

Under American law, every visiting alien must have a visa. About 80 percent of the visas issued here are for tourists and present little problem. The rest go to persons who want to work, either temporarily or permanently, and these people must enter a lengthy and complicated process that can take months and often years. The immigration lawyer finds ways to facilitate this process.

Parts of the immigration system are fraught with scandal and red tape. Some lawyers have mastered it by skirting the law, but no such charges have been made against Mr. Fraade and Embassy officials here say that immigration lawyers can perform a useful service.

"When Elton John comes to the U.S., he needs a temporary work permit," Mr. Fraade explained. "He's not going to queue up on Grosvenor Square." Of the more than 500 active clients on Mr. Fraade's books in Beverly Hills 90 percent are European.

Mr. Fraade's services have been employed by Roger Vadim, the film director, Joe Bugner, the boxer, Diana Dors, the actress, musicians Oscar Peterson and the Little River Band, Columbia Pictures, the University of Southern California, model agencies run by Eileen Ford, Wilhelmina and Johnny Casablancas, and virtually all of the toney French restaurants in Los Angeles. He has engineered temporary work permits for dozens of servants to the stars. Other clients are large employers of skilled workers, such as the California-based aircraft and silicon chip industries.

Describing himself as a "Europhile and Anglophile in particular," Mr. Fraade attires himself in English pin stripes and shirts bought from the international peacocks' shop, Turnbull and Asser. "I'm a suitoholic," he confessed. Having descended from Russian immigrants "of the pushcart variety," and having lived abroad, he said, helps him to identify with his clients. Shortly after he was born in Oklahoma City in 1942 his parents moved to New York, then, after the war, to Düsseldorf. "That gave me the introduction to Europe that marked me," said Mr. Fraade. The family later went West and Mr. Fraade was graduated from the University of California at Los Angeles. He attended Brooklyn Law School. "When I graduated in 1968 immigration law was not taught," he recalled.

"To stay out of the Army I taught school in Bedford Stuyvesant," he said, "then went into the special prosecutor's office

under New York State Attorney General Louis Lefkowitz in 1970. Meanwhile, I continued traveling to Europe."

"Through friends I met girls coming to New York who wanted to work as models," he said. He moonlighted by shepherding their visa applications through the Labor and Justice Departments. In 1975 he returned to California, passed the bar and set up the immigration department for a large law firm. He started his own practice last August in Beverly Hills.

Last month he placed a discreet ad in the London Financial Times announcing the opening of his London office. He got enough responses to indicate there was a potential market here for his services. "Coming to England is a logical extension of what's been happening in my practice," he said.

"I charge a flat fee," Mr. Fraade said, "from $3,000 to $7,500 depending on the case. The lower figure is more usual. I also try to do some pro bono work taking immigrant cases for no fee." In London the fee is slightly higher.

For immigrant visas, priority is given to relatives of United States citizens. Only two categories apply to immigrants wishing to work who have no American relatives. The sixth-preference category — skilled and semiskilled workers — has a backlog of six to eight months. The third preference — professionals, scientists and artists — has no backlog. "Vadim is clearly third preference," Mr. Fraade said. "But a top chef? The law's not so clear." Some 90 percent of his clients seeking permanent residency are in the third- or sixth-preference categories and his job

is often to convince visa officers of the validity of their claims. "Here the advocacy role can be helpful," said Alan Gise, United States consul general here.

Investors, however, are not given preference and, because the flow of immigrants is now so heavy that quotas are often filled by the preference categories alone, prospects are dim. Mr. Fraade has a solution.

On his latest trip he saw a client in Frankfurt whom he described as a top German industrialist. "He's convinced Europe is in a state of moral, economic and political decay and that Russia will take over. He won't make any more capital investments in Europe," Mr. Fraade said. "He wants to emigrate to America, the last bastion of capital enterprise. The structuring of a business affiliate lets him come on an E-2 Treaty-Investor visa — the next best thing to a green card." A "green card," which is in fact blue and white, is a permanent resident's permit.

Consular officials admit to mixed feelings about immigration lawyers but concede that, for corporations and investors in particular, they are useful. "The system is set up so no one should require a lawyer," Mr. Gise noted. "But in practice if you are an investor the immigration lawyer prepares the papers, oversees the transfer of funds, sees that requirements are met." Mr. Fraade has a client who wants to set up a subsidiary in California, which requires incorporation in that state. While his Beverly Hills office begins the incorporation procedure his brother Robert, in London, gathers the personal documents necessary for the client's visa, perhaps saving months.

Robin Laurance

Richard D. Fraade, immigration lawyer

Chapter 3

The Different Bases Or Avenues By Which An Alien May Get The "Immigrant" Type Of Visa (The Green Card): The Preference And Non-preference Categories

A. THE TWO MAIN BROAD CATEGORIES OF GREEN CARD APPLICANTS: NON-PREFERENCE AND PREFERENCE GROUPS

The United States government has established two broad general categories of persons who may immigrate permanently to the United States – that is, those who may apply for (or secure) immigrant types of visa or a green card. Such two categories are: **(1)** Those among them who are subject to an annual worldwide numerical limit (a quota); and **(2)** those among them who are exempt from, and hence are not subject to a quota, meaning that they may immigrate to the U.S. at any time notwithstanding what the worldwide demand for immigrant visas might be at the time.

Briefly summarized, generally those aliens who qualify for the green card on the basis of being an "immediate relative" of a U.S. Citizen, are not subject to any annual quota requirement and there are no limits as to the number of green cards that can be issued to such alien applicants; while those aliens who qualify for the green card in any other categories or on any other basis whatsoever (including both family-based and employment-based preferences, among others), are subject to annual quota. *In short, except for those who qualify for a green card on the basis of being an "immediate relative" of a U.S. citizen (see Section B below for the relevant definitions), all other applicants for a green card are subject to the constraints of an annual numerical quota.*

Preference vs Non-Preference

The first category of applicants mentioned above, the group that is subject to a numerical quota or limitation, is said to be subject to a "preference" (i.e., categories) system of visa allocation which determines the order of priority of their immigration classification based on the annual quota allotted. The other category of immigrant visa applicants, meaning the group that is not subject to any annual quota, is called the "non-preference" visa group. The preference group (those who receive a green card under a quota) fall into one of several classifications called PREFERENCES (see Section C below).

Under the Immigration Act of 1990, beginning from October 1, 1995, the worldwide annual quota for all immigrants (Green Cardholders) who can enter the United States every year, is 675,000. Of this overall number, the total number of green cards for persons who may qualify based upon family relationships to U.S. citizens and permanent residents, both in the preference and non-preference categories, is 480,000. That is, that category of immigrants which are not subject to any quotas, such as the immediate relatives of American citizens, are counted towards this maximum overall worldwide quota of 480,000. While out of the total number of visas issued to the preference aliens based upon family relationships, is set at 226,000, and the total annual limitation of quota for employment-based visas is set at 140,000.

B. COMPOSITION OF 'NON-PREFERENCE' IMMIGRANT VISA CATEGORY (no quota green cards)

As stated in Section A above, immigrants who qualify as "immediate relatives" of U.S. citizens - and those alone, among all immigrants - are NOT subject to quota limit, and have no numerical limitation on the annual number of green cards that can be issued to them. And such no-quota immigrants are also known as the *non-preference* visa category.

The following alien persons are defined as *IMMEDIATE RELATIVES* of a U.S. citizen:

- Spouses (including recent widows or widowers) of U.S. citizens
- Unmarried aliens under the age of 21 who have at least one U.S. citizen parent
- Parents of U.S. citizens, providing the U.S. citizens is 21 years of age and over.
- Stepchildren and stepparents of U.S. citizens, if the marriage creating the stepparent/stepchild relationship took place BEFORE the child's 18th birthday, or
- Parents and children related through adoption, if the adoption took place before the child reached the age of 16. Furthermore, the adopted child must have lived with the adoptive parent(s) for at least 2 years prior to the filing of the petition for a green card.

C. COMPOSITION OF 'PREFERENCE' VISA CATEGORIES (those subject to a quota)

Basically, although there are several preference classifications of immigrants falling under those who are subject to a quota limit on the annual number of green cards they can be issued (Section A above), this group of green card aliens - the so-called "preference" visa categories - actually cover only two general types of people: 1) certain kinds of family members of U.S. citizens or permanent residents, and 2) persons having some job skills wanted by U.S. employers.

The following alien persons comprise the preference visa applicants who are subject to an annual quota limit for a green card:

1. GROUP 1: 'Preference Relatives' or 'Family Preference' Classes of Applicants

Of the several immigrant visa preference categories available which are subject to a quota limit, the following ones, some 4 of them in number, are called PREFERENCE RELATIVE OR FAMILY PREFERENCE types because they are family-based or require family relationships with an American:

- *Family-based 1st Preference:* unmarried persons of any age who have at least one U.S. citizen parent. (This group is allotted a minimum quota of 23,400 visas per year).
- *Family-based 2nd Preference:* spouses and children under 21 years of age of green card holders, and unmarried sons and daughters of green card holders who are at least 21 years old at the time of filing of the petition (Allotted the minimum quota of 114200 per year).
- *Family-based 3rd Preference:* Married persons of any age, who have at least one U.S. parent. (Allotted a minimum quota of 23,400 per year)
- *Family-based 4th Preference:* Sisters and brothers of a U.S. citizen who (the citizen) must be at least 21 years old. (Allotted a minimum quota of 65,000 annually).

SCHEDULE OF 'PREFERENCE' CATEGORIES
OF IMMIGRANT VISAS (Those subject to a quota)

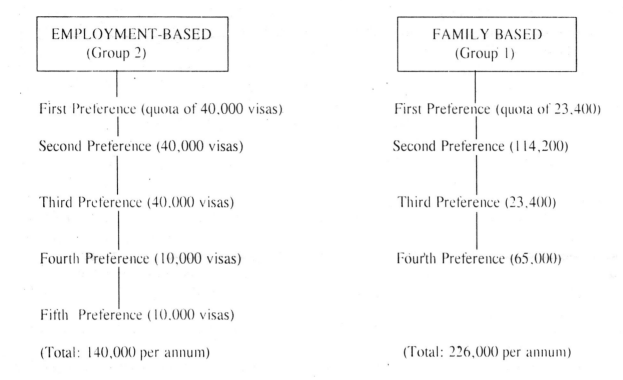

EMPLOYMENT-BASED (Group 2)	FAMILY BASED (Group 1)
First Preference (quota of 40,000 visas)	First Preference (quota of 23,400)
Second Preference (40,000 visas)	Second Preference (114,200)
Third Preference (40,000 visas)	Third Preference (23,400)
Fourth Preference (10,000 visas)	Fourth Preference (65,000)
Fifth Preference (10,000 visas)	
(Total: 140,000 per annum)	(Total: 226,000 per annum)

2. GROUP 2: 'Employment Preference' (i.e., Employment-based) Class of Applicants

The next major immigrant preference categories among those that are subject to a quota limit, are those which are employment-based or require an employment relationship with an American employer - the 'Employment Preference' classes. They are the following:

• *Employment 1st Preference:* Priority workers, including these three groups: persons of extraordinary ability in the arts and sciences in the fields of education, business or athletics; outstanding professors and researchers; and managers and executives of multinational companies. (Allotted an annual minimum quota of 40,000 visas).

• *Employment 2nd Preference:* Exceptional Ability Professionals - i.e., professionals with advanced degrees or exceptional ability. (Allotted annual minimum quota of 40,000 visas).

• *Employment 3rd Preferences:* Skilled and unskilled workers - i.e., a general category of aliens that include all other remaining aliens who seek immigrant visas on the basis of employment. (Annual minimum quota of 40,000 visas).

• *Employment 4th Preference:* Religious workers and a variety of worker categories. (Annual minimum quota of 10,000 visas)

• *Employment 5th Preference:* Individual entrepreneurs and investors capable of investing at least $1,000,000 in a U.S. business, or $500,000 in a "targeted employment" area (economically depressed area). (Allotted annual minimum quota of 10,000 visas).

3. Other Visa Preference Classes of Applicants

Other Green Card applicants who fall under the groups subject to a quota limitation, are the following:

(a) *Green Card Lottery Applicants or Diversity Immigrants.*

    As from October 1, 1994, another category of immigrant visa applicants (other than those applying based upon marital or family relationships and employment), was created - the so-called DIVERSITY IMMIGRANTS, more popularly known as the Visa Lottery. Under this program, an allotment of 55,000 visas are made available worldwide per year to people from various countries that are considered to be "low admissions" countries - that is, countries considered to send the fewest immigrants to the U.S. in recent times. Thus, the purpose of this program is to provide a separate avenue of entry to the U.S. for those persons who are from low admission regions and countries of the world, and therefore ensure some ethnic mix and a greater levelling of the immigration playing field for those from low admission places. This group of green cards are simply distributed by random selection by computer. (Procedure for getting the green card through the lotteries are outlined in Chapter 19).

(b) *Investors* (See Chapter 17 for procedures for getting the green card through the investor program.

(c) *Special Immigrants Green Cards*

    From time to time, congress enacts laws singling out certain persons as eligible for an immigrant visa. Groups of people so designated are treated as a part of the visa preference system and referred to as "special immigrants". As of this writing, aliens who fall under the special immigrants category, are:
* Ministers of religious or religious workers who are affiliated to a legitimate religious organization.
* Graduates of foreign medical schools who have been practising medicine in the U.S. as of January 9, 1987.
* Former employees of the Panama Canal Zone.
* Former long-time employees of a U.S. government agency in a foreign country who faithfully served the government for at least 15 years.
* Retired employees of designated international organizations who have lived in the U.S. for a certain number of years, and their spouses and unmarried children.
* Foreign children who have been declared dependent in juvenile courts in the United States.

    (Procedures for obtaining an immigrant visa through qualifying as special immigrant, are outlined in Chapter 16).

(d) *Refugees and Political Asylees Green Cards*

    Every year, some thousands of people from different parts of the world seek to enter or to stay in the U.S. based on political asylum or refugee grounds. This category of immigrants fall under the 'preference' group in that every year they have an annual quota of the number of green cards that can be granted, set by the President of the United States, which may vary from year to year and from country to country. (Procedures for obtaining an immigrant visa based on qualifying as a refugee or political asylee, are outlined in Chapter 18).

(e) *Temporary Protected Status' Visas*

    The U.S. government, through its Immigration and Naturalization Service (INS), may from time to time decide to give citizens of certain countries (they must already have been physically in the United State) a temporary safe haven in the United States when, in the judgment of the government, the conditions in the alien's homeland are of such dangerous condition as to warrant such a privilege. In such a situation, the alien would be granted an immigrant visa (a green card) on the grounds of his/her Temporary Protected Status (TPS). TPS is essentially similar to political asylum (in each instance the alien must have been physically present in the U.S), except that in the case of the TPS the visa is always temporary, and will never turn into an immigrant (i.e., permanent) visa.

(f) Amnesty Relief Visas

Under a 1997 law called the Nicaraguan Adjustment and Central America Relief Act (NACARA), people from a few designated countries who meet certain conditions are granted various kinds of immigration rights and reliefs depending on whether the alien is from Central America, Cuba or former Soviet Bloc country, Guatemala, or EL Salvador. The immigration rights and reliefs range from eligibility for permanent residence in the U.S. (immigrant visa), to suspension of deportation or cancellation of removal order.

Chapter 4

The Key Problem Areas For Aliens Seeking A Green Card On The Basis Of Having A Family Relationship With A U.S. Citizen Or Immigrant Visa Holder

In Sections A, B, and C of Chapter 3, we have explained that one way, indeed the major way, provided under the U.S immigration laws and procedures by which aliens may qualify for the immigrant visa (the Green Card) to the United States, is through having one kind of family relationship or the other with a U.S. citizen or a holder of an immigrant visa. In this chapter, we shall discuss the various specific categories of family relationships by which aliens can gain a green card, and the major issues, eligibility standards, and qualifications required of each category.

A. PERSONS WHO QUALIFY FOR IMMIGRANT VISA ON THE BASIS OF FAMILY RELATIONSHIP OR BEING A RELATIVE

As fully set forth in an earlier chapter (see Chapter 3, Sections B and C), with regard to family-based immigrant visa procedures, an alien can qualify for such a visa (a green card) on the basis of being a relative of, or having a family relation to, either a U.S. citizen or an immigrant visa holder in a few number of ways. *In this connection, it should be taken note of that family relationships of varying kinds with either a U.S. citizen or Permanent Resident constitute the most important basis on which the overwhelming majority of immigrant visas are sought or granted every year. Hence, the great significance of this chapter.*

The reason why a family relationship is so central is no mere accident: it has always been a deliberate and central policy aim of the immigration laws of the United States historically, to unify, re-unite and prevent the separation of family members as much as possible.

Briefly summarized, aliens who qualify on the basis of having a family relationship fall under the following categories or classifications as set forth in the U.S. immigration laws:

1. Immediate Relatives

Alien persons who qualify as an "immediate relative" of a U.S. citizen in any of the following ways:
• Spouses of U.S. citizens, including their widows and widowers, if they were married to the U.S. citizen for at least 2 years prior to the U.S. spouse's death, and are applying for an immigrant visa no later than 2 years after the U.S. citizen's death. The deceased spouse shall have been a U.S. citizen for at least 2 years prior to his/her death; the widow/widower shall not have legally separated from the U.S. citizen at the time of his/her death, and shall not have remarried.
• Unmarried aliens under the age of 21 who have at least one U.S. parent

• Parents of U.S. citizens, if the child (the U.S. citizen) is over the age of 21. (Stepparents and stepchildren qualify as "immediate relative" if the marriage creating the parent/child relationship took place before the child's 18th birthday: and adoptive parents and children qualify if the adoption took place before the child reached age 16 and the child had lived with the adoptive parent for at least 2 years prior to the petition for an immigrant visa).

NOTE: Note that an adult (over 21 years old) child of the parents of a U.S. citizen does not qualify under this particular visa category, since such children are not deemed the parents of a U.S. "child" under this specific provision.

2. Other Family Relatives

The other categories of aliens who are eligible for an immigrant visa, are those who qualify in various other ways as close family members to a U.S. citizen or an immigrant visa holder. These persons fall under the so called "preference relatives" categories, in that they are subject to a quota limitation (see Chapter 3 Section C).

They are:
   • **Family 1st Preference:** Unmarried aliens of any age, who have at least one parent who's a U.S. citizen.
   • **Family 2nd Preference: 2A:** alien spouses and children under 21 years old, of immigrant visa holders: 2B. Unmarried alien sons and daughters of green card holders who are at least 21 years of age.
   • **Family 3rd Preference:** Married aliens of any age who have at least one U.S citizen parent.
   • **Family 4th preference:** Sisters and brothers of U.S citizens who (the U.S citizen) is at least 21 years of age.

B. SOME ADVANTAGES OR DISADVANTAGES IN FILING AS 'IMMEDIATE RELATIVE' AS AGAINST A 'PREFERENCE RELATIVE'

1. No Quota Or Waiting For Immediate Relatives

As is emphasized in several places in this manual (see, for example Chapter 3, Section A), the process of obtaining the right to lawful U.S. Permanent Residency (immigrant visa status) is primarily governed by the immigrant visa "selection system" set forth under the immigration laws of the United States. The selection system is divided into two basic parts, namely:

> (i) that part covering those classes of intending immigrants who are exempt from (i.e. are not subject to) any numerical quotas or limitations; and
> (ii) that part dealing with those classes of intending immigrants who are subject to numerical quotas or limitations.

The reader should recall from Chapter 3, that with regard to qualifying for an immigrant visa through the general category for which some kind of family relationship with a U.S citizen or green card holder constitutes the basis for the visa eligibility, there's one major area of difference between those who qualify as *"immediate relatives"* and those who qualify as 'preference relatives': persons who qualify as *immediate relatives* are exempt from numerical restrictions and are permitted to gain immigrant visas in no specific or limited numbers, while all other kinds of relatives are not. *Hence, the important point we wish to make here, is simply this: that if you were to apply (if it were to be practicable for you to apply) as an "immediate relative" applicant (section A 1 above), you will have the distinct advantage of NOT being subject to a numerical quota or a "waiting list," and would be assured of having a visa number <u>immediately</u> upon your presentation of the required proof of qualification and documentations.*

Experts have estimated, for example, that each preference relative category can expect delays or waiting periods of the following magnitude: Family first preference, 2 years for nationals of all countries, and 11 years for Philippines, and 4 to 5 years for Mexicans; Family second preference, 4 years for nationals of all countries for family-based 2A, and 6 years for family-based 2B; Family third preference, 3 years for nationals of all other countries, and 9 years for Mexicans and at least 11 years for Philippines; and for Family third preference, a waiting period of at least 10 years for nationals of all other countries, and about 19 years for Philippines.

2. Accompanying Relatives Privileges Are Only For Preference Relatives

Aside from the advantage of no quota requirement and no waiting period which attach to immigrant visa aliens who qualify as immediate relatives, there is perhaps one other area where a family-based immigrant may have an advantage based on which among the two visa groupings he or she files under: the ability of the resultant immigrant visa recipient, or lack of it, to bestow immigrant visa status on his or her other relatives. Simply put, the rule is that so-called *accompanying relatives* (basically the spouse and children of the petitioning alien) who seek entry together with the alien, can ONLY be included with *preference relatives*, but not with immediate relatives.

Under the immigration rules, accompanying relatives (the spouse and children) of the petitioning alien receive a "derivative" visa which permits them to enter the U.S. together with the petitioning principal alien, and such relatives are considered to be accompanying the principal alien providing they receive their own immigrant visas within 4 months after the principal obtains his/her own immigrant visa (or adjustment of status), if its within the United States, or within 4 months after he/she departs from the foreign country. *However, beneficiaries of a visa petition who obtain their immigrant visa through being an immediate relative, cannot bestow an immigrant visa status on their other family members or relatives. Only visa beneficiaries who qualify as preference relatives can.* Thus, for example, if an alien (an immigrant visa or green card holder) becomes a U.S. citizen and files for and obtains an immigrant visa for his or her parents, the other children of the parents do not automatically qualify for immigrant visa. However, if you were to obtain an immigrant visa as a preference relative (say, through being an alien with a U.S. parent, or a brother or sister of a U.S. citizen, or a child of green card holder, etc), and you have a spouse or unmarried children under the age of 21, your spouse or unmarried children can automatically qualify for immigrant visas as *accompanying relatives* simply by proof of their family relationship to you. Also, if the relationship of spouse or child is created after the principal alien obtained his visa, or, if the principal alien were to marry after he/she had obtained the immigrant visa, then the family members would not be entitled to derivative immigrant visa status (they'll have to file a separate visa application and would be subject to worldwide numerical quota limitations).

In a word, the point is that as a rule, accompanying relatives or family members are always includable only with PREFERENCE RELATIVES, but not with immediate relatives.

All other things notwithstanding, aside from the two principal differences outlined above, the good news, though, is this: that the basic procedures and substantive visa issues involved in all family relationship-based immigrant visa petitions are virtually the same. Hence, we choose to discuss the basic general issues for all categories of family-based immigrant visa situations in this one chapter.

C. THE FIRST KEY PROBLEM AREA IN PROVING GREEN CARD QUALIFICATION: ESTABLISHING THAT A TRUE FAMILY RELATIONSHIP ACTUALLY EXISTS.

Perhaps the most important issue involved in being able to qualify for a permanent residency visa (immigrant visa) in any one of the family-based preferences, including the immediate relative of a U.S. citizen category, *is being able to provide sufficient evidence and verification that will satisfy the U.S. immigration authorities that a qualifying family relationship, does, in fact, exist between the sponsoring petitioner (i.e., the U.S. citizen or Permanent Resident), and the alien for whom the visa petition is filed,* the "beneficiary" of the petition. In this regard, to be eligible to file under the IMMEDIATE RELATIVE designation, as well as under most of the other family-based preference categories, qualification as a "CHILD" as defined under the Immigration Act, is a central pre-requisite - as a child either of one or both U.S citizen parents, or of a holder of a U.S. green card.

The core relationship which serves as the defining factor for all family-based rights and benefits accorded under the immigration law, is the PARENT-CHILD relationship. A "child", as defined under the law, means an unmarried person under the age of 21 years old. However, you should note that if an alien person does not qualify under this category because of age or marital status, he may still qualify for an immigrant visa under the first, second, or third, family preferences. Section 101 (6) (1) of the Immigration and Nationality Act defines the term "child" to include an unmarried person under the age of 21 years, who is:

a) **a legitimate child.**

b) **a stepchild** (where the mother or the father of a child married a person who is not the biological parent of the child), whether legitimate or illegitimate, as long as the child was not yet 18 years old when the marriage creating the status of stepchild occurred;

c) a **child legally legitimated** prior to the age o 18, provided the child is in the legal custody of the legitimizing parent at the time of the legitimization;

d) an illegitimate* child in relation to its natural mother, or in relation to its natural father if the father has or had a bona-fide parent-child relationship with the child;

e) an **adopted child** or children; and

f) **Orphans**,** provided certain conditions apply.

NOTE: A few helpful pointers need to be noted on children falling under the "adopted" and "orphan" backgrounds. For an adoption to be recognized as valid for U.S. immigration purposes, the following general conditions must be met: if the adoption occurs in a foreign country, that country's adoption laws apply; if it occurs in the U.S., the adoption laws of the adopting parent's intended state of residence in the U. S. apply. The adoption must occur BEFORE the child's 16th birthday, and the child must have been in legal custody of, and lived with the adopting parents, for at least two (2) years either before or after the adoption. In practice, this means that either a legal guardianship or an actual adoption court decree must have been issued two years before the visa petition is actually filed. You must be prepared to provide, in support of the visa petition for the child, that type of documentation required for an IMMIGRANT applicant who comes from the child's place of residence, as well as acceptable court papers or other documentations in proof that the adoption took place, in accordance with the laws of the place of the supposed adoption.

---

* For immigration purposes, the rule is that the issue of whether a person is "illegitimate" is generally determined according to the laws of the person's place or state of birth. For such countries which do not, for example, even make any distinction between legitimate and illegitimate children (e.g., African cultures and those of South America), or for those in which laws have been adopted abolishing the making of any distinction concerning legitimacy as between children, the issue is virtually irrelevant for immigration purposes. In such situations, either of the natural parents may petition for the child as all children under such situations must in effect be deemed "legitimate", or the natural parents could also petition for the parents if they otherwise meet the qualification.

** *In respect to orphan children:* generally, the orphan must have been a bona fide orphan, that is, both parents must have truly died or abandoned him, or where there's one surviving parent, he or she must have signed proper irrevocable surrender papers permanently giving up the child for adoption, with some of the papers showing that the surviving parent is incapable of supporting and caring for the child on his own; the petition for the adoption of the orphan must be filed before the child's 16th birthday; if the child is to be adopted in a foreign country, the adopting parents must show that they personally saw and approved of the child before the adoption was finalized.

It's important to recognize that, as a practical matter, because of the 2-year-residence-with-the-child requirement and the 2-year-legal-custody-with-the-child requirement, the only way the adopted child can get an immigrant visa is for one or both of the adopting parents to live or have lived with the alien child for at least 2 years. And if it will be difficult or impracticable for the petitioning parents to meet these requirements, the other alternative may be to attempt qualifying the child under the orphan child procedures (see Chapter 12). Or, to try to bring in the child as a non-immigrant (Volumes 1 of this manual), and then undertake the adoption proceedings in the United States.

The following are the types of showing often required to be provided to establish a valid child-parent relationship for immigration purposes:

• Evidence that the child lived with and was cared for as the child of the parent (or stepparent), or that the parent otherwise showed an active parental interest in the support and welfare of the child. (For example, proof of financial support, frequent visits or contacts with child by letter or other means, open acknowledgement of the child, evidence that the parent has held out the child as his own and provided for the child's needs, and, in general, any documented actions by the parent which reflect the existence of a parental relationship with the child).

• Documentary proof that the designated parent(s) are in fact the parent(s) – e.g., affidavits from persons present at the time of the pregnancy and birth of the child who can affirm the identity of the natural father and/or mother

• Marriage Certificate or other proof of the marriage between the parents, where applicable.

• The child's birth certificate, bearing the names of the U.S. citizen or green card holder as the parents

• Evidence of the legal termination of prior marriage, if either parents was previously married.

• In general, credible evidence that a bona-fide blood relationship exists between the child and designated parents – the blood relationship must be established by "clear and convincing" evidence; this evidence may include a blood test, if other evidence, such as the father's name on the birth certificate or a judicial determination of paternity, is not available.

D. THE SECOND KEY PROBLEM AREA IN GREEN CARD QUALIFICATION: ESTABLISHING THAT A QUALIFYING MARRIAGE ACTUALLY EXISTS.

Next to the definition of a "child", the definition of who qualifies as a "spouse" is the second most important issue involved in an alien being able to qualify as a "family member" for the purposes of eligibility for a grant of immigrant visa. *The primary issue in most such matters, is this: whether the underlying marriage upon which the claimed marital relationship is based, is valid and subsisting, including the validity of any prior divorces that may have been had by either spouse, if any.*

The basic rules governing this are as follows: that a marriage must be legally valid <u>at its inception</u> (from its very beginning); and the marriage must not have been entered into for the purpose of evading the U.S. immigration laws, i.e., as a fraudulent or "sham" marriage.*

One vital essential is that the alien spouse and the U.S. citizen or permanent resident must BOTH be parties to the marriage that is purported to be legally valid. In making a determination as to the validity of such a marriage, it is the law of the place where the marriage occurs that governs, in that the common view is that if the marriage happens to be valid and to enjoy official recognizance at the place where it is contracted, the simple principles of comity dictate that it be recognized in other jurisdictions just as well.**

---

*As established over the years by the courts, the test for making the determination as to whether a marriage was fraudulent at its inception, is roughly this: the marriage is fraudulent "If the bride and groom did not intend to establish a life together at the time they were married."(Bark vs. INS, 511 F.2d 1200 (9th Circuit, 1975).

**Note that all divorces granted by U.S. State courts are considered valid, as are subsequent marriages.

The exceptions when the above stated rules with respect to recognition of a foreign-contracted marriage do not apply and are hence not respected, included these:

i) When the parties to a marriage would be subject to criminal penalties for cohabiting in the U.S. jurisdiction where they reside or will reside; *ii)* where the marriage is deemed to be "against public policy" under U.S. social practices (e.g. a polygamous marriage or one between close relatives); and *iii)* where the marriage was by proxy, that is, the parties to the marriage were not physically present at the marriage ceremony in the presence of each other, and marriage was not consummated; and *iv)* in instances where one or both of the parties to the marriage have been previously married and then divorced, what may determine whether the present marriage of the parties is recognized as valid may well depend upon the validity of the prior marriage or marriages; thus, any such divorce(s) must be valid in the jurisdiction where the alien resided at the time of the divorce, and must also be accepted and deemed valid in the jurisdiction where the present marriage of the parties occurs.

Here are the major questions often posed on the issue of a marriage's validity:

1. Does the marriage, in fact, meet all the formal requirements of the jurisdiction (the place) in which it was entered into?

2. Is the marriage recognized as a valid lawful marriage in the alien's intended state of residence in the U.S.?

3. Does the qualifying marriage continue as a legal marriage, i.e., has no divorce or formal separation been entered into in the marriage in question?

4. Is it evident that the marriage was not entered into for the sole or primary purpose of obtaining an immigration benefit, such as an immigrant visa?

5. Were the parties entitled to enter into the current marriage on the basis that all prior marriages were legally terminated?

6. Is there no reason to believe that a fee or other consideration was given for the filing of the petition (other than, say, an attorneys fee or assistance in preparing the petition papers)?

E. THE NEW 1986 "SHAM MARRIAGE" OR MARRIAGE FRAUD LAW

Much of the documentation required to be supplied in support of visa petitions in which a marriage relationship is the basis, essentially centers on one question: establishing the bona-fide (the genuineness) of a marriage *at its inception*. Hence, the full apparatus of the Immigration and Naturalization Service (INS) investigatory procedures are directed at the discovery of such marriage relationships that are sham or fraudulent. In deed, in 1986 the U.S. Congress, concerned about doing something about the growing issue of sham marriages, passed a law, the Immigration Marriage Fraud Act, with provisions particularly designed to ferret out cases of sham marriages. In the year before the enactment of this law, the INS and many Congressional voices had asserted that about half the visa petitions that were based on marital relationships were fraudulent, and had been entered into solely for the purpose of obtaining a Green Card.

Thus, in an effort to eliminate, or at least drastically curtail, such "paper marriages", Congress passed a new law with special provisions designed to aid the INS examiners in the detection of fraudulent marriage relationships. By this provision (Section 241(c) of the Marriage Fraud Act thereof), any marriage formed or terminated within 2 years before or after the admission of the alien to permanent residence in the U.S., is "presumed" to be a fraudulent marriage, and would be the alien's "burden" to prove that such is not the case.

The law provides that an alien "shall be deported as having procured a visa or other documentation by fraud" and "to be in the United States in violation of this Act", if he or she obtains lawful permanent status on the basis of a marriage.

"Entered into less than two years prior to such entry of the alien and which, within two years subsequent to any entry of the alien into the United States, shall be judicially annulled or terminated, unless such alien shall establish to the satisfaction of the Attorney General that such marriage was not contracted for the purpose of evading any provisions of the immigration laws".

Particularly viewed with great abhorrence by the immigration authorities, is one particular variant of the marriage fraud, the situation commonly referred to as **"gigolo" marriages.** It refers to the situation in which a foreign national marries a U.S. citizen solely to procure an immigration benefit such as an immigrant visa, usually without the knowledge of the U.S. citizen. Often, in such a case, the matter comes to light when the U.S. citizen spouse discovers that the foreign national is not interested in maintaining the marital relationship, but has rather used the marriage for the purpose of obtaining the immigration benefit.

F. MAJOR FRAUD COMBATING PROVISIONS OF THE MARRIAGE FRAUD LAW

The following are the major provisions of the newly enacted law (the Marriage Fraud Act) designed to combat fraud in marriage for immigration purposes:

(The "alien spouse" is defined specifically as an alien admitted to permanent resident status within two years of the marriage upon which the application for residency is based).

1. All "alien spouses" of U.S. citizens and Permanent Residents are now granted permanent residency status only "CONDITIONALLY" for a period of two years, whenever the marriage upon which the immigration visa is based was formed within two years prior to the grant of the residence.

2. Thus, if an alien spouse obtains an immigrant visa within 2 years after marrying an America citizen or an immigrant visa holder, the immigrant card is <u>granted</u> <u>conditionally</u> and lasts for 2 years only. The couple is required to file a second visa petition (a joint one) within 90 days prior to the 2 years anniversary of the grant of conditional residence, so that the Immigration Service can re-evaluate the bona-fides of the marriage, and if determined then to be valid and still subsisting, a final actual, permanent immigrant visa will then be issued the alien spouse.

If, however, you are divorced at that point, or your U.S. spouse simply refuses to cooperate and jointly file the second visa petition with you, the INS will begin removal (deportation) proceedings against you (the alien spouse); it may automatically cancel both the alien spouse's immigration card and that of any unmarried children who may have also obtained a conditional immigrant visa by virtue of the couple's marriage.

There may be ways for the alien spouse to still keep his/her immigrant visa. The alien spouse may be able to obtain a "waiver" of the usual consequences and thus retain his or her immigrant visa if she can show one of the following three things by credible evidence:

- That he/she originally entered into the qualifying marriage in good faith - that is, that he(she) did not enter into it just to get a green card - but that the marriage is now legally terminated for good cause other than through the death of the spouse, and that the alien spouse was not at fault in failing to meet the requirements ordinarily prescribed for the removal of the conditional status; or
- that he/she is a victim of battery or extreme mental cruelty or abuse at the hands of the U.S. citizen or green cardholder spouse, or
- that if she were to be deported, such will cause you extreme hardship.

3. At any time during the two years of the alien spouse's conditional residency status, the Attorney General can, in his discretion, terminate such conditional status of the visa and subject the alien to deportation, if the marriage is terminated by divorce or annulment during the two years following the grant of immigrant residence, or if during that period credible information comes to the attention of the Attorney General that the marriage in question was entered into for the purpose of procuring the alien's entry into the U.S. as an immigrant or that an unlawful fee or other payment was given for procuring the alien's permanent residency.

4. Approval of a SECOND Preference petition is barred for a spouse of a permanent resident if the permanent resident obtained his own green card through marriage to the citizen or another resident within 5 years of the filing of the new second preference petition. (Aimed at preventing aliens from entering into marriages to obtain immigration benefits, then divorcing the sponsoring spouse and remarrying another alien to seek immigration for him or her).

5. A criminal penalty, up to 5 years in prison, and a fine of up to $250,000 if found guilty, added for knowingly entering into a fraudulent or sham marriage. Both the spouse and U.S. citizen spouse, alike, are subject to the criminal charges under the marriage fraud law. In addition, the permanent resident can be deported.

6. An alien can only qualify as fiancé(e) in the K nonimmigrant category if he or she has personally met the U.S. citizen sponsor within 2 years of the date of filing the K visa petition.

7. As an alien qualified to file for a green card on the basis of being married to a U.S. citizen, if deportation or exclusion proceedings have been started against you to remove you based on the grounds that the INS believes you are out of status or that you entered the U.S. illegally, and while such proceedings are pending you marry an American citizen, under the current law you now have the right, unlike previously, to file your petition for a visa or an application for Adjustment of Status. You and your American spouse are no longer prohibited, under current, as would have been the case under previous procedures, from proceeding with the visa filing process, and you will not now be forced to live outside the U.S. for 2 years before you may get your green card.

However, because you married under such suspicious circumstances while you were facing a possible deportation order, you (the newly-married alien) will invariably have to come up with a strong and convincing evidence of the type such that you can clearly establish to the INS that the marriage was entered into for love and in good faith with honest intention to establish a life together, and not simply for the purpose of getting a green card. (See Chapter 6, Section E for guidance on the kinds of documentary evidence required).

8. And finally, the penalty. Under the strict penalty imposed by the 1986 marriage fraud law, if the INS has reason to believe or to suspect that you (the alien as well as the U.S. citizen or permanent resident) have entered into a marriage merely for the purpose of obtaining a green card, or even that you helped someone else enter into a marriage for the purpose of evading the immigration laws, or if you have submitted papers to the INS based on such a marriage, you are subject to many stiff penalties. You can be prosecuted for a federal crime, and if found guilty, can be imprisoned for up to five years, or fined for up to $250,000, or both. In addition, permanent resident aliens as well as the alien spouse can be deported, and the alien involved in such a case will almost certainly lose the possibility of ever getting a green card in the future – no matter what other qualifications or relationships he/she may have in the future.

(The full and actual procedure for filing for an immigrant visa on the basis of having a marital relationship with a U.S. citizen or green cardholder, are outlined in Chapter 6)

Chapter 5

The Immigrant Visa Quota System: How It Works, And The Waiting Period Involved

A. PREFERENCE (QUOTA) IMMIGRANT VISAS HAVE TO UNDERGO A WAITING PERIOD.

As discussed in Chapter 3, while the non-preference category of immigrant visas or green cards (those set forth in Section B of Chapter 3) are not subject to any annual numerical limits or quotas, the other general categories of immigrant visas, called the 'preference' categories (Section C of Chapter 3), are subject to strict numerical quotas which will determine the order of priority of their immigration classification. *The basic significance between the preference and non-preference visa categories, is simply this: persons who qualify under the non-preference visa classification are exempt from any quota; and hence, there are simply no limits on the number of green cards that can be issued to such persons, and such aliens, once qualified, may immigrate to the U.S. at any time regardless of the worldwide demand for immigrant visas. On the other hand, persons qualifying under the preference visa classification are subject to an annual quota limitation, often meaning that they may face long delays and waiting periods in being lawfully admitted to the U.S.* The quotas determine how many immigrants worldwide can enter the United States each year, as well as how many immigrants can be granted immigrant visas from a particular country each year. In other words, there are essentially two separate quotas: one for each country, and one for the entire world.

Basically, the applicable law (the Immigration Act of 1990), provides for an over-all annual quota of 675,000 as from October 1, 1995 onwards, to be made available to all applicants worldwide each and every year. Out of this overall number allowed each year worldwide (675,000), each country is allowed a maximum quota of no more than 25,625 visas (i.e., no more than 7% of the 675,000 visas) per year* This situation produces, therefore, an odd state of affairs because the simple arithmetics of it just don't add up: since each country is allowed a quota of no more than 7% of the 675,000 overall amount, the multiplication of each country's quota (7%) by the total number of countries in the world, gets you a total much larger than 100.

Consequently, what this means in practical terms, is that the 7% allotment to each country is merely a theoretical maximum, not a practical or guaranteed number.

In practice, it has often turned out that immigrants from traditionally "oversubscribed" countries – that is, countries with huge numbers of visa applications each year (e.g. China, India, Korea, Mexico, the Philippines, Dominica Republic, Hong Kong, and the like) – generally undergo longer waiting (from 2 to 15 years) for a

---

*A few countries, called "dependent" countries, such as St. Kitts, Nevis, etc., are limited to just 2% of the yearly quota, while a country like Hong Kong is treated as a separate country for purposes of immigrant visa allocation.

green card than those in countries with far fewer applications (say, Great Britain, France, or Germany), since the demands for immigrant visa from such countries with huge request profiles far exceed the per-country limits allowed to them each year, as opposed to the situation with those from countries with a small number of immigrant visa applicants. Hence, as it often happens in practice, often applicants from a given country may not have used up (or even come anywhere close to using up) its per-country 7% immigrant visa allotment, and yet they will not be able to get immigrant visas essentially because the world-wide quota might have been exhausted.

A. HOW THE QUOTA OR PREFERENCE SYSTEM WORKS

The availability of immigrant visas is published each month by the Visa Section of the U.S. Department of State. Since each "PREFERENCE" category is allotted a set percentage of the world-wide number of visas allowed for the year, the State Department necessarily keeps a careful track of the number of visas used up by each foreign nation in the course of the year, as well as the number used up in each preference category. If the quota has been reached in a particular category before the fiscal year is over, the Department of State will not issue any more immigrant visas in that category for the rest of the fiscal year and will, in addition, state that visas are temporarily unavailable for that category, either for a particular country or worldwide. In each month, the Department publishes a statement – the **VISA OFFICE BULLETIN** – listing the visa availability world-wide for each preference category and individually by each country. (See an illustrative sample of this Bulletin in pp. 31-2)

Only a limited number of immigrant visas are, of course, available within the numerical system for each foreign country and within each preference category. Consequently, there is established a method by which to determine the order in which aliens are to receive consideration for an immigrant visa.

In general, an immigrant visa applicant is "charged" to the country of the applicant's birth (and not the country of his citizenship or nationality), and this determines the country against whose annual allotment of 26,625 visas a particular applicant's visa is to be charged. As often happens, the waiting list for certain countries (e.g. Mexico, the Philippines, India or Hong Kong) is longer than for other countries. When such a situation exists, the law would permit what is know as an **"alternate chargeability"** or **"cross-chargeability"** under certain circumstance. Thus, for example, if your spouse or parent was born in a different country having a shorter waiting list, you will be permitted to have your visa charged against your spouse's or parent's country of birth, thus allowing you to secure an entry visa sooner than you probably would otherwise have.

As a rule, when the demand from any single country exceeds the 26,625 visa limit in a given year, then for the year following, the visa availability for the natives of that country will be allocated according to the preference percentages for world-wide allocation of available visas.*

B. THE VISA PRIORITY DATE

One simple way to visualize the visa quota system is to envision yourself as standing amidst a long line of persons applying for a permit to enter the United State. To be able to get to the immigration officer's desk to even

---

*Such countries falling under this category are listed individually and clearly identified in the U.S. State Department's Visa Office Bulletin. For example, in 1982, natives of the People's Republic of China used up their full allotment of 20,000 immigrant visas which applied then for that year. Hence, in the following year, 1983, visas where required to be distributed to that country's natives on the basis of set percentages for each preference-category as follows:

Since, under the then prevailing law not more than 10% of the available visa could be used world-wide in the Third Preference category, then no more than 10% of the visas available to the Chinese natives could also be used in the Third Preference category in the year 1983, and so on and so forth. This way, by using the system of allocation, it is ensured that visas will be available in each preference category for that foreign state. For, otherwise, all 20,000 available visas might be used only by persons qualifying in the first few (top) preference categories, and the result will be that visas will be totally unavailable in the lower preference categories.

have your application considered on its merits, each person on the line has to take a number and wait until his number is called. This "number" represents, simply, the order by which each person on that line gets to the immigration officer's desk – the *"priority date"* in the terminology of U.S. Immigration Service. When the alien's priority date is reached, that's when his immigration application will be considered, but in the mean time, there'll be a awaiting period, often quite a long one, before you can get to that date. And it is this waiting period – that is, the waiting to get to the point where your visa application can merely be considered on its merits – that is often referred to when visa applicants hear of huge backlogs or excessive delays in getting an immigrant visa. A three-year backlog for person qualifying under, say, the Employment Third Preference, for example, means in practice that only persons who shall have filed visa applications or filed for labor certification 3 years earlier – those who shall have waited for at least 3 years – would be eligible for the immigrant visa as of today.

Immigrant visa applications (officially called "petitions" in immigration terminology) are considered chronologically on the basis of the "priority date" assigned to the application. The priority date is simply the date on which your petition is filed with the INS office or the American Embassy, or the date when your U.S. employer filed job application for you with the Department of Labor. (NOTE: Always keep safely the receipts of the fee paid to the INS or the return receipts of the registered mail from the post office. The dates on those documents are the PRIORITY DATE of your petition or application).

Each month, the State Department issues a Visa Bulletin (see pp. 35-6 for a sample copy) which establishes an immigrant visa "cut-off" date for each preference category. A CUT OFF DATE is simply the date before which a visa applicant in a preference category must have established a priority date in order for a visa to be made available to him or her. Thus, a cut off date simply announces which Priority Dates in each preference category are being processed by the Department of State for issuance of an immigrant visa: anyone whose priority date falls <u>before</u> this cut-off date, will be given a visa appointment within the month; and any whose Priority Date falls <u>after</u> the cut-off date, will have to wait. To put it another way, when natives of a particular country have used, or are projected to use, more than their country's visa allotment for any particular year, a date is established – a cut-off date – for each preference category before which a priority date must have been established in order for a visa to be made available for an applicant from that country. In this manner, the State Department is able to distribute visas so that the allotments for each preference category are maintained on a worldwide basis while the ceiling for each country is preserved.

The central important of an alien's PRIORITY DATE, it that it is, in effect, the date used to determine the alien's place on the "waiting list" for a visa as contained in the Visa Bulletin put out monthly by the U.S. State Department.

An alien whose application for a visa is in the stage of being processed, may check the priority date of his application by checking this Bulletin. (see sample of the Bulletin on pp. 35-6) With respect to those aliens whose petitions for the visa are based on having secured an approved LABOR CERTIFICATION, the Priority Date is the date on which a particular alien's application for Labor Certification (see p. 167 & 169) was first received and stamped by the local Employment Service in the U.S. It will be his Priority Date in the PREFERENCE Visa Category.* Then, if the alien later files a petition for a visa and has an employment-based preference petition approved based upon a profession or occupation, the alien is now placed into a higher preference – that is, the alien's preference priority date will be that same date on which the approved Labor Certification was first received

---

*For an alien seeking immigration based on close family relationship, the "priority date" is the date the visa petition is filed with the U.S. Embassy or the INS in the U.S.; for those based on an offer of permanent employment and needing labor certification, the "priority date" may be either the date the employer filed an application, or if an alien coming under a "blanket" Labor Certification needing no certification, it is the date of the filing of the visa petition with the INS.

by the Employment Service (and not the date on which the preference petition was submitted or approved). This, in other words, helps the alien, since he gets the advantage of the earlier priority date.

Here is the way this works in practice. Let's restate the basic rule in question here: an immigrant visa can be issued to an alien in the PREFERENCE category, only if there is an unused "available" visa from within the limited number of visas allotted the alien's country for the particular category in which the alien seeks to apply for the priority date. Another way this principle is often stated, is to say that the visa can be given the alien only if his priority (preference) date is "CURRENT" or "AVAILABLE." The visa is immediately "available" for a particular alien if the "waiting list" that existed shall have reached the priority date of the alien so that he does not have to wait on a list; and an alien's priority date is "current" for the alien's country and his preference category if any alien in that country and preference category may immediately apply for a visa inasmuch as there would be no waiting list for his country and preference category at that particular time.

EXAMPLE: Assume that in July 2000 the PRIORITY DATE for available visa numbers for the Employment-based Third Preference (as published in the State Department's visa Bulletin), is January 2001, and further assume that your U.S. employer filed for your Labor Certification with the Employment Service on September 1, 1999 – that is, the date on which the application for your Labor Certification was filed with the Employment Service. In other words, here, your own particular priority date will come before the current priority date for the employment-based third preference group as a whole (Jan. 1, 2001), meaning that a visa number would be immediately available to you.

HOW TO USE THE VISA TABLE

The State Department publishes a *Visa Bulletin* each month which reports the status of the various priorities. See Figure 5A below. The Bulletin contains the cut-off date. The *Bulletin* changes each month. The cut-off date may not necessarily change much from one month to the next, depending on how many petitions were filed during that month. A cut-off date may move one week for one preference category, two weeks for another preference category, or every month; or it may not even move at all for several months in your category. In short, simply be prepared to wait!

To use the Visa Table, the reader looks down the "PREFERENCE" column under the country of his/her place of birth in Figure 5A under the appropriate preference category (depending on whether the petition is family-based or employment-based). If it is not listed separately, the "All Chargeability Areas...." column heading of the list is used. The column to the left are then read downwards until the proper preference category is found either for family-based or for employment-based case. Finally, you look at the date or entry which appears at the intersection of Your Country of Birth line and the proper Preference column.

IF ENTRY IS "C"

If the entry is "C", it means that visas are available for any properly qualified applicant with any priority date. "C" means current.

IF ENTRY IS "U"

The entry "U" means Unavailable. No immigrant visas are available for any alien in that preference no matter how old his priority date. The waiting list if probably quite long, and the State Department will not be able to issue visas in that preference for that Place of Birth until the table entry changes.

IF ENTRY IS A DATE

If the visa table entry is a date, this is the "cut-off date," and this says that the alien must wait for the table date to be later than his priority date. The alien's priority date must be earlier than the table date for there to be a visa available for him. If the alien's priority date is not earlier, the alien must wait for the table entry to become "C" or until the date shown is later than his date.

D. HERE'S SAMPLE, EASY WAY TO DETERMINE YOUR VISA NUMBER AVAILABILITY OR PRIORITY DATE

The Visa Officer Bulletin, published each month by the U.S. State Department (see a sample on p. 35), reports on the status of the various priority dates and lists the visa numbers issued each month. And, a general way by which an alien would ordinarily try to determine whether a visa number for his particular visa preference category is available, or when his priority date becomes current, is by looking up such information from the monthly visa Bulletin; and if the alien should find that the date shown in the Bulletin for his country and preference is current and available (at the time that his petition is either filed or the decision is made on the petition), then he can conclude that he is eligible to get a visa. A copy of the Visa Bulletin can be gotten from any U.S. Embassy or from an INS office.

The process, however, of doing even that much – of going through the monthly visa Bulletin and trying to read and interpret the figures in the visa table by oneself – could often be unnecessarily confusing and burdensome to some, especially for a lay person. HENCE, OUR SIMPLE ADVICE IS THIS: don't even bother yourself trying to do it yourself; let the immigration experts and personnel in the field do the work for you. Just call up or visit any of the following parties in your area and ask for help in providing you with the information: a U.S. consular officer; a U.S. Immigration and Naturalization Service Officer; or the Visa Office Section of the U.S. State Department in Washington D.C. or, ask a local organization experienced and active in U.S. immigration matters. Ask to be informed about your status with respect to immigrant visa priority dates, whether the visa number for your particular preference category is available, and whether your priority date is "current". When calling, remember that visa numbers for the next month usually begin to be available during the last part of the present month.

The U.S. Department of State even has available for the public a tape or recorded message with visa availability information. The recording, updated each month with information on cut-off dates for the following month, can be heard 24 hours a day at this number: **202-663-1541.**

United States Department of State
Bureau of Consular Affairs

VISA BULLETIN

Number 74 Volume VII	Washington, D.C.

IMMIGRANT NUMBERS FOR MAY 1997

A. STATUTORY NUMBERS

1. This bulletin summarizes the availability of immigrant numbers during <u>May</u>. Consular officers are required to report to the Department of State documentarily qualified applicants for numerically limited visas; the Immigration and Naturalization Service reports applicants for adjustment of status. Allocations were made, to the extent possible under the numerical limitations, for the demand received by April <u>7th</u> in the chronological order of the reported priority dates. If the demand could not be satisfied within the statutory or regulatory limits, the category or foreign state in which demand was excessive was deemed oversubscribed. The cut-off date for an oversubscribed category is the priority date of the first applicant who could not be reached within the numerical limits. Only applicants who have a priority date <u>earlier than</u> the cut-off date may be allotted a number. Immediately that it becomes necessary during the monthly allocation process to retrogress a cut-off date, supplemental requests for numbers will be honored only if the priority date falls within the new cut-off date.

2. The fiscal year 1997 limit for family-sponsored preference immigrants determined in accordance with Section 201 of the Immigration and Nationality Act (INA) is 226,000. The fiscal year 1997 limit for employment-based preference immigrants calculated under INA 201 is 140,000. Section 202 prescribes that the per-country limit for preference immigrants is set at 7% of the total annual family-sponsored and employment-based preference limits, i.e., 25,620 for FY-1997. The dependent area limit is set at 2%, or 7,320.

3. Section 203 of the INA prescribes preference classes for allotment of immigrant visas as follows:

FAMILY-SPONSORED PREFERENCES

<u>First</u>: Unmarried Sons and Daughters of Citizens: 23,400 plus any numbers not required for fourth preference.

<u>Second</u>: Spouses and Children, and Unmarried Sons and Daughters of Permanent Residents: 114,200, plus the number (if any) by which the worldwide family preference level exceeds 226,000, and any unused first preference numbers:

A. Spouses and Children: 77% of the overall second preference limitation, of which 75% are exempt from the per-country limit;

B. Unmarried Sons and Daughters (21 years of age or older): 23% of the overall second preference limitation.

<u>Third</u>: Married Sons and Daughters of Citizens: 23,400, plus any numbers not required by first and second preferences.

<u>Fourth</u>: Brothers and Sisters of Adult Citizens: 65,000, plus any numbers not required by first three preferences.

EMPLOYMENT-BASED PREFERENCES

<u>First</u>: Priority Workers: 28.6% of the worldwide employment-based preference level, plus any numbers not required for fourth and fifth preferences.

<u>Second</u>: Members of the Professions Holding Advanced Degrees or Persons of Exceptional Ability: 28.6% of the worldwide employment-based preference level, plus any numbers not required by first preference.

<u>Third</u>: Skilled Workers, Professionals, and Other Workers: 28.6% of the worldwide level, plus any numbers not required by first and second preferences, not more than 10,000 of which to "Other Workers".

<u>Fourth</u>: Certain Special Immigrants: 7.1% of the worldwide level.

<u>Fifth</u>: Employment Creation: 7.1% of the worldwide level, not less than 3,000 of which reserved for investors in a targeted rural or high-unemployment area, and 300 set aside for investors in regional centers by Sec. 610 of P.L. 102-395.

4. INA Section 203(e) provides that family-sponsored and employment-based preference visas be issued to eligible immigrants in the order in which a petition in behalf of each has been filed. Section 203(d) provides that spouses and children of preference immigrants are entitled to the same status, and the same order of consideration, if accompanying or following to join the principal. The visa prorating provisions of Section 202(e) apply to allocations for a foreign state or dependent area when visa demand exceeds the per-country limit. These provisions apply at present to the following oversubscribed chargeability areas: INDIA, MEXICO, and PHILIPPINES.

5. On the chart below, the listing of a date for any class indicates that the class is oversubscribed (see paragraph 1); "C" means current, i.e., numbers are available for all qualified applicants; and "U" means unavailable, i.e., no numbers are available. (NOTE: Numbers are available only for applicants whose priority date is <u>earlier</u> than the cut-off date listed below.)

PREFERENCES

Family-based	All Charge- ability Areas Except Those Listed	INDIA	MEXICO	PHILIPPINES
1st	08APR96	08APR96	01FEB93	18JUL86
2A*	01MAR93	01MAR93	22JUN92	01MAR93
2B	08APR91	08APR91	08APR91	08APR91
3rd	22FEB94	22FEB94	15APR88	22DEC85
4th	01NOV86	01MAR85	08FEB86	22DEC77

*NOTE: For May, 2A numbers EXEMPT from per-country limit are available to
applicants from all countries with priority dates earlier than 22JUN92. 2A
numbers SUBJECT to per-country limit are available to applicants chargeable to
all countries EXCEPT MEXICO with priority dates beginning 22JUN92 and earlier
than 01MAR93. (2A numbers subject to per-country limit are "unavailable" for
applicants chargeable to MEXICO.)

Employment- Based	All Charge- ability Areas Except Those Listed	INDIA	MEXICO	PHILIPPINES
1st	C	C	C	C
2nd	C	C	C	C
3rd	C	01APR95	C	C
Other Workers	01APR90	01APR90	01APR90	01APR90
4th	C	C	C	C
Certain Religious Workers	C	C	C	C
5th	C	C	C	C
Targeted Employ ment Areas/ Regional Centers	C	C	C	C

The Department of State has available a recorded message with visa availability
information which can be heard at: (area code 202) 663-1541. This recording
will be updated in the middle of each month with information on cut-off dates
for the following month.

B. DIVERSITY IMMIGRANT (DV) CATEGORY

Section 203(c) of the Immigration and Nationality Act provides 55,000 immigrant
visas each fiscal year to provide immigration opportunities for persons from
countries other than the principal sources of current immigration to the United
States. DV visas are divided among six geographic regions. Not more than 3,850
visas (7% of the 55,000 visa limit) may be provided to immigrants from any one
country.

Chapter 6

Getting Your Immigrant Visa (The Green Card) Based On Your Being Married To A U.S Citizen Or Permanent Resident Alien

A. ALL THE VARIOUS KINDS OF FAMILY-BASED RELATIONSHIPS AVAILABLE FOR QUALIFYING FOR A GREEN CARD

As has been fully set forth in Chapters 3 & 4, within the family-relationship based immigrant visa categories – that is, those categories of green cards which are granted on the basis of being a relative of, or having a family relationship of some sort with a U.S. citizen or Permanent resident – one of the principal ways by which a green card may be obtained, is through marriage by the alien to an American citizen or to a permanent resident. (See Chapters 3 & 4 for further treatment). In this Chapter, we discuss the detailed eligibility requirements and the procedure for filing for and obtaining a green card for just those aliens who fall under this ONE family-related basis – BEING MARRIED TO AN AMERICAN CITIZENS OR TO A PERMANENT RESIDENT ALIEN.

B. BEING MARRIED EITHER TO A U.S. CITIZEN OR TO A PERMANENT RESIDENT ALIEN

As an alien, you may – if you're duly qualified, of course – obtain a green card through marriage in two basic ways: by being married either to an American citizen, or to permanent resident alien who holds a green card. If you qualify through being married to an American citizen, then you may file for the green card as an IMMEDIATE RELATIVE, with all the filing advantages associated with that class of aliens (basically, no quota required and no visa waiting period). But if you qualify through being married to a permanent resident, you will have to file for the green card under the Family Second Preference category (see Chapter 3 Sections B and C for the basic differentiations, as well as Chapter 4, Sections A and B).

C. THE VISA FILING PROCESS FOR THE ALIEN MARRIED TO A U.S. CITIZEN OR PERMANENT RESIDENT

To file for a green card based on your (an alien's) marriage to a U.S. citizen or permanent resident, follow the following procedures in the same order and chronology in which they are listed below:

1. First, be sure to have read, thoroughly, Chapter 4 of this manual, among others, most especially sections C, D, E, and F thereof, for some helpful advance guidance on what you need to have in order to be able to establish the actual existence of genuine family and/or marital relationship for immigration purposes.

2. NOTE that in the very initial phase involved in applying for any immigration visa (it's called the "petition" phase), it is the alien's sponsor or U.S. relative or family member, and NOT the alien himself or herself, who files

a "petition" on behalf of the alien, seeking to sponsor the said alien for the immigrant visa.* And, in this process, the legal term called the sponsoring U.S. citizen or permanent resident who is to sign the immigration papers for the benefit of the alien family member or worker, is "petitioner," while the alien person is called the "beneficiary."

3. Assuming that the alien for whom the visa is being sought is currently not in the U.S.* and that the visa petition is being filed in order to bring him or her to the U.S. from a foreign country, complete these forms:

Basic Forms Needed by The Sponsor in Petitioning for the Alien:
● Complete FORM 1-130, *Petition or Alien Relative.* (This Form, called the "Petition" for short, is the required form in all *family relationship-based* visa applications. It is to be completed (or, at least, to be signed only) by the U.S. citizen or Permanent Resident alien to whom the intending alien claims to have a close family relationship. (NOTE: Such form may actually be completed for the petitioner by the alien, providing it is the sponsoring U.S. citizen or Permanent resident who signs it at the end.) See illustrative sample of Form 1-130 on pp. 212.

● Form 1-360 – This is to be completed and filed ONLY in a situation when you (the alien person) are petitioning for a visa yourself as a battered spouse.

● Form G-325A. *The Biographic Information* form – see illustrative sample on p. 225). This form is to be completed in part by the sponsoring petitioner, and in part by the alien. Complete 2 copies – one by the husband and the other by the wife. The form is mostly used and applicable in petitions involving "Adjustment of Status" situations where the alien is already in the United State in a non-immigrant status and seeks to change to immigrant status. (See Chapter 20 for Adjustment of Status procedures). However, the form may be required in initial immigrant visa petition situations.

4. File the Completed "Petition" Forms
Now, to file the visa petition for the alien, you, the alien's U.S. citizen or permanent resident relative – the so-called "sponsor" or "petitioner" – must sign the completed petition forms, and submit them, along with the filing fees and the necessary supporting documents to the forms, with: the U.S. Immigration and Naturalization Regional Service Center. Simply mail the papers (always by certified mail with return receipt requested so that you'll have proof that the petition was received), to: The INS Regional Center for the area in which you (the alien's sponsoring petitioner) reside. There are four such centers spread across the U.S. and are not the same as the INS local office. (See Appendix B for the addresses of such INS locations).

[If the sponsor happens to be living outside the U.S., the petition may be filed by him at the nearest U.S. Consulate] For petitions for which the basis is employment or occupation-related, the sponsoring U.S. employer will generally file a petition only when the alien is *outside* the United States, or, if the alien is already in the U.S., then only if the alien's non-immigrant visa has expired or he has violated the terms of his non-immigrant visa (such as by dropping out of school or working without permission.) If the conditions are otherwise, it would ordinarily be the alien himself who has to file the petition, that is, as an "adjustment of status" case set forth in Chapter 20.

---

*In certain limited cases, however, such as cases involving a petition by a widow or abused spouse, the petition is allowed to be filed by the alien himself or herself.

**In a case, however, where the alien is already in the U.S. and he or she seeks a green card on whatever basis, the petition would have to be filed under a procedure called "Adjustment of Status." See Chapter 20 for the procedure.

Documentations Which May be Required in Support of the Sponsor's Petition in Family-Based Cases
To be attached to the basic PETITION form in support, are typically the following documents:

● BIRTH CERTIFICATE (or other equivalents, such as baptismal certificates, military service records, and the like) for both the petitioner and the alien "beneficiary" of the petition.

● PROOF OF U.S. CITIZENSHIP OF PETITIONER, or of his/her U.S. Permanent Residency status (Form I-551 or the "Green Card") – birth certificate, certificate of citizenship, naturalization certificate, or their equivalents, such as military service records, un-expired U.S. passport, baptismal certificate.

● Attach for BOTH spouses' color photographs that were taken within 30 days before the filing of the visa petition. (See Chapter 25, Section F for specification of the exact type and style of the photo required by the INS).

● Attach, most importantly for all petitions based on a marital a relationship, documents to prove that there is a valid marriage existing between the sponsoring petitioner and the alien spouse – any documentary proofs you can think of that will demonstrate that you did not marry mainly to obtain a green card: MARRIAGE CERTIFICATE of the petitioner to the alien, of course (only the civil registry certificate, not the marriage license or the church certificate, is acceptable unless your country accepts a church marriage certificate as an official document); wedding pictures of petitioner and beneficiary; any videos or snapshots of petitioner and beneficiary taken together before the marriage, and, even more importantly, since the marriage, and the like. (See items listed under Section 1 (iii) below for more of the kinds of proof that are acceptable).

● PROOF OF AGE of each alien (e.g., birth certificate or Declaration of age).

● ADOPTION DECREE (or other proof of legal adoption), if the alien is said to be an adopted child.

● DIVORCE DECREE (or death certificate thereof) from prior marriages by the petitioner and the alien, if parties were previously married.

● MARRIAGE CERTIFICATE OF THE COMMON PARENTS of the petitioner and the alien(s), in cases, for example, involving a brother or sister sponsoring a brother or sister.

● "SECONDARY EVIDENCE" type of data – such as affidavits (sworn statements) from people attesting to the necessary facts as to the close family relationship claimed, or letters, correspondence and other proof of communications which had existed between the petitioner and the alien.

● Pay the filing fee - $US80, in the form of a money order or certificate check made out to the "Immigration and Naturalization Service."

Do not send the originals of the documents at this time. Merely submit the photocopies of the documents for the moment, but be sure to have the originals readily available so that you can provide them to the INS officials for inspection and authentication when they are specifically asked for. [NOTE that, on the other hand, however, generally the documents submitted in the second phase of the visa processing, that is, in the "application" phase (Section D below), are usually required to be either the originals or the officially "certified" copies bearing a government seal of authentication].

NOTE: As a rule, the INS does not usually accept automatically the diplomas and schooling credentials earned in foreign institutions as valid or creditworthy or up to standard. Rather, for the INS to accept such documents, you (or the alien involved) would often need to submit the transcripts of the foreign schooling records to an accredited U.S. academic evaluator to be assessed. (See p. 194 for a list of some of such accredited agencies in the United States).

D. THE "APPLICATION" PHASE: UPON APPROVAL OF THE SPONSOR'S "PETITION," THEN IT IS THE ALIEN WHO MUST NOW FILE AN "APPLICATION" FOR THE ACTUAL VISA.

What happens after the alien's sponsoring petitioner (the U.S. citizen or green cardholder) has filed the petition for a green card for the alien spouse? The INS will consider the petition. If some material defects or omissions are found in the papers, such as unsigned forms or missing information or documents or payment, the INS will probably return the entire petition papers to the petitioner with a note or a Form 797, stating what corrections need to be made or what additional documents or information need to be supplied. Or, in certain cases, the INS may simple retain the papers already submitted but issue a request for the additional documents or information needed.

In any event, once the visa petition is approved by the INS, the INS will so inform the sponsoring petitioner by sending him or her either a NOTICE OF APPROVAL OF VISA PETITION (Form 1-191), or a *Notice of Action Form, Form 1-797*. And since the alien lives outside the U.S. in this case, the INS will forward the alien's entire file as well as a copy of the *Notice of Action (or Approval)* to the National Visa Center (NVC) located in Portsmouth, New Hampshire, which will in turn then send the file to the America Consulate in the alien's designated home country or current place of residence. Thereafter, the U.S. Consulate in the alien's home country notifies the alien himself (or herself) of the preliminary approval of the visa petition filed on his behalf, and forwards him a package of information and directives about how he may make the actual "application" for his immigrant visa at the area's U.S. Consulate there, and what documentations and proofs he would need to provide.

Basically, what it boils down to is that if the alien were to qualify as an "immediate relative" alien (Chapter 3, Section C, and Chapter 4, Section A1), meaning that he is therefore not subject to a quota or waiting period requirement, or if the alien qualifies under other family-based preference categories but his Priority Date is immediately current, meaning that there is no waiting period required for the alien and that his visa can begin to be processed immediately (Chapter 5, Section C), then what the alien would have received from the U.S. Consulate is the package of forms and information called the "Packet 3" type – meaning one that basically tells the alien what documents to prepare and assemble in order to be given an appointment for the visa interview with the Consulate Officials. The alien should expect this package within a month or two after the petition is approved. If, however, the alien qualifies under a family preference category, which means therefore that he is subject to some kind of a quota (a waiting period) for the visa number, and if his (her) Priority Date is not yet available or <u>current</u>, the alien will receive the kind of package called "Packet 3A" – basically a letter telling him that he will have to wait for some moment of time for the processing of his visa to be ready. And when it is ready, the alien will then receive Packet 3. In other words, if you are a preference alien of any kind (i.e., one who is subject to a waiting period ("quota") for the visa number to become available), even when you have an approved petition for an immigrant visa if your Priority Date is not yet <u>current</u> you must wait until it is current before you may file your visa application (the next step below). In any case, there is one good news regarding this: *the U.S. Consulate will usually advise the alien, any way, in the Packets 3 or 3A documents it sends the alien, about when it is that his PRIORITY DATE eventually comes up.* [See Chapter 5 for the way the waiting system works for the visa number to become available, and how to keep track of your quota progress through the U.S. State Department].

1. Procedures Involved In Filing the Visa Application

This phase in the visa processing formalities, you should note, is called the *"APPLICATION"* phase, as opposed to the *"PETITION"* phase, which is the first phase just concluded with the granting of the U.S. sponsor's or petitioner's initial petition on the alien's behalf. ***The difference here, in this "application" phase, is that from this point on in the visa processing, it is now THE ALIEN, himself, who has to make the formal request for the visa to the U.S. Consulate in his home country,*** and who has to carry out the remaining paperwork and see to the processing of the visa for the rest of the way, as the remainder of the steps required for concluding the visa processing now shift to the alien and to the U.S. Consulate in the alien's foreign country.

The information and instructions contained in the Packet 3 sent the alien (and to his sponsoring U.S. relative or employer) by the U.S. Consulate in the alien's home country, shall have generally told the alien what further steps he is to take in the processing of his visa. *Here's what you (the alien) do to kick off the filing of your application:*

● There are two primary forms you (the alien) should find included in Packet 3 – Form OF-230-1 and OF-169. You should first complete Form OF230, *Application for Immigrant Visa and Alien Registration - Part 1, Biographic Data.* Complete <u>only</u> the <u>first</u> <u>part</u> of this form at this stage. The second part of the OF230 is OF169. (See p. 220 for a sample of OF230 Part 1; and 2 is on p. 218 & 222). Secondly, upon the alien's completion of OF230 (the Part 1 thereof), promptly send it directly to the American Consulate. <u>Do so as soon as possible</u>; the Consulate officials will usually not begin working on your visa until they receive this form, as they will need the complete information from the Form OF230-1 to enable them begin the required security check into your background in the meantime.

● The Application fee may be required to be enclosed at this time. The area's U.S. Consulate will give the alien the applicable fee amount. As of this writing, the fee is $200 - $170 for the application, and $30 upon approval of the application.

1. Start Assembling the Necessary Supporting Documents

Next, you (the alien) should immediately begin to prepare and assemble the various documents enumerated in Form OF169, *Instructions For Immigrant Visa Applicants* (see sample of this on p. 218), in preparation for use in a visa appointment and interview with the Consulate officials later. And, as soon as you have available all the documents listed in Form OF-169, as applicable to you, and any others required by the Consulate, which may include some or all of those listed below, this is what you do: now, complete the Part 2 of the Form OF230 – that is, The Form OF-169 (this you sign at the bottom page), and the Form OF-230 Part 2, *Applicant For Immigrant Visa and Alien Registration – Sworn Statement,* reproduced on p. 222. (See sample of this form on p. 218). <u>Do not sign the OF-230, Part 2 form yet at this point</u> – wait until you are specifically asked to do so by the Consular officer. Mail only the form OF-169 (or take it down in person) to the Consulate office. Upon receipt of this form, this informs the Consulate that you (and all others, who are emigrating with you, if any) are now ready and prepared for the final processing of your application and to attend the visa appointment and interview.

Supporting Documents to be Attached to the Aliens' Application.

The following are the forms and examples of the supporting documents the alien applicant may have to complete and submit in an immigrant visa application phase:

● BIRTH CERTIFICATE: One certified copy for each person named for a visa in the application.

● Two (it could be more) passport-size color PHOTOGRAPHS of each alien, showing a full front view of the facial features, with the reverse side of each photograph signed (in full names) by the alien filing each application. (See Chapter 25, Section F for specification of the right style and manner of the photo).

● A current PASSPORT for each alien issued by the alien's country and valid for at least the next 6 months or so.

● A POLICE CERTIFICATE for each accompanying family member of the alien who is over 16 year of age – obtainable from the police or other appropriate authorities in each of all the countries where each alien had resided for more than 6 months. [If the alien is applying from within the U.S., the REPORT OF

FINGERPRINTING (Form FD 258, sampled on p. 224) may be used instead. The print is taken at a local police station or a local INS Office and recorded on the pre-coded card, then sent to the consulate or INS for referral to the FBI for a clearance report].

● COURT AND PRISON RECORDS, if any, for each applicable alien with a prior prison record.
● MILITARY RECORD for each alien, if applicable, for service in your country or any country.
● REPORT OF MEDICAL EXAMINATION for each alien. (The examination must usually be performed by a doctor or medical facility specially designated by the U.S. Consulate in the foreign country, who then furnishes the report to the alien to provide the Consulate).

Documentary evidence which ESTABLISH THE CLOSE FAMILY RELATIONSHIP THAT YOU CLAIM to have with your sponsoring U.S. petitioner, as applicable – e.g., marriage certificates, affidavits or sworn declaration of birth and family relationship by witnesses, adoption decree, correspondence and other proof of communication and family relationship which had existed between the petitioner and the alien, e.t.c. (Or, if more applicable, a death certificate, divorce decree, e.t.c. – whichever shows your true current marital status).

● EVIDENCE OF SUPPORT: If your visa application is family-based, or if it is employment-based but your relatives are your sponsors for your visa petition or own at least 5% of the company which is your sponsor, then you'll need to file Form I-864, *Affidavit of Support*. (See sample of the form on p. 241). Note that this form, the AFFIDAVIT OF SUPPORT, is to be made out and sworn to (signed) by the sponsoring U.S. citizen or Permanent Resident and his/her spouse, if married, showing that the sponsor promises that he will financially support you (the alien) and that you will not become a "public charge" to the U.S. government if admitted to the U.S. (A cover sheet to this form carries detailed instructions on the supporting documents, such as income records, statement of earning, bank records, evidence of property ownership, etc., to be attached to this affidavit).

If, on the other hand, your visa application is not family-based, and you do not have a job or offer of employment in the U.S., you should have your U.S. sponsor complete another version of the *Affidavit of Support*, Form I-134 (see sample of this form on p. 214).

● An approved LABOR CERTIFICATION from the U.S. Department of Labor – to be provided if applicable, such as when the alien has a job or an offer of employment by a U.S. company or employer and is filing under the Second, Third, Forth or Fifth employment-based preference category. The underlying documentary evidence upon which the certification has been obtained, is also to be attached. (When a labor certificate is submitted, it's customary in such cases to also enclose an EMPLOYER'S LETTER OR OFFER OF EMPLOYMENT – see the sample reproduced on pp. 176 & 177. For the procedures used in an actual, successfully processed prevous case, see "Explanatory Note" on p. 89.

● A few Consulates require the applicants to submit fingerprints. Most do not, however. Consulates requiring this will inform you of this.

● Form I-797, *Notice of Action* – include a copy of this form that has been sent you by the Immigration and Naturalization Service to notify you that your sponsor's visa petition had been approved.

What happens next? The Consulate examiners will take a quick, initial look at your application and make a preliminary assessment. And, once the examiners can determine either that you are not subject to a quota or that your visa number is immediately available ("current"), your application will be considered ready for further processing. At this point the Consulate will send you another batch of papers, known as PACKET 4. Packet 4 will provide you important relevant information, such as the following: a written notice or letter of appointment indication when you should come for your visa interview with the head of the Consulate's Immigrant visa section, the list of documents you are to provide, including those detailed in Form OF-169, directions on how and where you should have your medical examination taken before the interview date, and so on. And the Packet 4 may still have more forms to complete.

Now, take strict note of the date of *your visa interview appointment*. Also, be sure to make your medical examination appointment – it's usually scheduled for immediately before the visa interview, depending on the practice of specific consulates. The medical exam appointment letter will tell you where exactly to go (the name of the doctor or clinic, the address, etc), what specific tests or exams you are to take, the amount of the doctors' fee you are to pay for the exam, etc. Basically, the main purpose of the medical exam is to determine that you don't have the kind of medical conditions that would make you medically excludable under the law, such as tuberculosis or HIV (AIDS).

E. ATTEND THE VISA INTERVIEW

All alien applicants for an immigrant visa are subject to personal interview with the U.S. Consulate, although an interview is frequently waived for aliens under 14 years of age. Turn to Chapter 21, for the full procedures involved in this all-important visa interview.

However, simply be sure to bring with you to the interview appointment, all the completed forms and supporting documents you shall have gathered which apply in your case, including those listed in Sections C3 and D2 above which have not already been submitted. Do not mail your documents and paperwork to the Consulate. Rather, you are to bring them (the final papers you are required to provide) in person to your interview appointment. *This is when you will be expected to present the actual <u>originals</u> (or certified true copies) of the documents for the benefit of the Consular officers so that they can physically examine and authenticate the documents for their genuineness.* And it is also at this interview that you (each visa applicant) will have to sign the Form OF-230 application in the presence of the American Consul.

F. FINAL APPROVAL OF YOUR VISA BY THE CONSULATE OFFICE

In the end, upon the conclusion of the visa interview (Section E above), assuming that everything is in order with your visa application – that you have, for example, provided all the proofs and documentation required, and there's nothing in your background that makes you inadmissible under the immigration law, such as having a serious criminal record or contagious communicable disease – your application for a visa will probably be approved. You will be issued your "Green Card" (actually the card is not green in color) by the U.S. Consul in charge at the Consulate, a document formally known as the *Immigrant Visa and Alien Registration*, which bears your photograph and an official stamp of approval. Most of the times, however, the approved visa will merely be stamped in your (the alien's) passport for now, and the actual issuance of the Green Card to you will take place only after you've been admitted into the U.S.

As of this moment, you have been issued your immigrant visa. BUT REMEMBER THIS: You are NOT YET a <u>permanent</u> <u>resident</u>, though!

Your immigrant visa is valid for 6 months – it allows you to arrive in the U.S. within those 6 months.* And, technically, it is only at the moment when you make an entry into the U.S. with your immigrant visa in hand, that

---

*NOTE: At the time of your issuance of the visa, you will also usually be given back your original Form OF-230, along with the originals of your supporting documents and your medical x-rays. This is to enable you take these documents with you when you travel to the U.S. so that you can present them to the immigration authorities for verifications purposes upon your arrival at the U.S. port of entry.

you actually acquire the status of being a green card (an immigrant visa) holder. [See Chapter 22 for the formal admission process into the U.S. after approval of an alien's visa]. It is at that time that your passport is stamped and you are granted immediate authorization to work. And the permanent green card for you (and for others who accompany you as relatives, if any) are then ordered, and you get them in the mail in your new U.S. address a few months later. (IMPORTANT: Always be sure to inform the INS if you have any change in address upon arrival in the U.S. so that you do not face the potential problem of losing or misplacing your green card).

G. YOU MUST BE FORMALLY "ADMITTED" INTO THE U.S. AT A PORT OF ENTRY

The immigrant visa you've been issued is valid for 6 months – it grants you the legal authorization to arrive in the U.S. within those 6 months. *You must endeavor to arrive in the U.S. (at a port of entry) within the six months.* And, technically, it is only at the moment when you arrive at the U.S. port of entry and are formally "admitted" into the U.S. by the U.S. border inspectors, that you actually acquire the full status of being a permanent resident (an immigrant visa or green cardholder) of the United States. At that time, the U.S. border inspectors will stamp your passport as a legal immigrant admitted to stay and work in the United States. The actual card, called the Green Card, for you (and for others who accompany you as relatives, if any) are then ordered, and you get them by mail in your new U.S. address a few months later.

Note, however, that before you can be actually "admitted" into the U.S. even when you've obtained your approved visa, you must first have to successfully pass through the very important formalities involved in what is called *the inspection and admission process* into the United States. Turn to Chapter 22, *"Entering the United States: The Process of Getting Actually Admitted into the Country After You've Got Your Visa,"* for the procedures involved.

H. SPECIAL SITUATION: YOU MUST REMOVE THE 'CONDITIONAL RESIDENCE' STATUS
IF YOU MARRIED WITHIN 2 YEARS OF GETTING YOUR GREEN CARD

As fully explained in Chapter 4, Section F, as an alien qualified for a green card based on your being married to a U.S. citizen or a permanent resident, if you obtained your green card WITHIN two years after marrying the American citizen spouse or permanent resident, you have what is known as a "conditional" green card, and you are considered a "conditional permanent resident" – that is, your green card is granted you CONDITIONALLY, and for 2 years only, and you are required to file a second visa petition (a joint one with your spouse this time) within 90 days prior to the 2 years anniversary of the grant of the conditional residence, so that the INS can re-evaluate the bona-fide of the marriage, and only if the marriage is determined to be valid and still subsisting could the INS issue you a permanent immigrant visa. (See Chapter 4, Section F, for more on the conditional visa rules).

Hence, if you fall under this category and you obtained your green card approval within 2 years after marrying your American citizen permanent resident, here's what you must do: you and your spouse must apply to have the conditional status removed by filing a joint petition, within 90 days of the second anniversary of getting the green cards.

I. REMOVING CONDITIONAL RESIDENCE STATUS
Here Are the Basic Procedures
i. Complete and submit – it must be done WITHIN 90 days (the third month) before your second anniversary of becoming a conditional permanent resident – the following materials to an office of the Immigration and Naturalization Service in your place of residence in the U.S.:

●Form I-751, *Petition To Remove The Conditions On Residence.* You must have this form signed jointly by

BOTH you and your spouse. (See sample of this form on p. 237).
- Documentary evidence that you and your spouse are involved in a true, bona fide marriage. (See the list below)
- Filing fee of $80 in money order or certified check, made payable to the Immigration and Naturalization Service.

ii. Submit these items, by certified mail with return receipt requested, to the INS Regional Service Center nearest your place of residence. (See Appendix B for the addresses.) Retain your receipt of mailing from the post office for proof.

iii. Depending on the disposition of the INS officers towards your application, the INS may approve your petition without an interview. Or, it may decide that an interview is necessary before making a determination. In that case, you and your spouse will receive a notice of appointment for an interview from the INS. And, in the end, assuming that everything is in order with the INS – that the INS officers determine that you and your spouse had in fact married for love and are involved in a true marriage – the INS will approve your joint petition. Meaning that the 'conditional' status of your visa is removed, and that you are then a full-fledged permanent resident for all times thereafter.

The central key to prevailing in a petition to convert from a "conditional" to a "permanent" resident status, is simple: *just be able to present some good, documentary proof, documentations and explanations, that are consistent and truthful, demonstrating that you in deed married for love and with real commitment, and not merely to obtain a green card, and clearly showing that you and your spouse have established a life together.*

The following are some of the helpful kinds of documents you might submit to the INS to prove existence of a true marital relationship in your case:
- birth certificate of all children born of the marriage, if any, showing both parties as the parents.
- leases to the apartments the parties have occupied showing joint tenancy since the time of the marriage, telephone and utilities bills showing both your names as Mr. and Mrs.
- title to a house or other real property showing joint ownership.
- bank books or statements showing evidence of joint checking or saving accounts.
- hospital cards, union books, pay vouchers, or charge cards containing names of the parties as husband and wife or addressed to both as Mr. and Mrs.
- tax returns that are jointly signed and filed as a married couple for the years the parties have been married
- a letter on the company letterhead from both the husband's and the wife's current employer, giving important particulars, such as when employment began, amount of salary, marital status, dependants claimed, and the person to be notified in case of an emergency.
- registration of cars and other personal property in both names
- life and other insurance policies taken by the parties and listing each other as the insurance beneficiary.
- current testamentary Will showing one party as the spouse and beneficiary of the other's estate.
- wedding pictures and videos, and snapshots of other occasions showing the parties living together and in loving, marital situations.

Chapter 7
The K-1 Visa: A Special Entry Visa For Fiance(e)s Engaged To Marry A U.S. Citizen

A. WHAT IS A K-1 VISA

The K visa is singularly unique. Officially, it is classified as a NONIMMIGRANT visa. However, in reality, it is almost like an immigrant visa, if not exactly one. Hence, we are devoting here a separate chapter solely to discussing the eligibility standards and the procedures involved in obtaining the K visa.

The K visa is, in a word, for the alien living abroad who is a fiance or fiancee engaged to marry a United States citizen. The object of the K visa is to enable its alien holder who is a fiance or fiancee of a U.S. citizen engaged to marry the citizen, to gain entry into the U.S. SOLELY for the purpose of that alien marrying the U.S. citizen. If the alien is granted a visa, he of she must enter into the marriage with the U.S. citizen WITHIN 90 days of his or her entry into the U.S.; otherwise, the visa shall expire and the alien fiance or fiancee must return to his or her home country. No extensions are given on a K visa, the sole exception being in cases of illness or other like unforeseen emergencies; and no change of status to other categories, immigrant or nonimmigrant, is permissible for the K visa holder or the minor children accompanying such K visa holder, if any.

The K nonimmigrant category is unique in one major respect, namely: it differs from any other nonimmigrant classification in that it is the only nonimmigrant visa about which it is clear from the time of its issuance, and at the time of the alien's entry into the U.S. at the border, that the alien nevertheless intends to remain in the U.S. PERMANENTLY. (Under a provision of the Immigration Marriage Fraud Amendments of 1986, however, all K non-immigrants upon marrying the U.S. citizen spouse, are first subject to a 2-year period of "conditional permanent" residence, before they may secure permanent residency status).

B. HOW THE K-1 VISA WORKS

If you are an alien person engaged to or intending to marry a U.S. citizen, you will, with a K-1 visa, be able to come to the U.S. for the purpose of marrying the U.S. citizen; your U.S. citizen fiancee or fiance may bring you to America (he/she is to file a petition for you from the U.S.) by asking for you to be granted an entry visa into the U.S. for the sole purpose of undertaking the marriage – the K-1 visa. And, then, once you are granted a K-1 visa, if you also have any unmarried children who are under 21 years of age, they too would qualify for a visa, called the K-2 visa. With their K-2 visa, such children can accompany you to the U.S.; and further more, you can, as well, apply for a green card to have a permanent residence status in the U.S. once you actually get married to your U.S. citizen fiancee or fiance down to road.

C. THE UNIQUENESS AND BENEFITS OF THE K-1 VISA

K-1 visa is unique in that, though it is a nonimmigrant visa quite alright, once the K-1 visa holder gets married to the U.S. citizens, the visa can almost automatically be converted into a permanent residence visa or green card. The visa, while being issued by the U.S. Consulate abroad to the fiancee of a U.S. citizen, is perfectly understood to be a temporary visa that requires that the alien person contract an intended marriage within 90 days of his/her entry into the U.S. Yet, the visa just as clearly presumes that, once the marriage is contracted, the alien person will then apply for a permanent visa to the U.S. and will adjust his/her immigration status in the U.S. to a permanent residency status. In fact, the K-1 visa has no other real value or purpose – other than, in other words, to serve as a preliminary step to getting a permanent resident visa. Indeed, most couples, in apparent recognition of this reality, do not generally apply for the K-1 visa. Instead, they simply get married and then apply directly for the green card. For example, if you (a U.S. citizen) were to marry your alien fiancee (or fiance) in her country, you can simply file a petition for her for a green card to bring her in as "an immediate relative," a procedure that is much quicker, easier and less expensive. (No round trip expense, at least!) In consequence, as a practical matter, there is really one situation when the use of a K-1 visa is most proper and advisable: namely, when there is some good reason why the marriage between the two parties cannot take place either in the U.S. or in the alien's home country (e.g. the U.S. citizen is sick and bedridden or cannot take the time off to go abroad to marry, etc).

D. HOW TO QUALIFY FOR A K-1 VISA

Briefly summarized, to qualify for a K-1 visa, here are the basic requirements:

● the U.S. citizen, who must be the petitioner for the K-1 visa on the alien fiance(e)'s behalf, must establish that he/she is in deed a U.S. citizen.

● both parties in the couple, must establish that they are legally free and able to marry. (Each must be single and of legal age, and where either one has been previously married, proof of the termination of the marriage must be provided.)

● the alien fiance(e) must demonstrate genuine intention to actually marry the U.S. citizen within 90 days after entry into the U.S.

● the parties must establish that they have physically met and personally seen each other within the past 2 years prior to filing the visa petition. Except, however, that, in the case of those persons for which marriages are customarily arranged, or whose religious principles and practice prohibit couples from meeting before marriage (or where such a meeting would cause exceptional hardship), the requirement of pre-marital meeting may be waived for such persons, upon application. However, for such a waiver to be granted, the couple would need to make a showing to the U.S. Consular officer that both parties will be following as well all the relevant religious customs of the marriage.

E. HOW TO FILE FOR THE K-1 VISA

To file for a K-1 visa for your alien fiancee or fiance, follow these steps and procedures exactly in the same order and chronology in which they are listed below:

1. You (the U.S. citizen and petitioner) complete and sign these papers:

● Immigration Form I-129F, *Petition For Alien Fiance(e).* (See sample of this form on p. 210)

● Form G-325A: *Biographic Information*, for each person. Both the petitioner and the alien fiance(e) and accompanying children, if any, are to complete and sign this form. (See sample of this form on p. 225)

● Form I-134, *Affidavit of Support* (see the sample on p. 214), made out, signed and sworn to by the sponsoring U.S. citizen, whereby the petitioner promises that he (she) will financially support the alien and ensure that he (she) does not become a "public charge" to the U.S. government if admitted to the U.S. A cover sheet to this form carries detailed instructions and a list of the supporting documents (employment certification, statement of earnings, bank records, evidence of property ownership, etc) to be attached to this affidavit.

• COLOR PHOTOGRAPHS of the petitioner and the alien fiancé(e) that were taken within 30 days before the filing of the visa petition (see Chapter 25, Section F for specification of the exact type and style of the photo that's acceptable to the INS).

• PROOF OF AMERICAN CITIZENSHIP for the visa petitioner: birth certificate, certificate of citizenship or naturalization, U.S. passport, etc.

• DIVORCE DECREE/DEATH CERTIFICATES: Proof showing that any previous marriage in which either the petitioner or the alien were involved, if any, had been legally terminated.

• AFFIDAVIT by the U.S. citizen stating facts and information about how the fiancé and the fiancée met, how and why they decided to be married to each other, and their plans for the marriage and a married life together.

• PROOF that the U.S. citizen and the alien fiancé(e) have personally met each other within the past 2 years: photographs, videos, plane tickets, letters, etc.

• PROOF that the parties have an intention to marry within 90 days after the alien fiancé(e) arrives in the U.S.: personal letter from the parties themselves, letters from the religious or civic authority who will officiate at the marriage ceremony or a wedding, long-distance telephone bills, receipt showing advance payment made for reservation of the place where the wedding reception will be held, printed engagement or wedding invitation cards, etc.

• THE FILING FEE – it's $80 as of this writing, to be made out in the form of a money order or certified check, made payable to the "Immigration and Naturalization Service."

2. File The Completed Petition Forms and Papers

Now, you, the American citizen (variously called the "sponsor" or the "petitioner" in this process), are to file the visa petition for your alien fiancé(e). Simply, you sign the completed petition forms and submit them, along with the necessary supporting documents that are required, to the U.S. Immigration and Naturalization Service's regional office for the area in which you reside. (See Appendix B for the addresses of the INS). You may submit the above items in person by hand; or you may mail them, by certified mail with return receipt requested, and preserve the receipt of mailing.

NOTE: DO not sent the *originals* of the documents needed at this time. Only sent the photocopies for now. Retain the originals until the point when you're specifically asked to present them for inspection and verification.

F. FINAL STEPS IN CONCLUDING THE SECURING OF THE K-1 VISA

Upon your filing the petition papers with the INS office (Section E above), the INS will consider the petition, and, assuming that everything is in order, it will likely approve the visa petition. It will send you (as well as the alien beneficiary of the petition and the U.S. Consulate office in the foreign country where the alien is presently located). a written notification of the preliminary approval of the initial visa petition, called a NOTICE OF ACTION Form I-797. (See Chapter 6 at Section C and D thereof, for the detailed procedures of how this works). *But the important thing to note is that thereafter, from this point on in the Visa processing, all further steps required for concluding the visa processing now shift to the visa-seeker, THE ALIEN himself or herself, and the U.S. Consulate office in the foreign country where the alien is located.* The Notice of Action Form I-797 will contain instructions for the next steps that will need to be taken, including a listing of the additional information or documentation required to be supplied for the concluding phase of the visa processing.

The remainder of the procedures and steps called for in the processing of the alien fiancé(e)'s K-1 Visa from this point on till the end when the alien actually has the visa in his/her hand, are essentially the same as those outlined from Chapter 6, Section D thereof. Hence, turn to Chapter 6 Section D. *The Application Phase: Upon the Approval of the sponsor's "Petition," Then it is the Alien, who Must Now File An "Application" For the Actual Visa* (p. 39). Have the alien visa applicant finish up the remainder of the visa processing starting precisely from there.

NOTE: At the conclusion of the visa filing process and all the additional paperwork by the alien fiancé(e) at the American Consulate in his or her home country, the American Consul in charge of visa affairs there, upon being convinced that the American citizen and the alien fiancé(e) are genuinely engaged to be married and that they will likely marry upon the alien's arrival in the U.S., will grant the K-1 visa. The Consul will simple stamp the alien fiancé(e)'s passport with a K-1 visa. And if you (the alien) have any accompanying minor children (they must be under 21 years of age) for whom you have also requested a visa, the Consul will also stamp their passports with a K-2 visa, meaning that they are dependent upon the K-1 visa holder for their immigration status. *Your K-1 Fiancé(e) visa is, however, a NONIMMIGRANT Visa and only accords you [the alien fiancé(e)] a nonimmigrant status since, by it, you are simply promising to marry an American citizen.* You haven't married him or her yet. However, there's one immediately advantage of having the K-1 visa (aside, obviously, from your gaining entry into the United State): upon your arrival in the U.S., you can apply at once for an Employment Authorization card which will enable you to start working at once legally.

 Finally, note that as a K-1 visa holder, one principal precondition upon which the granting of your K-1 visa is based, is that you must, under the U.S. immigration law, get married to your U.S. citizen fiancé(e) WITHIN 90 days after you've arrived in the U.S. The rule is that if a K-1 fiancé(e) fails to marry his or her American fiancé(e) within the prescribed 90 days, or ever, the INS would start deportation proceedings against the K-1 alien as well as all the minor children who accompany the K-1 alien, if any; and if the K-1 fiancé(e) were to marry someone else other than his/her American petitioner, the K-1 alien (and any minor children who accompany the K-1 alien) will lose the right to receive a green card.

 On the other hand, if you follow through with the INS preconditions for granting you the K-1 visa and proceed to actually marry your American fiancé(e) within the required 90-day period – as the overwhelming numbers of K-1 fiancé(e) who come into America every year actually do-there's just one more step you'll need to take to finalize the securing of your green card. And this is: you must file the immigration Form 1-485 with the local INS office in the area where you live in the U.S. in a procedure known as "*Adjustment of Status.*" (See Chapter 20). You'll probably have a "conditional", Permanently residency status at this point. But at the end of your two years into the marriage, you can file to remove the conditional element and to convert to a permanent residence. (See Chapter 6 Section H for the procedures for removal of the conditional element for a green card which is based on marriage).

Chapter 8

Getting Your Immigrant Visa (The Green Card) Based On Being A Child Of A U.S. Citizen Or Permanent Resident: Filing As A Parent For Your Son Or Daughter

A. ALL THE VARIOUS KINDS OF FAMILY BASED RELATIONSHIPS AVAILABLE FOR QUALIFYING FOR A GREEN CARD

As has been fully set forth in the preceding Chapters 3 & 4, within the family-relationship-based immigrant visa categories provided for under the U. S. immigration laws – that is, those categories of green cards which are granted on the basis of being a relative of, or having a family relationship of some sort with, a U.S. citizen or Permanent Resident – one of the principal ways available therein by which a green card may be obtained, is through being a bona-fide child of an American citizen or Permanent Resident alien (green cardholder). In this chapter, we discuss the detailed eligibility requirements and the procedures for filing for and obtaining a green card for just those aliens who fall under this ONE family-related basis – BEING THE CHILD OF A U.S. CITIZEN OR PERMANENT RESIDENT ALIEN.

B. WHO QUALIFIES AS A PARENT WHO CAN PETITION FOR A GREEN CARD FOR A CHILD?

In furtherance of the fundamental goal and principle of encouraging family togetherness which generally underlies the U.S. immigration laws, a parent can petition to obtain a green card for his or her children, if he (she) meets a few basic requirements.

Basically, you qualify to do this if:

● You (the petitioner) are a U.S. citizen parent, and your alien child involved is <u>under</u> 21 years of age. (The child qualifies here under "Immediate Relative" classification – (see Chapter 3, Section B, and Chapter 4, Section A.1).

● You are a U.S. citizen parent, and your alien child involved is <u>over</u> 21 years of age and is not married. (The child comes under family-based First Preference classification – see Chapter 3, Section C.1, and Chapter 4, Section A.2).

● You are a U.S. citizen parent, and your alien child involved is over 21 years of age and married (The child qualifies here under the family-based Third Preference Classification – see Chapter 3, Section C.1, and Chapter 4, Section A.2)

● You are a lawful Permanent Resident alien (Green Card holder) parent, and your alien child involved is under 21 years of age and not married. (The child comes under Family-based Second – 2A Preference Classification). If the alien child is over 21 years of age and is not married (or has been married but is now divorced), then he/she would come under the Family-based Second 2B Preference classification.

C. WHO QUALIFIES AS A CHILD FOR WHOM YOU CAN PETITION FOR A GREEN CARD

Under the immigration law (see, especially Section 101(6)(1) of the Immigration and Naturalization Act) the term "child" is defined to include the following: a legitimate child; a stepchild; a legally legitimized child; an illegitimate child; an adopted child; and orphan child. The proper definition of who is a "child" is very important in this connection as it determines what kind of documentations and proofs will be required by the INS in supporting the petition for a green card in a given case.

i. Legitimate Child

A woman and man who conceive a child, are known as the biological or natural parents of the child. Under the INS procedures, when a child is born to a man and a woman who are married to each other, the child is deemed their LEGITIMATE child. Usually, as a U.S. citizen or Permanent Resident parent, you can show that you are the father or mother of such a person, your natural child or children, simply by submitting the child's birth certificate with your (the parents' names) fully listed on it as the parents. When you, the petitioning parent, are the child's father, then you must also submit your marriage certificate showing that you're married to the mother of the child.

As a parent petitioning for a green card for a child, it is somewhat easier to establish the parent-child relationship through a mother as compared to a father: for the most part, all you have to do, in the case of a mother, is have the birth certificate showing the names of the mother and of the child and the relationship between the woman and the child is automatically established even if the woman is not (or was never) married to the child's father. But not so with the father! If the father and mother of the child are not married to one another at the time of the birth of the child, and the child's birth certificate does not bear the man's name, there's trouble for the man; he'll have to produce some other documentation or proof in order to establish that the child is indeed his child – documentation and proofs ranging from a properly executed document of acknowledgement of paternity before a civil court, to a blood test or signed affidavits from the mother or other parties.

Aside from having a legitimate child, a child could also be a "LEGITIMATED" child. In the terms of the INS, a "legitimated" child is a child born to a man and a woman who, though not married to each other when the child was born, did marry each other *before* the child turned 18.

ii. Stepchild

When you, the mother or the father of a child, marry another person other than the natural or biological parent of that child, a stepparent relationship is created between that new parent (the non-biological parent) and the child. But, under the immigration rules, for there to be any immigration benefit (a green card), that marriage between the child's (one) parent and the stepparent must have to have occurred BEFORE the child turns 18 years of age.

If you are a stepchild, your U.S. stepparent may petition for you for a green card under two basic condition: 1) the marriage creating the family relationship took place before the stepchild's 18th birthday; and 2) the marriage that created the stepchild/stepparent relationship is still in existence at the time of the filing of the petition for the green card for the stepchild. (In the eyes of the INS, if the marriage which created the stepchild/stepparent family relationship has ended, that relationship also ceases to exist).

iii. Adoptive Child

For the purpose of immigration, a person is considered to be an "adopted child" in the eyes of the INS, if these basic conditions are present:

● If that person (the adoptive child) has been adopted strictly according to the adoption laws of the country of his or her birth, or of the American state of the adopting parent; and

- If the adoption of that person occurs before he or she turns 16 years of age.
- The adoptive U.S. parent (the petitioning party for the grant of immigrant visa) must have had legal custody of the adoptive child for at least two years prior to the petition for a green card – meaning that either a legal guardianship or an actual adoption decree must have been issued on such a child at least 2 years prior to the filing of the petition for a green card.
- The adopted child must have physically lived with the adoptive parents before the petition is filed.

In short, the process involved in filing for a green card for a adopted child, is quite complex, and would require that the adoptive parent petitioning for the adopted child submit almost all of the same documents as do parents who petition for their natural children, while requiring some additional requirements that are particular for adoptive children and parents. Hence, for this reason, the procedures involved in filing for a green card for adopted children, both as petitioners or beneficiaries, are treated in separate chapters – See Chapters 11 and 12.

iv. Illegitimate Child

As a U.S. parent (whether a citizen or green cardholder), you may petition for a green card for your illegitimate child(ren). Simply put, if you and the other parent of the child were not married at the child's birth, the child will be treated as illegitimate. If you are the mother, legitimacy is irrelevant in the eyes of the immigration authorities, and you can file the petition exactly as you would for any legitimate child. However, if you are the father, you are required to present some other extra documents that would prove two other additional elements – your paternity of the child, and either the legal legitimization or the existence of a genuine parent/child relationship.

D. HOW TO FILE FOR THE GREEN CARD

To file for a green card for your child(ren) based on your (a U.S. citizen or Permanent Resident) being the parent of an alien child(ren),* simply follow these steps and procedures exactly in the same order and chronology· in which they are listed below:

1. First, be sure to have read, thoroughly, Chapter 4, for some helpful guidance on certain definitions and concepts which are relevant to establishment of true parent-child relationship under the U.S. immigration law.

2. *Complete These Forms*

Assuming that the children at issue are currently not in the U.S. and that you are filing to bring them in from a foreign country, complete:

- FORM I-130, *Petition For Alien Relative.* This form (obtain it free of charge from the INS) is to be completed and signed by the U.S. parent, called the visa "petitioner." (See sample copy of this form on p. 212)
- FORM G-325A: *Biographic Information.* This form is to be completed in part by the sponsoring petitioner, and in part by the alien beneficiary. The form in mostly used and applicable in petitions involving "Adjustment of Status" situations (see Chapter 20) where the alien is already in the U.S. in a nonimmigrant status and seeks to change to immigrant status. However, it may be required in some initial immigrant visa petition situations. (See p. 225 for sample of this form).

3. File the Completed Forms & Papers

Now, to file the visa petition for your alien child(ren), you – the so-called "sponsor" or "petitioner" –

---

* The Green Card procedures specific for adopted children, are set forth separately in Chapters 11 and 12 to allow for a comprehensive treatment which the matter deserves.

must sign the completed forms and submit them (along with the necessary supporting documents), to the U.S. Immigration and Naturalization Service's District Office in the United States. File them in the office covering the area in which you, the sponsor, reside, or where the alien's prospective employment is located, where employment is applicable. (See Appendix B for the addresses of the INS locations)

Documentations Which May Be Required In Support Of The Sponsors' Petition

To be attached to the basic PETITION forms in support, are typically the following documents:

- PROOF OF U.S. CITIZENSHIP OR PERMANENT RESIDENCE OF PETITIONER: For the petitioning U.S. citizen, your birth certificate, certificate of citizenship or naturalization, U.S. passport, and the like. For the petitioning Permanent Resident, a showing of your green card, unexpired re-entry permit or passport with an unexpired stamp indicating admission to the U.S. as a permanent resident.
- CHILD'S BIRTH CERTIFICATE showing the names of the petitioner(s) as the mother and/or father of the child.
- MARRIAGE CERTIFICATE of the child's common parents (the petitioners), if petitioner is filing as the father; and the marriage certificate of the child's mother or father and the stepparents, if petitioner is filing for either of the child's stepparents, showing the names of the particular stepparent's husband or wife who has become the child's stepparent. If petitioner is filing as a stepparent, present also your (the stepparent's) birth certificates to show the names of your (stepparent's) natural parents.
- MOTHER'S MARRIAGE CERTIFICATE: Present this to show child's mother's change of name, where child's mother has since changed her maiden name because she had married someone else. (Similarly, if child is a daughter who has changed her maiden name because of marriage, present her marriage certificate to show that the child on the birth certificate and the child on the immigration form are the same person).
- If you (the petitioner) are the father of the child and you are either unmarried to the child's mother at the time of his/her birth, or unable to present a birth certificate of the child that bears your name as the father, then you must submit evidence proving that, at least up to the time the child turned 21 years of age, a real father-child relationship existed between the two of you: evidence of having lived together in the same house with the child at least until his/her 18th birthday, evidence of maintaining personal contact with the child and of having provided financial support for the child, school records, with the man's name registered as the father, photographs, letters and birthday cards sent to the child and received by him/her, Christmas cards, evidence of entering the child's name as a beneficiary in the man's life insurance, income tax returns showing the child as a dependent, cancelled checks or other common financial records showing that petitioner has regularly contributed money to the child's support.
- DIVORCE DECREE/DEATH CERTIFICATES: present divorce decree or death certificates as well, showing that previous marriages in which you and your present spouse were involved, if any, had been legally terminated.
- If you are a father petitioning for an illegitimate child,* present documents providing proof for: your paternity to the child (e.g., submission of the child's birth certificate with your name entered therein as the father, blood test results, sworn affidavits from at least two people who can confirm that there was a father-child relationship, including the child's mother identifying you as the child's father, etc); and/or legitimization papers (documents such as civil court papers obtained according to the procedures and

---

*NOTE: Certain countries have abolished the legal differences between legitimate and illegitimate children - e.g. China, Haiti, and Jamaica, which only recently passed such laws abolishing the distinction between children born in marriage and out-of-wedlock. The father still has to show, however, that such a law was changed before the child became 18 years old. And if this can be so shown, the petitioner will not need to present all those proofs stated above.

documents called for by the laws of the country where the child was born), as well as evidence that real parent/child relationship has existed between you and the child.

- •Attach, for the sponsoring parent and each of the child(ren), color photographs that were taken within 30 days before the filing of the visa petition. (See Chapter 25, Section F, for specification of the exact type and style of the photo required by the INS).
- •The filing fee - $US80, in the form of a money order or certified check made payable to the "Immigration and Naturalization Service."

Now, submit the above items (you may submit them in person or mail them, always by certified mail with return receipt requested, and preserve the receipt of mailing) to the nearest INS Regional Service Center. (See Appendix B for the addresses.)

NOTE: Do not send the *originals* of the documents needed at this time. Merely submit the photocopies of the document for now. Retain the original until the point when you're specifically asked by the INS or consulate to present them for inspection and verification.

E. THE FINAL STEPS IN CONCLUDING THE SECURING OF THE GREEN CARD FOR YOUR CHILD(REN)

Upon your filing the petition papers with the INS office (Section D above), the INS will consider the petition and, assuming that everything is in order, it will likely approve the visa petition and send you (as well as the alien beneficiary of the petition and the U.S. Consulate in the foreign country where the alien in presently located) a written notification of the preliminary approval of the initial visa petition. (See Chapter 6 at Section D thereof, for the detailed procedures of how this works). BUT HERE'S THE IMPORTANT THING TO NOTE HERE: that, hereinafter, from this point on, all further steps required for concluding the visa processing now shifts to the visa-seeker, the alien child himself or herself, and to the U.S. Consulate's office in the foreign country where the child is located.

The rest of the procedures and steps called for in the processing of the alien's green card from this point on till the end when the alien actually gets the visa in his/her hands, are essentially the same as those outlined in Chapter 6 from Section D thereof. Hence, turn to Chapter 6, Section D, The *"Application" Phase: Upon the Approval of the Sponsor's "Petition," Then You, the Alien, Must Now File an "Application" For The Actual Visa* (p. 39). Have your alien visa applicant finish up the remainder of the visa processing starting precisely from there.

Chapter 9

Getting Your Immigrant Visa (The Green Card) Based On Being A Parent Of A U.S Citizen: Filing As A Child For Your Father Or Mother

A. ALL THE VARIOUS KINDS OF FAMILY BASED RELATIONSHIPS AVAILABLE FOR QUALIFYING FOR A GREEN CARD

As has been fully set forth earlier in the preceding Chapters 3 and 4, within the family-relationship-based immigrant visa categories provided for under the U. S. immigration laws - that is, those categories of green cards which are granted on the basis of being a relative of, or having a family relationship of same sort with, a U.S citizen or permanent Resident – one of the principal ways available therein by which a green card may be obtained, is through being a bona fide parent of an American citizen. In this chapter, we discuss the detailed eligibility requirements and the procedures for filing for and obtaining a green card for just those aliens who full under this one family-related basis – BEING A PARENT OF A U.S. CITIZEN.

B. WHO QUALIFIES AS A CHILD WHO CAN PETITION FOR A GREEN CARD FOR A PARENT.

Consistent with the most fundamental goal and principle of encouraging family togetherness which generally underlines the U.S. immigration laws, a person can petition to obtain a green card for his or her parents, if he (she) meets a few basic requirements.

Basically, you qualify to do this if:
- you are a U.S. citizen; and
- you are 21 years old or older at the time of your filing the petition on behalf of your parents.

C. WHO QUALIFIES AS A PARENT FOR WHOM YOU CAN PETITION FOR A GREEN CARD?

Basically, your parent(s) qualify as your "mother" and /or "father" for immigration purposes, if they were married to each other; either before you were born, or after you were born but before you turned 18 years old. However, the immigration law still allows for a child to be able to file for an immigrant visa for a parent under various kinds of scenarios - even when one's parents were not married to each other at the time of one's birth, or even in a stepchild-stepparent situation, or in adoptive child/parent situations, etc.

i. Stepmother or Stepfather Situation

If your father or mother married someone other than your natural or biological parent before you turn 18 years of age, the person he or she marries becomes known as your STEPMOTHER OR STEPFATHER. As a U.S. stepchild, you may petition for a green card for your stepparents under two conditions: 1) the marriage creating the family relationship must have taken place before your (the stepchild's) 18th birthday, and 2) the marriage that created the stepchild/stepparent relationship between you and your stepparent must still be in existing at the time of your filing the petition for the green card.

ii. Adoptive Parents Situation

As an adopted child, you can petition for a green card for your adoptive mother and father, if you meet the following conditions:
- you were adopted before your 16th birthday; and
- you are an American citizen, and are 21 years old or older at the time of your filing the petition for the green card for your adoptive parents.

NOTE: In each and all of the situations involved in this chapter, you will be able to file the green card petition for each of them as your "Immediate Relative," thus being able to secure the green card for them with no quota requirement and more quickly. (see Chapter 3 Section B, Chapter 4 Section A.1, and Chapter 5)

D. HOW TO FILE FOR THE GREEN CARD

The file for a green card for your parent(s) based on your (the U.S. citizen child) being the child of an alien mother or father, follow these steps and procedures in exactly the same order and chronology in which they are listed below:

1. First, be sure to have read, thoroughly, Chapter 4, for some basic helpful general guidance on certain definitions and concepts relevant to establishment of true parent-child and family relationship under the U.S. immigration law.

2. *Complete These Forms.* Assuming that your parents are currently not in the U.S. and that you are filing to bring them in from abroad, complete:
- FORM I-130, *Petition for Alien Relative.* This form (obtain it from the INS) is to be completed and signed by the U.S. child, called the visa "petitioner". (See sample copy of this form on p. 212).
- FORM G-325A: *Biographic Information.* (See p. 225 for a sample of this form).

3. File the completed petition Form & Papers:

Now, you are to file the visa petition for your alien parent or parents. Simply, you (variously called the "sponsor" or the "petitioner") sign the completed petition form and submit it, along with the necessary supporting documents that are required (see the list below), to the U.S. Immigration and Naturalization Services' District office for the area in which you reside. (See Appendix B for addresses of the INS locations).

Documentations Which May Be Required in support of the Sponsor's PETITION:
- PROOF OF U.S. CITIZENSHIP OF PETITIONER: Your birth certificate, certificate of citizenship or naturalization, U.S. passport, and the like.
- YOUR BIRTH CERTIFICATE, showing your name and your mother's name, if filing only for your mother; and showing your name and the names of both of your parents, if filing for your father.
- MARRIAGE CERTIFICATE of the common parents, if you are filing for your father; and the marriage certificate of your mother or father, if you are filing for either of your stepparents, showing the name of her husband or his wife who has become your stepparent. If filing as a stepchild, present also your (the step child's) birth certificate to show the names of your (the stepchild's) natural parents.
- ADOPTION DECREE (or other proof of legal adoption), if you are an adopted child filing for your alien adop—

tive parent(s); plus a statement showing the dates and places you have lived together with your adoptive parents.

- MOTHER'S MARRIAGE CERTIFICATE: Present this to show mother's change of name if your mother has since changed her maiden name because she had married someone else.
- If you and your father did not live together before you turned 18, or even if you lived with him before your 18th birthday, you need to present proof that, at least up to the time you turned 21 years of age, there was a father-child relationship between you – by way of presenting evidence of maintaining personal contact and provid ing financial support, school records, photographs, letters and birthday cards sent you, Christmas cards, evi dence of entering your name as a beneficiary in his life insurance, evidence of father and child having resided in the same place, income tax returns showing the child as a dependent, etc.
- DIVORCE DECREE/DEATH CERTIFICATES: Present, as well, divorce decrees or death certificate (if applicable), showing that previous marriages in which you and your present spouse were involved, if any, had been legally terminated.
- If you are a U.S. illegitimate child petitioning for a green card for your father, you must be able to present documents providing proof for these two element: the paternity of your father (e.g. having his name on your birth certificate, or taking a blood test), and either legitimization papers (documents such as civil court papers obtained according to the procedures called for by the law of the country where the child was born), or the existence of real parent/child relationship.
- Attach for you and your applicable parent(s) color photographs that were taken within 30 days before the filing of the visa petition (see Chapter, Section F for specification of the exact type and style of the photo required by the INS).
- The filing fee – it's $80 as of this writing, in the form of a money order or certified check, made payable to the "Immigration and Naturalization Service."

You may submit the above items by hand; or you may mail them, by certified mail with return receipt requested and preserve the receipt of mailing, to the nearest INS Regional Service Center. (See Appendix B for the addresses).

NOTE: Do not send the originals of the documents needed as this time. Only send the photocopies. Retain the originals until the point when you're specifically asked by the INS or the consulate to present them for inspection and verification.

E. FINAL STEPS IN CONCLUDING THE SECURING OF THE GREEN CARD FOR YOUR PARENTS

Upon your filing the petition papers with the INS office (Section D above), the INS will consider the petition, and, assuming that everything is in order, it will likely approve the visa petition and send you (as well as the alien beneficiary of the petition and the U.S. Consulate office in the foreign country where the alien is presently located) a written notification of the preliminary approval of the initial visa petition. (See Chapter 6 at Section D thereof, for the detailed procedure of how this works). BUT HERE'S THE IMPORTANT THING YOU SHOULD NOTE HERE: that, hereinafter, from this point on in the visa processing, all further steps required for concluding the visa processing now shift to the visa-seeker, the alien parent himself or herself, and to the U.S. Consulate's Office in the foreign country where the parent is located.

The remainder of the procedures and steps called for in the processing of the alien parent's green card from this point on till the end when the alien actually has the visa in his/her hand, are essentially the same as those outlined in Chapter 6, from Section D thereof. Hence, turn to Chapter 6, Section D, *Upon the Approval of the Sponsor's "Petition", Then You, the Alien, Must Now File an "Application" For The Actual Visa* (p. 39). Have your alien visa applicant finish up the remainder of the visa processing starting precisely from there.

Chapter 10

Getting Your Immigrant Visa (Green Card) Based On Being A Brother Or Sister Of A U.S. Citizen

As has been repeatedly emphasized in several Sections of this books, perhaps the single most fundamental goal and principle which generally underlies the immigration laws and policies of the United States, is to unite families and to encourage family togetherness. In furtherance of this, one family-related-basis among many provided under the U.S. immigration law by which a foreign person can obtain a green card, is through being a bona fide brother or sister of a U.S. citizen.

Persons who qualify under this category as brothers and sisters of American citizens, fall under one category out of the nine categories of green card applicants, namely, under the Family Fourth Preference. (See Chapter 3, Section C, and Chapter 4, Section A.2 for a discussion of the immigrant visa *preference* classification and preference system). This group of aliens are, of course, subject to a quota limitation and a visa waiting period requirement.

A. BASIC REQUIREMENTS FOR GREEN CARD ELIGIBILITY UNDER THIS VISA CATEGORY

Basically, you qualify as an alien (foreign) person for whom a U.S. citizen can petition for a green card as a brother or sister, if the following conditions are present:
- The person who is petitioning for the green card for you, is a U.S. citizen, and is at least 21 years of age at the time of the filing of the visa petition.
- You, the alien person or green card beneficiary (the person for whom the green card is being sought), are truly a genuine, legitimate brother or sister of the U.S. citizen petitioner.

B. WHO QUALIFIED AS A LEGITIMATE BROTHER OR SISTER

Under the U.S. immigration law, any two or more alien persons who have (who can fully demonstrate by documentary evidence that they have) both parents (i.e., full-brothers and full-sisters), or at least one common parent (i.e., half-brothers and half-sisters), with an American petitioner, fully qualify. And the same is also true, within certain parameters, for aliens who are stepbrothers and stepsisters of American citizen, or their adopted brothers or sisters.

i. Full and Half Brothers and Sisters

If the U.S. citizen's mother and father were married, and had other children (or a child) who are the alien persons for whom the green card petition is being filed, those persons (the alien green card-seekers) are legitimate brothers and sisters of the U.S. citizens. And if you (say, the U.S. citizen petitioner) and another person (the alien) have the same mother or father, but not BOTH parents in common, that other person is then your half-brother or half-sister. For documentary proof: submit the birth certificates of both the petitioner and the alien brother or sister which will have the parents' names listed to show that both parties have the same father and mother, or that they have at least one common mother or father. If you are in a half-brother or half-sister situation and the only common parent involved in your case is just your father, then you'll additionally need to document that your father was married to your mother at the time of your birth, as well as to your sibling's mother at the time of his or her own birth – e.g., the civil marriage certificates for the two marriages, divorce decrees or death certificates to show that all prior marriages involving your father had been legally terminated, photographs demonstrating a marital, family, or romantic relationship between your father and the two mothers, old photos showing you and your other siblings together in family situations, and the like. Also, it is frequently valuable to obtain sworn affidavits from people who know the family or the relationship claimed (from the mother, for example, especially where there are no birth certificates or other official documents which show the common parentage existing between the children, or from an older aunt or uncle). Such affidavit will state that such persons know of the birth of the child to the parent claimed, and of the relationship and life together between the claimed parent and child.

ii. Stepbrothers & Stepsisters

When your mother or father marries another person other than your mother or father, that other person is your STEPPARENT, and if that other person has children from a previous marriage or relationship, those children of your stepparent would be your stepbrother or sister. But here's the catch: for purposes of the U.S. immigration, however, in order for you (the U.S. citizen) to be able to file for a green card for an alien as a stepbrothers or stepsisters, that marriage that took place between your natural father or mother and the stepparent must have occurred BEFORE you turned 18 years of age.

Hence, for documentary proof: Submit items such as your birth certificate; the birth certificate of your stepbrother or stepsister involved; marriage certificate of your mother or father and the stepparents, clearly showing the names of the particular stepparents' husband or wife who had become the petitioner's stepbrother's or stepsister's stepparent; divorce decrees or death certificates to show that all previous marriages involving the stepparents, if any, had been legally terminated, etc. Where you (or your stepsister) have changed your maiden or previous names because of marriage, you should present your marriage certificate to show that your names on the birth certificate and the person on the immigration form are the same person.

iii. Adopted Brother and Sister

If your mother and father have adopted a child into your family, under the immigration rules that child is your adopted brother or sister – so long as that adoption had been undertaken according to the laws of the state or country where undertaken. Or, if you have been adopted by parents who have other children of their own, their children also become your brothers and sisters, just as well, upon your being adopted into their family. But here's the catch: for purposes of the U.S. immigration, however, such adoption is valid and acceptable if, and only if, the adoption decree occurs <u>before</u> the 16th birthday of your adopted brothers or sisters, if they are the petitioning parties, or before your own 16th birthday, if you are the adopted person.

For documentary proof: submit adoption-related papers for the adopted person, including adoption decree; birth certificates showing your name and the name of your adopted sister's or brother's parents as the same, etc. As the U.S. petitioner, if you are the adopted person, the adoption decree must show that the adoption took place before you were 16 years of age, and that it took place before your adopted sisters or brothers were 16th years of age, if they are the adopted parties and the petitioners for you.

C. HOW TO FILE FOR THE GREEN CARD

To file for a green card for your alien brother or sister, follow these steps and procedures in the same order and chronology in which they are listed below:

1. First, be sure to have read, thoroughly, Chapter 4 for some basic helpful general guidance on certain definitions and concepts relevant to the establishment of true parent-child and family relationship under the U.S. immigration law.

2. *Complete These Forms*

Assuming that your brothers and sisters are not currently in the U.S. and that you are filing to bring them in from abroad, complete:

- FORM 1-130, *Petition For Alien Relative*. This form (obtain it from the INS) is to be completed and signed by the U.S. citizen brother or sister, called the visa "petitioner." (See sample of this form on p. 212)

3. *File The Completed Petitions Forms & Papers*

Now, you (variously called the "sponsor" or the "petitioner" in this process), are to file the visa petition for your alien brother(s) or sister(s). Simply, you sign the completed petition form and submit it, along with the necessary supporting documents that are required (see the list below), to the U.S. Immigration and Naturalization Service's District Office for the area in which you reside. (See Appendix B for addresses of the INS locations.)

Documentations Which May Be Required In Support of the Sponsor's Petition

- PROOF OF U.S. CITIZENSHIP for the sponsoring petitioner: birth certificate, certificate of citizenship or naturalization, U.S. passport, etc.
- Simply look for the same types of documents that can demonstrate the kind of sibling relationship claimed which apply to you, including those listed for each of the different sibling categories in Section B above – for siblings who are full and/or half brothers and sisters, stepbrothers or sisters, or adopted brothers and sisters.
- Attach for you and your applicable brother(s) and sister(s) color photographs that were taken within 30 days before the filing of the visa petition. (See Chapter 25, Section F for specification of the exact type and style of the photo that's acceptable to the INS).
- The filing fee – it's $80 as of this writing, in the form of a money order or certified check made payable to the "Immigration and Naturalization Service."

You may submit the above items in person by hand; or you may mail them, by certified mail with return receipt requested, and preserve the receipt of mailing, to the INS Regional Service Center covering the residence of the American petitioner (See Appendix B for the addresses)

NOTE: Do not send the *original* of the documents needed at this time. Only send the photocopies. Retain the originals until the point when you're specifically asked by the INS to present them for inspection and verification.

D. FINAL STEPS IN CONCLUDING THE SECURING OF
THE GREEN CARD FOR YOUR BROTHER OR SISTER

Upon your filing the petition papers with the INS office (Section C above), the INS will consider the petition, and, assuming that everything is in order, it will likely approve the visa petition and send you (as well as the alien beneficiary of the petition and the U.S. Consulate office in the foreign country where the alien is presently located) a written notification of the preliminary approval of the initial visa petition. (See Chapter 6 at Section D thereof for the detailed procedures of how this works). BUT HERE'S THE IMPORTANT THING YOU SHOULD NOTE HERE: that hereafter, from this point on in the visa processing, all further steps required for concluding the visa processing now shift to the visa-seeker, the alien brother or sister himself or herself, and to the U.S. consulate office in the foreign country where the parent is located.

The remainder of the procedures and steps called for in the processing of the alien brother's or sister's green card from this point on till the end when the alien actually has the visa in his/her hand, are essentially the same as those outlined in Chapter 6, from Section D, thereof. Hence, turn to Chapter 6, Section D. *The "Petition" Phase: Upon The Approval o the Sponsor's "Petition," Then You, the Alien, Must Now File an "Application" For The Actual Visa* (p. 39). Have your alien visa applicant finish up the remainder of the visa processing starting precisely from there.

Chapter 11
Getting An Immigrant Visa (The Green Card) Based On Adoption Of A Non-orphan Alien Child

A. ALL THE VARIOUS KINDS OF FAMILY BASED RELATIONSHIPS AVAILABLE BY WHICH AN ALIEN CAN QUALIFY FOR A GREEN CARD

In Chapters 3 and 4, we fully explain that within the family-relationship-based immigrant visa categories – that is, those categories of green cards which are obtainable on the basis of being a relative of, or having a family relationship of some sort with, a U.S. citizen or Permanent Resident - one of the ways by which a green card can be obtained, is through being a bona-fide child (or parent) of an American citizen or Permanent Resident alien (green cardholder). And, as also explained in those same chapters, among those who are classifiable as "children" under the U.S. immigration law for whom a U.S. parent or permanent resident alien may file a petition for the grant of a green card, are persons who are adopted alien children of such persons. In this chapter, we discuss the detailed eligibility requirements and the procedures for filing for and obtaining a green card for just those aliens who fall under this one family-related basis – BEING THE ADOPTED CHILD OF A U.S. CITIZEN OR PERMANENT RESIDENT ALIEN.

B. WHO QUALIFIES FOR A GREEN CARD THROUGH ADOPTION

As is repeatedly emphasized in several parts of this book, in furtherance of the fundamental goal and principle of encouraging family togetherness which is the hallmark of American immigration law and policy, alien children can get green cards through their American parents, just as alien parents can get green cards through their American children. The same rights remain available to adopted children and adoptive parents, providing they meet certain requirements. Under the U.S. immigration law, "adopted children" are classified into two types - orphan children and non-orphan children. Both classes of adopted children are eligible for green cards, but the difference is that the requirements for qualification for a green card for those who qualify as orphans are different, indeed vastly different, from those who qualify as non-orphans.

C. THE TWO CLASSES OF ADOPTED CHILDREN: ORPHANS AND NON-ORPHANS

1. Orphan Adopted Child

Basically, the process of adoption of foreign-born orphan children, is essentially the special immigration equivalence of obtaining a green card for an abandoned alien (foreign born) child. As defined under the U.S. immigration law, a child falls under the category of an "orphan" child under these conditions, and can therefore qualify for a green card eligibility only under the "orphan child" category if:

- The child is under 16 years of age at the time the visa petition is filed.
- Both of the child's natural parents are either deceased, or have permanently and legally abandoned the

child, or the child is living with a "sole or surviving parent" who is incapable to care for the child and has irrevocably released him or her, in writing, for adoption.
●The child shall have been living outside the U.S. and, if not already adopted by the U.S. parents, must either be in the custody of the adopting parents or of an agent who is acting on their behalf in accordance with the local law.
●Only *U.S. citizens* may petition for a green card for an orphan; non-orphans, on the other hand, may have either a U.S. citizen or permanent resident as their petitioners.

Thus, under such a strict definition, a child who has BOTH parents, is not an "orphan" for U.S. immigration purposes, even if the parents are unable to care for him and want to surrender him for adoption. Consequently, as is actually the case, often there may be children who are otherwise legally free for adoption according to foreign law, but may not be eligible for a U.S. immigration visa as orphans because those children are unable to fit the U.S. definition of who an orphan child is.

In deed, such somewhat strict conditions required under U.S. law for meeting the immigration definition of an "orphan" has evoked what some immigration law experts have called the "orphan limitation" problem in international adoptions – the view that the law limits immigration to a group of children that is much narrower than those legally free and available for adoption in foreign countries.

2. Non-Orphan Adopted Children

A non-orphan is any person who is already legally adopted, but whose adoption was finalized prior to his or her 16th birthday. It does not matter how old the child is at the time the visa petition is filed, only when he was adopted. Unlike an orphan child, the non-orphan child is neither orphaned nor abandoned by his or her natural parents. In addition to already being legally adopted, the child must have been in the legal custody of, and living with, the adoptive parents for at least two years prior to the application for a green card – meaning that either a legal guardianship or an actual adoption decree must have been issued on behalf of such a child at least 2 years prior to the filing of the green card petition.

Often, however, a child may meet the visa requirements of both the orphan and the non-orphan categories. The U.S. parent intending to obtain a green card for such a child can then choose between the two options in terms of which one will make for a simpler visa application filing. For example, for an orphan visa application filing, the U.S. parents do not have to meet the two-year cohabitation and legal custody requirement which applies with the non-orphan child. And, furthermore, petitioning parents in orphan adopted situations need not have physically met with the child before doing the adoption or visa paperwork: they can file the visa petition on the child behalf right away, and need not have to wait till the legal adoption shall have been completed. On the other hand, for the case involving non-orphan visa application filing, the age of the child at the time of the petition is not relevant, and the child will not need to be under the age of 16 at that specific time, as is the case with an orphan filing. Furthermore, to file for a green card for an orphan child, you can only do so if you are a U.S. citizen; on the other hand, only if you are filing for a non-orphan could you be merely a green card holder.

In this chapter, and for the remainder of this chapter, we shall address only the process of obtaining an immigrant visa (a green card) for an ADOPTED CHILD – that is, for the NON-ORPHAN CHILD situation. (The procedures for obtaining a green card under the ORPHAN child category, are outlined in Chapter 12)

D. BASIC CONDITIONS FOR GREEN CARD ELIGIBILITY IN NON-ORPHAN SITUATION

You may, as an American adoptive parent, file a petition to secure a green card for an alien child who falls under the definition of being your "adopted child" (non-orphan classification), if the following conditions are present:

- you (the petitioning parent) are either a U.S. citizen or a lawful Permanent Resident
- the alien adoptive child at issue shall have already been legally adopted, and the adoption procedures done in strict accordance with the adoption laws of the country of his or her birth, or of the America State of the adopting parents
- the alien child's adoption shall have occurred BEFORE he or she turned 16 years of age.
- the alien child must have been in legal custody of, and physically residing with, the adoptive U.S. parent or parents for at least two years prior to the petition for the green card, either before or after the adoption decree shall have become final – meaning that either a legal guardianship or an actual decree of adoption must have been issued on such a child at least 2 years prior to the filing of the petition for a green card.*
- the alien adopted child must have physically lived with the adoptive parents at some point in his/her life before the petition is filed
- the American adoptive parent(s) must be able to meet certain requirements. Generally, as part of standard adoption procedure in most U.S. states' jurisdictions, they must satisfactorily complete a HOME STUDY or an investigation by a state public or government-licensed private adoption agency in the U.S., or otherwise satisfy such a requirement if the adoption takes place in a foreign country or in a U.S. state where an investigation is compulsory.

E. HOW TO FILE FOR A GREEN CARD FOR THE NON-ORPHAN ADOPTED CHILD

Basically, the procedure for filing for and obtaining a green card for a child adopted by a U.S. citizen parent or green cardholder under the category of non-orphan, are precisely the same as those which apply for blood-related children of U.S. citizens and green cardholder fully described in Chapter 8.

To file for a green card for your adopted child(ren) based on your being the U.S. parent of a non-orphan adopted alien child, simply follow these steps and procedures in the same order and chronology in which they are listed below:

1. First, be sure to have read, thoroughly, Chapter 4, for some helpful further guidance on certain definitions and concepts which are relevant to the establishment of true parent-child relationship under the U.S. immigration law.

2. Complete These Forms
Assuming that the children at issue are currently not in the U.S. and that you are filing to bring them in from a foreign country, complete:
- FORM 1-130, *Petition For Alien Relative*. This form (obtain it free of charge from the INS) is to be

*Note that, as a practical matter, because of these requirements, the only way the adopted child can practically get a green card, is for at least one of the adopting parents to live or have lived in the foreign country with the alien child. If the 2-year residency or legal custody requirement is difficult to achieve because the resulting separation may be too emotionally traumatic for the petitioning adopting parents or the adoptive child, for example, then another alternative may be to process the immigration papers under the orphan child procedures (see Chapter 12). Or, one other alternative would be for the child to enter the U.S. on a temporary, non-immigrant visa, say as a student or a visitor. You may then initiate adoption proceedings for him (her) in the United States. Except, however, that under this option you cannot file a green card petition for the child as a "relative" until 2 years shall have passed after the adoption. Note, however, also, that under the current U.S. immigration law, a child who enters the U.S. as a nonimmigrant or on a tourist or student visa, cannot be adopted as an ORPHAN child. What you will need to do in such a situation, would be to make sure you inform the U.S. consular office in the foreign country that you plan to adopt the child so that the child would be given an "Advance Parolee" designation. You could argue, for example, that you must have the child came with you to the U.S. in order to be able to complete the adoption process.

completed and signed by the U.S. parent, called the visa "petitioner." (See sample copy of this form on p. 212)

● FORM G-325A: *Biographic Information*. This form is to be completed in part by the sponsoring petitioner, and in part by the alien beneficiary. The form is mostly used and applicable in petitions involving "Adjustment of Status" situations (see Chapter 20) where the alien is already in the U.S. in a nonimmigrant status and seeks to change to immigrant status. However, it may be required in some initial immigrant visa petition situations (see p. 225 for sample of the form).

3. Now, File The Completed "Petition" Forms and Papers

Now, to file the visa petition for your alien child(ren), you – the so-called "sponsor" or "petitioner" – must sign the completed forms and file them (along with the necessary supporting documents), with the U.S. Immigration and Naturalization Service's District Office in the United States. File in the office covering the area in which you, the sponsor, reside, or where the alien's prospective employment is located, where employment is applicable. (see Appendix B for the addresses of the INS locations)

Documentations Which May be Required in Support of the Sponsor's Petition

To be attached to the basic PETITION form in support, are typically the following documents:

● PROOF OF U.S. CITIZENSHIP OR PERMANENT RESIDENCE OF PETITIONER: For the petitioning U.S. citizens, submit your birth certificate, certificate of citizenship or naturalization, U.S. passport, and the like. For a permanent Resident, present your green card, unexpired reentry permit or passport with an unexpired stamp indicating admission to the U.S. as a permanent resident.

● CHILD'S BIRTH CERTIFICATE showing the names of the petitioner(s) as the adopting mother and/or father of the child by reason of the adoption decree.

● ADOPTION PAPERS: present adoption-related papers for the adopted child, such as the court adoption decree showing adoption prior to the child being 16 years of age; documents that show that the adoptive parents had legal custody of child for at least 2 years prior to the petition, and that the adopted child had resided with the adoptive parent(s) for at least 2 years.

● MARRIAGE CERTIFICATE of the child's common parents (the petitioner), if petitioner is filing as the father; and the marriage certificate of the child's mother or father and the stepparents, if the petitioner is filing for either of the child's stepparent, showing the names of which one of the stepparent's husband or wife has become the child's stepparent. If petitioner is filing as a stepparent, present also your (the stepparent's) birth certificates to show the names of your (the stepparent's) natural parents.

● MOTHER'S MARRIAGE CERTIFICATE: present this to show the child's mother's change of name, where child's mother has since changed her maiden name because she had married someone else. (Similarly, if child is a daughter who has changed her maiden name because of marriage, present her marriage certificate to show that the child on the birth certificate and the child on the immigration form are the same person).

● If you (the petitioner) are the father of the child and you are either unmarried to the child's mother at the time of his/her birth, or unable to present a birth certificate of the child that bears your name as the father (or if the child is adopted), then you must submit evidence proving that, at least up to the time the child turned 21 years of age, a real father-child relationship existed between the two of you: evidence of having lived together in the same house with the child at least until his/her 18th birthday, evidence of maintaining personal contact with the child and of having provided financial support for the child, school records, with the man's name registered as the father, photographs, letters, and birthday cards, sent to the child and received by him/her, Christmas cards, evidence of entering the child's name as a beneficiary in the man's life insurance, income tax returns showing the child as a dependent, canceled checks or other common financial records showing that petitioner has regularly contributed money to the child's support, etc.

- •DIVORCE DECREE/DEATH CERTIFICATES: present divorce decree or death certificates as well, showing that previous marriages in which you and your present spouse were involved, if any, had been legally terminated.
- •If you are a father petitioning for an illegitimate* child, present documents providing proof for your paternity to the child (e.g., submission of the child's birth certificate with your name entered therein as the father, blood test results, sworn affidavits from at least two people who can confirm there was a father child relationship, including sworn statement by the child's mother identifying you as the child's father; and/or provide legitimatization papers (documents such as civil court papers obtained according to the procedures and documents called for by the law of the country where the child was born), as well as evidence that real parent/child relationship has existed between you and the child.
- •Attach, for each of the sponsoring parent and the child(ren), separate color photographs that were taken within 30 days before the filing of the visa petition. (see Chapter 25, Section F for specification of the exact type and style of the photo that's acceptable to the INS).
- •The filing fee – $US80, in the form of a money order or certified check, made payable to the "Immigration and Naturalization Service."

Now, submit the above items (you may submit them in person or mail them, by certified mail with return receipt requested and preserve the receipt of mailing) to the nearest INS Regional Service Center. (See Appendix B for the addresses).

Do not send the originals of the documents that are needed at this time. Merely submit the photocopies for the moment, but retain the originals until they are specifically asked for by the INS officials for their inspection and authentication. [Note that, on the other hand, however, generally, the documents submitted in the SECOND PHASE of the visa processing, that is, in the "application" phase (Section F below), are usually required to be either the originals or officially "certified" copies bearing a government seal of authentication].

NOTE: As a rule, the INS does not usually accept automatically the diplomas and schooling credentials earned in foreign institutions as valid or creditworthy or up to standard. Rather, for the INS to accept such documents, you (or the alien involved) would often need to submit the transcripts of the foreign schooling records to an accredited U.S. academic evaluator for its assessment. (See p. 194 for a list of some of such accredited agencies in the United States).

F. FINAL STEPS IN CONCLUDING THE SECURING OF THE GREEN CARD FOR YOUR NON ORPHAN

Upon your filing the petition with the INS office (Section E above), the INS will consider the petition, and, assuming that everything is in order, it will likely approve the visa petition and send you (as well as the alien beneficiary of the petition and the U.S. Consulate office in the foreign country where the alien is presently located) a written notification of the preliminary approval of the initial visa petition. (See Chapter 6 at Section D thereof for the detailed procedures of how this works). BUT HERE'S THE IMPORTANT THING YOU NEED

---

*NOTE: Certain countries have abolished the legal difference between legitimate and illegitimate children – e.g., China, Haiti and Jamaica, which only recently passed such laws abolishing the distinction between children born in marriage and out-of-wedlock. The father still has to show, however, that such a law was changed before the child became 18 years old. And if this can be so shown, the petitioner will not need to present all those proofs stated above.

TO NOTE HERE: that, hereafter, from this point on in the visa processing, all remaining further steps required for concluding the visa processing now shift to the visa-seeker, the alien non-orphan child himself or herself, and to the U.S. Consulate office in the foreign country where the child is located.

The remainder of the procedures and steps called for in the processing of the alien non-orphan child's green card from this point on till the end when the alien actually has the visa in his/her hand, are essentially the same as those outlined in Chapter 6, from Section D thereof. Hence, turn to Chapter 6 Section D, *The "Petition" phase: Upon the Approval of the Sponsor's "Petition," Then the Alien Must Now File an "Application" For The Actual Visa* (p. 39). Have your alien visa applicant finish up the remainder of the visa processing starting precisely from there.

NOTE THE FOLLOWING, HOWEVER

1. Note that, an alien child adopted by a U.S. citizen (but not one adopted by a Green Cardholder) who falls under the category of a NON-ORPHAN, is considered an *"immediate relative"* of the U.S. citizen; while an alien non-orphan child who is adopted by a green cardholder, falls under the *"preference relatives"* category of immigrants. Recall (see Chapters 3, 4 and 5) that "immediate relative" aliens may immigrate to the U.S. in unlimited number; they are not subject to a quota. "Preference relative" aliens, however, are subject to some quota. Note, also, that foreign adopted orphan children (Chapter 12) are, as well, not subject to any quota limitation or waiting period.

2. Note that a new law passed by Congress in 2000, called the **Child Citizenship Act,** grants automatically citizenship to most adopted children born abroad, provided they are under 18 years of age and at least one parent or legal guardian of the child is an American citizen. Thus, by virtue of the new law, a child of American parents, whether born in the U.S. or adopted oversea, has now essentially one and the same status under the law as an American. And there's no more legal distinction between the two.

Chapter 12
Getting An Immigrant Visa (Green Card) Based On Adoption Of An Orphan Child

A. WHO QUALIFIES FOR A GREEN CARD THROUGH ADOPTION?

As is repeatedly emphasized in several parts of this book, in furtherance of the fundamental goal and principle of encourage family togetherness which is the hallmark of American immigration laws and policy, children can get Green Cards through their American parents, just as parents can get Green Cards through their American children. The same rights remain available to adopted children and adoptive parents, providing they meet certain requirements. Under the U.S immigration law, "adopted children" are classified into two types – orphan children and non-orphan children. Both classes of adopted children are eligible for green cards, but the difference is that the requirements for qualification for a green card for those who qualify as orphans are different, in deed vastly different, from those who qualify as non-orphans.

B. THE TWO CLASSES OF ADOPTED CHILDREN: ORPHANS & NON-ORPHANS
1. Orphan Adopted Child

Basically, the process of adoption of foreign-born orphan children, is essentially the special immigration equivalence of obtaining a green card for an abandoned alien (foreign-born) child. As defined under the U.S immigration law, a child falls under the category of an "orphan" child under these conditions, and can therefore qualify for a green card eligibility only under the "orphan child" category, if:

- The child is under 16 years of age at the time visa petition is filed.
- Both of the child's natural parents are either deceased, or have permanently and legally abandoned the child, or the child is living with a "sole or surviving parent" who is incapable to care for the child and has irrevocably released him or her, in writing, for adoption.
- The child shall have been living outside the U.S. and, if not already adopted by the U.S. parents, must either be in the custody of the adopting parents or of an agent who is acting on their behalf in accordance with the local law.
- Only U.S citizens may petition for green cards for orphans; non-orphans may have either U.S. citizens or permanent residents as their petitioners.

Thus, under such strict definition, a child who has both parents is not an "orphan" for U.S. immigration purposes, even if the parents are unable to care for him and want to surrender him for adoption. Consequently, as is actually the case often, there may be children who are otherwise legally free for adoption according to foreign law, but who may not be eligible for a U.S. immigrant visa as orphans because those children are unable to fit the U.S definition of who an orphan child is.

In deed, such somewhat strict conditions required under U.S. law for meeting the immigration definition of an "orphan" has evoked what some immigration law experts have called the "orphan limitation" problem in international adoptions – the view that the law limits immigration to a group of children that is much narrower than those legally free and available for adoption in foreign countries.

2. Non-Orphan Adopted Children

A non-orphan is any person who is already legally adopted, but whose adoption was finalized prior to his or her 16th birthday. It does not matter how old the child is at the time the visa petition is filed; only when he was adopted. Unlike an orphan child, the non-orphan child is neither orphan nor abandoned by his or her natural parents. In addition to already being legally adopted, the child must have been in the legal custody of, and living with, the adoptive parents for at least two years prior to the application for a green card – meaning that either a legal guardianship or an actual adoption decree must have been issued on such a child at least 2 years prior to the filing of the green card petition.

Often, however, a child may meet the visa requirements of both the orphan and the non-orphan categories. The U.S. parent intending to obtain a green card for such a child can then have the choice of choosing between the two options in terms of which one will make for a simpler visa application. For example, for an orphan visa application filing, the U.S. parents do not have to meet the two-year cohabitation and legal custody requirement which applies with the non-orphan child. And, furthermore, petitioning parents in orphan adoptions need not have physically met with the child before doing the visa or adoption paperwork; they can file the visa petition on the child's behalf right away and need not have to wait till the legal adoption shall have been completed. On the other hand, for the non-orphan visa application filing case, the age of the child at the time of the petition is not relevant and the child will not need to be under the age of 16 at that specific time, as is the case in an orphan filing. Furthermore, to file for a green card for an orphan child, you may only do so if you are a U.S. citizen; on the other hand, only if you are filing for a non-orphan could you be merely a green cardholder.

In this chapter, and for the remainder of this chapter, we shall address only the process of obtaining an immigrant visa (a green card) for an alien orphan – that is, in an orphan child situation. The procedures for obtaining a green card under the NON-ORPHAN child category, are outlined in Chapter 11.

C. WHO QUALIFIES AS AN ORPHAN CHILD FOR PURPOSES OF ELIGIBILITY FOR GREEN CARD

To summarized, an alien (foreign born) child may be classified under the U.S. immigration law as an orphan if he (she) meets the following condition:

- He (she) is under 16 years of age and both parents are dead or have disappeared; or
- He (she) is under 16 years of age and the "sole or surviving parent" with whom he is living is incapable of caring for him and has irrevocably released him for adoption and immigration to the U.S.; or
- He (she) is under 16 years of age and the both parents have permanently abandoned him, or have became separated or lost from him, and the legal authorities in the child's country have granted legal and permanent custody of the child to an orphanage on account of the abandonment or separation.
- In addition, to be classified as an orphan, the child must be living outside the U.S. and, unless already adopted by the U.S. parents, must be either in the natural parent's custody or in the custody of an agent authorized by them in accordance with the local law.

D. GENERAL CONDITIONS FOR GREEN CARD ELIGIBILITY IN ORPHAN SITUATIONS

- You (the U.S. visa petitioner) must be a U.S. citizen in order to be eligible to file a visa petition for an orphan child; green card holders are not eligible to do so.
- The orphan child must be less than 16 years of age at the time the visa petition is filed
- Petitioning American citizen, if not married, must be at least 25 years of age. (There are no age restrictions if the petitioner is married).

•The adopting U.S. parents (or parent) may, at their option, file the petition for a green card on the child's behalf either before the legal adoption is completed or after. However, adopting parents who have not finalized the adoption proceedings (who do not have the actual adoption decree in their hands) must first submit to and satisfy certain pre-adoption requirements existing under the laws of their U.S. State, including a home study by the state government or an approved agency, before they may undergo the final processing for the green card.

E. AS A PROSPECTIVE U.S. ADOPTIVE PARENT, YOU MUST FIRST MEET THE PRE-ADOPTION REQUIREMENTS, INCLUDING A HOME STUDY

An underlying policy objective of the U.S. immigration law relating to adoption of foreign children, whether for orphans or non-orphans, is to protect the adoptive child primarily by ensuring that the adopting U.S. parents will properly care for the child. Consequently, in all applications for a green card involving an adoption, both where the prospective adoptive child has been located and where he has not, the adopting parents are strictly required to undergo, and to meet, certain pre-adoption requirements before an adoption decree may be finalized or a green card petition approved for an orphan child. Thus, if you are adopting or planning to adopt an orphan child in the United States, you must first comply with strict pre-adoption requirements set by your state of residence before you may proceed with adoption.

A major component of the pre-adoption requirements of almost every state, is a HOME STUDY conducted by the state government or an approved agency. The purpose of the home study is to enable the responsible state agency handling the adoption to investigate the future parents of the alien child and the future home of the child and the ascertain that the adopting couple (or single person) is psychologically and financial fit to act as a parent for the child. Thus, only with a favorable recommendation of the home study state official or agency would the orphan visa petition with the INS (or even his adoption petition with state court) be pre-approved.

To contact the local branch of the agency that oversees adoptions in your state, simply look in your local telephone book under "Adoptions", "Child Welfare" or "Social Services"; or call the adoption services agency of your state government located in the capital city of your state.

F. PROCEDURES FOR FILING FOR A GREEN CARD FOR AN ORPHAN CHILD

Under the immigration procedures, there are two basic ways you (the U.S. visa petitioner) may go in the petition process for an orphan child's green card: you may file a petition for the alien child's green card either BEFORE he completes the legal adoption, or AFTER you've done so. Consequently, American couples (or single persons) who are planning to adopt foreign-born children but have not yet found a specific child to adopt, may still proceed with applying for a green card for a child using a method known as *"advance processing"* visa application procedures.

The principal value of the use of the advance processing method, is that it enables the U.S. citizens who have not yet located a specific child to adopt, to accomplish the immigration paperwork in anticipation of the adoption. The INS will process the documentation relating to that part of the procedures that relate to the prospective ADOPTIVE PARENTS first; so that at a later date it will then address that part of the documentations and the procedures relating only to the CHILD when the child becomes available.

1. Orphan Adoption By Advance Processing Method: Where The Child Has Not Yet Been Found

Brief summarized, the process of filing for a green card for an alien child runs roughly this way: first, you'll need to file for the child a visa "PETITION" in an INS regional office in the United States, or in the U.S. embassy (consulate) in the country where the child currently resides. This first step is called the "petition" phase. Then, assuming the petition is approved by the INS, a second or additional set of papers are filed, this time, thought, with the U.S. Embassy in the country of the child's residence. This second step is called the "application" phase.

The Petition Phase: In No-child-available Situation

For an orphan child adoption situation where the child to adopt has not yet been found and the adopting U.S. couple is going abroad to locate an orphan child but wish to apply for advance processing to speed up the immigration process once the child is found, or even for a situation where the adoption is undertaken after the child's arrival in the U.S. but a speedier processing of the immigration is desired, the following documentations are to be filed by the adopting parents with the *Immigration and Nationalization Service* in the U.S.:

- FORM 1-600A, *Application for Advance Processing of Orphan petition* (used in advanced processing filing only). {See sample copy on p. 233}
- INS FORM 1-130, *Petition for Alien Relative.* See sample of this form on p. 214 [NOTE: these forms are completed and signed by the American adopting parent (or both parents, if married), who are the "petitioners' in this whole undertaking. The forms, upon being completed, are accompanied by the necessary supporting documentations.

Such documentation would generally include:
- Proof of marital status – a certified copy of the petitioner's marriage certificate, if applicable.
- The fingerprints of each prospective adoptive parent on Form FD-258. It is a good idea to submit two forms FD-258 for each prospective adoptive parent in case the first set of fingerprints turns out to be illegible. (Sample of form is on p. 224).
- Proof of termination of any prior marriages of the prospective U.S. citizen petitioner and spouse, or unmarried prospective petitioner, if applicable.
- Proof of the marriage of the prospective petitioners and spouses, if married.
- Proof of the prospective petitioner's United States citizenship. The types of proof acceptable for this are explained in detail on Form 1-600A. (See sample of this form on p. 233).
- A favorable HOME STUDY REPORT and recommendation. This is a report on the ability of the adoptive or prospective adoptive parent(s) to care for a child or children. If the home study is not yet available, it must be submitted within one year from the date of filing the advance processing application or the application will be considered abandoned.
- Attach, for each of the adoptive parents and the adoptive child (where available), color photographs that were taken within 30 days before the filing of the visa petition. (See Chapter 25, Section F for specification of the type and style of the photo acceptable to the INS).
- The appropriate filing fee ($155 as of this writing), in the form of a money order or certified check, made out to the "Immigration and Naturalization Service." [Note that the application is considered abandoned if the adopting parties are unable to locate an orphan within one year, at which point a new fee (as well as a new advance application) will be required if the parties wish to continue with the alien child adoption]

2. Petition Papers & Documentations When The Child Has Been Found.THE "PETITION" PHASE:

For an adoption where the child to adopt has already been found, the U.S. adopting parents can, if they wish, immediately file a visa petition for the child at the INS Regional office in the U.S., even if the advance application has not yet been approved, or even filed. The documentation needed to accomplish the first step of the immigration process – the PETITION phase – is identical to that required for situations involving where the child to be adopted has not yet been found as described in Section F.1 above*, but with the following exceptions: it will be necessary at this Step One petition phase, to include certain documents which were not required in the no-child-available

*Except, perhaps, Form 1-600A, which you may exclude if you are not filing for advance processing

case – such as the child's birth certificate or other proof of his/her age; evidence that the child's natural parents are dead or have legally abandoned the child, etc., as listed below.

For an adoption involving where the orphan child to adopt has already been found, you (the petitioning prospective U.S. adopting parents) will need to file the following documentations with the INS:

- All the documents listed in Section F.1 above*; PLUS:
- The birth certificate of the orphan child or other proof of his/her age (to show that the child is under 16 years of age when the visa petition is filed);
- Death certificate of the orphan child's natural parents or proof of legal abandonment of him or her by both parents;
- Either a report of home study that favorably recommends the child's adoption by the adopting parents, or other written proof by the adopting parents that they have satisfactorily complied with the pre-adoption requirements of their state, including a home study done by the state government or an approved agency, if the adoption is to be completed in the U.S.; and
- The adoption decree, if an adoption of the child had already been completed.

Note that, in the situation involving advanced processing when the child to be adopted is not yet found, upon the U.S. citizen petition's submission of the advance processing petition papers to the INS (See Section F.1 above), the INS will promptly commence its own investigation of the adopting parents. And if the preliminary application is approved (it usually takes a minimum of 90 days), the INS will promptly notify the adopting parents by sending them a document known as a NOTICE OF ACTION Form 797. Once the advance processing is approved, when the child to be adopted is finally found, at that point that's when the petitioning parents must then submit the remainder of the documents – the last batch of papers listed immediately above. This action must be taken within 18 months after the approval of the advanced processing application. You need not to make another payment of $155 fee with this second batch of papers since it was already paid at the time of your submission of the advanced · processing papers.

G. NOW, FILE THE "PETITION" PAPERS

Upon completing and gathering the above forms and documentations as applicable to you (see Section F.1 or F.2 above), the U.S. adoptive parent(s) may now file (submit) these papers – called the "petition" papers in this phase of the visa processing operations – either to the nearest INS local office in the United States, or the U.S. Embassy in the country of the child's residence, but most adopting parents residing in the U.S. generally file the papers with the U.S.- based INS office. (See Appendix A for a list of U.S. Embassies, and Appendix B for the INS). American adopters who are resident abroad or travelling abroad to adopt the child or to identify one, however, would usually file at the U.S. Embassy in which the child lives.

NOTE: (1) Foreign orphan children, just like aliens who fall under the category of 'immediate relative' aliens, are not subject to any quota limitations or a waiting period as they are part of the persons who are defined as 'immediate relatives' of Americans (Chapter 3, Section B). They may immediately immigrate to the U.S. in unlimited numbers each year.

(2) A new law passed by Congress in 2000, called the Child Citizenship Act, confers automatic citizenship to most adopted children born abroad, provided they are under 18 years of age and at least one parent or legal guardian of the child is an American citizen. Thus, by virtue of the new law, a child of American parents, whether born in the U.S. or adopted abroad, has now essentially one and the same status under the law – an American. And there's no more legal distinction between the two.

H. FINAL STEPS IN CONCLUDING THE SECURING OF
THE GREEN CARD FOR THE ALIEN ORPHAN CHILD

Upon your filing the petition papers with the INS office (Section G above), the INS will consider the petition, and, assuming that everything is in order, it will likely approve the visa petition and send you (as well as the alien beneficiary of the petition, which is the adoptive child or his custodian, and the U.S. consulate office in the foreign country where the alien child is presently located) a written notification of the preliminary approval of the initial visa petition. (See chapter 6 at Section C.4 thereof, for the detailed procedure of how this works). In deed, if you had filed for an advanced processing, the INS shall have approved your petition for your adoptive child's green card immediately following its approval of your advanced processing application upon your finding and identifying the child to adopt (Section F.2 above). And you would have been sent a document by the INS called the *Notice of Action* Form 797 to indicate approval of the advanced processing. And if, on the other hand, the visa petition had been directly filed with, and approved by the U.S. Embassy abroad, the petition file will simply remain there awaiting the next steps in the child's immigration proceedings. BUT HERE IS THE IMPORTANT THING FOR YOU TO NOTE HERE: that, *hereinafter, from this point on in the visa processing, all further steps required for concluding the visa processing now shift to the visa-seeker, the alien child himself or herself, and to the U.S. consulate office in the foreign country where the child is located.*

The rest of the procedures and steps called for in the processing of the alien child's green card from this point on till the end when the alien actually gets the visa in his/her hand, are essentially the same as those outlined from Chapter 6, Section D thereof. Hence, turn to Chapter 6, Section D, *The Application phase: Upon the Approval of the Sponsor's "Petition", then you, the Alien, must now file an "Application" For The Actual Visa* (p. 39). Have your alien visa applicant (the child or his/her current custodian or handlers) finish up the remainder of the visa processing starting precisely from there.

Note The Following, However:

In normal visa processing situations where the alien beneficiary of the petition (the person for whom the visa is being sought) is an adult person, this phase of the visa processing – the "application" phase – will usually be expected to be undertaken, not by the adult visa sponsor or petitioner, but by the visa beneficiary himself or herself. However, adoptive parent petitioners should take note of a few special differences in this particular instance as the process often involves, not adults but underage children, as the visa beneficiary. First, while, in general, the remainder of the papers which need to be completed in this "application" phase of the visa processing should normally be expected to be done by the alien beneficiary of the visa petition, in this instance, however, it is still the American adoptive parent(s) who would largely complete the application papers and then file them, on behalf of the orphan child, with the American Embassy in the child's home country. In deed, it is customary in such instances involving a minor orphan, for the INS office to send the Packet 3 (a package of application forms and instructions for their completion and processing) directly to the American adopters, and to request such adopters to return the paperwork to the Embassy. And still a little later, when the Embassy officials are ready to undertake the final processing of the visa, it is often to the American adopters (and usually the child, as well) that the Embassy sends the second batch of papers and instructions (Packet 4) informing them about how and where the orphan is to go to take the medical examination and to appear for the final visa interview, etc. (Note that very young children, and under 14 years of age, are usually exempt from having a visa interview).

The point, then, is that you should be fully aware that in this particular instance, it is YOU, the American adopter and petitioner, that would often have to complete the main forms and prepare the principal documents required and return them to the consulate office on the child's behalf. And that   the onus falls on you to coordinate the entire document preparation and gathering tasks with the orphan child, along with perhaps an adult person who is stationed in the child's current place of residence who will be taking the child through the consulate.

Finally, note that, after the adoptive child shall have been admitted to the U.S. as a permanent resident or green cardholder, the American petitioner(s), his/her prospective adoptive parents, are legally expected to proceed <u>promptly</u> to formally adopt the child. They are to do so in accordance with the legal adoption rules and procedures of their state of residence. But what if, for some strong reason whatsoever, the American parents never undertake the legal adoption of the child after he (she) gets here? Strangely enough, the law on that is the orphan's immigration status will remain unaffected: the child will still retain the green card and his legal status as a lawful permanent U.S. resident, anyway. Yet, it still is illegal for one to file an orphan petition for a green card simply for the purpose of bringing the child to America but with no genuine intent to carry out the adoption of the child. Such U.S. petitioner is still potentially subject to criminal prosecution by the U.S. government for filing a fraudulent petition.

However, if adopted, under a new law, the Child Citizenship Act passed by Congress in 2000, the child (provided he's under 18 years of age and the adoptive parents are U.S. citizens), is automatically an American citizen.

Chapter 13

Getting Your Immigrant Visa (The Green Card) Based On Having Employment Or Job Skills: First Preference Priority Workers

A. ALL THE DIFFERENT KINDS OF EMPLOYMENT-RELATED BASES AVAILABLE FOR QUALIFYING FOR A GREEN CARD.

As has been fully set forth earlier in Chapter 3, Section C.2, within the employment-based immigrant visa categories – that is, those categories of green cards which are granted on the basis of having an employment or certain job skills – there are basically five separate preferences or groupings within which a qualifying alien may fall. (See Chapter 3, Section C.2 for a detailed breakdown).

In this Chapter, we discuss the detailed eligibility qualifications and the procedures for filing for and obtaining a green card under just ONE of those five employment related bases for qualifying: THE EMPLOYMENT <u>FIRST</u> PREFERENCE OR PRIORITY WORKERS CATEGORY.

EMPLOYMENT-BASED (EB) GREEN CARD CATEGORIES

- FIRST Preference (Priority Workers)
- Persons of Extraordinary Ability (Nobel Prize winner, Lee Iacocca of General Motors caliber of managers)
- OUTSTANDING PROFESSORS/RESEARCHERS (Researchers, scientists of Jonas Salk caliber)
- International Executives

- SECOND Preference
- (Exceptional Ability Professionals: Masters + Degree Professionals)

- THIRD Preference (Skilled and/or unskilled workers)
- Professionals with Baccalaureate Degree
- Two-year training or experience
- General or unskilled labor

- FOURTH Preference (Special Immigrants)
- Certain juveniles
- Ministers of religion
- Retired former employees of U.S. government abroad

- FIFTH Preference (Entrepreneur Investor)
- Employment creation investors

B. PRIORITY WORKERS CATEGORY: ALIENS WHO QUALIFY

There are three principal characteristics which distinguish this preference category: they have a high level of achievement; a Labor Certification (a certificate of job approval or authorization from the U.S. Department of Labor)* is not required as a prerequisite for obtaining this visa; and the alien does not need to be "sponsored" by a U.S. employer in order to be eligible, but may, himself, simply file the petition on his (or her) own behalf.

There are 40,000 visas made available under this category to aliens annually on a first-come, first served basis. There are three sub-categories of immigrant making up the Priority Workers:
- Persons of extraordinary ability in the arts and sciences, field of education, business, or athletics
- Outstanding professors and researchers
- Multinational corporate executives or managers.

1. Persons of Extraordinary Ability

To qualify as a PRIORITY WORKER under this sub-category, the alien must have risen to the very top of his/her field in the sciences, arts, education and business or athletics. *The high level of achievement must be demonstrated by:*
- proof of national or international acclaim, and public recognition in the given field of endeavor which is sustained over a reasonable period of time and is extensively documented
- documentary evidence of such achievement of a highly reliable nature
- proof of intent by the alien to continue work in the U.S. in the field of endeavor which is the subject of the acclaim
- proof that and arguments about how the alien's work in the U.S. will substantially benefit the United States in the future

The alien's required high level of achievement can be demonstrated in any of the following ways:
- proof of receipt of a major internationally recognized award, such as the Nobel Prize, Olympic Gold Medal, or, for a motion picture director or actor, the Academic Award. Or, in lien of such famous or extraordinary award, the alien must present evidence and proof of AT LEAST THREE of the following:
- receipt of a lesser national or international prize or award for excellence in the particular field of endeavor
- membership in associations that require merit and outstanding achievements for membership, as judged by nationally or internationally recognized experts in the given field
- published material about the alien's work or accomplishments in professional journals, major trade publications, or other major media. Published material must include the title, date, and author of the publication, and must be translated into English.
- participation by the alien on a panel, or as an individual, as a judge of the work of professional colleagues in the same field of endeavor or a related field.
- evidence of original scientific, scholarly, or artistic, athletic or business-related contributions of major significance made by the alien
- copies of scholarly articles written by the alien that have been published in professional journals or other major media, such as national or international newspapers, magazines, etc.

---

*NOTE: True, as an alien qualifying under the Priority Worker category (or a Schedule A Applicant), you'll not need to file for or to obtain a Labor Certification from the U.S. DOL. However, you (the alien) still need to submit with your visa petition, all the relevant documents and proofs necessary to establish your qualification for the specific job or occupation you claim – basically the kinds of documentations detailed in this Sections B & C herein, for each subcategory involved.

- display of the alien's work at artistic exhibitions, showcase or competition, in more than one country.
- performance in a leading role for organizations or establishments that have a distinguished reputation.
- command by the alien of a high salary or other significantly high remuneration for services in relation to what others in the field receive
- commercial success in the performing arts, as shown by box office receipts or by records, cassette, compact disk or video sales.
- other evidence of comparable nature to demonstrate that you're extraordinary, if you do not have any of the above enumerated credentials, or if these types of evidence do not readily apply to your occupation.

NOTE: For persons applying under Extraordinary Ability category, they need not have an offer of employment in the United States. They need only submit, however, a clear proof that they're seeking entry into the U.S. to continue work in their field of work, and generally how they plan to do so.

2. Outstanding Professors and Researchers

To qualify as a PRIORITY WORKER under this subcategory, the alien must have risen to the level of one of the outstanding professors and top researchers of his or her country and of the world. Documentations or evidence of the following nature are needed:

- proof of a firm job offer made to you by a research institute or university in the U.S., and/or of a firm commitment that it's willing and able to employ you (the alien) in your field of expertise, and in a tenured permanent teaching or research position, and not simply a temporary appointment.
- PROOF OF INTERNATIONAL REPUTATION AND ACCLAIM possessed by you in your particular academic field, with evidence consisting of AT LEAST TWO of the following:
- receipt of major international prizes or award for outstanding achievement
- membership in academic associations which require outstanding achievement for membership
- published articles in professional publications by others about your work.
- participation on a panel, or as an individual, judging the work of others in the same field of expertise
- original scientific or scholarly research contributions to the field of expertise
- authorship by you of scholarly books or articles in journals with international circulation by you.
- proof of at least 3 years of teaching or research in your field of expertise.
- proof that the U.S. employer is a private employer, as differentiated from a university or other educational institution, that the private employer has at least 3 other persons employed in full-time research, and has some accomplishments in the field.

3. Multinational Corporate Executives or Managers

To qualify as a Priority Worker under the multinational EXECUTIVE or MANAGER preference subcategory, the alien must have been employed, during the 3 years just preceding the visa application, as an executive or manager for at least 1 year by the same multinational corporation* or firm which is to employ him or her in the

NOTE: To qualify as a "multinational corporation" or business entity for our purposes here, the corporation must meet certain distinction characteristics under the immigration law. Namely, it must be a corporation which: (1) has different branches located in two or more countries but owned and controlled by the same corporation or individual; and which (2) has a subsidiary, or affiliate located in the U.S. but is owned and controlled by the same group of individuals, each owing the same share. Furthermore, the foreign and the U.S. corporation must be ones which are under the control of the same person, company or group, or merely an internationally-recognized accounting firm organized in the U.S. and affiliated with a world-wide coordinating organization owned and controlled by the member accounting firms. Finally, the multinational corporation, to qualify under the immigration law requirements, must be truly "doing business" in the U.S. – that is, providing goods and services on a regular, continuous and routine basis, and not merely present as an agent or an office in the U.S.

U.S. Furthermore, the alien must intend to continue rendering services, in a managerial or executive capacity, to the same employer. The petitioning company (the employer) must have been in business in the U.S. for at least one year prior to the filing of the immigrant visa petition.

THE CENTRAL QUESTION, OF COURSE, IS: how exactly do you define the key terms *"executive"* and *"manager"* in this context? In actuality, the definition of these two terms is closely identical to the way they are defined under the requirements for aliens seeking the L-1 nonimmigrant visa [see Chapter 11 of the Volume 1 of this book authored by the same author].For the purposes of the immigrant visa category (as well as the nonimmigrant L-1 intra company transferee visa, more fully described in Chapter 11 of Volume 1), the immigration law defines the "executive" and "manager" in the specific terms following below.

a) *Manager*
An alien person qualifies as a manager if he/she has ALL of the following characteristics:
- he/she manages the company or a department of the company
- he/she supervises and controls the work of other supervisory, professional or managerial employees, or manages an essential function within the company, or a department or subdivision of the company. (Note that, in other words, a mere first-line supervisor, defined as a supervisor below the level of middle management, does not qualify as a "manager" in this specific context; rather, for a first line supervisor to qualify in this context, he must be supervising persons of professional caliber).
- he/she has the authority to hire and fire the person under his(her) supervision. If no other employees are supervised, he must function at a senior level within the organization.
- exercises the official discretion and authority to establish goals and policies, and to make decisions concerning the day-to-day operations of that portion of the organization or function for which he/she has responsibility.
- receives only general supervision from higher executive, board of directors, or stockholders.

b. *Executive*
An executive alien person qualifies as an EXECUTIVE if he (she) has ALL of the following characteristics:
- directs the management of the organization (the company) or a major part of it.
- establishes the goals and policies of the organization or a major part of it.
- has wide discretionary authority on major decisions concerning the company.
- receives only general supervision or direction from higher level executives, a board of directors, or stockholders of the organization.

By way of a summary, here's one immigration expert's rather vivid but concise and helpful definition of the above named two key terms: "Show me a person who can hire and fire employees (who he supervises and controls), and I will show you a manager. On the other hand, show me a person who has authority to sign company checks and make policy decisions, and I will show you an executive".*

C. HOW TO FILE FOR A GREEN CARD
To file for a green card for an alien person based on the alien being a professional or worker under the employment-based First, Second, Third, Fourth or Fifth Preference categories, simply follow these steps and procedures in EXACTLY the same order and chronology in which they are listed below:

*C. James Cooper, Jr., a long-term Denver, Colorado immigration attorney and author, author of the *Immigration Tapes (Text)*.

1. First, be sure to read, thoroughly, Chapter 3 for some helpful basic information on the different employment-based green card preferences or categories that are available under the U.S. immigration law.

2. Assuming that the alien for whom the visa is being sought is currently not in the U.S.* and that the visa petition is being filed in order to bring him or her into the U.S. from a foreign country, here are the paper to prepare:

> ● Form ETA 750 Part A and B, *Application For Alien Employment Certification* (see sample of this form on p. 167, and the "EXPLANATORY NOTE" on p. 89). This form needs to be filed only by aliens whose employment-based preference category is subject to Labor Certification – basically, every other category except for persons applying either as Priority Workers under the employment first preference, or in occupations listed under "Schedule A"**. Assuming the alien in this case is subject to Labor Certification, then the aliens prospective U.S. employer would be the is one who must prepare and sign Part A of Form ETA-750; the alien completes and signs Part B, and the U.S. employer files the whole form for the benefit of the alien with the Department of Labor (DOL), basically demonstrating to the DOL that there are no Americans or permanent residents in the state in which the alien will be working who are ready, willing or able to do the work that the alien is being hired to do at the prevailing wage. (The rather elaborate procedures for filing for a Labor Certification is in Chapter 23). The ETA-750 used in an <u>actual</u> case filing is reproduced on pp. 167, 169 and the EXPLANATORY NOTE for the filing of this form is on p. 89).

If this given case is subject to a labor certification, then you will, at this point, wait until AFTER the application for labor certification has been filed with the DOL. You must first get the DOL approval of the labor certification application <u>before</u> you may file the actual petition (the papers below) for the immigrant visa on behalf of the alien. However, to petition for a green card when an alien is qualified for Schedule A job, the U.S. employer merely prepares and files directly with the INS Service Center, both Form ETA-750 and Form 1-140 (along with the usual necessary supporting documents for visa petition), clearly showing that the alien qualifies for a Schedule A occupation. (See Chapter 23 for a full treatment of the labor certification procedures).

3. *Now, prepare the following forms for filing with the INS office*
- Immigration Form 1-140, *Immigrant Petition For Alien Worker*. This form (obtainable free of charge from the INS) is to be completed and signed by the alien's intended U.S. employer – known as the alien's "spon sor" or "petitioner." (See samples of this Form on p. 180, and on p. 216 also)
- FORM G-325A, *Biographic Information*. (See p. 225 for a sample). This form is to be completed by the principal alien and each relative accompanying him/her who is over 14 years of age and below 79, if any.
- If Labor Certification applies, proof of the approved Department of Labor's Certification – this is represented by the Form ETA-750, Part A, which the DOL shall have returned to the sponsoring U.S. employer with a red and blue stamp marked on it to indicate approval of the labor certification application. Filing fee -- attach this, it is $75 as of this writing, in the form of a money order or certified check made payable to the "Immigration and

---

*In a case, however, where the alien is already in the U.S. and he or she is seeking a green card on whatever basis, then the petition would have to be filed under a difference procedure called "Adjustment of Status" (see Chapter 20 for this procedure).

**What is a 'Schedule A' occupation? Under the U.S. immigration procedures, the nation's Department of Labor specifies, from time to time, that certain occupations and professions that are of significance to the health of U.S. economy are in short supply in the United States. And alien professions who belong to such professions that are declared by the DOL to be in such supply, are exempt from or automatically granted Labor Certificate. Occupations or professions which are so declared by the DOL to be in short supply, are listed in a document - the Schedule A. The list shifts and changes from time to time. As of this writing, the principal occupations on the current Schedule A list, are registered nurses and physical therapists.

Naturalization Service".

4. *File the Completed Petition Forms & Papers*

Now, to file the visa petition for the alien, you, the alien's prospective U.S. employer – the so-called "sponsor" or "petitioner" – must sign the completed forms (and have the alien(s) sign the ones they need to), and then submit them, along with the filing fees and the necessary supporting documents to the forms, to: the U.S. Immigration and Naturalization Service's regional center. Simply mail the papers by certified mail, with return receipt requested, to the INS Regional Center covering the area in which the alien's prospective employer's business is located. There are four such centers spread across the U.S. and are not the same as the INS local offices. (See Appendix B for the addresses of the INS regional center locations).

Supporting Documents Which May Be Attached To Sponsor's Petition

Attach to the papers you file with the INS, the necessary supporting documents which apply to the alien's particular employment preference or category. The following documents may typically be required:

● EVIDENCE OF JOB OFFER: Supporting letters or written offer of employment or sworn affidavits from the alien's U.S. petitioner-employer, giving the alien's job specifications, salary, and facts as to whether the employment is permanent or temporary. (See sample of such a letter on pp. 176 & 177)

NOTE: Except for only ONE out of the three subcategories that make up the employment First Preference Priority Worker group, namely, the subcategory of *Persons of Extraordinary Ability*, for every other employment preference whatsoever, the alien must first have a job offer from a U.S. employer in order to apply for a green card. In other words, unless an employment-based alien is applying under a person of 'Extraordinary Ability' within the priority workers' 1st Preference category, he/she must first have a job offer.* In this connection, note that while ALL aliens applying either as Priority Workers under the employment first preference (all three subcategories) and those in occupations listed under "Schedule A," are not required to have a <u>Labor Certificate</u>, nevertheless only ONE specialized, tiny sub-group of employment-based alien applicants are not required to have a <u>specific job offer</u> from a U.S. employer to qualify: namely, those belonging to just <u>one</u> of the three sub-categories of the employment First Preference, 'Persons of Extraordinary Ability' subcategory. To put it another way, while all aliens, only, qualifying either as employment First Preference Priority Workers or Schedule A applicants do not have to have a labor certification, all employment-based aliens whatsoever, except only for those qualifying under just the 'Persons of Extraordinary Ability' subcategory in the employment first preference Priority Worker group, must generally have a specific job offer from a U.S. employer.

● JOB EXPERIENCE EVIDENCE: Letters or affidavits from the alien's previous (and/or present) employers, professors or professional colleagues (see samples of such letter on pp. 178, 179 & 182.)
● Certified copies of CERTIFICATES, DIPLOMAS, SCHOOL TRANSCRIPTS, and other documents and proofs of educational qualification, job skills or professional status for the job or position claimed. (see sample of this on pp. 178 & 179.)

---

*In strict terms, there's one more other group of aliens which is exempt from having to have a specific job offer before they may apply for a green card, and that other group are those who qualify as having 'exceptional ability' in the sciences, arts and business, under the employment-based Second preference. Under the rules, however, in practice most people in this preference necessarily have to have a U.S. job offer, still, as the alien in this preference who qualifies is required to apply for a waiver in order to be exempt from having a job offer or a labor certification, and would have to meet certain stringent conditions in order to qualify. For example, for an 'exceptional ability' alien to qualify for exemption from the usual job offer requirement, he (she) would have to be able to show that his coming to the U.S. will <u>substantially</u> "benefit" the economic, cultural or educational interests of the United States — that is, that his presence in the country, and his use of his talents and skill from being present there, will have a favorable impact on the country, economically, culturally, educationally and/or in terms of employment, etc., which would be <u>national</u> in scope as well as <u>substantial</u>.

- SWORN AFFIDAVITS FROM CREDIBLE AUTHORITIES OR EXPERTS in the alien's field of expertise testifying that the alien has the special technical training or specialized experience claimed – e.g. the skill to use a particular machine or speak a foreign language that such a job calls for.
- PUBLISHED MATERIALS BY OR ABOUT THE ALIEN in newspapers, magazines, professional journals, etc.
- Proof of PROFESSIONAL LICENSES, membership in professional societies, achievement awards, and the like.
- CERTIFICATE AWARDS from trade union or technical schools, apprenticeship schools, etc.
- LICENSES or trade union certificates.
- FOR PHYSICAL THERAPIST Petition: submit copy of the alien's U.S. State license in the state where he(she) will work, or a letter from that state's physical therapy licensing agency.
- FOR REGISTERED NURSES' petition: submit copy of the alien's nursing license issued by the specific U.S. State where he (she) will work, or evidence of his passing the Commission on Graduates of Foreign Nursing School (CGFNS) examination.
- IN GENERAL, gather and provide the kinds of documentations which will apply in proving the alien's qualification under the particular employment preference category to which the alien belongs as set forth in the applicable Section B(1), (2) or (3) above.
- VERIFICATION DOCUMENTS from the U.S. employer to prove that the business entity actually exists, and that it can afford to employ and to pay the alien the required salary, and that it earns sufficient income to be able to do so. You may provide, for example, the company's U.S. tax returns for the past 2 years; or bank statements for the company and the balance sheet, plus the profit and loss statements. Publicly held corporations and larger, better known companies that are nationally or internationally known, may generally not have to produce such documents; for such companies, the corporate annual reports would usually suffice.

Do not send the <u>originals</u> of the documents needed at this time. Merely submit the photocopies of the documents for the moment, but be sure to have the originals readily available so that you can provide them to the INS officials for inspection and authentication when they are specifically asked for. (NOTE that generally, however, on the other hand, the documents submitted in the second phase of the visa processing, that is, in the "application" phase (Section D below), are usually required to be either the originals or officially "certified" copies bearing a government seal of authentication).

NOTE: As a rule, the INS does not usually accept automatically the diplomas and schooling credentials earned in foreign institutions as valid or creditworthy or up to standard. Rather, for the INS to accept such document, you (or the alien involved) would often need to submit the transcripts of the foreign schooling records to an accredited U.S. academic evaluator for its assessment. (See p - for a list of some of such accredited agencies in the United States).

D. THE "APPLICATION" PHASE: ONCE THE SPONSOR'S "PETITION" IS APPROVED, THEN THE ALIEN, HIMSELF, FILES AN "APPLICATION" FOR THE VISA

What happens after the alien's sponsoring petitioner (the U.S. employer) has filed the petition for a green card for the alien? The INS will consider the petition. If some material defects or omissions are found in the papers, such as unsigned forms or missing information or documents or payment, the INS will probably return the entire petition papers to the petitioner with a note, or a Form 797, stating what corrections need to be made or what additional documents or information need to be supplied. Or, in certain cases, the INS may simply retain the papers already submitted but issue a request for the additional documents or information needed.

In any event, once the visa petition is approved by the INS, the INS will so inform the sponsoring petitioner by sending him or her either a NOTICE OF APPROVAL OF VISA PETITION (Form 1-191), or a *Notice of Action* form, Form 1-797. And since the alien lives outside the U.S. in this case, the INS will forward the alien's entire file as well as a copy of the *Notice of Action* (or Approval) to the National Visa Center (NVC) located in Portsmouth, New Hampshire, which will in turn then send the file to the American Consulate in the alien's designated home country or current place of residence. Thereafter, the U.S Consulate in the alien's home country notifies the alien himself (or herself) of the preliminary approval of the visa petition filed on his behalf, and forwards him a package of information and directives about how he may make the actual "application" for his immigrant visa at the area's U.S. Consulate there, and what documentations and proofs he would need to provide.

Basically, what this boils down to is that if the alien were to qualify as an "immediate relative" alien (Chapter 3, Section B), meaning that he is therefore not subject to a quota requirement, or if the alien qualifies under other preference categories but his Priority Date is immediately current, meaning that there is no waiting period required for the alien and that his visa can begin to be processed immediately (Chapter 3, Sections C.1 or C.2, and Chapter 5, Sections C and D), then what the alien would have received from the U.S. Consulate is the package of forms and information called the "Packet 3" type – meaning one that basically tells the alien what documents to prepare and assemble in order to be given an appointment for the visa interview with the Consulate Officials. The alien should expect this package within a month or two after the petition is approved. If, however, the alien qualifies under a preference category, which means therefore that he is subject to some kind of a quota (waiting period) for the visa number, and his (her) Priority Date is not yet available or <u>current</u>, the alien will receive the kind of package called "Packet 3A" – basically a letter telling him that he will have to wait for some moment of time for the processing of his visa to be ready. And when it is ready, the alien will then receive Packet 3. In other words, if you are a preference alien of any kind (i.e., one who is subject to a quota or waiting period for the visa number to become available), even when you have an approved petition for an immigrant visa if your Priority Date is not yet <u>current</u>, you must wait until it is current before you may file your visa application (the next step below). In any case, there is one good news regarding this: *the U.S. Consulate will usually advise the alien, any way, in the Packet 3 or 3A documents it sends to the alien, about when it is that his PRIORITY DATE eventually comes up**. [See Chapter 5 for the way the waiting system works for the visa number to become available, and how to keep track of your quota progress through the U.S. State Department].

1. Procedures Involved In Filing the Visa Application

This phase in the visa processing formalities, you should note, is called the "APPLICATION" phase, as opposed to the "petition" phase which is the first phase just concluded with the granting of the U.S. sponsor's or petitioner's initial petition on the alien's behalf. The difference here, in this "application" phase, is that from this point on in the visa processing, it is now <u>THE ALIEN</u> himself, who has to make the formal request for the visa to the U.S. Consulate in his home country, and who has to carry out the remaining paperwork and see to the processing of the visa for the rest of the way, as the remainder of the steps required for concluding the visa processing now shift to

---

*Generally speaking, as an alien qualifying under an employment-based preference (or category), you will be subject to some sort of a quota requirement and a waiting period for a visa number to become available. However, the way the preference system is set up, the higher the preference, the less skilled the jobs and the longer the waiting period you'll likely have to have. For example, for the periods up to January 1998, there were no waiting periods whatsoever for persons falling under the employment First Preference; aliens in the employment Second Preference had only a waiting period of some 8 months for people from India and 10 months for people from China; those in the employment Third Preference had only a waiting periods of 4 years for professionals and skilled workers from China, and of 3 years for professionals and skilled workers from Philippines, and up to 7 years for "other workers" from all countries; for those in the employment Fourth Preference, the waiting period was 8 months for religious workers from all countries; and for those in employment Fifth Preference, there was no waiting period – but that's apparently because there were relatively very few visas available in this category.

the alien and to the U.S. Consulate in the alien's foreign country.

The information and instructions contained in the Packet 3 sent the alien (and to his sponsoring U.S. relative or employer) by the U.S. Consulate in the alien's home country, shall have generally told the alien what further steps he is to take in the remaining processing of his visa. *Here's what you (the alien) do to kick off the filing of your application:*

- There are two primary forms you (the alien) should find included in Packet 3 – Form OF230-1 and OF-169. You should first complete *Form 0F230, Application for Immigrant Visa and Alien Registration - Part 1, Biographic Data.* Complete only the first part of this form at this stage. The Part 2 of the OF230 is OF169. (See p. 220 for a sample of OF-230, Part 1; and Part 2 is on pp. 218 & 222).
- Secondly, upon the alien's completion of OF230 (the Part 1 thereof), promptly send it directly to the American Consulate in the alien's country. Do so as soon as possible; the Consulate officials will usually not begin working on your visa until they receive this form, as they will need the completed information from the FORM OF 230-1, to enable them begin the required security check into your background in the meantime.
- The application fee may be required to be enclosed at this time. The area's U.S. Consulate will give the alien the applicable fee amount. As of this writing, the fee is $200 - $170 for the application, and $30 upon approval of the application.

2. Start Assembling the Necessary Supporting Documents

Next, you (the alien) should immediately begin to prepare and assemble the various documents enumerated in Form OF-169, *The Instructions For Immigrant Visa Application* (see sample of this on p. 218), in preparation for their use in a visa appointment and interview with the Consulate officials later. And, as soon as you have gathered all the documents listed in Form OF-169, as applicable to you, and any others required by the Consulate, which may include some or all of those listed below, this is what you do: now complete the Part 2 of the Form OF-230, that is, the Form OF-169 (this you sign at the bottom page), and the Form OF-230, Part 2, *Application For Immigrant Visa and Alien Registration – Sworn Statement* (reproduced on P. 222). Do not sign the OF-230, Part 2 form yet at this point – wait until you are specifically asked to do so by the Consular officer. Mail only the form OF-169 (or take it down in person) to the Consulate office. Upon receipt of this form, this informs the Consulate that you (and all others who are emigrating with you, if any) are now ready and prepared for the final processing of your application and to attend the visa appointment and interview.

Supporting Documents to be Attached to the Alien's Application

The following are the forms and examples of the supporting documents the alien applicant may have to complete and submit in an Immigrant visa application:

- BIRTH CERTIFICATES: One certified copy for each person named for a visa in the application
- TWO (it could be more) passport-size color PHOTOGRAPHS of each alien, showing a full front view of the facial features, with the reverse side of each photograph signed (in full names) by the alien signing each application. (See Chapter 25, Section F for specification of the right style and manner of the photo).
- A CURRENT PASSPORT for each alien issued by the alien's country and valid for at least the next 6 months or so.
- A POLICE CERTIFICATE for each accompanying family member of the alien who is over 16 years of age – obtainable from the police or other appropriate authorities in each of all the countries where each alien had resided for more than 6 months. [If the alien is applying from within the U.S., the REPORT OF FINGER PRINTING (Form FD258, sampled on p. 224) may be used, instead. The print is taken at a local police station or a local INS office and recorded on the pre-coded card, then sent to the Consulate or INS for referral to the FBI for a clearance report].

- COURT AND PRISON RECORDS, if any, for each applicable alien with a prior prison record.
- MILITARY RECORD for each alien, if applicable, for service in your country or any country.
- REPORT OF MEDICAL EXAMINATON for each alien. (The examination must usually be performed by a doctor or medical facility specifically designated by the U.S. Consulate in the foreign country, who then furnishes the report to the alien to provide the consulate).
- EVIDENCE OF SUPPORT. If your visa application is family-based, or if it is employment-based but your relatives are your sponsors for your visa petition or own at least 5% of the company which is your sponsor, then you'll need to file Form 1-864, *Affidavit of Support.* (See sample of form on p. 241). Note that this form, AFFIDAVIT OF SUPPORT, is to be made out and sworn to (signed) by the sponsoring U.S. citizen or Permanent Resident and his/her spouse, if married, showing that such sponsor witnesses that he will financially support you (the alien) and that you will not become a "public charge" to the U.S. government if admitted to the U.S. A cover sheet to this form carries detailed institutions on the supporting documents, such as income records, statement of earnings, bank records, evidence of property ownership, etc., to be attached to this affidavit. If, on the other hand, your visa application is not family-based, and you do not have a job or offer of employment in the U.S., you should have your American-sponsor complete another version of the *Affidavit of Support,* Form 1-134 (see sample of this on p.214).
- An approved LABOR CERTIFICATION from the U.S. Department of Labor – when applicable, such as when the alien has a job or an offer of employment by a U.S. company or employer and is filing under the Second, Third, Fourth or Fifth employment-based preference category. The underlying documentary evidence upon which the certification has been obtained are also to be attached. (When a labor certificate is submitted, it's customary in such cases to also enclose an EMPLOYER'S LETTER OR OFFER OF EMPLOYMENT – see the samples reproduced on pp. 176, 177, 178 & 179). Samples of Approved Labor Certification are reproduced on 172, 173 & 174. The full procedures for obtaining labor certification are in Chapter 23; for the labor certification procedures used in an actual case, see "Explanatory Note" on p. 89.
- A few Consulates require the applicants to submit fingerprints. Most do not, however. Consulate requiring this will inform you of this.
- Form 1-797, *Notice of Action* – include a copy of this form that has been sent you by the Immigration and Naturalization Service to notify you that your sponsor's visa petition had been approved.

What happens next? The Consulate examiners will take a quick, initial look at your application and make a preliminary assessment. And, once the examiners can determine, either that you are not subject to a quota or that your visa number is immediately available ("current"), your application will be considered ready for further processing. At this point, the Consulate will send you another batch of papers, known as PACKET 4. Packet 4 will provide you important relevant information, such as the following: a written notice or letter of appointment indication when you should come for your visa interview with the head of the Consulate's immigrant visa section, the list of documents you are to provide, including those detailed in Form OF-169, directions on how and where you should have your medical examination taken before the interview date, and so on. And Packet 4 may still have more forms to complete.

Now, take strict note of the date of your visa interview appointment. Also, be sure to make your medical examination appointment – it's usually scheduled for immediately before the visa interview, depending on the practices of specific consulates. The medical exam appointment letter will tell you where exactly to go (the name of the doctor or clinic, the address, etc), what specific tests or exams you are to take, the amount of the doctor's fee you are to pay for the exam, etc. Basically, the main purpose of the medical exam is to determine that you don't have the kind of medical conditions that would make you medically excludable under the law, such as tuberculosis or HIV (AIDS).

E. ATTEND THE VISA INTERVIEW

All alien applicants for immigrant visa are subject to personal interview with the U.S. Consulate although an interview is frequently waived for aliens under 14 years of age. Turn to Chapter 21 for the full procedures involved in this all-important visa interview.

However, simply be sure to bring with you to the interview appointment, all the completed forms and supporting documents you shall have gathered which apply in your case, including those listed in Sections C.4 and D.2 above which have not already been submitted. Except for Form OF-230-1, which you (the alien) shall have submitted to the Consulate as soon as you received it, and Form OF-169, which you shall have sent in to the Consulate as soon as you were ready to request for an interview, you will need to submit, in person, virtually all the application forms and documentations you've prepared. Virtually all of the same documents you (or your U.S. sponsor) first filed in the petition phase, may be required to be submitted again to the Consulate, in addition to other documents. Do not mail your documents and paperwork to the Consulate. Rather, you are to bring them with you in person to your interview appointment. This is when you would be expected to present the actual <u>originals</u> (or certified true copies) of the documents for the benefit of the Consular officers so that they can physically examine and authenticate the documents for their genuineness. And it is also at this interview that you (each visa applicant) will have to sign the Form OF-230 Application Part 2 (see p. 222 for the sample) in the presence of the American Consul.

F. FINAL APPROVAL OF YOUR VISA BY THE CONSULAR OFFICE
Finally, upon the conclusion of the visa interview (Section E above), assuming that everything is in order with your visa application – that you have, for example, provided all the necessary answers and proofs required, and that there's nothing in your record that makes you inadmissible to the U.S. under the immigration law – your application for immigration visa will probably be approved on the spot. The U.S. Consul in charge at the Consulate will inform you there and then of the approval, and you may be asked to return later in a certain day when you will be issued your visa. Or, oftentimes, you may be informed of the visa decision through the mail.

In any event, to evidence the grant of immigrant visa to you, the U.S. Consul will usually place a stamp in your passport at this time to serve as your temporary "green card" for the meantime. (you will usually receive the actual "green card", formally called the *Immigrant Visa and Aliens Registration Number*, which will bear your photograph, fingerprints, and an official   U.S. stamp of approval, latter on when you are already in the U.S.)*

As of this moment, you have been issued your immigrant visa. BUT REMEMBER THIS: though you have your immigrant visa in hand, you are NOT YET a permanent resident of the United States, though!

G. YOU MUST NOW BE FORMALLY "ADMITTED" INTO THE U.S. AT A U. S. PORT OF ENTRY
The immigrant visa you've been issued is valid for 6 months – it grants you the legal authorization to arrive in the U.S. within those 6 months. You must endeavor to arrive in the U.S. (at a port of entry) WITHIN the six months. And, technically, it is only at the moment when you arrive at the U.S. port of entry and then formally get "admitted" into the U.S. by the U.S. border inspector, that you actually acquire the full status of being a permanent resident (an immigrant visa or green cardholder) of the United States. At that time, the U.S. border inspectors will stamp your passport as a legal immigrant admitted to stay and work in the United States. The actual card, called the green card (actually, the card is not green in color) for you (and for others who accompany you as relatives, if any), are then ordered, and you get them by mail in your new U.S. address a few months later.

But, note that before you can be actually "admitted" formally into the U.S. even with your approved visa in hand, you have to successfully pass through the very important formalities involved in what is called the 'inspection and admission' process into the United States. Turn to Chapter 22, *"Entering the United States: The Process of Getting Actually Admitted into the Country After You've Got Your Visa,"* for this procedure.

---

*NOTE: At this time of your issuance of the visa, you will also be given back your original Form OF230, along with the originals of your supporting documents, and your medical X-rays. This is to enable you take these documents with you when you travel to the U.S. so that you can present them to the U.S. immigration border inspectors for their verification when you apply for entry ("admission") into the U.S. upon your arriving at the U.S. port of entry.

Chapter 14

Getting Your Immigrant Visa (The Green Card) Based On Having Employment Or Job Skills: Second Preference Or 'Exceptional Ability' Professionals

A. ALL THE VARIOUS KINDS OF EMPLOYMENT-RELATED BASES AVAILABLE FOR QUALIFYING FOR A GREEN CARD

As has been fully set forth earlier in Chapter 3, Section C.2, with regard to employment-based immigrant visa categories – that is, those categories of green cards which are obtainable on the basis of employment or job skills – there are 5 separate preferences or groupings within which a qualifying alien can fall, ranging from the employment-based First preference or priority worker, to employment-based Fifth Preference or Entrepreneur investor. (See esp. Section C.2 of Chapter 3 for a detailed breakdown)

In this Chapter, we discuss the detailed eligibility qualifications and the procedures for filing for and obtaining a green card under just ONE of those five employment-related bases for qualifying – THE EMPLOYMENT SECOND PREFERENCE or Exceptional Ability Professionals category.

EMPLOYMENT-BASED (EB) GREEN CARD CATEGORIES

- FIRST Preference (Priority Workers)
  - Persons of Extraordinary Ability (Nobel Prize winner. Lee Iacocca of General Motors caliber of managers)
  - OUTSTANDING PROFESSORS/RESEARCHERS (Researchers, scientists of Jonas Salk caliber)
  - International Executives

- SECOND Preference
  - (Exceptional Ability Professionals: Masters + Degree Professionals)

- THIRD Preference (Skilled and/or unskilled workers)
  - Professionals with Baccalaureate Degree
  - Two-year training or experience
  - General or unskilled labor

- FOURTH Preference (Special Immigrants)
  - Certain juveniles
  - Ministers of religion
  - Retired former employees of U.S. government abroad

- FIFTH Preference (Entrepreneur Investor)
  - Employment creation investors

B. EXCEPTIONAL ABILITY ALIEN PROFESSIONALS: ALIENS WHO QUALIFY

This category is reserved for only the most accomplished or talented professionals who have a lot to contribute to America in the arts, sciences, education, or business fields. The qualification that the Priority Worker is required to meet under the "extraordinary ability" standards of the employment-based First preference category treated in the preceding Chapter 13, is very similar to the "exceptional ability" standards required to be met by the qualifying alien under the present employment-based Second preference category. But with just some few differences. One major difference lies in the nature of the alien's reputation required: the Extraordinary Ability Priority Workers aliens are required to be acclaimed and recognized not only in their own countries, but also INTERNATIONALLY; Exceptional Ability aliens, on the other hand, need only be acclaimed and recognized just in their own native lands. The First preference type of professionals (the Extraordinary Ability Priority Worker of Chapter 13), are to be renowned in the sciences, arts, education, business, or athletics; the Second preference aliens of 'exceptional ability' being addressed in this Chapter, on the other hand, are renowned in the sciences, arts, or business ONLY, but talent in athletics is not included. In sum, generally speaking, 'extraordinary ability' first preference category of aliens are generally of a higher caliber; they are said to be in the top 2% to 3% of their field internationally. In contrast, an 'exceptional ability' Second preference category alien does not need to have such top notch degree of acclaim to qualify.

Aliens who qualify as professionals in various fields are eligible, such as the following: social workers, librarians, and high school teachers with a Masters' degree (or those with only a bachelor's degree who have 5 years of continuous experience in their field), lawyers, high-achiever performing artists, business executives or presidents of enterprises, artists such as nationally acclaimed painters, sculptors, authors and writers, arts dealers and experts, scientists, etc.

C. THE KINDS OF EVIDENCE/DOCUMENTATIONS REQUIRED FOR PROOF OF QUALIFICATION

Aliens in the employment-based SECOND PREFERENCE group are allotted 40,000 visas every year on a first-come, first-served basis.

To qualify for an immigrant visa under this category as an alien of EXCEPTIONAL ABILITY, you (actually the alien's would-be U.S. employer) are required to provide evidence on the alien from at least three of the following categories of documents:

- Official academic degree, diploma, certificate or similar academic record, from a college or university showing that the alien has a U.S. baccalaureate degree or a foreign equivalent degree relating to his or her area of exceptional ability
- Written articles by or about the alien about his/her success or achievements in their business, trade or profession; testimonials and letters of recommendation from renowned members of the alien's peer group; public records and reports describing awards or prizes given the alien, such as, say, an outstanding entrepreneur or business leader or executive award, and annual reports of the alien's company.
- Evidence (such as letters from current or former employers) showing that the alien had had at least 10 years of full time experience in the field for which he/she is being sought.
- A license to practice the profession, or certification for a particular profession.
- Evidence that you (the alien) have commanded a high salary or other remuneration for services, which show exceptional ability (at least $US75,000 - $US100,000 per year).
- Evidence of the alien's membership in professional associations.
- Evidence of recognition for achievements and significant contributions to the alien's industry or field by peers, governmental entities or professional or business organizations.

- For a PERFORMING ARTISTS, for example: you may present playbills, reviews, magazine a. showing your national and/or international acclaim and credibility as a performing artists (a classical lead singer, etc), and its nature and extent, or as a popular actor or actress in the cinema, theatre, etc.
- For AN ARTIST OR ART DEALER OR EXPERT: you may present critical reviews by or about the alien and/ or his (her) work, in art magazines or cultural pages of newspapers, reporting awards or prizes won by the alien in national competitions, and discussing the alien's abilities as a painter, sculptor, nationally recognized author or writer, etc.
- For a SCIENTIST, for example: you may present articles in the alien's professional or academic field, magazines and newspapers, by and about the alien relating to his research work; books and reports of critical acclaim published about the alien's scientific research or study, evidence of awards, prizes or fellowships earned by the alien.

D. LABOR CERTIFICATION IS REQUIRED.

An important requirement for the grant of visa to aliens in this preference category, is that the alien would have to have found a U.S. employer who is willing and able to hire him, and that the alien's U.S. prospective employer must first file with the U.S. Department of Labor and obtained a document called the "labor certification" – a document which, in essence, certifies that there are no Americans or permanent residents in the alien's intended State of residence who are ready, willing and able to do the job for which the alien is being hired, and at the prevailing wages. The process is called obtaining *Labor Certification*. (See Chapter 23 for the rather complex procedures involving in obtaining labor certification).

The Immigration and Naturalization Service (INS), may, however, waive the labor certification requirement for some aliens in this preference – if and when it can be persuaded that it would be in the *national interest* of the U.S. to do so. By this rule, called the *"national interest waiver"* rule, if the employer will be able to make a good case that the particular job will benefit the national interest – that, because of unique or exceptional abilities in the science, arts or business possessed by a given alien, the alien will "substantially benefit the national economic, cultural, or educational interests or welfare of the United States"–then the alien can ask the INS to waive the requirement of a job offer from an employer before he may file a visa petition. But, unless the alien can make such a case to the INS, then his prospective U.S. employer must file for a labor certification for the alien, and must first secure an approved Labor Certification BEFORE the sponsor may file a visa petition for the alien.

NOTE: Under the immigration procedures, the visa processing authorities will consider comparable evidence that is appropriate to the alien's application in the event that the alien cannot exactly fit into the specific types or categories of documentations listed above. Thus, if these categories do not apply to your profession, you can try to submit other documentations which nevertheless demonstrate that you are of 'exceptional ability' caliber, and offer a reasonable explanation why the kind of evidence or documentations listed above do not apply to your particular situation. *The point of importance for you to note, is that the mere possession of a degree, diploma, or certificate from a college or university, or a license to practice a particular profession or occupation, is not sufficient evidence of exceptional ability by itself; and that, to qualify as having exceptional ability, there must be something beyond the basic qualification.* And, secondly, that in some cases having a college degree or other formal basic qualification may, in fact, not be necessary at all as long as you can present other evidence of other kinds which can demonstrate that you have national recognition and acclaim in your field of expertise. A performing artist (a classical guitarist, a lead singer in a rock group, or popular actors or actresses in the cinema), may present playbills, reviews, magazine articles and awards; business executive could present articles by or about them and their success in business, testimonials from members of their peer group, awards as outstanding entrepreneurs or executives, or annual reports of their companies; nationally recognized painters, sculptors, authors or writers.

could present evidence of art exhibits, reviews in cultural magazines, and awards or prizes won in national competitions; and scientists can present magazine, journal, or newspaper articles about their work or research, accolades from scientific journals, books published by or about them, and proof of awards or fellowships earned by them.

E. HOW TO FILE FOR THE GREEN CARD

To file for a green card for an alien person based on the alien being a professional with EXCEPTIONAL ABILITY under the employment Second preference category, simply follow the same steps and procedures in EXACTLY the same order and chronology in which they are listed in Chapter 13, starting from Section C thereof (p. 78).

EXPLANATORY NOTES
(To illustrate the procedures for 2nd or 3rd Preference Cases as used in this Manual)

1. As emphasized in several parts of this manual (see, for examples Chapter 25, Sections A, B, C), immigration forms are notorious for frequently changing. Please take note that the sample petition Form 1-140 reproduced and used here for illustrative purposes (pp. 180-1), has long been superseded by a revised edition which is now currently in use as of 1991 (see p. 216 for a sample of this version). However, we still employ the old, outdated form here for illustration, because of the fact that the petition of Mr. Arun (Doe) which is discussed here, concerns an actual case (as well as actual documentations), which have previously been filed and successfully used and processed by an alien(s) in obtaining a Green Card—materials generously made available to the present author and publisher for illustrative purposes, courtesy of C. James Cooper, Jr., the Denver, Colorado immigration lawyer and specialist. As would be observed on the bodies of these forms, the names, personal and business addresses, and other identifying information of sorts, have been deleted on these sample Cooper forms and documentations, but merely out of concern to protect the privacy of the parties involved.

2. In this specific case, which, you should be reminded, is a true actual case previously processed, the alien, originally as Indian national from New Delhi therein, had first entered the U.S. on an F-1 (i.e., a nonimmigrant) student visa in August 1983. After having received a Master's Degree in Computer and Information Science and having had some practical training, the alien got a job offer from a company in Fort Collins, Colorado, for a position as a Software and Development Engineer, a temporary position, which then meant that he needed an H-1 (temporary worker) visa. The alien's prospective employers filed a petition for an H-1 Visa for the alien, Form 1-129B. Then, at the same time, since in this particular instance the alien was perfectly "in status" as a student as of that time and was therefore qualified to file, he filed Form 1-506, *Application For Change of Nonimmigrant Status,* from within the U.S. requesting to change his status from his non-immigrant F-1 student status, to the non-immigrant H-1 (temporary worker) status. The application was granted and the alien's status changed to H-1 status. Then, subsequently, the alien's Colorado-based employer decided they needed his services permanently; the employer then started the process for securing a permanent residence for the alien.

3. Since the alien's educational and work experience apparently qualified him for the 3rd Preference (the equivalent category today is 2nd Preference) immigrant visa, the employer recognized that he first needed to apply for a Labor Certification from the Department of Labor stating that there was a shortage of qualified, able, willing and available U.S. workers for the specific position in question; the employer applied and was granted this certification. (See Chapter 23 for labor certification procedures, generally; sample labor certification application form for Mr. Arun (Doe), Form ETA-750A & B, are reproduced on pp. 167, 169, respectively, and sample letter from the U.S. Department of Labor approving certification, is reproduced on p. 74). Secondly, at the same time, immediately after receiving the Labor Certification (i.e., <u>no</u> <u>later</u> <u>than</u> 60 days of receiving that), the employer file also the *Form 1-140* visa petition with the Immigration Service to classify the alien under the 3rd (it would be the 2nd and 3rd under current law) preference visa category. (Sample Form 1-140 for Mr. Arun (Doe's) case is reproduced on pp. 180).

4. And third, at the same time that the 1-140 petition was filed, the alien himself (the "beneficiary" of the petition) also filed an Application to Adjust his Status to that of a permanent resident, Form 1-485. (See procedures for "Adjustment of Status" fully outlined in Chapter 20). And To his Form 1-140 petition, Mr Arun (Doe), of course, attached various supporting documents – the employer's letters of offer of employment (see pp. 176 & 178), the Biographic Data Form G-325A (see a blank copy of this form on p. 225), certified copies of his college degree and diplomas, fingerprints, photographs, medical examination reports, his alien's Arrival-Departure Record, Form 1-94, his approved Labor Certification notification letter (see copy on p. 174), and the underlying documentations on which it was granted, etc. (See sample of Mr. Arun (Doe's) Form 1-485 on pp. 180-1, but <u>note</u> that this form has since been superseded by a revised edition which is now currently in use.

5. Finally, note that, in short, the procedure followed in the above situation (as in all such situations) is similar to the ADJUSTMENT OF STATUS process set forth in Chapter 20 of the manual. Note, also, that if Mr. Arun (Doe) had filed under the 6th Preference category which was one other job category available <u>at</u> <u>the</u> <u>time</u>, he may not <u>simultaneously</u> file an Application to Adjust Status to Permanent Resident (Form 1-485) <u>at</u> <u>the</u> <u>same</u> <u>time</u> that he filed the Form 1-140 petition. The reason this is so is that the 6th preference was generally noted for having chronic backlogs of visa numbers; and inasmuch as the rule is that an alien is <u>not</u> eligible to adjust his/her status in the U.S. if there is a backlog of visa numbers in the particular preference involved, he would have to designate in the petition (part 4 of the current Form 1-140 at p. 216) an American Consulate abroad closest to his residence to which his visa case should be sent for processing upon approval of the petition.

Chapter 15

Getting Your Immigrant Visa (The Green Card) Based On Having Employment Or Job Skills: The Skilled & Unskilled Worker Alien

A. ALL THE VARIOUS KINDS OF EMPLOYMENT-RELATED BASES AVAILABLE FOR QUALIFYING FOR A GREEN CARD

As has been fully set forth earlier in Chapter 3, Section C.2, with regard to employment-based immigrant visa categories – that is, those categories of green cards which are granted on the basis of employment or job skills – there are 5 separate preferences or groupings in which a qualifying alien can fall, ranging from the employment-based First preference or priority worker, to employment-based Fifth Preference or Entrepreneur investor. (See Section C.2 of Chapter 3 for a detailed breakdown)

In this Chapter, we discuss the detailed eligibility qualifications and the procedures for filing for and obtaining a green card under just ONE of those five employment-related bases for qualifying – THE EMPLOYMENT <u>THIRD</u> PREFERENCE or Skilled and Unskilled Worker category.

EMPLOYMENT-BASED (EB) GREEN CARD CATEGORIES

- FIRST Preference (Priority Workers)
  - Persons of Extraordinary Ability (Nobel Prize winner. Lee Iacocca of General Motors caliber of managers)
  - OUTSTANDING PROFESSORS/RESEARCHERS (Researchers, scientists of Jonas Salk caliber)
  - International Executives

- SECOND Preference
  - (Exceptional Ability Professionals: Masters + Degree Professionals)

- THIRD Preference (Skilled and/or unskilled workers)
  - Professionals with Baccalaureate Degree
  - Two-year training or experience
  - General or unskilled labor

- FOURTH Preference (Special Immigrants)
  - Certain juveniles
  - Ministers of religion
  - Retired former employees of U.S. government abroad

- FIFTH Preference (Entrepreneur Investor)
  - Employment creation investors

B. WHO IS A SKILLED AND/OR UNSKILLED WORKER ALIEN

This preference could be summed up as a general category that includes all the other remaining aliens who seek immigrant visa to the U.S. on the basis of employment – the butcher, the baker, the college graduate alien with less than 5 years experience, the alien who is not a performing artist or business entrepreneur, in short, the alien who may be skilled or unskilled but is an essential part of the overall workforce of the United States. As with the second preference category, aliens who qualify under this THIRD PREFERENCE category, are also allotted 40,000 visas annually, plus any visas from the first two employment-based preference which are unused, if any.

C. LABOR CERTIFICATION IS REQUIRED

As with the SECOND Preference aliens, an important requirement for a grant of visa to aliens in this THIRD preference category, is that the alien must have a job offer from a U.S. employer and a Labor Certification that is issued by the U.S. Department of Labor, certifying that there are no American workers who are willing, available, and qualified to do the proposed job for the prevailing wage, as determined by the State's Employment Security Agency. (See Chapter 23 for the elaborate procedures involving in obtaining Labor Certification).

D. ALIENS WHO QUALIFY

To qualify for this employment-based THIRD Preference group, you must qualify under one of these three sub-categories: skilled worker; professionals with no advanced degrees; and unskilled workers. The first two of these subcategories - namely, the skilled workers and the professionals with no advanced degree – share 30,000 of the 40,000 visas allotted to The Third Preference group.

1. Skilled Workers

Alien in specific industrial or business positions with special skills who are capable of performing a job requiring at least two years of specialized training or experience but do not necessarily require a college degree. The job must also be permanent – not seasonal or temporary

NOTE: It is the Department of Labor (DOL) that decides how much training or experience is required of a particular worker or position in order to be classified as a skilled worker or position. Hence, to be on the safe side, be sure to consult extensively with the DOL and/or with an experienced immigration lawyer or other professionals before applying for a labor certification under this SKILLED WORKER visa category.

2. Professionals Without Advanced Degrees

Professionals of sorts who have only a bachelor's degree from a university college. You'll probably qualify, if you:
- have a bachelor's degree (only)
- are considered a member of a profession
- have less than 5 years of work experience, and
- are not necessarily nationally (or internationally) acclaimed.

The following worker categories, for example, will fit into this group: an architect, accountant, business manager, computer systems analyst, chemist, dietitian, business executive, fashion designer, insurance actuary, journalist, lawyer, medical technologist, airline pilot, pharmacist, scientist, teacher, veterinarian, zoologist, hotel managers (large hotels only), physicians, engineers, physical therapist, chemist, etc.

3. Unskilled Workers

This subcategory is for aliens who are capable of filling positions requiring less than 2 years of training or experience. Only 10,000 of the 40,000 visas allotted to the whole Third Preference category per year, is allocated to this unskilled worker subcategory. And, as a result of this limitation, the backlog and waiting period for this subcategory is very considerable. Indeed, currently, the unskilled worker subcategory is said to be experiencing about 7 to 9 years delay, such that for all intents and purposes the visa is practically unavailable.

The U.S. Department of Labor has established a list of the types of job which will not be given a Labor Certification because it considers that there will always be qualified Americans and permanent resident aliens available and able to take such jobs. These are called *"Schedule B" occupations* (see the list below).

Schedule B Occupations

The following is the U.S. Department of Labor's current list of the types of jobs which belong to the Schedule B occupations – i.e., jobs for which no Labor Certification may be given for the reason that the government believes there are more than enough Americans and permanent residents available to take such jobs.

Assemblers
Attendants – amusement and recreation
　　service, parking lots and service station
Bartenders
Bookkeepers
Caretakers
Cashiers
Charworkers and cleaners
Chauffeurs and taxicab drivers
Cleaners in hotels and motels
Clerks – general, grocery stores and hotel and motel
Clerk typists
Cooks, short order
Counter and fountain workers
Dining room attendants or waiters
Electric Operators
Electric truck operators
Floor workers
Groundskeepers
Guards
Helpers, and industry

Household domestic service workers or housekeepers
　　– unless they have one year of prior paid experience
Janitors
Keypunch operators
Kitchen Workers
Laborers
Loopers and toppers
Material handlers
Nurses' aids and orderlies
Packers, markers and bottlers porters
Receptionists
Sailor and deck
Sales clerks, general
Sewing machine operators and handstitchers
Stockroom and warehouse workers
Street car and bus conductors
Telephone operators
Truck drivers and tractor drivers
Typists (lesser skilled only)
Ushers
Yard workers

A Waiver May Be Filed

In theory, the law allows for some exceptions to the rule that no labor certification may be given for certain types of jobs such as those listed in Scheduled B. It allows that under certain strict circumstances, a U.S. employer may apply to request that a Labor Certification be granted for an alien (as well as to file a national interest waiver for the job at the same time), even if a job is listed as a Schedule B occupation: namely, in a situation where, after having fully advertised and posted a notice with the labor union and made other necessary recruiting efforts, an employer's efforts have failed and the employer is truly unable to find an American or permanent resident alien in the area to take the job, though the job is of a Schedule B occupation caliber. This is the theoretical law! *In practice, however, the reality is that by and large the Department of Labor will generally not approve an employer's application for a waiver of a Schedule B occupation – except, perhaps, in very limited, rare cases involving extraordinary circumstances.*

E. HOW TO FILE FOR THE GREEN CARD

To file for a green card for an alien person based on the alien being a worker (skilled or unskilled) under the employment Third Preference category, simply follow the same steps and procedures in <u>EXACTLY</u> the same order and chronology in which they are listed in Chapter 3, starting from Section C thereof (p. 78).

See, also, the "EXPLANATORY NOTE" on p. 89 for the visa filing procedures of an actual case previously filed and successfully processed, with the actual documentations used thereof.

Chapter 16

Getting Your Immigrant Visa (The Green Card) Based On Having Employment Or Job Skills: Special Immigrants

A. ALL THE VARIOUS KINDS OF EMPLOYMENT-RELATED BASES AVAILABLE FOR QUALIFYING FOR A GREEN CARD

As has been fully set forth in Chapter 3, Section C.2, with regard to employment-based immigrant visa categories – that is, those categories of green cards which are obtainable on the basis of employment or job skills – there are 5 separate preferences or groupings in which an alien can fall, ranging from the employment-based First preference or priority worker, to employment-based Fifth preference or entrepreneur investor category. (See Section C.2 of Chapter 3 for a detailed breakdown).

In this Chapter, we discuss the detailed eligibility qualifications and the procedures for obtaining a green card as it applies in just ONE, of those five employment-related bases for qualifying – THE EMPLOYMENT <u>FOURTH</u> PREFERENCE or 'Special Immigrants' category.

EMPLOYMENT-BASED (EB) GREEN CARD CATEGORIES

- FIRST Preference (Priority Workers)
  - Persons of Extraordinary Ability (Nobel Prize winner, Lee Iacocca of General Motors caliber of managers)
  - OUTSTANDING PROFESSORS/RESEARCHERS (Researchers, scientists of Jonas Salk caliber)
  - International Executives

- SECOND Preference
  - (Exceptional Ability Professionals: Masters + Degree Professionals)

- THIRD Preference (Skilled and/or unskilled workers)
  - Professionals with Baccalaureate Degree
  - Two-year training or experience
  - General or unskilled labor

- FOURTH Preference (Special Immigrants)
  - Certain juveniles
  - Ministers of religion
  - Retired former employees of U.S. government abroad

- FIFTH Preference (Entrepreneur Investor)
  - Employment creation investors

B. SPECIAL IMMIGRANTS: RELIGIOUS WORKERS, FOREIGN MEDICAL GRADUATES, PRESENT/RETIRED EMPLOYEES OF INTERNATIONAL ORGANIZATIONS ETC.

Occasionally, Congress passes a law making Green Cards (immigrant visas) available to one category of people or the other who have not been included in the regular "visa preference" system, but fit into a special situation. Such immigrants fall, therefore, under a category called SPECIAL immigrants. This is the FOURTH preference immigrants of the employment-based visa group.

NOTE: *A significant advantage of this visa preference category, is that the applicants are NOT required to go through the complex process of securing a labor Certification.* They need to have, however, a job offer in the U.S.

A total of 10,000 visas are allocated each year for all special immigrant categories taken together – the FOURTH preference employment-based immigrants plus any left over visas from the higher employment-based categories. Currently, except perhaps for non-clergy religious worker applicants (these may experience a short wait of 6 months or so), the visas for all alien applicants in this category are available on current basis, and the visa petitions are normally approved within four months, as compared to the average of 6 months it takes generally for green card applicants.

C. WHO QUALIFIES AS A SPECIAL IMMIGRANT?

The bulk of the Fourth-preference Special Immigrants, are primarily comprised of ministers of religion (50% of the total visas for this group) and former employees of the U.S. government in foreign countries. Special immigrant green cards are available to aliens who fall under the following groups: religious workers, foreign medical graduates, and retired or present employees of international organizations.

a. Religions Workers

To qualify as a "religious worker", you must fall under one of these two subcategories: clergy, and "other" religious workers. A clergy is defined as a person authorized by a recognized religious denomination to conduct traditional religious functions – a minister, priest, brother, nun, rabbi, Buddhist monk, commissioned officer of the Salvation Army or of the Christian Science Church, and ordained deacons, and the like. Persons falling under the "other religious worker" subcategory would be those who are authorized to perform normal religions duties done by liturgical workers but who are not ordinarily considered part of the clergy – religious instructors or counselors, catechists, cantors, missionaries, religious translators or broadcasters, workers or professionals in religious hospitals, such as nurse or doctors, and the like.

In general, to qualify for a green card as a RELIGIOUS WORKER, you must meet the following requirements:

    i) You must be a member or a minister, for at least the past 2 years, of a recognized religious denomination that: (1) has a recognized creed, a form of worship, a distinct history and established places of worship and congregation with a standard system of training and selection for its officers; (2) is a bona fide religious group operating in the United States – it must have some form of religious government, assets and methods of operation, religious services and ceremonies; and (3) has non-profit status in the U.S. (i.e., must be incorporated and have tax-exempts status under the U.S. laws, or at least be recognized by the INS as a non-profit organization).

    ii) Immediately before applying for the immigrant visa, you (the applying alien) must have been engaged in a "religious vocation, profession, or occupations" in your country in a religious organization continually for at least 2 years. (A "religious vocation, profession, or occupation" is simply defined as a job or function which falls under any one of either the traditional religious functions subcategory outlined above (minister, priest, etc), or any of the other religious worker subcategory of persons who perform religious work done by various liturgical workers (religious instructors, counselors, catechists, etc).

iii) You (the applying alien) must have been offered a position in the United States by that religious group of which you have been a member for at least the past two years to work for them in the U.S. in a "religious vocation, profession or occupation" as a minister of that religion, or in some other capacity related to the religious activities in the U.S. And your sole purpose in coming to the U.S. must be to work in that capacity for the religious group.

Religious workers are by for the largest single group within the entire 'Special Immigrants' employment-based 4th preference category. They are allocated one-half of all the visas available in this category.

NOTE: Note that you are not considered eligible as a 'religious worker' if you are merely employed with a religious denomination in a clerical, janitorial, mechanical, nonprofessional (requiring at least a college degree or its equivalent) capacity, such as being a receptionist, secretary, janitor, chauffeur, electrician, gardener, fundraiser; if your employment with the religious denomination is for a period of LESS than 2 years immediately preceding the visa application; or if the religious denomination with which you have been employed is one which has no affiliation in the U.S.

Non-Immigrant Visas Are Available, Also, For Religious Workers

Readers should note that, the same Immigration Act of 1990 which established eligibility for IMMIGRANT (i.e. permanent) type of visas (Green Cards) for those who qualify as religious workers, also created eligibility for NON-IMMIGRANT type of visas for those same kinds of aliens who qualify as religious workers. (Readers interested in the applicable procedures for obtaining *non-immigrant* visa as a religious workers should refer to R-1 visa procedures in Volume One of this manual for a comprehensive treatment.) *For our purposes here, what is important to know, is that, in practice, religious workers are eligible for immigrant visa or green card (one that allows them to stay and work in the U.S. permanently), as well as for non-immigrant visa, which is one that allows them to stay and work in the U.S. on a fixed, more temporary time basis. And, what is also of immediate importance for readers to know, is that one good news, here, is that the requirements for obtaining the immigrant visa as a religious worker are essentially the same as those required for obtaining the non-immigrant visa as a religious worker.*

These are, of course, some important differences which exist between the privileges and limitations enjoyed by religious workers who wind up with an immigrant visa, and those who wind up with a non-immigrant visa. Basically, the differences in eligibility requirements and privileges between the religious worker applying as immigrant visa alien and those applying as non-immigrant visa alien, are as follows:

• The status of a religious worker as a NON-IMMIGRANT in the U.S. is valid for only 5 years. After 5 years, the alien religious worker who functions as a priest, nun, rabbi, or what have you, has to go back to his home country (unless, of course, he is somehow eligible to change to another non-immigrant status or to apply for an immigrant visa).
• The 'special immigrant' category of religious workers requires two years of continuous work experience be

fore the petition for a visa may be filed; the requirement for non-immigrant R visa, on the other hand, is just 2 years membership in the religious denomination which has an affiliate in the U.S.

- The 'special immigrant' categories taken together, is allotted 10,000 immigrant visas yearly; there is no quota restriction, on the other hand, on the number of non-immigrant visas that can be granted to religious workers who are qualified for a visa, and every religious denomination in the U.S. that needs religious workers can sponsor persons as non-immigrants without limitation.

b. Foreign Medical Graduates

Another group of aliens which qualify for inclusion as 4th preference SPECIAL IMMIGRANTS, are foreign medical graduates. If you are a graduate of a foreign medical school who came to the U.S. with an H or J visa, you qualify as a special immigrant if you do meet the following requirements:

i) you were licensed to practice medicine in any state in the U.S. on or by January 9, 1978, and have continuously lived and practiced medicine in the U.S. since January 10, 1978;
ii) if you came to the U.S. on a J-1 visa and were subject to the 2-year home residency requirement, you are eligible if you either got a waiver of the home residency requirement or got a no objection letter from your home government.

c. Present or Retired Employees of International Organizations, Their Spouses and Relatives

As an alien, you qualify for an immigrant visa under the 'special Immigrant' category, if you meet the following requirements:

- you are a retired employee of an international organization who has worked for such an organization for at least 15 years prior to your retirement on a G-4 or N visa; you have lived in the U.S. for at least 7 years and have been physically present for at least half of those 7 years immediately before your applying for the immigrant visa; and you applied for the immigrant visa within 6 months of your retirement.
- You are an unmarried son or daughter of an officer, employee, retired officer or employee of an international organization; and you have lived in the U.S. for 7 years, and were physically present in the U.S. for at least half of those 7 years while you were between the ages of 5 and 21 before applying for the immigrant visa; your application was before your 25th birthday; and you have a G-4 or N type of nonimmigrant visa.
- you are a surviving spouse of a deceased officer or employee of an international organization who had been so employed for at least 15 years; the deceased officer or employee has lived in the U.S. for at least 7 years, and you (the surviving spouse) have been physically present for at least half of those 7 years on a G-4 or N visa before the death of your spouse and before applying further visa; and you apply for the visa within 6 months of the death of your deceased spouse.

d. Others Who Can Qualify as Special Immigrants

The following other persons can qualify for an immigrant visa as special immigrants:

- residents of the Panama Canal Zone on or before April 1, 1979, who were employed for at least one year either by the Panama Canal Company or the Canal Zone government on or before October 1, 1979, or Panamanians by birth who were employed by the U.S. government in the Canal Zone for at least 15 years prior to October 1, 1979.
- alien persons who have been employed abroad by the U.S. government for at least 15 years, and whose immigration has been approved by the U.S. Secretary of State due to exceptional circumstances, based on the recommendation of the principal officer in charge of the U.S. foreign office in which the alien was employed.
- foreign nationals who are minors and have been declared dependent by a juvenile court located in the U.S., and

determined by the court to be eligible for long-term foster case, and that it is in the minor's best interest for him or her to remain in the U.S.
- Spouses and children of special immigrants under the age of 21 can automatically get green cards, as accompanying relatives of special immigrant by simply providing proof of their family relationship to the special immigrant.

D. HOW TO FILE FOR THE GREEN CARD

To file for a green card for an alien person based on the alien being a SPECIAL IMMIGRANT under the employment FOURTH preference category, simply follow the same steps and procedures in EXACTLY the same order and chronology in which they are listed in Chapter 13, starting from Section C thereof (p. 78).

HOWEVER, TAKE NOTE OF THE FOLLOWING FACTS WHICH ARE PECULIAR TO THE SPECIAL IMMIGRANT VISA CATEGORY:

1. For the petition, the form you are to file with the INS is Form1-360, *Petition for Americans, Widows or Special Immigrants* (see sample on p. 226), in lieu of the Form 1-140.

2. In filing as a Special Immigrant, know that you (the alien) are allowed the option in this instance to person ally file the petition by yourself – i.e., to be the "petitioner" for the visa. That is to say that, here, you (the alien) are not required (except ONLY in the case of the non-clergy religious workers) to have a U.S. petitioner sponsor you for the green card petition. Thus, the Form 1-360 may be filed, for example, either by the religious worker visa-seeker himself, or by the sponsoring U.S. religious organization. You should note, however, that, as a practical matter, though the worker may personally file the petition quite alright, in practice the INS gives more weight to petitions filed by the sponsoring organization.

3. If you (an alien) are located abroad, say in your home country, you can personally file your own visa petition by mailing your papers to the INS office in the U.S. Or, you can have your sponsoring organization in the U.S., if any, do it for you. However, in the "application" phase of your visa processing, which follows after your initial petition has been approved (Chapter 13, Section D), you would be able to file your application in the U.S. ONLY IF you are physically inside the U.S. already, using the method called 'Adjustment of Status' (see Chapter 20). Otherwise, if you are outside the U. S., then your only option is to do the application at the appropriate consulate in a foreign country.*

4. Basically, since the primary object of the petition is to show that you meet the legal requirements of some special immigrant category or the other, what you need to provide is simply the kinds of supporting documentations that show you belong to the particular Special Immigrant sub-category you claim, as described in Section C of this Chapter.

The following documentations may be typical For Each Sub-Category:
FOR RELIGIOUS WORKERS.
- all diplomas, certificates and transcripts, showing your academic and professional qualifications (e.g., certificate of ordination or authorization to conduct religious worship as a member of the clergy, diploma from

---

*NOTE: If you have been or are now working or living illegally in the U.S., or have violated U.S. immigration or other laws, you probably may not be able to stay in the U.S. and get your green card. Or, you may possibly subject yourself to a 3- or 10-year waiting period, just for being out of status for 6 or 10 months, for example. Hence, if you are in such a situation, be sure to read thoroughly the chapter on inadmissibility (Chapter 24) and probably consult with a competent immigration lawyer in this instance, before proceeding with a visa application.

religious institutions, or other written proof that the alien is qualified in a religious vocation or occupation).
- letter from the sponsoring religious organization in the U.S. detailing the type, nature and structure of its organization, number of followers in both the U.S. and your home country, facts about your job offer in the U.S., including the job title, duties, salary, qualification requirements, and duration of the employment, etc, and showing that the job or services you will perform is of a religious or professional nature.
- a letter from authorized official of the religious organization in the alien's foreign country, which verifies the alien's membership in the organization for at least 2 years, and details the kind of religious work and employment he (she) has had within the organization during that period.
- written proof that the religious organization (or an affiliate) which will employ the alien in the U.S. is a bona fide nonprofit religious organization, and is exempt from taxation by the U.S. Internal Revenue Service, such proof as may be required from the religious organization to show its nonprofit status.

FOR FOREIGN MEDICAL GRADUATES
- original Form 1-94 card, whether current or expired, or a passport bearing a visa stamp showing you (the alien) were admitted to the U.S. with a J or H visa prior to January 9, 1978
- medical license issued by a U.S. state before January 9, 1978, or a letter from the state's medical board verifying that you were licensed as a doctor
- proof that you have been continuously employed as a physician since January 9, 1978, that you've maintained continuous residence in the U.S. since your entry into the country (e.g. letter from your employers or your U.S. personal income tax returns or W-2 forms for each year, your utility bills, bank records, etc).
- Form 1 AP-66, given to you when you got your J visa, if you came into the U.S. on a J-1 Visa (you must enclose a "No Objection" letter from your home country or an embassy of the country, if you were subject to 2-year foreign residency requirement).

FOR RETIRED EMPLOYEES OF INTERNATIONAL ORGANIZATIONS
- Copies of your passport or 1-94 card covering the past 15 years and clearly showing notations for your entries and departures
- U.S. Income tax returns or W-2 forms for past 15 years
- Letters from the international organization detailing your periods of employment with the organization and your visa status, and giving the number of days you worked in the U.S.
- Bank statements showing personal regular deposits and withdrawals made during the period
- Letter from your employer in the U.S. giving your official retirement date, which must be within 6 months before you apply for the green card.

Chapter 17

Getting Your Immigrant Visa (The Green Card) Based On Having Employment Or Job Skills: Entrepreneur/Investor Immigrants

A. ALL THE VARIOUS KINDS OF EMPLOYMENT-RELATED BASES AVAILABLE FOR QUALiFYING FOR A GREEN CARD

As has been fully set forth in Chapter 3, Section C.2, with regard to employment-based immigrant visa categories – that is, those categories of green cards which are obtainable on the basis of employment or job skills – there are 5 separate preferences or grouping in which an alien can fall, ranging from the employment-based First preference or priority worker, to employment-based Fifth preference or entrepreneur/investor category. (See Section C.2 of Chapter 3 for a detailed breakdown).

In this Chapter, we discuss the detailed eligibility qualifications and the procedures for obtaining a green card as it applies in under just ONE of those five employment-related bases for qualifying – THE EMPLOYMENT FIFTH PREFERENCE or employment-creation Entrepreneur/Investor category.

EMPLOYMENT-BASED (EB) GREEN CARD CATEGORIES

- FIRST Preference (Priority Workers)
- Persons of Extraordinary Ability (Nobel Prize winner, Lee Iacocca of General Motors caliber of managers)
- OUTSTANDING PROFESSORS/RESEARCHERS (Researchers, scientists of Jonas Salk caliber)
- International Executives

- SECOND Preference
- (Exceptional Ability Professionals: Masters + Degree Professionals)

- THIRD Preference (Skilled and/or unskilled workers)
- Professionals with Baccalaureate Degree
- Two-year training or experience
- General or unskilled labor

- FOURTH Preference (Special Immigrants)
- Certain juveniles
- Ministers of religion
- Retired former employees of U.S. government abroad

- FIFTH Preference (Entrepreneur Investor)
- Employment creation investors

B. THE EMPLOYMENT-CREATION ENTREPRENEUR/INVESTOR ALIEN

The Immigration Act of 1990 established a new category of immigrants: aliens, who are probably millionaires in their home countries, who can qualify for a green card through making a sizable financial investment in the United States. Such aliens constitute the employment-based FIFTH preference category. The category is allocated 10,000 immigrant visas per year for foreign persons (and their spouses and minor children) who invest a minimum amount of capital in a new enterprise that creates employment, with 3,000 of those visas reserved for persons investing in rural areas or areas of high unemployment. The law providing for this visa category in the Immigration Act of 1990, comes directly out of the basic economic philosophy and objective of the Congress of the United State to vitalize the economy of the U.S. and to create employment for Americans. Its basic strategy is simple: to offer a green card to a financially able alien, in return for his or her setting up a commercial enterprise that will give jobs to American workers. Thus, this category of immigrant visa aliens are called *"employment creation aliens."*

C. WHO QUALIES FOR A VISA THROUGH INVESTMENT?

Immigrant visas through investment are available to any alien who invests an amount which ranges from a low of $500,000 if the business is located in a *"targeted employment areas,"** up to a high of $3,000,000 for an enterprise located in a region deemed to be of low unemployment. Under the procedures of the Immigration and Naturalization Service (INS), here is how the relevant investment levels are set:

- If the city or town picked by the alien investor is one designated by the state's Attorney General to be a "targeted employment area," the level of investment required may be as low as $500,000. (A total of 3,000 of the 10,000 visas allotted to this preference category annually are reserved for this level of investment).
- If the area picked by the alien investor is not one of the targeted employment areas, but has an unemployment rate significant below (150% below) the national average, then the level of investment required may be more than $1 million, though not to exceed $3 million.
- If the area picked by the alien investor is designated by the Attorney General to be a high unemployment area, the investment level required is $1 million.

Generally speaking, the standard investment is $1 million. In all situations, however, the investment must create at least 10 full-time jobs for U.S. citizens, permanent resident aliens, or other immigrants lawfully authorized to work in the U.S., not counting the investor himself or the investor's immediate family, or independent contractors. The workers must each work at least 35 hours a week.

It should be noted that under the relevant immigration law, it is only the state government of the chosen area that has the responsibility to identify which parts of the particular state qualifies as a high unemployment area, and to notify the INS the locations that qualify. Thus, unless the state government of your area of intended investment has specifically designated that area as a rural or targeted employment area or high employment area for the purpose of green card acquisition through investment, an area may not qualify. Accordingly, several states, including California, Florida, New York, Texas and Washington, have been known to make such designations, among others.

D. WHAT IS THE NATURE OF THE INVESTMENT REQUIRED?

Under the administrative regulations of the INS for this program, the entire investment does not have to be made in cash. The investment or capital can take the form off cash alone, or cash plus cash equivalents, such as bank deposits, loans, mortgage notes, and personal loans. Or it can take the form of the value of equipment, inventory or

---

*Defined as either a city or town of less than 20,000 inhabitants; or an area outside the boundaries of a city or town of more than 20,000 inhabitants; or any place that is certified by the state government as having a high unemployment (150% of the national average).

other tangible property. The source of the investment capital must be lawful. That is, it is required to come from legitimate sources of wealth. This requirement was added by the INS as a precautionary measure to guard against underworld or drug cartel kingpins obtaining green cards through this visa category.

The investment funds could be from any of the normal sources of legitimate wealth: it could be from savings or from selling stocks or real property in the foreign country; it could be funds borrowed from banks with real property or stocks or bonds in the foreign country used as collateral, or borrowed from friends, relatives or investors who believe in your business project; or it could be from an inheritance. Borrowed funds may be used however, only as long as the alien investor remains personally liable in the event of default and the loan is not secured by assets of the business that is being purchased. The investment must involved a business, such as a trading enterprise or a manufacturing plant or service-oriented company, and must be one which requires the alien investor's participation or management skills to provide jobs to the area.

The law establishing this alien employment creation program basically requires the investment to be made in a completely new commercial enterprise, and the investment is expected to be well underway when the green card application is made. However, under the administrative regulations of the Immigration and Naturalization Service (INS), a qualified investment includes the purchase of an existing business so long as the enterprise's net worth, after the completion of the sale, is at least 140% of the value of the enterprise prior to the date of the acquisition or that there is a 40% increase in the level of employment. In other words, an investor can purchase an existing enterprise so long as he (she) increases its net worth or the number of employees by at least 40%. What this means, in other words, is that this requirement will preclude an investor from merely purchasing an ongoing business without causing any substantive improvement in the capital or employment levels of the enterprise.

In addition, the regulations provide that an investment by an alien investor qualifies for a green card under this program when such investment is employed for the purchase and overhaul of a financially troubled or undercapitalized business enterprise by a foreign person so long as the acquisition will save jobs. A 'troubled business' is defined as one that has been in existence for at least two years and has experienced loss during those two years equal to at least 20% of its net worth. In any event, a total of $1,000,000.00 (or $500,000.00 if applicable) must be invested and ten jobs must have been created or preserved. An investor buying a troubled business is prohibited from laying off any employees. Experts have noted, in this connection, that being able to reorganize an existing business as a feature of this visa category, is very interesting because, they say, business consultants agree that in most instances it is preferable to purchase an ongoing business enterprise, rather than for a person to attempt the development of a business from the beginning – especially, in the case of a foreign person. Since there is a highly developed industry in the United States for the acquisition and sale of existing commercial enterprises, what would be probably more advisable, and wiser, they assert, is for a prospective foreign investor to readily utilize the services of professionals such as corporate and business lawyers, real estate brokers and business brokers, and others, in the identification of a suitable acquisition.

This employment-based, 5th Preference visa category requires that the investor manage the business PERSONALLY and does not anticipate that the investor be merely a passive financier. There is an exception allowed to this rule, and that is in the case of a limited partner of a limited partnership formed in accordance with the requirements of a certain uniform limited partnership law. In such a situation, it is generally recognized that the requirement that the investor directly manage and/or supervise the investment may not be practicable because the limited partnership act referred to, by its very terms, defines the limited partner as a passive investor and a limited partnership interest is primarily a security interest and will support an employment creation investor visa.

Finally, the law provides a number of measures to discourage fraud by immigrant investors by providing for fines of up to $250,000.00 and jail for up to five years. In addition, the law makes the grant of permanent residence to immigrant investors "conditional," and establishes a two-year trial period during which the Immigration and Naturalization Service is to determine whether the enterprise was in fact established, whether or not the capital was in fact invested, and whether the alien did sustain the enterprise. Within the 90 days period prior to the end of the two-year period, the investor must file an additional petition with the Immigration and Naturalization Service requesting that the conditional status of residence be removed.

E. HOW TO FILE FOR THE GREEN CARD

To file for a green card for an alien person based on the alien being an entrepreneur/investor immigrant under the employment FIFTH preference category, simply follow the same steps and procedures in EXACTLY the same order and chronology in which they are listed in Chapter 13, starting from Section C thereof (p. 78).

HOWEVER, TAKE NOTE OF THE FOLLOWING FACTS WHICH ARE
PECULIAR TO THE ENTREPRENEUR/INVESTOR VISA CATEGORY

1. For the petition, the form you are to file with the INS, is FORM 1-526, *Immigrant Petition By Alien Entrepre neur* (see sampie on p. 231), in lieu of the Form 1-140.

2. The filing fee for this petition, as of this writing, is $155, payable to the INS by money order or by certified check.

3. In filing as a entrepreneur/investor immigrant, know that YOU (the alien) are the one who personally files the petition on your own behalf on this instance – i.e., you are the "petitioner." Thus, you do not need an American sponsor in filing for this visa. You may file your petition, whether you are at the time living in the U.S. already or outside of it, by directly sending the papers to the INS Regional Service Center in the U.S. covering the area closest to where the business in which you are investing is located. (See Appendix B for the list of addresses).

4. Note that, while you can, whether from within or outside the U.S., personally file your visa papers in the U.S., in the first phase (the "petition" phase) of your visa processing, in the second phase (the "application" phase) of the visa processing, however, which follows after your initial petition has been approved (Chapter 13, Section D), you would be able to file your application in the U.S. ONLY IF you are physically inside the U.S. already, using the method called 'Adjustment of Status' (see Chapter 20). Otherwise, if you are outside the U.S., your only option for filing your application is to do so at the U.S. consulate in a foreign country*

5. Basically, since the primary object of the petition is to show that you have either made or are in the process of

---

*If you are in the U.S. legally on a nonimmigrant visa with a current Priority Date (Chapter 5), you can probably apply quite safely for your green card from either inside or outside the U.S. whichever you prefer. And if you are in the U.S. illegally or entered the U.S. legally under the Visa Waiver Program (see Chapter 2, Section D), you may still file your green card application inside the U.S. if you can demonstrate that you had a visa petition or labor certification application on file by January 14, 1998, and are willing to pay a penalty fee of $1,000. On the other hand, if you have been or are now working or living illegally in the U.S., or you are out of status or have violated U.S. immigration or other laws, you probably may not be able to stay in the U.S. and get your green card. But, if you file at a U.S. Consulate abroad, you may possibly subject yourself to a 3- or 10-year waiting period, that being "overstay" bar imposed by the law against individuals who were out of status for 6 or 10 months after April 1, 1997. Hence, if you are in such a situation, be sure to read thoroughly the chapter on Grounds for Inadmissibility (Chapter 24), and probably, consult with a competent immigration lawyer in this instance, before proceeding with the visa application.

making a qualifying business investment in the U.S., what you need to provide is simply the kinds of supporting documents that demonstrate that you've met these conditions, as set forth in Sections C and D of this chapter.

The following documentation may be typical:

- copies of articles of incorporation or other legal charter or business license of the company, and outstanding stock certificates (if the business is a corporation)
- agreement of partnership, joint venture, or business trust (if the business is a partnership), or license or other official authorization to do business in the form of sole proprietorship, if applicable.
- notarized affidavit of the secretary of the company, or of the official records keeper of the business, giving the names and addresses of each owner of the company, and the percentage of the company owned by each.
- in the case of a business which is in a *targeted employment area*, letter from the U.S. state government certifying that the business is located in a rural area or area of high unemployment.
- in the case of investment made in an existing business, proof (e.g., stock purchase or investment agreement, certified financial statements, personnel and payroll records) that capital was transferred, and evidence that it resulted in a substantial increase (at least 40%) in the networthy of the existing business or of the number of employees.
- tax returns of the company for the past 2 years, if business has been in operation for that long, tax returns (for corporate, partnership or personal income, inheritance, franchise, property) filed within the past 5 years in the U.S. or outside the U.S., to show that the invested capital was obtained by legitimate means.
- payroll records of the company (better, if for at least the past 2 years, if possible), personnel records including copies of Form 1-9 for the 10 or more employees, or the business plan showing when such employees will be hired, and how the business will find the resources or generate the income to meet the payroll
- letters from banks, bank statements, showing the average account balance of the business; purchase contracts, bank loan agreements, statements of bank transfers into the business
- evidence of deposit of funds in the business bank account, and evidence of sources of the funds.
- invoices, sales receipts, contracts for purchase, and bills of sale for the purchase of assets and capital goods and the business inventory for use in the U.S. enterprise.
- statement of entry in the U.S. Customs Service commercial entry documents for proof of transfer of foreign property to the U.S., bills of lading and transit insurance policies.
- accountant's financial statements, including profit and loss statements and balance sheets of the U.S. enterprise for the past 2 years, as available.
- lease agreements for the business premises, construction contracts and blueprints for building the business building or remodeling of the business premises.
- comprehensive business plan with cash flow projections for the next 3 to 5 years.
- loan or mortgage document, promissory note, security agreement, or other evidence of secured borrowing, if any was made.
- foreign business registration records by the alien entrepreneur.
- detailed statement describing the business, enterprise and its business, where the investment funds are coming from and how the investment will be used; an itemization of full-time positions that will be filled with American workers, including their duties, salaries, and when each position will become available; a statement of your position or title as the day-to-day manager of the operations and/or the executive officer for policy making and planning, including your specific duties, and salary.

6. You Must Remove The Conditional Status Of The Visa.

Finally, note that for person who get the green card under the alien entrepreneur visa category, the initial green card you get (after you have been granted your green card application) is a *"conditional" green card*. That is, it is valid for two years <u>only</u>, and you are required to file a simple, second set of immigration forms within 90 days prior to the 2 years anniversary of the grant of the conditional visa, so that the INS can reevaluate to be certain that you (the alien) actually made the investment you are supposed to make. The object of this law by the U.S. Congress, is to be sure that aliens do not begin to use investments as a fraudulent means of obtaining green cards.

This is called ***"removing the conditional status"*** of the green card. It's a simple procedure. The INS will try to contact you to remind you of this requirement at the time when it's due to be done, but it's still your own responsibility to do it. All you have to do (about 21 months after receiving the green card), is file Form 1-829, *Petition By Entrepreneur To Remove Conditions* (see sample on p. 239). And if you can provide proof that you actually made the investment and established a commercial enterprise that you're supposed to have done, the conditions on your temporary green card will be removed, and you'll retain a <u>permanent</u> green card.

Chapter 18

Getting The Immigrant Visa (A Green Card) Based On Being A Refugee Or Political Asylee

One important route by which an alien person could gain eligibility for admission to the United States as an IMMIGRANT (green card holder), is through qualification as a REFUGEE seeking political asylum. Under the Refugee Act of 1980, foreign nationals who qualify as refugees or political asylees, namely people fleeing persecution from their own countries, have found a haven in the United States, in keeping with America's history and reputation as "the land of opportunity and last beacon of hope." Such persons may obtain U.S. permanent residency (i.e., an immigrant visa), and without need to have to obtain either a Labor Certification or a U.S. job offer. Those fleeing war or natural disaster, on the other hand, are equally taken in and receive what is called *Temporary Protected Status* (TPS).

A. CONDITIONS FOR QUALIFICATION:

To qualify for the refugee or political asylee status (both are also called the "conditional entrant" status in reference to the fact that such persons have to meet certain special conditions to qualify), the alien has to meet *one or more* of the following conditions:

    i) he (she) must have been fleeing from his home country either to escape actual persecution or because he merely has "a well founded fear of persecution....on account of race, religion, nationality, membership in a particular social group or political opinion," or

    ii) he must have been unable or unwilling to return to his home country because of such reasons;

    iii) he must have been uprooted from his homeland by catastrophic natural calamity, civic disturbance or military operation, as defined by the President of the United States, and cannot return to his usual home.

Under the law, the standards for determining who is a *"refugee"* and who is an *"asylum"* seeker, are virtually identical. The difference is only one of slight technically: the refugee is one from a third country outside his homeland who then seeks admission to the United States; in contrast, an asylee (one applying, for asylum) must already be in the United States or at a port of entry thereof. (For example, an Iranian in France who seeks admission to the U.S. on the claim of persecution, is a "refugee"; however, if he were already in the U.S., even if he could not have a passport or a visa, he would be thought of as an "asylum" seeker). In addition, a refugee may be a person who, in the discretion of the President of the United States, is declared by the president to be a refugee, even when such person is still residing in his (her) own country. The status of refugee or political asylum does not extend, however, to anyone who may have ordered, incited, assisted or participated in the persecution of any person on account of race, religion, nationality, membership in a particular social group, or political opinion. Nor does it extend to a person who has become "firmly settled" in their adopted countries – that is, one who may have been granted permanent residency or citizenship by that country, or has achieved independence because of their education, employment, exercise of profession or business affairs in the adopted country.

If you are married or have children under the age of 21, upon your getting a refugee or political asylee status your spouse and children (those under 21) can also be granted the same status automatically as your accompanying relatives by providing proof of their family relationship to you. Such status of accompanying relatives are not recognized under the Temporary Protected Status, however. Instead, each family member must qualify for TPS on his or her own

The area of refugee law is frequently subject to changes both in the interpretation of the law and in the political inclination of the United States, depending on the events in the world. Certain political, ideological and sociological conditions in a country, a part of the world, or the world, may at a given point cause the United States to assume that a member of a particular group qualifies as a refugee or asylee, while denying that status to other groups who may seem similarly situated.

Do you get accorded automatic refugee or asylee status by the U.S. government just merely for the fact that you managed to make your way to the United States (or a port of entry thereof) screaming 'persecution' 'persecution'? Not at all! In deed, by current estimates, in recent times there are anywhere from 30,000 to 40,000 applications each and every year flooding in to America worldwide in quest of asylum in the United States, of which only a fraction, about 25% thereof, is granted by the Immigration Service. (In 1984, for example, there were 32,344 such applications, of which just 8,278 were granted).

To be sure, the alien applicant has a right to expect one thing: not to be returned to the country where he or she would face persecution. This does not mean, however, that he has an automatic right to asylum in the United States. In deed, the reader should know that an alien, even if fully and legally eligible for asylum in the United States, still does not have an automatic right to it and could still be turned down by the U.S. authorities. *The point, simply, is that in the final analysis, how a specific case gets to be decided upon depends almost entirely on ONE factor: the "discretion" and disposition of the Immigration and Naturalization Service (INS) officers*. As provided for by the Refugee Act of 1980, and supported by several court rulings, since, aliens with well-founded fear of persecution "may be granted asylum in the discretion of the Attorney-General." In practice, there is an annual limitation, fixed by the U.S. Attorney General or the President, on how many asylum applications will be granted in a given year. And generally, such determination as to who to grant asylum is justified on the basis of the humanitarian concerns and the national interest of the United States. The officials of the INS, which is an agency of the U.S. Attorney General's Department of Justice, are said, by one source, to "almost always" base their determinations solely on the "advisory opinion" (written report of recommendation) supplied them by the U.S. State Department's Bureau of Asylum and Humanitarian Affairs on every such application submitted.

What is a 'Well-founded Fear of Persecution'?

A crucial issue upon which most asylum cases almost always rests, is this: being able to establish to the satisfaction of the INS (and the State Department) officials, just want constitutes a "well-founded fear of persecution" on the part of a given alien? The standards set by Federal Courts for assessing this seem to amount to the following i) some "objective facts" (i.e., elements such as presentation of testimony, written documentations or other evidence) must support the alien's subjective fears of persecution, his fears that he would face danger in his homeland or that other people there had suffered persecution for similar reasons; ii) the alien must present "specific facts" tending to show that he will be so singled out for persecution; and iii) as handed down in the 1987 Supreme Court's 6-3 decision (INS. v. Cardoza-Fonseca), an applicant need not have to show that there's a "clear probability" that he would be persecuted in his home country but simply that "persecution (in the home country) is a reasonable possibility." As the court put it in its rather liberal interpretation of the law, an applicant probably meets the objective eligibility standard for asylum if he demonstrates "a 10 percent chance of being shot, tortured, or otherwise persecuted."*

B. WHO QUALIFIES AS A REFUGEE

As outlined above, concerning the refugee status the key requirement for qualification as a refugee, is that the alien's unwillingness or inability to return to his home or other country be founded either on actual persecution or a well-founded fear of persecution on account of his race, religion, nationality, membership in a particular social group, or political opinion. In order to prove that you (the alien) are subject to these conditions, you must prove first that the government is oppressive and tyrannical, and for that reason denies you the protection otherwise afforded to nationals of that country through the legal or political institutions of that country. Second, you must prove individual persecution or a well-founded fear of persecution.

The first requirement, namely, proof as to the general oppressive nature of the foreign regime, is easier to provide than the second requirement, i.e., proof as to the persecution of the particular alien applicant. Usually there will be more documentation available about the regime's behavior in regard to human rights, and in certain instances the United States may already have recognized the oppressive nature of the foreign government in question. There are various documentary sources and human rights organizations which maintain information on the state of human rights of the citizens in certain countries, and such information can be made available to an applicant for refugee status. The refugee applicant must prove that the home country's institutions and/or policies do not accord protection to individual citizens. If the Department of State of the United States does agrees with an applicant's assertion of the home country's despotic nature, the applicant is in luck for a grant of green card; otherwise, the applicant bears a heavy burden of persuasion and proving his/her case.

The second requirement, namely, proof of individual actual persecution or a well-founded fear of persecution of the visa applicant, is very often the greatest obstruction to a finding of refugee status particularly when it is asserted by an individual who is not a member of a group that has been recognized as such by the Department of State. The applicant must present documented evidence that individually or as a member of a group, the alien will be subject to persecution. For obvious reasons, for the Immigration and Naturalization Service the mere assertions or presentation of self-serving statements by the applicant claiming persecution, is hardly ever taken at face value or accepted as sufficient. To be sure, the law provides that the burden of proof may be established solely by the testimony of the refugee or asylee. However, in practice, this is not easy to accomplish. In practice, generally unless the applicant is a member of a distinct group of persons whom the United States government identifies and accepts as a persecuted group in a foreign country, the individual must provide documentary proof as to his/her personal exposure. And meeting this requirement, the immigration experts say, presents a greater burden to an applicant for asylum, since, by definition, they assert, that person is already outside of the home country and probably within the national border of the United States. Thus, it is said, generally it is difficult, if no impossible, at that point to obtain and present the type of documentary proof which the INS requires.

---

*NOTE however, that the sweeping "discretionary" powers granted the Attorney General under the Refugee Act, still remain overriding, nevertheless, and that his view on any given application still prevails. In practice, the fact, for example, that a person genuinely feared that he might be injured in a civil strife or violence in his country, has been dismissed by the Carter and Reagan Administration officials as insufficient grounds to grant asylum, as they contend that many who came from, say, Pakistan, Haiti, Guatemala, San Salvador and other Central and Latin American countries, are (were) fleeing poverty and economic conditions, and not political persecution. Accordingly, by recent State Department account, applicants from a handful of strife-torn and/or poor countries, such as Cuba, Haiti, Iran, EL Salvador, and Nicaragua, comprise two-thirds of the request for asylum in recent years, while the most often approved are (or had been) those from Iran, Afghanistan, South Africa and Ethiopia.

In addition to the above two requirements for eligibility, the alien applicant for refugee or asylee status also must be innocent of any acts of persecution himself, and must otherwise be a person of good moral character.

C. WHO QUALIFIES AS AN ASYLEE

As stated earlier in Section A above, the principal difference between the asylum and refugee categories, is that the former applies to those aliens who are already IN the United States, while the latter applies to persons who are OUTSIDE the United States. Under the applicable immigration law, the grant of asylum to an application is purely discretionary, and the Attorney General acting through his representative in the Immigration and Naturalization Service, may withhold the granting of asylum for any caused he deems a good cause, say, for example, for the reason that an alien secretly enters the U.S. and bypasses the normal refugee process which was otherwise available to him. In such an event, the grant of asylum could be denied him by the INS officials on that basis. A total of 10,000 green cards are set aside annually for aliens (including their spouses and children) who are granted political asylum and are eligible to adjust their status in the U.S.

The following categories of persons are NOT eligible to file for asylum in the United States:
- an alien who may be removed, pursuant to a bilateral or multilateral agreement existing between the U.S. and another government, to a third country in which the alien would have access to a full and fair procedure for determining a claim to asylum or equivalent temporary protection, unless the INS finds that it is in the public interest for the alien to receive asylum in the United States.
- an alien who files his or her application later than one year after entry into the U.S., unless the alien can demonstrate to the satisfaction of the INS that changed conditions in the country have caused the delay in filing. This would apply to an individual who entered the United States in some non-immigrant status and then, because of changes in the home country, cannot now return without being subject to persecution.
- an alien who has previously applied for asylum and has had such application denied.

The law does not allow an alien to appeal the decision of the INS to any court with respect to a decision on any of the above points.

In general, asylum is not available to an alien if the INS determines:
1. That the alien ordered, incited, assisted, or otherwise participated in the persecution of any person on account of race, religion, nationality, membership in a particular social group, or political opinion;
2. that the alien, for reason of having been convicted of a particularly serious crime by a final judgement, constitutes a danger to the community of the United States;*
3. that there are serious reasons for believing that the alien has committed a serious nonpolitical crime outside the United States prior to his/her arrival in the United States;
4. that the alien is inadmissible as a terrorist or as a member of a terrorist organization; or
5. that the alien was firmly resettled in another country prior to arriving in the United States.

D. HOW TO FILE FOR THE GREEN CARD: REFUGEE APPLICANTS
1. The applicant for REFUGEE status (he/she is outside his/her own country of nationality, but also outside the U.S.), prepares and gathers the following forms and documents:

---

*Note that an alien who has been convicted of an aggravated felony is considered to have been convicted of a particularly serious crime and thus not eligible for asylum. The law governing qualification for refugee status also gives the INS the authority to create new conditions under which an alien will be ineligible for asylum, a notably unusual provision under U.S. law in that as a general proposition on administrative body is hardly ever given the power to create additional conditions for ineligibility under the law.

- Form 1-590, *Registration for Classification as Refugee*
- Form G-325A, *Biographic Information* – for any applicants who are 14 years of age or over (sample on p. 225).
- Two photographs of each applicant taken within the last 30 days (see Chapter 25, Section F for the prescribed style and manner of photo pose).
- *Affidavit of Financial Support* – find a responsibility person or organization who is to be your sponsor, to sign a sworn statement to be responsible for the expense of your transportation to the place of resettlement in the U.S. and a means of support for you once you arrive there. (NOTE: typically, such promises of financial sponsorship come from relatives who are already in the U.S., or from private charitable organizations such as churches and refugee-assistance organizations). If the sponsoring party is a relative, the relative should simply fill out the immigration Form 1-134 (see sample on p. 214), and if the sponsoring party is an organization, it should provide you a written sponsorship agreement.
- Detailed, personal sworn statement setting forth your fears and an account of any past persecution in your country, and detailing your reasons for seeking refugee status, and why you fear to return to your country.
- Newspaper articles describing the types and conditions of persecution you would face if returned to your home country
- Affidavits from people or organizations who have personal knowledge of, or have personally experienced, similar persecution you claim in your home country.
- Written reports on human rights conditions about your country provided by organizations like the Amnesty International, Central America Resource Center, the Americas Watch Committee, or the U.S. State Department's Country Reports
- Statements or letters (possibly sworn or notarized) of any witnesses, friends, relatives, respected leaders of the community, news reports from people outside your country.
- Documents of personal identification for each applicant – such as birth certificate, marriage certificate, divorce and death certificates showing termination of any previous marriages; notarized affidavits from you and/or other people familiar with you and your family situation.

2. The refugee applicant applies for the refugee status at one of the INS overseas offices around the world (they are not the same as the U.S. embassies or consulates although many such offices are located within the consulate or embassy buildings) by submitting the application papers <u>in person</u> (and never by mail). At present, the places where one can file a refugee application, are:

Athens, Greece	Kuala Lumpur, Malaysia
Bangkok, Thailand	Lusaka, Zambia
Belgrade, Serbia & Yugoslavia	Madrid, Spain
Buernos Aires, Argentina	Manila, Philippines
Cairo, Egypt	Mexico City, Mexico
Djibouti, Gulf of Eden Mexico City, Mexico	Mogadishu, Somalia
Frankfurt, Germany	Naha, Okinawa
Gaborne, Botswana	Nairobi, Kenya
Geneva, Switzerland	New Delhi, India
Havana, Cuba	Panama City, Panama
Hong Kong, China	Rio de Janeiro, Brazil
Islamabad, Pakistan	Rome, Italy
Jakarta, Indonesia	Seoul, South Korea
Karachi, Pakistan	San Jose, Costa Rica
Khartoum, Sudan	Singapore
Kinshasa, Congo	Tokyo, Japan
	Vienna, Austria

3. Upon the applicant submitting his (her) application papers to the INS application office, he will be notified by mail where and when to come to be interviewed by the overseas immigration officer. Immediately prior to the interview, the refugee and any accompanying relatives must undergo a medical examination. (The procedures for these exams as well as the fees charged, will be explained to the alien in the alien's interview appointment letter). The medical exams are conducted by designated private doctors for a fee, which vary from as little as $50 to more than $150 per exam, depending on the country involved. The fingerprint of the refugee (and those accompanying him or her, if any) will also be taken at an Application Support Center (there is a $25 fee for this) run by the INS. [See Chapter 21 for the full procedures involved in general visa interviews]

4. Following the interview by the overseas immigration officer, if he determines that you meet the essential legal requirements (that you have, in fact, been persecuted or that you have a well-founded fear of persecution because of race, religion, nationality, political opinion, or membership in a particular social group), the applicant would be designated a "refugee" and the application granted. The applicant will be given a "parole visa". Thereafter, from the time your application is approved, you have 4 months in which you must enter the U.S.

5. Upon your entry into the United States, after one year of your physical presence in the United States – you must not have violated certain U.S. immigration or other laws or regulations during this period – then you, as well as your spouse and children, if applicable, may apply for the green card through the "Adjustment of Status" procedure. (See Chapter 20). And if all goes well, you will be given your green card. The green cards will be dated from the time of your first arrival in the U.S. as refugees.

E. HOW TO FILE FOR THE GREEN CARD: ASYLEE APPLICANTS

1. The applicant for ASYLUM prepares and gathers the following forms and documents:
- prepare all of the same forms and supporting documents listed in Section D.1 above – except for Form 1-590 and the *Affidavit of Financial Support* or Form 1-134 therein, both of which do not apply in asylum applications. Then, add these two forms herein:
- Form 1-589, *Request For Asylum In the United States* – make one original and three copies (see sample on p. 114). NOTE that this form has since been superceded by a later version of the form, titled *Application For Asylum and For Withholding of Removal*. However, we reproduce the old form on p. 114 for illustrative purposes to illustrate the same kinds of details and information required, as shown in this form which represents an actual asylum case successfully processed by an alien.
- Form 1-765, *Application For Employment Authorization*. (if applicant wants immediate employment in the U.S.).

2. The Asylum applicant has to apply for the asylum status in one out of only 4 Regional Service Centers that handle all asylum applications in the U.S. (see below). Where you must file depends on where you live.

CALIFORNIA SERVICE CENTER: If you live in: Arizona, California (southern part only), or Nevada (southern part).

TEXAS SERVICE CENTER: If you live in: Alabama, Arkansas, Colorado, District of Columbia, Georgia, Louisiana, Maryland, Mississippi, New Mexico, North Carolina, Oklahoma, Pennsylvania (western part), South Carolina, Tennessee, Texas, Utah, Virginia, West Virginia, or Wyoming.

VERMONT SERVICE CENTER: If you live in Connecticut, Delaware, Maine, Massachusetts, New Hampshire, New Jersey, New York, Pennsylvania (eastern part), Rhode Island or Vermont

NEBRASKA SERVICE CENTER: If you live anywhere else in the United States.
(See Appendix B for the complete list and addresses)

NOTE: Under a recent immigration rule, as of April 1, 1997, you must file an asylum application *within one year* after you arrived in the U.S. to be eligible for asylum. Exceptions: Unless you can show either same changed circumstances which have caused a major effect on your eligibility for asylum (e.g., changes in political conditions in your country), or extraordinary circumstances with direct connection for why your application wasn't filed on time, such as events or factors beyond your control relating to the late filing. Furthermore, another newer rule is that you cannot file your application for work authorization until your case has been pending for 5 months after you have filed the Form 1-589, or your case has been approved, whichever one comes first.

You file the application by mail to the INS Regional Office that applies to you, if you are not currently involved in any removal (i.e., deportation) proceedings with the INS. And, if you are currently involved in any removal proceedings, then you must file your application with the court and the immigration judge that is handling your case.

3. Upon the applicant submitting his (her) application papers to the INS (or the immigration court, where applicable), the INS will initially review the application to determine if these is a legal reason to "summarily" deny his (her) application, such as a serious criminal conviction record. If that is the case, the application will quickly be denied and the applicant will face deportation proceedings. However, if there's no cause for a summary denial of the application, the applicant will be notified by mail when and where to come (it will be at one of the INS Asylum offices) to be interviewed by an asylum officer.

In the meantime, the INS may sent your application to an agency of the U.S. Department of State, the Bureau of Human Rights and Humanitarian Affairs (BHRHA), for a review. The BHRHA reviews your application and makes comments on the application as to the accuracy of the assertions of the application on the conditions in the foreign country and the experiences described, and in regard to whether the applicant, or people similarly situated as him, who returned are likely to be persecuted, and makes a nonbinding recommendation to the Asylum officer on whether one of the grounds for denial may apply to the applicant. (The BHRHA recommendations are nonbinding, but, in practice, they carry a lot of weight with the INS Asylum officers!). Indeed, under current regulations, the applicant is entitled to be promptly told, in person, the decision or recommendation of the BHRHA on his application, and the applicant is to be given an opportunity to respond to the BHRHA comments.

4. The asylum applicant will go through a similar personal interview, medical examination and finger printing formalities as in a refugee application case, as set forth in Section D.3 above.

5. Following the interview by the Asylum officer, if the case is not approved, the application will not automatically be denied; rather, the application is referred to a removal (i.e., deportation) proceedings before an immigration judge, where the applicant can, again, apply for a political asylum before a judge.

If your application is approved, you (the alien applicant) will be designated as an "asylee." Thereafter, one year after your application to grant you asylum has been approved – and if you continue to be a refugee or asylee, and have not violated certain criminal laws of the U.S., and have been assigned an immigrant visa number with a current Priority Date -- then you, as well as your family, if applicable, may apply for the green card through the "Adjustment of Status" procedure (see Chapter 20). And if all goes well, you will be given your green cards.

Form I-589 REQUEST FOR ASYLUM IN THE UNITED STATES Page I

INS Office:
Denver, Colorado

Date:

1. Family Name ███████ | First ███████ | Middle Name NMN

2. A number (if any or known)

All other names used at any time (include maiden name if married)
None

3. Sex ☐ Male ☒ Female

4. Marital status ☐ Single ☐ Divorced ☒ Married ☐ Widowed

I was born: (Month) **July** (Day) **4** (Year) **1957** in (Town or City) **Addis Ababa** (State or Province) **Shoa** (Country) **Ethiopia**

Nationality — at birth **Ethiopian** | At present **Same** | Other nationalities **None**

If stateless, how did you become stateless?
I am stateless because I left Ethiopia without an exit visa (permission from the present regime), and would not return to my country, since I know I would be imprisoned for life or killed.

Ethnic group **Amahra** | 7. Religion **Christian/Coptic** | 8. Languages spoken **Amahric, English, French**

9. Address in United States (In care of, C/O, if appropriate)
(Number and street) **Colorado Boulevard,** (Apt. No.) ███ (City or town) ███, (State) **Denver, Colorado** (Zip Code) ███

10. Telephone number (include area code) **303-**███████

Address abroad prior to coming to the United States
(Number and street) ███ (City) **Nairobi** (Province) **Kenya** (Country)

My last arrival in the U.S. occurred on: (Mo/Day/Yr)
May 9, 1982

As a ☐ Visitor ☒ Student ☐ Stowaway ☐ Crewman ☐ Other (Specify)

At the port of (City/State)
New York City, New York

Means of arrival (Name of vessel or airline and flight number, etc.)
P.A. 189

☒ was ☐ was not inspected

Date authorized stay expires (Mo/Day/Yr)
May 31, 1984

My nonimmigrant visa number is _____ **A 2**███ _____, it was issued by the U.S. Consul on **May 31, 1982** (Mo/Day/Yr)
(If none, state "none")
at **Nairobi, Kenya**
(City, County)

14.

Name and location of schools attended	Type of school	From Mo/Yr	To Mo/Yr	Highest grade completed	Title of degree or certification
...r L.O.P.H. School, Addis Ababa	Elementary/Secondary	9/66	8/74	8th	Promoted
...enilk II Comprehensive Sec. School, Addis Ababa	Compre.	9/74	8/77	12th	Graduated

15. What specific skills do you have?
Typing, IBM key punch operator, children's counselor at YWCA

16. Social Security No. (if any)
None

17. Name of husband or wife (wife's maiden name)
Yilma ███████

18. My husband or wife resides ☒ with me ☐ apart from me (if apart, explain why)
███████ **Colorado Boulevard,** ███████ **Denver, Colorado,** ███████
Address (Apt. No.) (No. and street) (Town or city) (Province or state) (Country)

Form I-589
(Rev. 3-1-81)

NOTE: This form (and the addendum on p. 116) reproduced here by courtesy of Denver, Colorado immigration attorney, C. James Cooper, Jr., is an actual application submitted on behalf of a political asylum seeker from Ethiopia. The supporting documents in this case were hundreds of pages long; however, what is included herein is only but a few excerpts from some of the documentations so as to give the reader just an idea of what is often needed to get a political asylum, especially when the applicant happens to come from certain countries.

(OVER)

FORM I-589

in the U.S. Is spouse making separate application for asylum? ☒ Yes : No (If not, explain why)

26 . U.S. are children included in your request for asylum? ☐ Yes ☐ No (If not, explain why)

N/A

I have ____ sons or daughters as follows: (Complete all columns as to each son or daughter. If living with you, state "with me" in last column; otherwise give city and state or foreign country of son's or daughter's residence.)

Name	Sex	Place of birth	Date of birth	Now living at
███████	M	Addis Ababa	3/31/78	████ ████ Addis Ababa

Relatives in U.S. other than immediate family

Name	Address	Relationship	Immigration status
███ ████	██ Pennsylvania St. ███, Colorado	Brother	Political Asylee
█████ ████	██ Dexter Street ███ Colorado	Sister	Same as above
████ ████	██ Pennsylvania St. ███, Colorado	Sister	Same as above

Other relatives who are refugees but outside the U.S.

Name	Relationship	Country where presently located
██ ███	Cousin	Kenya
███ ████	Cousin	Kenya

List all travel or identity documents such as national passport, refugee convention travel document or national identify card.

Document type	Document number	Issuing country or authority	Date of issue	Date of expiration	Cost	Obtained by whom
ssport	P04████	Ethiopia	11/15/80	11/16/82	$100	myself

Why did you obtain a U.S. visa?

I intended to travel to the United States, where I have friends and relatives.

27. If you did not apply for a U.S. visa, explain why not?

N/A

28. Date of departure from your country of nationality (Mo/Day/Yr)

September 23, 1981

29. Was exit permission required to leave your country? ☒ Yes ☐ No (If so, did you obtain exit permission ☐ Yes ☒ No (If not, explain why) I was denied exit permission by my government to travel to U.S. as a punishment for non participation in its political activities. My brother-in-law, who is a station manager for Ethiopian Airlines in Nairobi with the help of some influential friends was able to get me out of the country to Nairobi.

(2)

30. Are you entitled to return to country of issuance of your passport ☐ Yes ☒ No Travel document ☐ Yes ☐ No Or other document ☐ Yes ☐ No (If not, explain why.) I will not be able to return to my country, since I left without permission and through contacts of my brother-in-law, who will be in great trouble if I were to return. In addition, my return will mean my imprisonment for leaving, because of the restriction the Kebele (political cell unit) has put me.

31. What do you think would happen to you if you returned? (Explain) My life would be in jeopardy. It was my refusal to participate in the Kebele and the youth league that turned my life into a nightmare. Accusation of being a remnant of the old regime, a Christian, to that of being a sympathizer of the Ethiopian People's REvolutionary Party (EPRP) and the Ethiopian Democratic Union (EDU) were directed at me, which led to repeated interrogation in the Kebele, followed by detention and imprisonment in the Kebele.

32. When you left your home country, to what country did you intend to go? Even though I intended to travel to the United States, I was forced to stay in Nairobi with my brother-in-law for nine months, because of the travel restrictions to the U.S. and Western Europe my government put on me due to non-participation in its program.

33. Would you return to your home country? ☐ Yes ☒ No (Explain) I have seen enough horrors in my country to never want to go back under its existing conditions. The new regime makes no distinction between young or old, men or women. The new regime's brutality embraces all who still believe in God, family, and the traditions that have existed for thousands of years. I would be subject to physical abuse and tort

34. Have you or any member of your immediate family ever belonged to any organization in your home country? ☐ Yes ☒ No (If yes, provide the following information relating to each organization: Name of organization, dates of membership or affiliation, purpose of the organization, what, if any, were your official duties or responsibilities, and are you still an active member. (If not, explain) I have only been affiliated with the Ethiopian Orthodox Trinity Church as a member of the youth choir. However, my brother, Asmareye ████████, was accused of being a member of the E.P.R.P., and was taken by the Kebele one morning, who advised my family that he died. We never received his body. My cousin, Nardos ██████, was held by the Kebele on similar charges, and was killed with three bullets, which necessitated our paying $300 in order to bury her. Both my brother and my cousin were 17 years of age.

35. Have you taken any action that you believe will result in persecution in your home country? ☒ Yes ☐ No (If yes, explain) I left Ethiopia without an exit visa, which is punishable by long-term imprisonment and possibly death. While in Ethiopia, I refused to participate in the Kebele's political activities, and because of that, have been imprisoned, interrogated, tortured and denied attendance at work, church or social activities.

36. Have you ever been ☒ detained ☒ interrogated ☐ convicted and sentenced ☒ imprisoned in any country? ☒ Yes ☐ No (If yes, specify for each instance: what occurred and the circumstances, dates, location, duration of the detention or imprisonment, reason for the detention or conviction, what formal charges were placed against you, reason for the release, names and addresses of persons who could verify these statements. Attach documents referring to these incidents, if any).

SEE ATTACHED SHEET (p. 118 herein)

37. If you base your claim for asylum on current conditions in your country, do these conditions affect your freedom more than the rest of that country's population? ☒ Yes ☐ No (If yes, explain) While every Ethopian has been affected by the change, I was affected a great deal more because of the label put on my father as a former landlord, my strong ties to my religion, and the suspicion put on my family and me as E.P.R.P. and E.D.U. supporters and the resulting murders of my brother and cousins. It is these family and religious reasons and my personal disinterest in the present regime which forced me to flee from one province to another to elude the constant harrassment by the Kebele people.

38. Have you, or any member of your immediate family, ever been mistreated by the authorities of your home country/country of nationality? ☒ Yes ☐ No. If yes, was it mistreatment because of ☐ Race ☐ Religion ☐ Nationality ☐ Political opinion or ☐ Membership of a particular social group? Specify for each instance: what occurred and the circumstances, date, exact location, who took such action against you and what was his/her position in the government, reason why the incident occurred, names and addresses of people who witnessed these actions and who could verify these statements. Attach documents referring to these incidents.

SEE ATTACHED SHEET (p. 118 herein)

39. After leaving your home country, have you traveled through (other than in transit) or resided in any other country before entering the U.S.? ☒ Yes ☐ No (If yes, identify each country, length of stay, purpose of stay, address, and reason for leaving, and whether you are entitled to return to that country for residence purposes. I stayed in Nairobi, Kenya, for nine months after leaving Ethiopia and before my arrival in the United States. I was helped by my brother-in-law, who is a station manager for the Ethiopian Airlines. Because of his help and his American friends, I was able to get to the United States. I would not be able to return to Kenya, since I have no residency status there.

40. Why did you continue traveling to the U.S.? Because my brother and sisters were here and offered to help me. My fiance (I am now married to him) was also here, and friends of both of us.

41. Did you apply for asylum in any other country? ☐ Yes—Give details ☒ No—Explain why not Because I have always believed that no other country would match America's idealism for freedom, justice and equality for all. The United States' tolerance for religious, racial and political diversity is a well-known fact world-wide.

DIE SHEET

(3)

(over)

FORM I-589

42. Have you been recognized as a refugee by another country or by the United Nations High Commissioner for Refugees? ☐ Yes ☒ No (If yes, where and when)

43. Are you registered with a consulate or any other authority of your home country abroad? ☐ Yes—Give details ☒ No—Explain why not

I have not contacted them, not only because they would not recognizë me, but also I have absolutely no intention to ever get involved with them. I feel very worried about the safety of my parents and my son should the present regime learn of my whereabouts.

44. Is there any additional information not covered by the above questions? (If yes, explain)

Because of the conditions that have developed in my country, I would never return there, even if forced to do so. I fear for my child's and parents' safety but am more fearful of my own life if I returned to Ethiopia.

45. Under penalties of perjury, I declare that the above and all accompanying documents are true and correct to the best of my knowledge and belief.

_____   November 4, 1983
(Signature of Applicant)   (Date)

_____   _____
(Interviewing Officer)   (Date of Interview)

ACTION BY ADJUDICATING OFFICER   ☐ GRANTED   ☐ DENIED

_____   _____
(Adjudicating Officer)   (Date)

Advisory opinion requested ☐   _____
                                                (Date)

(4)

(FORM I-589 - ATTACHMENT)
REQUEST FOR ASYLUM IN THE U.S. - ~~██████~~ Hirut

Response to Question 36:

I have been detained, interrogated, tortured and imprisoned numerous time in my country, Ethiopia. Several reasons were cited for these harrassments: my family connections (former landowners); the alleged membership of my brother and cousin to the now-defunct, Ethiopian Peoples Revolutionary Party, which resulted in their murder during the operation referred to as "red against white" terror; my strong religious belief; my refusal to participate and convert to the new tenets of the communist philosophy to which the youth league adheres, all of which resulted in my being looked upon as anti-government.

Most of my detention, interrogation, torture and imprisonment took place at Higher 13, Kebele 11. The new regime has sliced the city into Kebeles to restrict movement of the inhabitants and to gain virtual control over the lives of the people. Each Kebele has unrestricted power to detain, interrogate, torture, imprison, and even the right to kill within each one's jurisdiction. The Kebeles are comprised of people who belonged to the lowest strata during the former regime and they used their newly-acquired power to settle scores on the people who had scorned them prior to the present regime take-over.

The Kebele staff in the district in which I lived were former koolies (street sweepers, day laborers and simple loafers), who showed no mercy and used their uninhibited power ruthlessly. I owe my life to a former koolie who used to do odd jobs for our family and never forgot the humane way my family treated him. He was responsible for my releases and the application of minimal methods of torture, compared to other people, who were put to extreme pains.

There were no formal charges, no records kept, no representation by a lawyer, no public disclosures--in short, there were no legal or formal procedures followed in any of these arrests, detentions and even death. Any Kebele member can conduct his/her own investigations. During the period of 1975-1979, at the height of the Kebele power, I was summoned and detained frequently. I would be beaten with a leather-covered wire whip on any place of my body, and have some deep scars as a result of that; I would be tied up, so that my body looked in the shape of a ball and suspended with a stick in my mouth. Movement was impossible. The longest detention (most detentions lasted two to three days at a time) was in June of 1977, where I was questioned on the whereabouts of my brother and cousin and the extent of my involvement and sympathy to their cause. I was kept for two weeks in our Kebele cell with a number of other students crammed in one room. I maintained my innocence and lack of interest in politics and cited my previous interrogations which had produced no results for the Kebele. I was finally released with the help of the former koolie, who still showed kindness to me.

From then on it became a routine to be summoned by one of the members of the Kebele for more interrogation. It was a mere exercise of authority with no foundations to the variety of accusations. Since they had absolute authority, no one checked on their erratic behavior. I could not keep my salaried job or go to church or attend social functions. I were only allowed to work for the Kebele or attend their propaganda lectures every night, and if I did neither, I was imprisoned. The torture and threats of rape filled my life with constant terror and nightmares.

Response to Question 38:

As mentioned in the response to Question 36, I was tortured, scarred and threatened with rape. My brother and a first cousin were murdered because of their so-called affiliation with the E.P.R.P. We have never received the body of my first cousin for burial. My father (a former landowner) was charged with corruption as a member of the former regime, even though he was never involved in such activites, and he is harrassed by being assigned to night guard duties, although he is old and in poor health, and held a high position in the community prior to the present regime take-over. My husband, Yilma ██████ can verify these statements. Mis-treatment happened so often from 1975 that I am unable to state certain dates of these many occurrences.

THE NEW YORK TIMES, MONDAY, MARCH 27, 1989

A13

Western Nations Are Raising Barriers to Refugees

By HENRY KAMM
Special to The New York Times

GENEVA, March 25 — While 12 million people are officially counted as refugees who have fled persecution or violence in their homelands, the Western nations that have been the principal upholders of the right of asylum are raising barriers to keep them out.

Those nations are afflicted, in a phrase that has gained currency among refugee workers, with "compassion fatigue." The main reason is a growing perception of an unending flow of people from lands of poverty in search not of safety but of economic betterment. The exiles' assertions that they are seeking political asylum are met with increasing disbelief.

Challenges to the requests for asylum affect not only recent refugee groups, such as Central Americans in the United States and Iranians and Sri Lankans in Europe, but also Vietnamese boat people, who for many years were granted refugee status, if not always asylum, without serious question.

1.6 Million Indochinese Accepted

Today, in the United States, Western Europe, Canada and Australia — which have so far taken in 1.6 million out of the 1.7 million Indochinese refugees — official and public attitudes have never been so negative.

And at the Office of the United Nations High Commissioner for Refugees, the exiles' chief international advocate, and among governmental specialists and private refugee organizations, a new pessimism is widespread.

"All the organizations that deal with refugees, national or international, are aware that procedures to determine who is and who is not a refugee are now being used to accept as few as possible and not to determine who needs protection and who does not," Jean-Pierre Hocke, the High Commissioner, said in an interview here.

Throughout Western Europe, where since 1986 the number of asylum seekers has for the first time risen above 200,000 annually — it was only in 1980 that the number reached 100,000 — acceptance rates have sunk alarmingly. Nations are reticent about statistics, but according to the disparate figures made available to the High Commissioner's office, acceptance rates now average from 7 percent to 14 percent.

Governments say little about the number of people turned back at their borders before they can present asylum requests. In an exception, the West Germany Interior Minister, Friedrich Zimmermann, was reported by the news magazine Der Spiegel to have said 124,000 aliens were denied entrance last year.

Switzerland, which before this decade averaged 70 percent acceptance, is down to about 7 percent. The West German approval rate has dropped from 16 percent in 1986 to short of 12 percent in the first six months of last year. In France, considered one of the more liberal nations in asylum policy, acceptances declined from 40 percent in 1986 to 32 percent since then.

'Reaction of Hostility'

"A general reaction of hostility, fear toward refugees has become apparent, sometimes virulent in nature," said Michel Moussali, representative of the High Commissioner's office to the European Community. "Several countries have decided to revise their procedures and adopt restrictive and dissuasive measures, with the declared aim of preventing the arrival of false refugees but in fact striking indiscriminately at economic migrants and true refugees."

Measures have been adopted by the United States, which automatically puts under detention, often for as long as two years, Central American asylum seekers who arrive with documents that are judged to be "not in order," said Roger Winter, director of the United States Committee for Refugees, a nongovernmental organization.

He also cited the interdiction at sea of more than 18,000 Haitian asylum seekers. "Such highly visible actions that our Government has taken contribute to the undermining of refugee protection," Mr. Winter said in a telephone interview.

The United States Immigration and Naturalization Service reported in March that requests for political asylum from Central Americans had gone up from 7,000 in 1985 to more than 50,000 in 1988.

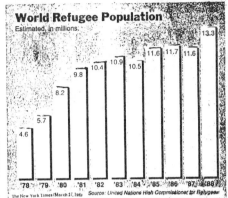

World Refugee Population
Estimated, in millions.

4.6 5.7 8.2 9.8 10.4 10.9 10.5 11.6 11.7 11.6 13.3

'78 '79 '80 '81 '82 '83 '84 '85 '86 '87 '88

The New York Times/March 27, 1989   Source: United Nations High Commissioner for Refugees

Denmark's Attitude: Sternness Gains

In Western Europe, policies described as "humane deterrence" have been generally adopted since the mid-1980's. They include increasingly restrictive visa requirements, penalties levied on airlines that deliver travelers without visas, denial of work permits while asylum applicants wait, often for years, for final decisions on their requests, reduction of welfare payments and other benefits during the waiting period and long-term lodging in barracks-like collective quarters, without minimal privacy.

Symptomatic, yet surprising because of a long history of humanitarianism, is the change in Denmark's attitude. "I think we've reached a point where it can't get worse," said Finn Slumstrup, information director of the Danish Refugee Council.

When in 1985 and 1986 the number of people granted asylum annually rose from around 1,000 to more than 6,500, a vocal minority began to warn that Danish homogeneity and national culture were threatened. The fact that many of the refugees were from Lebanon, Sri Lanka and Iran and joined about 23,000 migrant workers from Turkey, added a racist, and an anti-Muslim, note to the campaign, Mr. Slumstrup said in a telephone interview.

A revised immigration law and stern administrative procedures followed in 1986. Together, they made it difficult for asylum seekers to be admitted into Denmark.

As a result of the range of restrictive measures, the number of people granted asylum in Denmark has been cut in half since 1987.

"There is still sympathy for refugees, but they must be the 'right' refugees," Mr. Slumstrup said. "Boat people lived up to the image. They were undernourished, dressed in rags. They can't be reasonably well-dressed and well-fed, like the jet people of the 80's."

The United Nations agency operates under an international convention concluded in 1951 that defines a refugee as a person who, "owing to well-founded fear of being persecuted for reasons of race, religion, nationality, membership of a particular social group or political opinion, is outside the country of his nationality."

"The convention responded to the outflow of refugees from Eastern Europe," Mr. Hocké said. "Persecution was the key word, and it concerned individuals. Today, nine-tenths of the refugees are to be found in the third world. It means large groups fleeing from violence, not individuals needing protection from persecution."

Attitudes began to change in the early 1980's; the term "compassion fatigue" was first used in 1980, by Senator Alan K. Simpson of Wyoming. That period saw mass arrivals in Europe of asylum seekers fleeing from war in Lebanon and the revolutionary regime in Iran and culminating in the scattered arrivals of about 50,000 Tamils asking for shelter from civil strife in Sri Lanka.

"It is the high number of non-Europeans that caused the negative reactions," said Robert Van Leeuwen, deputy head of the Regional Bureau for Europe and North America of the High Commissioner's office. "The public, not helped by politicians who fail to play their educative role, is becoming more xenophobic. There is significant racism, and then the politicians play to that."

Refugee officials in general, while noting restrictive American measures toward Caribbean and Latin American asylum seekers, believe that the immigrant character of the United States and its multiracial makeup have kept negative attitudes there at a lower level.

Claims of Persecution: Harder Scrutiny

Mr. Hocké said that increasingly traditional asylum countries no longer accept a refugee's subjective judgment that the fear that impelled him to flee was well-founded. Young Tamil men have been told by most European Governments that they could have escaped from the conflicting pressures of their Government and the Tamil rebel groups to other regions of Sri Lanka instead of taking the long trip westward.

Most of the Tamils remain in the limbo of awaiting final rulings; fewer than 100 are believed to have been deported so far.

While the High Commissioner's office has maintained a stand on behalf of Tamil refugees in Europe, many in the organization and other refugee workers are concerned over a significant revision of its 14-year-old policy of support for asylum claims by Vietnamese boat people, the largest group of refugees leaving their country to apply for permanent asylum.

In an interview, the head of the agency's Asian activities went so far as to denounce the earlier policy.

"It is fairly obvious that for a number of historic and political reasons we didn't handle the Indochinese refugees very wisely," said Sergio Vieira de Mello, director of the High Commissioner's regional bureau for Asia. He was discussing the policy of recognizing their refugee status without individual screening.

Mr. Vieira de Mello noted that Hong Kong had now instituted severe screening measures and that Thailand and Indonesia had adopted a policy of pushing off refugee boats.

A Plan of Action: Caveats Introduced

The High Commissioner, together with the United States and other principal resettlement countries, submitted a Plan of Action to a 35-nation conference in Kuala Lumpur, Malaysia, this month. Vietnam and Laos took part.

The plan, which was not made public, was adopted without significant change. It stresses legal emigration possibilities and urges the granting of temporary asylum in countries where boat people land. But it considers it "imperative" that "organized clandestine departures be deterred." It urges the enforcement of "official measures" against organizers of departures.

The document makes no reference to the United Nations Universal Declaration of Human Rights, whose Articles 13 and 14 state, "Everyone has the right to leave any country, including his own," and "Everyone has the right to seek and enjoy in other countries asylum from persecution."

By implication, the Plan of Action also appears to recognize the possibility of forced repatriation to Vietnam for those rejected in screening. "In the first instance every effort will be made to encourage the voluntary return of such persons," it says, adding that "alternative methods of return" are to be examined if "after the passage of reasonable time" voluntary return makes insufficient progress.

Last month, Simon Ripley, a Briton who served as legal consultant to the High Commissioner's office in Hong Kong, resigned in protest against the screening. In a report submitted with his resignation, Mr. Ripley noted that of 313 cases screened, only 2 were found to qualify for refugee status.

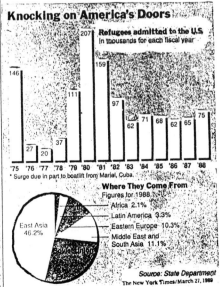

Knocking on America's Doors

Refugees admitted to the U.S. in thousands for each fiscal year

146 27 20 37 207 159 111 97 62 71 68 62 65 75

'75 '76 '77 '78 '79 '80 '81 '82 '83 '84 '85 '86 '87 '88

* Surge due in part to boatlift from Mariel, Cuba.

Where They Come From
Figures for 1988

East Asia 46.2%
Africa 2.1%
Latin America 3.3%
Eastern Europe 10.3%
Middle East and South Asia 11.1%

Source: State Department
The New York Times/March 27, 1989

Chapter 19
Obtaining A Green Card Through The DV-I Visa Lottery Program

A. THE GENERAL NATURE OF THE DV-I VISA LOTTERY PROGRAM

Under the Immigration Act of 1990, the U.S. Congress created, effective from the year 1995 and thereafter, a green card category designed to benefit aliens from countries that are determined to have sent the fewest number of immigrants to the U.S. in recent years. There are 55,000 green cards given out per year under this program. Natives of countries determined by the INS (Immigration and Naturalization Service) according to a mathematical formula specified by the law, are allowed to compete for these visas.* This program is identified by the visa symbol, DV-I, and because the method used to select those who receive the visas is essentially by random drawing, the program is formally known as the **"VISA LOTTERY"** or **"Green Card Lottery."**

Thus, each year, these 55,000 places are allocated according to a formula whereby each of the qualified regions of the world is allocated a given percentage of the 55,000 green cards. No qualifying country within any one region, however, may receive more than 7% (3,850) of the 55,000 worldwide total lottery green cards in any given year.

Under the visa lottery program, the law apportions the 55,000 immigrant visas among six geographic regions – Africa, Asia, Europe, North America, Oceanic, and the three areas of South America, Central America and the Caribbean, according to a formula based on which countries, and which regions of the world, sent the fewest number of immigrants to the U.S. during the previous 5 years, in proportion to the size of their populations. A greater share of the available visa numbers goes to those regions with low admissions than the high admissions regions.

The law requires that there must be a new application period every year (usually in late winter or early spring), and a separate registration by each applicant for each year's DV-1 visas. Thus, a visa registration submitted one year by an applicant, is not held over to the next, and if you are not selected in a given application year, you'll need to re-apply afresh for the next year's period in order for you to be considered again.

B. QUALIFYING COUNTRIES UNDER THE DV-1 PROGRAM

The Immigration and Naturalization Service (INS) determines the countries whose nationals may be entitled to the lottery green cards. The countries are then grouped by regions. The eligible countries and the numbers allotted to each region may change each year, depending on the variations in the immigration rates. The eligible countries and the total number of green cards allotted to each geographic region in 1999, for example, are as follows:

---

*As of this writing, the following countries are excluded from the lottery system and do not qualify: Canada, China, Dominican Republic, El Salvador, India, Jamaica, Mexico, Philippines, South Korea, Taiwan, United Kingdom and dependent territories (except Northern Ireland), Vietnam.

AFRICA:	(21,409)	All countries on the continent
ASIA:	(7,254)	All countries EXCEPT the following: China-mainland born and Taiwan born, India, Philippines, Vietnam, and South Korea. (Hong Kong is eligible).
EUROPE:	(23,024)	All countries EXCEPT the following: Great Britain (United Kingdom) and its dependent territories, (Northern Ireland is eligible), Poland.
NORTH AMERICA:	(8)	The Bahamas is the ONLY eligible country included in the North America region. Canada is NOT eligible.
OCEANIA:	(837)	All countries.
SOUTH AMERICA, CENTRAL AMERICA, and the CARIBBEAN:	(2,468)	All countries EXCEPT Mexico, Jamaica, El Salvador, the Dominican Republic, and Colombia.

C. STEP ONE IN THE DV-1 VISA APPLICATION PROCESS: REGISTRATION

The first step in applying for a DV-1 visa, is to get registered in the program. The object of registration is simply to place your name among those who may be selected, through the lottery drawing system, to receive the green cards. Your registration simply identifies you as an alien who apparently comes from an eligible country. It does not mean that you are necessarily eligible for a green card.

As stated earlier in this Section A above, there is a new application period for each given year for DV-1 visa that are to be issued during each Fiscal Year (i.e., from October 1 through next September 30th). For example, for the Fiscal Year 1995 (i.e., from October 1994 through September 1995), the application period for registration for the DV-I visa of that Fiscal Year, began at 12 a.m. (Eastern U.S. time) on June 1, 1994, and ended at midnight of June 30, 1995. Applications are required to be typed or clearly printed in English language. To simplify the process, simply make a clear photocopy of the form on p.). Completely complete the form, including affixing your passport photo. Then mail it to the very one of the following 6 addresses which applies to the region of your native country:

ASIA:	DV-I program National Visa Center Portsmouth, NH **00210** U.S.A.
SOUTH AMERICA, CENTRAL AMERICA, AND CARIBBEAN:	DV-I Program National Visa Center Portsmouth, NH **00211** U.S.A.

EUROPE: DV-I Program
                               National Visa Center
                               Portsmouth, NH **00212**
                               U.S.A.

AFRICA: DV-I Program
                               National Visa Center
                               Portsmouth, NH **00213**
                               U.S.A.

OCEANIA: DV-I Program
                               National Visa Center
                               Portsmouth, NH **00214**
                               U.S.A.

NORTH AMERICA   DV-I Program
(Bahamas only)   National Visa Center
                               Portsmouth, NH **00215**
                               U.S.A.

NOTE: It is most important to use the correct postal zip code for your specific region as listed above. If, for example, your native country is Nigeria, which is, of course, in Africa, then the "postal zip code" for Africa would be the correct one to be used, which is **00213**.

Note, also, that the application must be sent by regular or air mail ONLY – not by hand delivery, by fax, or by registered or certified mail. And thirdly, you must be sure to do this: type or clearly print on the mailing envelop (on the upper left hand corner of the front of the envelop), your full name and return address and the name of the country or area of which you are a native. *Failure to do any of these three things, may disqualify you.*

Only one application may be submitted by, or in the name of each applicant during the registration period. (Submission of more than one application will disqualify the person from registration). Do not mail separate registrations for children (person under age 21) unless they qualify on their own and are willing to immigrate without you.

Applications must be sent ONLY to the addresses above (by the regular mail or air mail only), and may be mailed from within the United States or abroad. Applications received at the DV-I program address either BEFORE or AFTER the application period, or delivered to any other address, will not be processed for registration. Only ONE application may be included in each envelope.

Size of Envelops:
The envelope in which each application is mailed must be BETWEEN 6 inches and 10 inches (15cm to 25cm) IN LENGTH, and BETWEEN 3½ inches and 4½ inches (9cm to 11cm) IN WIDTH. This is necessary to assist the automated processing of the mail.

D. INFORMATION YOU MUST INCLUDE IN THE REGISTRATION APPLICATION
Each application must be in the following format:
A. Applicant's Full Name
Last Name, First Name and Middle Name

B. Applicant's Date And Place Of Birth

Date of birth: Day, Month, Year

      Example: 15 November 1981

      Place of Birth: City/Town, District/County/Province, Country

      Example; Munich, Bavaria, Germany.

C. Name, Date And Place Of Birth Of Applicant's Spouse And Children, If Any.

The spouse and child(ren) of an applicant who is registered for DV-I status are automatically entitled to the same status. To obtain a visa on the basis of this derivative status, a child must be under 21 years of age and unmarried. (NOTE: DO NOT list parents of the applicant as they are not entitled to derivative status.)

D. Applicant's Mailing Address

The mailing addresses must be clear and complete, since it will be to that address that the notification letter for the persons who are registered will be sent. A telephone number is optional.

E. Applicant's Native Country If Different From Country Of Birth

See the answer to Question I n Section E below regarding the meaning of "native" for the purpose of the DV-I program.

E. FREQUENTLY ASKED QUESTIONS ABOUT DV-I REGISTRATION

1. *How Is The Term "Native" Of A Country Under The DV-I Law Defined? Are There Any Basis Upon Which Persons Who Have Not Been Born In A Qualifying Country May Be Eligible For Registration?*

Native means BOTH someone born within one of the qualifying countries AND someone entitled to be 'charged' to such country under the provisions of Section 202 (b) of the Immigration and Nationality Act. Applicants for DV-I registration may be charged to the country of birth of a spouse; a minor dependent child can be charged to the country of birth of a parent, and an applicant born in a country of which neither parent was a native or a resident at the time of his/her birth, may be charged to the country of birth of either parent. An applicant who claims the benefit of alternate chargeability must include a statement to that effect on the application for registration, and must show the country of chargeability on the upper left hand corner of the envelope in which the registration request is mailed

2. *May Persons Who Are In The U.S. Apply For Registration?*

Yes, an applicant may be in the U.S. or in another country, and the application may be mailed in the U.S. or from abroad.

3. *Is Each Applicant Limited To Only One Application During This DV-I Registration Period?*

Yes, the law allows only ONE application by or for each person during the DV-I registration period. SUBMISSION OF MORE THAN ONE APPLICATION WILL DISQUALIFY THE PERSON FROM REGISTRATION. (NOTE: More than 400,000 applications were DISQUALIFIED during the 1993 and 1994 visa lotteries, for example, due to multiple applications. Applicants may be disqualified at the time of registration or at the time of the visa interview if more than one entry is detected).

4. *May A Husband And A Wife Each Submit A Separate Application?*

Yes, if otherwise qualified, a husband and a wife may each submit one application for registration; if either is registered, the order would be entitled to derivative status.

5. *Must Each Applicant Submit His/Her Own Request, Or May Someone Act On Behalf Of An Applicant?*

Applicants may prepare and submit their own request for registration, or have someone act on their behalf. Regardless of whether an application is submitted by the applicant directly, or is assisted by an attorney, friend, relative, etc., ONLY <u>ONE</u> APPLICATION MAY BE SUBMITTED IN THE NAME OF EACH PERSON. Only one notification letter will be sent for each case registered, to the address provided on the application.

6. *What Are The Requirements For Education Or Work Experience?*

The law and regulations which govern the DV-I program require that every applicant must have at least a high school education or its equivalent or, within the past five years, have two years of work experience in an occupation requiring at least two years training or experience. This is basically the only qualification required of an applicant for eligibility for the visa. "High school education or equivalent" is defined as successful completion of 12-year course of elementary and secondary education comparable to that of a high school diploma degree in the United States. Qualifying work experience shall be based upon the most recent edition of the Dictionary of Occupation Titles published by the Employment and Training Administration of the United State Department of Labor.

Documentary proof of education or work experience should NOT be submitted with the application, but must be presented to the Consular officer at the time of formal immigrant visa application.

7. *How Will Cases Be Registered?*

At the National Visa Center, all mail received will be separated into one of 6 geographic regions and individually numbered. After the end of the application period, a computer will randomly select cases from among all the mail received for each geographic region. Within each region, the first letter randomly selected will be the first case registered, and the second letter selected the second registration, etc. It makes no difference whether an application is received early or late in the application period, all applications received during the mail-in period will have an equal chance of being selected within each region. When a case has been registered, the applicant will immediately be sent a notification letter, which will provide appropriate visa application instructions. The National Visa Center will continue to process the case until those who are registered are instructed to make formal application at a U.S. consular office or until those able to do so apply at an INS office in the United States for change of status. The National Visa Center will provide additional instructions on the steps to take to pursue the applications for DV-I visas.

8. *May Applicants Already In The U.S. Adjust Their Status With The INS?*

Yes, provided they are otherwise eligible to adjust status. Registered applicants who are physically present in the United States may apply to the Immigration and Naturalization Service (INS) for adjustment of status to permanent resident. Applicants who adjust, however, must first mail completed forms OF-230, Part 1, and DSP-122 to the National Visa Center. (These forms will be included with the registration notification letter). Applicants must ensure that the INS can complete action on their cases before September of the given year, since on that date registrations for the current Fiscal year DV-I program terminate.

9. *Will Applicants Who Are Not Registered Be Informed?*

No, applicants who are not registered will receive no response to their registration request. Only those who are registered will be informed. All notification letters are expected to be sent within about 3 months of the end of the application period. Anyone who does NOT receive a letter will know that his/her application has not been registered.

10. *How Many Applicants Will Be Registered?*

A total of about 90,000 persons, both principal applicants and their spouses and children, will be registered. Since it is likely that some of the first 55,000 persons who are registered will not pursue their cases to visa issuance, this larger figure should ensure use of all DV-1 numbers, but it also risks some registrants being left out. All applicants who are registered will be informed promptly of their place on the list. Each month visas will be issued, according to registration lottery rank order, to those applicants who are ready for visa issuance during that month. Once all of the visas for the Fiscal Year have been issued, the program for that year will end. *Registered applicants who wish to receive visas must be prepared to ACT PROMPTLY on their cases.*

11. *Is There A Minimum Age For Applicants For Registration Under The DV-1 Program?*

There is NO minimum age for submission of an application for registration, but the requirement of a high school education or work experience for each principal applicant at the time of visa issuance will effectively disqualify most persons who are under age 18.

12. *Will There Be Any Special Fee For Registration In The DV-1 Category?*

There is NO FEE FOR SUBMITTING A REQUEST FOR REGISTRATION, and NO FEE should be included with the letter sent to the mailing addresses indicated above. (DV-1 applicants, like all other immigrant visa applicants, must of course pay the regular visa fees to the U.S. immigration authorities at the time of the visa processing and issuance).

13. *Are DV-1 Applicants Especially Entitled To Apply For A Waiver Of Any Of The Grounds Of Visa Ineligibility?*

No. Applicants are subject to all grounds of ineligibility specified in the Immigration and Naturalization Act and there is no special provision for the waiver of any grounds of visa ineligibility other than those ordinarily provided in the Act.

14. *May Applicants Who Are Already Registered For An Immigrant Visa In Another Category Apply In This Registration For The DV-1 Category?*

Yes, such person may seek DV-1 status through this registration as well.

15. *How Long Do Applicants Who Are Registered On The Basis Of This Application Period Remain Entitled To Apply For Visas In The DV-1 Category?*

Under the law, persons registered following this DV-1 application period are entitled to apply for visa issuance ONLY DURING CURRENT FISCAL YEAR, i.e., from October 2000 through September 2001 Fiscal year, for example. That is, there is no carry-over of benefit into another year for persons who are registered but who do not obtain visas during the given Fiscal year.

There is absolutely no advantage to mailing early, or mailing from any particular locale. Every application received during the mail-in period will have an equal random chance of being selected. However, more that one application per person will disqualify the person from registration. Also, failure to include the applicant's native country and full name and address on the envelope (on the top left hand corner thereof) will disqualify the application.

F. STEP TWO IN THE DV-1 VISA APPLICATION PROCESS: FILE THE VISA APPLICATION

The second step in applying or the green card through the lottery program, is for you to file the actual application for the visa. The application is, in effect, the formal request for you to be issued a green card. And you file this only

If (and AFTER) you are fortunate enough to be among the winners of the visa lottery – meaning those who receive a notification by the National Visa Center that your registration was selected for green card processing.

This second step, called the "APPLICATION" process for a green card, may be undertaken either at an INS office in U.S., or in your home country at a U.S. Consulate there. If you are already in the U.S. legally on a nonimmigrant type of visa, you may apply for the lottery green card either inside or outside the U.S., depending on which one you prefer. If, on the other hand, you are already in the U.S. but illegally or entered legally under the visa waiver program, it's possible that you may still file your lottery green card application inside the U.S., providing you are not subject to any of the applicable grounds of inadmissibility or other bars to getting a green card under the U.S. immigration laws (see Chapter 24). The vast majority of lottery green card applications, will necessarily be filed and processed at the consulates abroad, however, since most winners would not already have been resident in the U.S. In any case, you should note that it is generally felt that the Consulate would probably process such cases faster than the INS offices in the U.S. would. Consequently, it may be more advisable for you to consider having your lottery green card application processed in your home country. This consideration is especially relevant and important in this instance for one vital reason: ***under the DV-I law, if the visa is not issued you by the end of the fiscal year (September 30th) for and in the year you were picked, your application lapses and becomes invalid.*** In any event, generally if the INS determines that you are inadmissible, you will often be notified outright and be given or sent the necessary forms and information for filing a waiver if it is determined that a waiver is necessary. You'll need to complete Form 1-601 (see sample on p. 235), and attach the applicable filing fee ($95 as of this writing). You may file this application with the consulate office in your native country for onward transmittal to the applicable INS office in the U.S. (only the INS can process or approve the waiver). Or, you may file it directly with the applicable Immigration and Naturalization Service office in the United 'States.

LOTTO VISA 200__ ✓ ?

APPLICATION FOR
DIVERSITY IMMIGRANT VISA PROGRAM 200__ ↙ ?

PLEASE TYPE OR PRINT THE INFORMATION REQUESTED BELOW

1. APPLICANT'S FULL NAME (LAST NAME SHOULD BE <u>UNDERLINED</u>)

<u>Last Name,</u>   <u>First Name</u>   <u>Middle Name</u>

_____, /......................... /................................

PHOTOGRAPH

(Attach a recent, preferably less than 6 months old, photograph of the <u>applicant</u>, <u>spouse</u> and all <u>children</u>, 2.0 inches (37 mm) square in size, with <u>name</u> and <u>date of birth</u> on the back. The photograph (not a photocopy) should be attached to the entry with clear tape--do NOT use staples or paperclips, which can jam the mail processing equipment.)

2. APPLICANT'S DATE AND PLACE OF BIRTH

Date: Day_____, Month_____, Year_____

Place: City/Town_____.

District/County/Province_____

Country_____

3. NAME, DATE AND PLACE OF BIRTH OF APPLICANT'S SPOUSE AND CHILDREN (IF ANY)
If you are selected, your unmarried children under 21 years of age and your spouse can also apply for visas.

NAME (Last, First and Middle Names)	DATE Day, Month, Year	PLACE OF BIRTH (City/Town; District/County/Province; Country

Spouse:_____, __/____/____ _____. _____. _____

Child 1._____, __/____/____ _____. _____. _____

Child 2._____, __/____/____ _____. _____. _____

Child 3._____, __/____/____ _____. _____. _____

Child 4._____, __/____/____ _____. _____. _____

Child 5._____, __/____/____ _____. _____. _____

If more space is necessary please use a separate paper.

4. APPLICANT'S MAILING ADDRESS AND TELEPHONE NUMBER(OPTIONAL) Please Print in CAPITAL LETTERS

STREET, BUILDING NO AND APT. _____

NEIGHBORHOOD/VILLAGE_____CITY_____

PROVINCE/STATE_____ZIP CODE_____COUNTRY_____

TELEPHONE NUMBER: Country Code_____. City Code_____. Local Number_____

5. APPLICANT'S NATIVE COUNTRY IF DIFFERENT FROM THE COUNTRY OF BIRTH:_____

6. SUBMIT A RECENT PHOTOGRAPH OF YOURSELF. 1 AND ½ INCHES SQUARE (37mm x 37mm) WITH YOUR FULL NAME PRINTED ON THE BACK. Photograph should be taped to the upper right corner of the application with clear tape, do NOT use staples or paperclips.

7. SIGNATURE OF APPLICANT (WITH NORMAL SIGNATURE)_____

DV-200-? Program
National Visa Center
Portsmouth, NH 00__ ↙   Enter the proper zip code for you

Chapter 20

"Adjustment Of Status": How A Non-Immigrant Alien Can Change To Immigrant Or Permanent Residency Status (The Green Cardholder), While Living In The U.S.

Ordinarily, the authorized legal process by which an alien gets admitted to the United States as a PERMANENT RESIDENT (i.e., as "Green Card" holder), is for the alien to apply for and obtain an immigrant visa in a foreign country outside the United States, usually at a U.S. Consulate in a foreign country, and then be admitted from <u>OUTSIDE</u> into the United States as an "immigrant" by virtue of the immigrant visa. However, suppose the alien is already physically present in the United States in a non-immigrant status of one kind or another. Can he or she then change to an immigrant (i.e., green card) status from <u>WITHIN</u> the U.S. at some point along the line? The answer is, YES. He may apply to do so – under certain conditions.

The process by which a nonimmigrant alien changes his or her status from a nonimmigrant, to an immigrant status (i.e., to the status of green card holder or a lawful permanent resident of the U.S.), is called *ADJUSTMENT OF STATUS.*

A. ALIENS WHO ARE NOT ELIGIBLE TO APPLY FOR ADJUSTMENT OF STATUS

As conceived under the relevant immigration laws and policies of the United States, adjustment of status is viewed as a form of relief from deportation and as a "privilege" which is granted only in the discretion of the Attorney-General of the United States. It is held that adjustment of status is a "privilege" in that it relieves the alien of the potential burden of having to return to his home country to make an application there for an immigrant visa. A trip to the alien's home country to make such a visa appointment, for example, may well have interfered with the alien's present business activities and could be prohibitively expensive, according to this line of reasoning. In light of such fundamental premise that permitting adjustment of status is a "privilege" and not a right, certain legal requirements and restrictions are therefore imposed upon the nonimmigrant alien with respect to being permitted to adjust his or her status.

Consequently, certain aliens who fall under certain categories are not eligible to adjust their status in the United States, even when they otherwise possess the prerequisite conditions (such as having a visa petition or labor certification pending as of April 30, 2001, or having a current Priority Date).

Aliens who are NOT Eligible For Adjustment of Status in the U.S., Include the Following:

1. Aliens who at the time of entering the United States had gained entry surreptitiously as stowaways.
2. Aliens who entered the U.S. as, or had their status changed to, J-1 or J-2 EXCHANGE VISITORS (see Chapter 6 of Vol.1 of this manual), and were subject to the requirement of having to return to their home countries to live for a 2-year period before applying for a change of status, and had not been granted a waiver of that requirement.

3. Aliens who would not have been admissible to the U.S. anyway, based on any part of Section 212 (a) of the Immigration and Nationality Act – that is, the laws listing the grounds for, and the classes of aliens subject to "exclusion" from been admitted (see Chapter 24).

4. Aliens who are granted "conditional status" (pp. 27, 104 of this manual), or are admitted as fiancés or fiancées pending the conferral of full permanent residency status, but who had failed to marry the person who had specifically petitioned for them.

5. Aliens who marry (and seek a permanent residence based on that marriage) while exclusion or deportation hearings are pending – unless, however, they can otherwise demonstrate that the marriage was entered into in good faith and not for the purpose of obtaining the immigrant visa.

6. Aliens who failed to appear at the scheduled removal or deportation proceeding or asylum interview.

7. Aliens who failed to depart the U.S. as required by a deportation order; or failed to meet a voluntary departure date.

B. ADJUSTMENT OF STATUS FROM WITHIN THE U.S. IS GENERALLY PREFERABLE FOR THE ALIEN

Normally, the permanent visa (green card) is issued the alien from OUTSIDE his/her country at a U.S. Consulate abroad, usually in his/her own native country. The Adjustment of Status procedure, however, enables the alien person in the United States to receive the permanent visa (green card) from WITHIN the U.S. As an alien person already resident in the U.S. who is a beneficiary of a family-based or employment-based petition for a visa, you can apply for the permanent residency visa in one of TWO ways: you can seek to receive your lawful status without leaving the United States – that is, through the "adjustment of status" route; or you can seek to do so by going back to your original country of residence and applying for a green card through the consular visa processing way (see from Chapters 6 to 19).

An important question is, assuming you have a choice between the two methods of securing your green card, which one is better or more preferable for you?

Most experts contend that seeking to gain the immigrant status (to get the green card) by the "adjustment" process from WITHIN the United States, holds certain advantages over seeking to do it through the normal process – that is, by applying for and getting the immigrant visa from OUTSIDE the United States. Consequently, seeking such a visa by the adjustment of status method in the U.S., has been said to be "preferable" by legal practitioners and immigration experts.

The following are among the major advantages of securing an immigrant status visa status via the "adjustment of status" route from within the U.S.:

1. By adjusting status from within the U.S., the alien who is already in the U.S. needs NOT travel to a U.S. consulate in his home country or other foreign country to apply for the immigrant visa, thereby saving on travel expenses, and relieving him from having his business activities or family life disrupted.

2. As a rule, the adjustment of status process frequently leads to speedier and faster grant of the permanent residency (i.e., immigrant) status than does regular visa processing, depending on the type of petition filed and the consular post abroad in which the visa application would otherwise have been made.

3. For those classes of aliens whose claim for eligibility for admission as immigrants is based on occupational qualifications, the alien filing for adjustment of status (i.e., from within the U.S.) can usually be granted employment authorization as early as the date of filing of the adjustment of status application; whereas, with regard to visa

petitions filed from foreign countries, as a general rule no explicit employment authorizations is granted the alien during the processing of the application.

4. Perhaps the most important advantage lies in the far greater legal constitutional protections that the alien filing from within the U.S. could enjoy over one doing so from a foreign country. To put it simply, as an alien seeking adjustment of status from within the U.S., you are automatically allowed all the privileges, rights and immunities of the United States constitution, the same as a person would enjoy who is fully a U.S., citizen.

To begin with, once you have been inspected at a port of entry and been properly admitted into the U.S., if the immigration officials should at any time thereafter deny you a visa to remain in the country, it is on the shoulders of the immigration officials themselves, and NOT on yours, that the burden now squarely falls to show that you are indeed a person deserving to be deported. In deed, under the applicable law, in a "deportation" hearing to determine your immigration status you need not even have to show (as you will have to in an "exclusion" hearing situation) that you are a person absolutely entitled, beyond a reasonable doubt, to enter the United States.

The second point is that if you filed a visa petition in the United States and it is denied, access to the Federal Courts, as well as to formal administrative appeal bodies, are readily available to you in full. Just like any regular U.S. citizen, you as well are entitled to hire an experienced immigration lawyer or to seek the aid of any of the many domestic U.S. immigration organizations involved in protecting the rights of aliens in the U.S. You may have such experts or organizations represent you and fight on your behalf to secure your rights through the courts and administrative bodies. Thus, if, for example, the first INS officer to rule on your adjustment application case (he's usually the area's District Director) turns you down, then you are at least in a position to appeal your case to higher authorities – first, to a U.S. immigration judge, and if still unsatisfied, then next to the Board of Immigration Appeal in Washington D.C., and if need still be, then finally to the U.S. Court of Appeals.

In contrast to the above situation, for an alien who applies for the immigrant visa through a U.S. consulate in a foreign country, the decision of one official and one official alone – the U.S. consul – is, for all practical purposes, final and virtually unappealable to any higher authority![1]

C. ALIEN PERSONS WHO QUALIFY FOR ADJUSTMENT OF STATUS

Based on the 1996 immigration law, many strict conditions which existed under prior immigration procedures regarding adjustment of status were eliminated and the U.S. government now essentially encourages persons to adjust their status from within the United States, rather than to travel to a U.S. Consul abroad to apply for a green card. To be entitled to an Adjustment of Status, the alien person must be eligible to receive a permanent resident visa immediately. That is, the Priority Date for the preference visa category you have must be "current". In other words, if you are a beneficiary of a Preference Petition[2] which is currently backlogged, you will not be eligible for adjustment of status. For example, the priority date for the unskilled category under the Third employment-related preference (Chapter 15), is generally deemed to be 6 to 7 years in arrears. Hence, if you have an approved employment-based Third preference petition, for example, and are already in the United States, you would not be eligible to file for an adjustment of status – unless and until the priority date is current. Once your priority date under this preference is current, you may then file for adjustment of status by filing the application forms (see Section D below) and paying the normal filing fee ($130 as of this writing), if you are in status and are otherwise eligible for

---

[1] Sure. in theory at least. a Consul's decision can be reviewed by the U.S. Department of State in Washington D.C. But the Department's role is only advisory and the Department may not order the Consul to approve a petition. Secondly, most aliens residing in a foreign country will hardly ever dare, much less afford, the expense or trouble to challenge a Consul's negative decision before a U.S. government agency located far away in Washington D.C.

[2] A preference petition would be basically any alien visa petition other than those filed by "immediate relatives" (Chapter 3. Section B. Chapter 4. Section A.1) of U.S. citizens. Such aliens, because they are subject to a quota limitation, would also be subject to priority dates. (See Chapter 5. Section B. C).

adjustment.

Aliens who are eligible for Adjustment of Status to receive a green card from within the U.S., fall under two basic groups – those who may do so outright WITHOUT having to pay an EXTRA CHARGE, and those who may do so but with an extra charge imposed.

1. *Aliens Eligible Without Having To Pay Extra Charge*
You may adjust your status without having to pay any extra fee particular to adjustment if you fall under these groups:

- You are an 'immediate relative' of a U.S. citizen (see Chapter 3, Section B, Chapter 4, Section A.1)[3] and had entered the U.S. with a visa and were inspected by an immigration officer at the time of the entry, and been either properly admitted into the U.S. in some nonimmigrant classification or been "paroled" into the U.S. (i.e., allowed in, pending decision in a deportation or exclusion hearing).
- Providing you were inspected and otherwise properly admitted into the U.S., and were not admitted "in transit" or as an alien crewman or as a terrorist or undesirable alien, you are still eligible to adjust your status, even if you have violated other immigration laws, such as overstaying your visa or working without authorization, if you meet the following conditions:
  i. You are legally married to a U.S. citizen or legal alien;
  ii. You are either the parent of a U.S. citizen who is at least 21 years of age, or of the minor child of a U.S. citizen or legal alien.

To put it another way, in general, so long as you had entered the U.S. properly – basically by having been inspected by an INS inspector – and have maintained your legal nonimmigrant status while you lived in the U.S., upon application for a change of status, you can probably get your green card without having to leave the U.S.[4] Persons falling under this category listed above, may apply for adjustment of status   (once their priority date is current for individuals who are preference aliens), by filing the appropriate papers and paying the regular filing fee. (If you happen to be married to an American citizen but had entered the U.S. without being inspected, or entered as a crewman or stowaway, then your only option would be to use the penalty method outlined under Section C.2 below)

2. *Aliens Who May Become Eligible By Payment Of A Penalty Extra Fee*
BUT what if you do not qualify within the group of people listed in Section C.1 above – that is, you do not qualify as an 'immediate relative' of a U.S. citizen – but you are out of status, and have worked without authorization or entered the U.S. without being properly inspected? Then, you may still apply for an adjustment but only under one condition: if you are "grandfathered in" - that is, if you can use the old penalty rule which allowed the adjustment of status by otherwise ineligible applicants upon their paying a $1,000 penalty fee.

Here are the basic rules for aliens falling under this group:
(a) If you do not qualify within any of the group of persons listed in Section C.1 above – that is, if you do not qualify as an 'immediate relative' of a U.S. citizen – but are out of legal status, and have worked without authori-

---

[3,4] You should note that if you are married to a U.S. citizen, however, generally you can still adjust your status within the U.S. even if you have fallen out of legal status or had worked without authorization - providing you did not enter the U.S. without being properly inspected, and did not enter as a crewman or stowaway.

zation or entered the U.S. without being properly inspected, once your priority date is current, you may still apply for adjustment of status by filing your visa petition (or labor certification application) and paying a $1,000 penalty fee – on or by April 30, 2001.[5]

(b) If you are an alien on whose behalf an employment-based visa petition is being filed under the First, Second or Third preference employment categories (Chapters 13, 14 or 15 of the manual, respectively), or if you are a Special Immigrant (Chapter 16), once your priority date is current, you may generally apply for adjustment of status by paying a $1,000 penalty fee for filing the adjustments of status application.

You can still adjust your status in these circumstances under either of the above sub-groups, even if: you gained admission into the U.S. without a valid visa or inspection by immigration officers; even if you entered the U.S.; "in transit" en route to another country but went on to stay or to work in the U.S.; even if you last entered the U.S. as a crew member or in any other capacity on board a ship or aircraft; and even if your sponsoring relative is a green card holder and you have entered the U.S. with a visa but overstayed your visa time or worked without a valid authorization of the INS.[6]

To put it another way, you are, if you do not qualify as an 'immediate relative' alien but qualify only as one kind of preference[7] alien or the other, prohibited from applying for adjustment of your status until and <u>UNLESS</u> your PRIORITY DATE is <u>current</u>, even if you have an approved petition indicating that a visa number is available. Once your priority date is current, you may apply to adjust your status – so long as you are in status. If, however, you are out of status, or have worked without authorization or entered the U.S. without being inspected by an INS official, your only avenue for adjustment of status would be to apply paying a $1,000 penalty fee, and to have filed your visa petition or labor certification ON OR BY April 30, 2001. *In sum, except for "immediate relatives" of U.S. citizen (including the spouses of green card holders) and those who use the monetary penalty route, virtually any other aliens would generally need to have maintained their nonimmigrant status and not have worked without authorization in order to be eligible to do their change of status from a nonimmigrant status to immigrant status from <u>within</u> the U.S.*

NOTE: Note that under a new ground of inadmissibility provided for in the 1996 Immigration Reform Law, aliens who were *unlawfully present* in the United States for 6 months after April 1, 1997, who subsequently left the U.S. voluntarily before the commencement of any removal proceedings, and who now seek formal admission into the U.S. (whether by adjustment of status or by applying for an immigrant or nonimmigrant visa), are subject to a stringent restriction: such alien is barred from re-entering the U.S. for 3 years; and if the unlawful presence had been for 1 year or more, the waiting period for which he's barred from reentering the U.S. is 10 years from the date of the alien's departure from the U.S. The term "unlawfully present" has a complex definition but generally means the overstay by a foreign person of the time authorized by the INS for the person to remain in the U.S., as usually noted on the Arrival-Department Record (Form 1-94). This is interpreted by the INS to include the time required by an alien to remain in the U.S.

---

[5] The original cutoff date for this was January 14, 1998. However, by The Legal Immigration and Family Equity Act of 2000 (LIFE Act) Congress replaced that original eligibility cutoff date so that it's now April 30, 2001. However, the LIFE Act also added a new "physical presence" requirement namely, that immigrants need to prove that they were actually present in the U.S. on the date of the enactment of this measure, which is Dec. 21, 2000, in order to be eligible to use this new provision.

[6] One exception to this general rule is with respect to aliens for whom the visa petition is employment-based. For such aliens, the limit for which you could have worked without authorization or overstayed your visa, is for a total period of 180 days.

[7] A preference alien would be basically any alien other than those who do not qualify as "immediate relatives" of U.S. citizens. (See Chapter 3 and 4). Such alien, because they are subject to a quota limitation, are also subject to a priority date (Chapter 5).

while in formal removal proceedings. Furthermore, this bar to reentry do not apply to any period of time which the alien spent under the age of 18; or for which he had a "bona fide" asylum application pending; or for which he was the beneficiary of a family unity protection application, or during which he was a "battered woman or child."

D. STEP-BY-STEP PROCEDURES FOR APPLYING FOR ADJUSTMENT OF STATUS

So you want to file to adjust your status from a non-immigrant, to IMMIGRANT status, while you are already living in the United States? Just follow the following general procedures step-by-step in the EXACT order in which they are listed below:

STEP 1: DETERMINE THAT YOU MEET THE GENERAL ELIGIBILITY REQUIREMENTS TO APPLY FOR ADJUSTMENT OF STATUS

See Sections A, B and C of this chapter. Do you, hopefully, fall under any one or more of the categories of aliens who may apply under either Section C.1 or C.2 above?

STEP 2: DETERMINE THAT THIS IS A PROPER TIME WHEN YOU MAY FILE AN ADJUSTMENT APPLICATION

First, before you rush to go file the adjustment of status application forms, there is one thing you had better done FIRST: determine that this is a proper time when you may file for an adjustment. There are a number of strict rules that control when and how you may apply for an Adjustment of Status, and *it is very essential that you follow such rules* if you are to ensure that your application papers will be processed quickly and successfully. Basically, you determine whether it is the proper time when you are to apply or not, by doing this: determining that you have either an approved (or approvable) Immediate Relative or Preference petition; or, if your case is one for which no preference petition is required (e.g. as in the case of NONPREFERENCE classification or SPECIAL IMMI-GRANTS), then you need only be able to present appropriate evidence of eligibility for such nonpreference or special immigrant status. In simple terms, here's what you do: First, check the latest U.S. Department of States' Visa Bulletin. Is an immigrant visa number available to you under the category for which you qualify at the time of this application? (See Chapter 5, especially Section D thereof, for how to do this). If it is, then this is the proper time for you to file your adjustment application. And if it is not, then it is not the proper time for you to file. Secondly, are you going to file, as most people have to do, under one of the many immigrant PREFERENCE categories (Chapter 3, Section C.1 and C.2)? Unless you happen to be among the relative few who qualify as "immediate relative" and "special immigrant" aliens who are exempt from the numerical limitation requirement outlined   in Chapter 5, you would probably have to file under one of the preference categories. If you do, then here's what you have to do: either you have previously filed the visa petition under your chosen preference classi-fication and secured an approval for it, or, if that is not the case, then simply prepare the visa petition and be prepared to submit it concurrently with your application for adjustment.

Recall a basic rule of relevance here: namely, that an adjustment application may be accepted ONLY IF the alien applicant has shown that he is qualified for the immigrant visa at the time of the application (or will be when the papers already on file in a pending application are approved). If the applicant does not have a nonpreference priority date (from having an approved Labor Certification, for example), and does not have a nonpreference petition on file with the INS, then the applicant cannot qualify for an immigrant visa, meaning that the adjustment application cannot be accepted. If there is an immigrant visa "available" to the alien, the alien who believes he meets the qualifications for adjustment can file his adjustment application at the same time that he files the petition that will make him eligible for the preference classification. He does not have to wait for the preference petition to be approved so long as he will be eligible for an immigrant visa if and when the petition is approved.

EXAMPLE: let's say you are going to file a "Schedule A" labor certification application and an employment-related Third Preference petition. Now, if according to the figures from the latest Visa Bulletin the Third Preference is "current" (meaning available) for your home country, this means that approval for your Third Preference petition will make you eligible for an immigrant visa *immediately*; hence, under this situation you CAN file an adjustment application *at the same time* that you file your Schedule A application and the Preference Petition. But, let's say that, on the other hand, everything else remains the same as in the above example but except for one thing: that the latest Visa Bulletin shows that visas are NOT "current" for the employment-related Third Preference category for your country. Then, in that case, approval of Third Preference petition will not make you eligible for an immigrant visa *immediately*, and hence you CANNOT file an adjustment application at this time, and you must wait and file when a visa is available for you. Now, suppose a visa number becomes available while your Schedule A application and Preference petition are awaiting approval? You can then do one of two things: either file the adjustment application and ask the INS to put it together with your previously filed Schedule A application and preference petition papers; or, in the alternative, you can wait and file the adjustment application after the Schedule A application and preference petition have been approved – so long as a visa is immediately available to you and you continue to meet all the adjustment requirements.

The Sequential Order And Timing Of The Papers To File

The whole point of the above discussion, in short, is simply to emphasized that there are a number of strict rules that determine when and how you may apply for an Adjustment of Status which will need to be followed in order to ensure a quick, proper and successful application. In any case, to simplify the whole process, simply follow these procedures in filing for an adjustment of status:

1. First, if you meet the following conditions, namely, if you either qualify as an 'immediate relative' of a U.S. citizen (basically a spouse, parent or minor child of a U.S. citizen, as more fully outlined in Chapter 3, Section B), or you are over 21 years of age, are unmarried and a child of a U.S. citizen and have maintained your legal status in the U.S. and never worked illegally, and your present Priority Date is current, then you may file the following documents with the INS at the same time:

    (i) Form 1-130, *Petition For Alien Relative*, to be filled out by the petitioner sponsoring the alien. (Applicable only in situations involving a petition based on a family relationship to a U.S. citizen. See illustrative sample of the form on p. 212).

    (ii) Form 1-485, *Application To Register Permanent Residence or Adjust Status*, to be filled out by the alien 'beneficiary' (see illustrative sample of this form on p. 229).

NOTE: Form 1-485A, which is a supplement to Form 1-485, is required <u>ONLY</u> in a situation when the alien visa petitioner is subject to the $1,000 penalty fee for residing in the U.S. illegally and is eligible to file because he/she had a visa petition or labor certification on file before April 30, 2001. The form is intended only to determine if you are subject to the penalty.

    (iii) Then file, also, the first group of other documents listed on p. 136 under ADDITIONAL DOCUMENTS.

2. On the other hand, if you are any kind of Employment Preference alien (i.e., one subject to a quota and some waiting period) on whose behalf a petition based upon employment has been filed, and you have already received a Labor Certification (see Chapter 23), then here's the sequential order of the papers you are to file:

(i) First, file Form 1-140, *Immigrant Petition For Alien Worker*, with the local INS office. This form is to be filled out and signed by the alien's prospective U.S. employer. (See illustrative sample of the form on pp. 180 & 216).

(ii) File FORM 1-485, *Application to Register Permanent Residence or Adjust Status*, with the INS. But only AFTER the FORM 1-140 petition is approved and your Priority Date is "current" (See Chapter 5, Sections C and D), may you file this form. (See illustrative sample of this form on p. 229). See "Explanatory Note" on pp. 89 and 141 for explanation about the employment of the FORM 1-140 on p. 180 in actual, previously filed successful cases.

NOTE: You may file FORM 1-485A, also, which is a supplement to FORM 1-485, ONLY WHEN your situation is such that you are subject to the $1,000 penalty fine for residing in the U.S. illegally and are eligible to file because you had a visa petition or Labor Certification on file before April 30, 2001. The form is intended only to determine if you are subject to the penalty.

(iii) Then file, also, the second group of other documents listed on p. 136 under ADDITIONAL DOCUMENTS.

STEP 3: FILE THE ADJUSTMENT APPLICATION, WITH THE SUPPORTING DOCUMENTS ATTACHED

You are now in the position to submit ("file") your application for Adjustment of Status to the INS. What do you do? You submit the application papers outlined in STEP 2 above (could be done in person or be mail, depending on the procedures of the particular local INS office) to the office of the Immigration and Naturalization Service (INS) covering the alien's place of residence in the U.S. (see listing of INS offices in Appendix B)

If the FORM 1-140 preference petition is applicable in your case, and is being filed at the same time as the application for adjustment, BOTH papers should be filed at the same INS office; if it is being filed without the application for adjustment, the filing would be with the INS office covering the place of the alien's intended employment. A nominal fee is charged by the INS for the filing of the adjustment application. A separate application need to be submitted for each member of the alien's family (the spouse and unmarried children under 21 years of age) being applied for.

Typical Documents you may attach:

A number of supporting documents and forms are to accompany the primary adjustment of status application forms. Thus, along with the applicable forms listed in STEP 2 above, you may also attach the following to your submission, as and if applicable:

- The alien's (each alien's) BIRTH CERTIFICATE or an equivalent
- Passport-size color PHOTOGRAPHS of each alien. Be sure they are taken according to INS requirements (see Chapter 25, Section F)
- INS Form G-325A, BIOGRAPHIC INFORMATION, to be filled out by the alien. (See sample on p. 225).
- INS Form 1-94, RECORD OF ARRIVAL AND DEPARTURE, which must have been obtained by the alien at the time of his original entry into the United State, usually attached to the alien's passport when he (she) entered the country. It serves as proof that the alien had a visa and was examined by U.S. immigration officers
- FORM 1-864, AFFIDAVIT OF SUPPORT (see sample of form on p. 241). This must be filled out, signed and notarized on the alien's behalf, by the person who is sponsoring the alien (he/she must be a U.S. citizen or green cardholder), and by both spouses, if they are married. It's to be filed in all family-based green card petitions, as well as in any employment-based petitions where the alien's relatives are the alien's sponsors or

own at least 5% of the sponsoring company. Or, if you have an employment, you may simply submit a letter of employment from your employer in the U.S., in stead, giving your job history, position, and salary, along with a copy of your pay stub showing your current earnings. (See sample of such letter on pp. 171, 176, 177, 178, and 179). *Or, another version, FORM 1-134, AFFIDAVIT OF SUPPORT, may also be used, and should simply be completed and sworn to by a close relative in the U.S., and his/her spouse, if married, and given on behalf of the alien. (See sample of FORM 1-134 on p. 212).*

• Form 1-765, *Permission to Accept Employment.* (Complete this form, ONLY IF you want advanced permission to work.)

• The Alien's PASSPORT (used for proof of the alien's identity and nationality)

• FINGERPRINT CARD (same as FORM-FD-258 sampled on p. 224). The fingerprinting is made either at a local INS office or at a local police department directed by the INS, and the fingerprint card duly filled out and signed by the official who did the fingerprinting. (Fingerprinting is not application for aliens 14 years of age or younger).

• Report of MEDICAL EXAMINATION. (The exam must be done by a doctor or medical facility specifically designated by the INS to perform such service, and the report is usually made by the examining doctor on FORM FS 398, Forms 1-486A, OF 157, 1-693, or an equivalent.)

• FILING FEE. Include the filing fee to file Form 1-485 in money order or certified check made payable to the INS. It is currently $130, if the petitioner is 14 years old or over, or $100, if under 14 years of age.

Additional Documents Particular to Petitions Based On FAMILY RELATIONSHIPS:

• BIRTH CERTIFICATE (or other equivalents, such as baptismal certificates, military service records, and the like) for both the petitioner and the alien "beneficiary" of the petition, to establish the family relationship between the U.S petitioner and the alien, if any is claimed.

• PROOF OF U.S. CITIZENSHIP OF PETITIONER, or of his/her U.S. Permanent Residency status

• MARRIAGE CERTIFICATE of the petitioner to the alien, if applicable.

• PROOF OF AGE of each alien (e.g., birth certificate or Declaration of age).

• ADOPTION DECREE (or other proof of legal adoption), if the alien is an adopted child. (see, also Chapters 11 and 12)

• DIVORCE DECREE (or death certificate thereof) from prior marriages by the petitioner and/or the alien, if any.

• MARRIAGE CERTIFICATE OF THE COMMON PARENTS of the petitioner and the alien(s), in cases, for example, involving a brother or sister sponsoring a brother or sister.

• "SECONDARY EVIDENCE" type of data – such as affidavits (sworn statements) from people attesting to the necessary facts as to the close family relationship claimed, or letters, correspondence and other proof of communications which had existed between the petitioner and the alien.

• For an alien family member (a child or a spouse) accompanying or following to join an alien already qualified for visa issuance in the U.S., you must further furnish such documents as are necessary to establish the family relationship claimed: birth certificates, marriage licenses, sworn statements (affidavits), letters and proof of other forms of communications which had existed between the petitioner and the alien.

Additional Documents Particular For Petitions Based On JOB-RELATED PREFERENCE VISA Categories:

• Alien LABOUR CERTIFICATION (if applicable), with the underlying documentary evidence upon which the certification had been obtained attached (See Chapter 23 for the labor certification procedures). See illustrative sample of Approved Labor Certification on pp. 172 & 174).

• STATEMENT OF QUALIFICATION OF ALIEN, Form ETA 750B. (See illustrative sample on pp. 176 &

177).

- JOB OFFER FOR ALIEN, Form ETA-750. (See illustrative sample on pp. 167-8).
- Certified copies of CERTIFICATES, DIPLOMAS, SCHOOL TRANSCRIPTS, and other documents and proofs of educational qualification, job skills or professional status. (See, for example, "Explanatory Note" on p. 89, paragraph 3 thereof)
- AFFIDAVITS FROM CREDIBLE AUTHORITIES OR EXPERTS testifying to alien's technical training or specialized experience.
- PUBLISHED MATERIALS BY OR ABOUT THE ALIEN in newspapers, magazines, professional journals, and the like.
- Proof of PROFESSIONAL LICENSES, membership in professional societies, achievement awards, and the like.
- Affidavits from present or former employers, professors or professional colleagues
- EMPLOYER'S SUPPORTING LETTER OR OFFER OF EMPLOYMENT) from the alien's U.S. petitioner-employer. (For sample, see pp. 171 & 176)
- CERTIFICATE OF AWARDS from trade union or technical schools, apprenticeship schools, etc.
- LICENSES or trade union certificates.

STEP 4: THE IMMIGRATION OFFICER EXAMINES YOUR APPLICATION & THE DOCUMENTATIONS FILED

What happens next, after you've filed your adjustment-of-status application papers with the INS office? The INS examiners will take a quick look at your submission and make a preliminary assessment, and, assuming that the examiners are able to determine (from the figures from the Department of State's Visa Bulletin) that a visa number is immediately available to the alien at the particular time of the filing of the said application, the application will be considered timely filed and hence will be retained for processing.

Following that, the INS visa processing examiners will more closely examine the application papers to evaluate the alien's eligibility for admission. *Among the key questions they would seek answers to are such questions as the following:* is it clear in this given case that there are no grounds on which the alien can be excluded from the U.S. under Section 212 of the Immigration Act? (See Chapter 24). Does the alien seemingly meet the qualifications under all immigration laws and regulations? Did he (she) come into the U.S. properly, after having undergone an inspection at a U.S. port or through being paroled into the U.S. pending an exclusion hearing? And if not, does he qualify anyway according to the legal requirements? *Are there any indications or reasons to believe, that the alien has entered the U.S. with a preconceived intent to become an immigrant and to permanently reside in the U.S.?* Has he in the past ever overstayed the time authorized him under the nonimmigrant visa he currently or previously had? Has the alien engaged in unauthorized employment after January 1, 1977? Has he maintained a valid status since entry into the U.S. and as of the time of the adjustment application? In other words, to put it in one sentence: does the alien lack any of the important qualifications for adjustment of status, or violate any of the conditions and prohibitions for gaining eligibility enumerated in Chapter 24 of this manual? And if he has, might he be eligible for a green card anyway under any of the categories listed in Section B of this chapter?

STEP 5: ATTEND THE IMMIGRATION VISA INTERVIEW

The INS will send you an interview appointment date after your filing is processed. Usually, spouses cases require an interview; other cases may or may not require one. You (the alien and each one applying with him or her) will need to be interviewed by the INS following the preliminary screening of the application. The Immigration and Naturalization Service (INS) district office, upon scheduling the interview, will usually send or give you an interview appointment notice telling you the date and place set for the adjustment interview to be held, if any has been planned for your case. In deed, often the MEDICAL EXAMINATION information and IMMIGRATION INTERVIEW appointment papers (FORM 1-486 or 1-693 or its equivalent), may be sent you (the alien). with the date and place for the alien to appear for the immigration interview marked on the said papers. (The INS-approved doctor, upon completion of the alien's medical exam, will simply complete FORM 1-489A and return it to the alien in a sealed envelope for him to deliver to the INS officers at the interview).

Now, depending on the procedures followed by your particular INS office, the interview may be held on the same day as the date of the filing of the application, or, more often than not, it may be scheduled weeks or even months later. If applicable in your situation, the interview may also cover the 1-140 Preference Petition filed by you, in which case the U.S. employer involved may also have to be invited for the INS interview.

The primary objective of the interview should be well understood. It is essentially this: to enable the interviewing officers to better determine whether the facts set forth by the alien in his underlying visa petition papers are accurate, or whether fraud is involved, and whether the alien meets the qualifications for adjustment as set forth under the law, or is deserving of being granted an adjustment anyway as a matter of discretion. Hence, the interviewer basically uses the face-to-face meeting and the personal exchanges at the interview to counter-check any questions or apparent contradictions in the application papers for consistency, the aim being to fill in any material gaps or omissions on any questions occurring from the documentations submitted.

Again, depending on the precise processing procedure employed in the given INS district office of your filing, the required security clearances, which take 60 days to complete, may be made either prior to the interview or thereafter. In any case, whether made prior to or after the interview, the process by which such security checks are made are essentially the same: the INS forwards copies of the alien's Biographic Information form, FORM G-325A, to the FBI, the CIA, and the consular office located in the alien's country of nationality or last residence, and waits for at least 60 days. (Such checks are limited only to applicants over 14 years of age). If no response is received within the 60 days period, then it is assumed that no adverse information exists against the alien(s) in question.

Finally, the INS examiner will contact the State Department's Visa Section (usually by telephone and on the day of the interview) to assure that a visa number is available for the applicant. (See Chapter 21 for a fuller treatment of the visa interview procedures).

NOTE: Be reminded that, at all times while your adjustment of status application is being processed, you must remain in your legal nonimmigrant status. If you should allow your legal status (e.g., as an F-1 student, or H-1B professional, etc) to lapse, it may complicate your adjustment application or even make it impossible for you to obtain the permanent residence status. Furthermore, you should endeavor (you or your spouse or your minor children) not to leave the U.S. during this period, unless you do so AFTER having first applied for and received advance permission from the INS to be able to reenter the U.S. – known as Advance Parole application

NOTE, however, that in any case, under the INS rule, if you happen to have been out of status for a period of 6 months or more after April 1, 1997 before filing your immigrant visa application, you are not permitted to travel outside the U.S. until your application is approved. If you do, you would have to wait for 3 years for your application to be approved, or 10 years if you were out of status for over 360 days.

STEP 6: GRANT OF YOUR VISA BY THE INS

Finally, upon the conclusion of the visa interview, assuming you've provided all the requisite documents and verifications, and that you are not inadmissible in terms of the immigration law, and providing that a visa number is immediately available, for your particular visa category, the INS official may inform you there and then that your Adjustment of Status application is approved. Or, the INS official may simply inform you that the decision will be sent you in the mail.

The INS officer will request you to bring your passport to the INS office. It will be stamped (and/or your FORM I-94 as well) with employment authorization notation, and you will be assigned an "A" (file) card number which will become your permanent resident identification number on your GREEN CARD when you get the actual card.

You will usually receive the actual "GREEN CARD" (actually it's not at all green in color), formally called, *Immigrant Visa and Alien Registration Number*, which bear your photograph and a stamp of approval of the U. S. government, by mail in about 3 to 6 months.

E. WHAT ARE THE CHANCES THAT THE INS MAY NOT RULE FAIRLY OR OBJECTIVELY ON YOUR ADJUSTMENT APPLICATION?

True, the granting of an alien's application to allow him to change from nonimmigrant to immigrant status is considered a "privilege" extended by the immigration service, rather than a right, and the INS officer is deemed to have sweeping "discretionary" powers either to grant such an application or to deny it. Admittedly, it is to be clearly borne in mind that even when the alien can show that he or she meets all the statutory requirements called for to warrant the granting of adjustment, it is still possible, in deed totally within the realm of the INS's "discretion," that the INS may still refuse to grant the adjustment, should its officers mere feel, for example, that the alien does not deserve such a privilege. Nevertheless, with all that said, it should be stated, in all fairness to the INS, that as a practical matter by and large the rules under which the INS decides the fate of adjustment applicants hardly ever allow the INS to deny such application on arbitrary basis – that is, without some good reason.[8] (Reasons such as, say, violation of the prohibition against unauthorized employment, or of having entered the U.S. with an apparent pre-conceived intent to remain permanently resident there, or of making material false statements to a U.S. Consul in the alien's home country or in the adjustment application, or of failing to have maintained valid nonimmigrant status since entry in the U.S., and the like, for example.)

Probably the most common basis for denying an adjustment application is ENGAGING IN UNAUTHORIZED EMPLOYMENT on the part of an alien. Nevertheless, even in such cases the general rule followed by the INS in addressing them is that in the absence of some "adverse factor," approval of adjustment application is usually granted, and even in those circumstances where such adverse factors are present, the principle is that those adverse factors are weighed against any "unusual or even outstanding equities" (i.e., factors that are favorably countervailing) in the alien's favor in determining whether to grant adjustment.

The second most prominent basis for denying adjustment applications by the immigration service, is ENGAGING IN SHAM MARRIAGES. As a rule, immigration officials scrutinize adjustment applications that are based on marriage of the alien to a U.S. citizen or permanent resident alien, more carefully. The belief, common among immigration officials, is that this category of immigrant visas (that is, those based on marriage relationships) is the most abused among all immigrant visa categories, and that many such aliens enter into sham marriages simply for

---

[8] See In the Matter of Arai. 13 I & N. 494, 496 (B. I. A. 1970)

the purpose of securing immigrant visa eligibility through the marriage relationship. Consequently, if you are an alien in a marriage relationship situation you should generally expect to be questioned closely regarding what your preconceived intention might have been at the time of your last entry into the U.S. as a nonimmigrant, the objective being to ascertain that the marriage was not entered into fraudulently, solely for the purpose of gaining eligibility for an immigrant visa, and that you and your supposed spouse truly intend to establish a life together in a bona fide marital relationship at the time when you entered into the marriage.

For a helpful insight, you'll find reproduced on pp. 148 a QUESTIONNAIRE used by consular and immigration officials in interviews and investigations where the bona fides (the honesty or legitimacy) of a marriage is a concern.

The Principal "Discretionary" Factors Considered by the INS in Deciding on Adjustment Applications.

As summarized from the relevant major court and administrative decision on the matter, the following are the principal factors which influence the decision of the immigration officials as they exercise administrative "discretion" on an adjustment application:

1. The existence of true family ties in the United States
2. Likelihood of hardship resulting to the alien and the petitioner and difficulty in traveling abroad.
3. Length of residence in the U.S.
4. Evidence of preconceived intent to remain permanently in the U.S. at the alien's time of last entry into the U.S. as a nonimmigrant (e.g., entering the U.S. as a nonimmigrant just weeks before making application for adjustment of status)
5. Repeated violations of the immigration laws or entry into the U.S. as an undesirable nonimmigrant
6. Whether the applicant is a person of good moral character.
7. The candor of the applicant at the adjustment interview and in his application papers
8. Circumstances clearly demonstrating, through the timing of the filling of the adjustment application, for example, that the only reason the alien entered the U.S. was to make his application for permanent resident. (For example, entering the U.S. as a nonimmigrant, and within a relatively short time marrying a U.S. citizen (or permanent resident) who had borne the alien a child and whom he had known for a considerable length of time before the marriage, would raise a question of preconceived intent to marry a citizen and remain in the U.S. permanently)

On the other hand, immigration experts knowledgeable in the matter, suggest certain conditions as being helpful in getting a more favorable disposition by immigration officers in visa cases that are based on marriage relationship: existence of photographs that show the spouses together, such as wedding album or marriage reception pictures, guest list of persons who attended the wedding, and the letters, gifts and greeting cards which have been exchanged between the couple; keeping a joint bank account or joint credit cards by the couple, having mutual wills, use of the husband's last name by the wife, and evidence that the parents and families of the parties have met and approved of the marriage, and so on.

F. WHAT ARE YOUR REMEDIES IN THE EVENT YOUR APPLICATION IS DENIED?

A few courses of action are open to you should your application for adjustment be turned down for whatever the reasons. First, you may simply forget about the application that had been filed on your behalf in the United States altogether, and just make out another application for immigrant visa and file it anew at the U.S. consulate in your home country. (Following the same procedure as in Chapter 6 thru. 19 of this manual). Or, alternatively, you may seek a re-consideration of your Application for Adjustment: you simply appeal your case firstly to the Board of Immigration Appeals in Washington D.C., and following that, you may make a second but final appeal to the U.S. Court of Appeals, if need be. (See Chapter 22, Section D thru. H thereof, for detailed discussion of immigration appeals and hearing procedures.

EXPLANATORY NOTES
(to the forms and procedures used in Chapter 20)

"Adjustment of Status" procedures (the subject matter of Chap. 20 at p. 128), are very closely similar to the same procedures described with respect to the filing of Mr. Arun (Doe's) petition for 3rd Preference immigrant visa, as set forth in "Explanatory Note" on p. 89, starting especially from paragraph 3 thereof.

In that specific case discussed in "Explanatory Note" on p. 89, which is an actual case previously and successfully processed, for a Green Card through adjustment of status, Mr. Arun (Doe), an Indian national who had first come into the U.S. on a F-1 student visa, had, upon obtaining advanced degree in Engineering, subsequently applied for and obtained a change of status to the non-immigrant H-1 temporary worker) status. Thereupon, the alien's employers subsequently sought to get him a permanent residence – a 3rd preference visa as of that time – that would ensure his services to them on a permanent basis.

First, the employers applied for and obtained a labor certification approval from the U.S. Department of Labor for the position in question, following essentially the same procedures as those outlined in Chap. 23 of this manual. Then, *secondly,* at the same time, immediately after receiving the labor certification (i.e., no later than 60 days of that), the employer filed the immigrant visa petition, Form 1-140, with the Immigration Service in Denver, Colorado, requesting to classify Mr. Arun (Doe) under the 3rd preference (at the time it could also have been the 6th preference) visa category. (See sample of a actual Form 1-140 for Arun reproduced on pp. 180-1, but note that the newer edition form currently in use, is reproduced on pp. 216; sample labor certification application Forms ETA 750A & B use for Arun are reproduced on pp. 167-170, and the letter from the Dept. of Labor approving certification is reproduced on p.174).

And *thirdly*, at the same time that the 1-140 petition was filed, the alien "beneficiary" of the petition also filed an application to adjust his status to that of a Permanent Resident, Form 1-485 (see p. 229) from within the U.S., and to this petition the alien attached the relevant supporting documents – the employer's letter of offer of employment (see copy on pp. 176 & 178), the alien's *Biographic Information* Form G-235A (a blank copy of this form is on p. 225), the alien's letter of approved Labor Certification (see p. 174), and the underlying documents on which it was granted, his fingerprints, photographs, birth certificate, passport, medical examination report, certified copy of alien's college degree and diplomas and his Arrival-Departure Record, Form 1-94, etc.

In this particular instance, the alien was able to simultaneously file for adjustment of status (Form 1-485) with the visa petition (Form 1-140), because he was in a position to do so in that the petition was for the 3rd preference for which there was relatively little or no backlog of visa numbers as of that time. In contrast, however, the 6th preference category job positions at the time were generally noted for having chronic backlogs of visa numbers, and had the petition been filed in the 6th preference category, Mr. Arun (Doe) would not have been eligible to adjust his status from within the United States; rather, he would have had to designate in his petition an American Consulate abroad closest to his residence to which the visa case should be sent for processing upon approval of the petition.

CONCERNING FAMILY-BASED IMMIGRANT VISA PETITIONS

Now, let's say that, on the other hand, this adjustment of status petition was based, not on employment or occupation, but on a marriage or blood relationship to a U.S. citizen or a Green Card holder -- essentially those falling under the Family-based 1st, 2nd, 3rd or 4th preferences, and the "immediate relatives" categories. In such a situation, the procedures would remain basically the same as those outlined above, EXCEPT that: i) Rather than provide evidence of professional or job qualifications, such as a Labor Certification or school diplomas and the like, you merely have to provide evidence relevant to establishing the claimed family relationship, such as marriage and birth certificates, adoption papers, and the like; and ii) you'd have to file visa petition FORM 1-130, *"Petition for Alien Relative,"* (see sample on pp. 212-3), rather than the petition FORM 140. The rest of the usual procedures will remain essentially the same as are outlined in Chapters 6 to 12, as applicable to you, and/or Chapter 20 of this manual.

Chapter 21
The Visa Interview

A. YOU MAY OR MAY NOT BE SUBJECT TO AN INTERVIEW

As a rule, U.S. consulates abroad hold personal interviews on almost all green card applications (except for aliens under 14 years of age), while the personal interviews in Adjustment of Status applications in the United States are held by the INS in only some application, depending on the nature of the visa sought, and the facts involved in a given case. Asylum and refugee cases, for example, and cases involving an alien applying on the basis of a marriage or adoptive relationship to a U.S. citizen or permanent resident, will usually require a personal interview often with both the alien and the U.S. citizen or permanent resident. In any event, whenever an interview is required in your case, the U.S. Consulate or the INS in charge in your case will usually send you a written notice of the interview appointment. (In a Consulate situation, that information will come with the Packet 4).

B. BRING THE ORIGINAL DOCUMENTS WITH YOU FOR VERIFICATION

Generally, whatever forms you'll need to complete for the processing of the application, and whatever supporting documents you might have gathered in support of the application, you'll have to take them with you PERSONALLY to the interview. You do not mail the papers and documents this time. This is when you would be expected to present the actual originals (or certified true copies) of the documents for the responsible immigration officials to inspect them for verification purposes.

C. THE GENERAL NATURE OF THE INTERVIEW

What happens at this all-important interview? The consular officials will conduct a quick, preliminary check of your application and the supporting documents you submitted in regard to their formats and contents to see that your submissions are at least complete and that the forms are completely filled out. The consular or INS official will usually require you to "execute" (i.e., to sign) the application form(s) in his presence. The interviewing officer will also review the report of your medical examination made out by the designated physician who performed your medical exam. You will pay the consular officer the application filing fees required, if you have not already done so by now. In consular applications, some U.S. Consulates would accept payment only by certified check, money order, or travelers check, while others would accept cash.

In any case, assuming that the papers submitted seem at least complete and in order, the officer will assign a "case number" to your application. (Make sure you collect a receipt of filing from the officer, for your own records).

Briefly summed up, the primary objective of the visa interview is to enable the interviewing Consular or INS officer to verify the information set forth by the alien in the underlying visa petition and application papers (and, where it applies, in the Labor Certification paper as well), in terms of their accuracy and the genuineness of the supporting documents submitted. The interviewing officer is interested in scrutinizing the alien and the documents submitted for any indication of fraud or misrepresentation of the facts in the application papers. Thus, the interview process basically involves verification of your application's accuracy and inspection of your documents to confirm the statements in the application papers. Hence, the interviewer basically uses the face-to-face meeting and personal exchanges at the interview to counter-check and clarify any questions, or apparent contradictions in the application papers for consistency, with a view to filing in any material gaps or omissions occurring from the papers submitted.

The visa interviewer will closely examine the alien's application papers from the standpoint, as well, of evaluating the alien's legal eligibility for admission into the United States. He or she will want answers to questions such as these: is it clear in the specific case involved, that there are no grounds under the relevant U.S. immigration law on which this alien can be excluded from entry or staying in the U.S.? Does this alien seem to meet the qualifications required for the particular visa applied for under the relevant immigration laws and regulations? Does the alien, for example, truly or genuinely possess the close family relationship to a U.S. citizen or permanent resident claimed; or the occupational qualifications or other eligibility requirements claimed in the alien's petition or application papers?

In general, by almost every account, the one central issue about which most problems occur in immigrant visa interviews, has to do with verification of the alien's claims as to his qualification for a job, when the visa petition is employment based, or as to the existence of a true family relationship to a U.S. citizen or Permanent Resident alien, especially in regard to claims of the existence of a marriage between the alien and his/her sponsoring U.S. petitioner.

D. SPECIAL SCRUTINY IN MARRIAGE-BASED APPLICATION INTERVIEWS

As a rule, immigration officials scrutinize with a special degree of attention and carefulness, applications that are based on claimed family relationships, especially marriage relationships, of an alien to a U.S. citizen or Permanent Resident. The belief prevalent among immigration officials, is that this category of immigrant visas is the most fraud-ridden and abused of all immigrant visa classifications, and that many aliens enter into "sham" marriages with U.S. citizens or permanent residents with the sole intent of gaining eligibility for an immigrant visa through such a relationship but without a genuine intention to maintain the marital relationship.

Hence, if the interviewing consular officer should, even remotely, feel that the existence of a close family relationship you claim (say, as between one spouse to another, or a parent and a child, or one brother or sister to another etc) is in any way not credible, you can rest assured that this will be one area of intense interest and questioning the consular officer will concentrate on. If, for example, you are in a marital relationship situation with a U.S. citizen or a green cardholder wherein you had married while temporarily in the United States, you should generally expect to be questioned closely by the interviewing officer regarding what your preconceived intention might have been at the time of your last entry into the U.S. as a non-immigrant. And you should, in that event, be prepared to answer questions and to present credible evidence sufficient to convince the Consular (or INS) personnel that the marriage was legitimate and was not entered into fraudulently just so that you can gain eligibility for an immigrant visa. You'll be asked questions which are intended to verify that you and your U.S. spouse truly intended to establish a life together in a bona-fide marital relationship at the time you entered into the marriage.

For a helpful insight, you'll find reproduced on p. 148 *a Questionnaire used by Consular and immigration officials* in interviews and investigations in which a major concern is to determine the bona-fides (the honesty or legitimacy) of a marriage. (See, also, Chapter 4, Sections D thru. F for more on the problem areas involved in establishing that a bona-fide marital and other family relationships truly exist for immigration purposes.)

E. FORMAT OF SUSPECTED "MARRIAGE FRAUD" INTERVIEWS & INS INVESTIGATION

Typically, in an 'immediate relative' situation where both the alien and his/her U.S. citizen or permanent resident spouse reside in the United States, the format is to interview the spouses separately[1]. At the interview, the couple will be separated and exactly the same questions will be asked each one on various specific personal issues about their relationship and marital life together. The questions are normally diverse enough as to preclude the possibility that the spouses could anticipate or prepare the answers in advance of the interview, and, except for questions of sexual nature concerning the sexual habits of the couple, virtually every area of the couple's marital relationship could be probed. The questions asked will basically be related to matters which spouses who actually live together should normally know about each other and that perhaps no one else would know.

Typical questions will relate to matters such as: the division of household chores, the food preferences of the spouses, what type of food was eaten by the couple on a particular day or occasion, the nature and setting of the couple's living room, questions about where things are kept, the number of rooms in the couple's marital residence, on which side of the sitting room or on which chair the respective spouses sit, the color preferences of the parties, on which side of the bed the respective spouses sleep, what time of the day each spouse typically wakes up to prepare for work or goes to sleep or returns from work, the kinds of sports programs or T.V. programs or movies preferred by each, and matters of this nature.

Then, following the separate questioning, the interviewer compares the answers of both spouses to the questions to determine that there are no serious inconsistencies between the two sets of answers. And if the immigration (or consular) examiner is be left with any serious doubts as to the legitimacy of the marriage, he can do one of two things: either deny the visa application outright, or refer the case to the Investigation Section of the INS which then assigns the matter to an inspector for a "field investigation" of the marriage relationship. Such investigations would often involve things like making unannounced visits to the couple's designated home address at unusual hours (e.g., in early mornings or late at night) to determine if the parties really lived together, visiting the spouses' place of employment to check the information listed in the employment records regarding the marital status, contacting the landlord of the couple's residence or the neighbors to ask questions about the couple, etc.

Indeed, the immigration and consular authorities have designed a list of factors – *"WARNING SIGNS"* – as a guide for them in determining whether a given marriage may have been fraudulently entered into for the purpose of getting an immigration benefit. They are: **(1)** that the couple has not know each other for very long; **(2)** they have only seen each other for a brief period or a few times prior to the marriage; **(3)** they do not presently live together or have never lived together; **(4)** they married only after the alien spouse becames the subject of a deportation proceeding; **(5)** they come from very different racial, cultural or religious backgrounds; **(6)** they do not speak a common language; **(7)** there is a big age difference between the couple; and (8) the alien spouse paid a large sum of money to the U.S. citizen or Permanent Resident.

On the other hand, immigration experts knowledgeable in the matter suggest certain conditions as being helpful in getting a more favorable disposition by immigration officers in visa cases that are based on marriage relationship: the existence of photographs that show the spouses together, such as wedding album or marriage reception pictures, guest list of persons who attended the wedding, and letters, gifts, and greeting cards which have been exchanged between the couple, keeping a joint bank account or joint credit cards by the couple, having mutual

---

[1] In situations where the alien spouse [or fiancé(e)] lives in her native country, the alien spouse is interviewed alone there, and the U.S. relative who resides in the U.S. is not usually required to attend the interview.

wills, use of the husband's last name by the wife, and evidence that the parents and families of the parties have met and approved of the marriage, and so on.

F. THE CENTRAL KEY TO A SUCCESSFUL VISA INTERVIEW: ABSOLUTE TRUTHFULNESS

The central point for the alien in having a successful and trouble-free visa interview, can be simply summed up in one sentence: ABSOLUTE HONESTY AND TRUTHFULNESS ON THE PART OF THE ALIEN. Experts widely experienced in the intricacies of securing a visa under the U.S. immigration laws and procedures, are almost unanimous in advising that the single, most common, underlying factor which generally spell the doom of most aliens whose applications for a visa are denied, is MISREPRESENTATION OF THE FACTS AND LACK OF CANDOR ON THE PART OF THE ALIEN.

Christopher E. Henry, a long time New York attorney and vastly experienced U.S. immigration expert, sums up his advise to U.S. visa applicants this way:[2]

"It is extremely important to always be truthful when applying for a visa, both on your written application and during any interview which may be conducted. Visa fraud (which is defined as any misrepresentation made during the application process) is a very serious crime; any person who commits visa fraud may be barred perma- nently from the United States. *Committing visa fraud is often more dangerous to a visa applicant than whatever the applicant was trying to cover up in the first place......*" Henry states that the interviewer's "questions will usually be direct and straightforward, but not always," adding that "part of the process is to try to trick you into admitting your 'real' motive for wanting to go to America," or into lying. Henry, pronouncing an applicant's lack of truthfulness the most "exceedingly stupid thing for a visa applicant to do," cites as a classic example a situation where an applicant will have a criminal conviction which, in and of itself, isn't really all that serious and may not have been a bar at all to his being granted a visa, but which becomes a serious problem for the applicant only "because the person is afraid that the visa application will be rejected and therefore lies about the conviction on the application and/or during the interview." And then, lo and behold the U.S. Consulate, which invariably has access to all kinds of information provided it by the intelligence agencies of other governments anyway, uncovers the misrepresentation about the alien's prior conviction, and thus the alien is denied the visa application for the reason of lying about the conviction (committing visa fraud) alone, even though the crime itself may have been no bar to the granting of a visa.

Finally, C.James Cooper, a veteran immigration expert who has been through same hundreds of visa interviews in the course of his long professional career as an immigration lawyer, offers this fitting words of advice and wisdom for the would-be visa interviewee:[3]

"Whatever you do, never let the other side see you get a little nervous when dealing with government officials. This is normal. But remember, immigration officials are law enforce- ment personnel and have been carefully trained in the art of interviewing foreign nationals. They have been taught that, generally, persons who appear to be nervous, ill at ease, who perspire, have sweaty palms, and do not make direct eye contact, may be hiding something.

---

[2] Christopher E. Henry, author. How To Win The U.S. Immigration Game (The O'Brien Press, Dublin: 1989)

[3] C. James Cooper, author The Immigration Tapes (Text)

Immigration officials are suspicious of anyone who appears to be uptight. Although it is understandable why a person would be nervous and full of anxiety under the scrutinizing eyes of an immigration or consular officer, you will be more successful if you understand the process and know what to expect. Therefore, your composure and mannerisms when dealing with an immigration or consular officer are very important. Although you should not act as though you know everything or be too confident, *you should try to be relaxed and appear to be as believable as possible. The impression you make may be the deciding factor on whether or not your visa will be granted."*

G. HOW DO YOU BEST PREPARE FOR AN INTERVIEW?

Bear in mind, once again that, basically, the interviewer's main questions and interest will generally center upon the information you have already given in your answers to the questions on the application forms and documents you've submitted to Consular or INS office, and that his primary task is to review your papers and ask you questions based on those answers and information you have submitted in order to verify the accuracy of the facts and information you've provided. Most such interviews are actually brief – some 20 to 30 minutes or so long. And sometimes the same questions will be repeated several times, especially in cases where your U.S. employer (or relative) has filed the visa petition for you.

Hence, actually, the most important and best way you can "prepare" for a visa interview, is this: *relax; just answer the questions asked you by the interviewer truthfully and simply.* Don't try to be smart or clever with the interviewer; he's more than likely to "see through you." If you don't quite understand a question, say so, ask for a clarification before you answer. Or, where you can't understand the English used by the interviewer, or you're confused by his accent or intonation, don't be embarrassed or bashful – ask for a language interpreter.

QUESTIONNAIRE USED TO ESTABLISH INTENTIONS
OF MARRIED COUPLE.

Name_____ Date_____

File No._____

1. State your true and full name and any other names by which you are known.
2. State your spouse's full name and any other names by which he or she is known.
3. What is his/her date and place of birth?
4. Where do you presently reside? With whom and for how long?
5. When, where and how did you meet your spouse for the first time?
6. Who introduced you to him/her?
7. For how long did the courtship last? And how was it done?
8. How long did the two of you go steady before marriage?
9. Did you have any dates prior to marriage? Where and what did you do on those dates?
10. Who made the necessary arrangements for your wedding?
11. Where and when did you get married (specify place, time and date)?
12. What is the name of the officer, judge, priest or minister who solemnized your marriage? And who contracted him?
13. Approximately how many people were present during the wedding? If there are eight or less people who attended, list their names and your relationship to them.
14. What are the names of the witnesses at your wedding? And who chose them?
15. If a reception was help after the wedding, list the place, time and number of people who attended.
16. Were there pictures of the wedding, and/or the reception? If there were, pictures should be shown to the interrogation officer.
17. Where and for how long did you spend your honeymoon? Was the marriage consummated?
18. List all the places where you lived with your spouse and the inclusive dates when you lived at such places.
19. Aside from the two of you, who else lived in the above listed places?
20. Where are you presently working? What is the nature of your job? What hours do you work? And how much do you receive a month?
21. Where does your spouse work? What is the nature of his/her job? What hours does he/she work? And how much does he/she earn?
22. What are your parents names and present whereabouts?
23. What are your sibling's names and their addresses?
24. Was your spouse ever introduced to your parents and siblings? (If so, when and where?)
25. What are your spouse's parents' names and present addresses?
26. What are your spouses siblings' names and present addresses?
27. Have you ever been introduced to your spouse's parents and siblings? (If so, when and where?)
28. Did you give or receive a wedding ring or an engagement ring?
29. Was the ring engraved? Where was it purchased?
30. How many children do you have? List all their names, ages and present addresses.
31. By what means and how often did you hear from your spouse before and after your marriage?
32. If your spouse has already left for the U.S., how often has he/she visited you?
33. Where did you stay during those visits and what did you do?
34. Have you given or sent any gifts to your spouse? (What and when?)
35. Have you received any gifts or presents from your spouse? (What and when?)
36. Who is arranging for your travel documents? Any travel agent or atorney?
37. Who filled out the petition for you? Where was it filled out?
38. How often did you and your spouse go to your travel agent/attorney?
39. Who paid for your travel agent or attorney?
40. Who will pay for your traveling expenses and how?
41. Monetary support. How much and how often?
42. The following documents and/or papers were shown to the interviewer/witness:

	Date	Quantity
Letters	_____	_____
Photos (Wedding)	_____	_____
(Reception)	_____	_____
Money Order Receipts	_____	_____

I have read the foregoing statement and it is a true and correct record of my declaration.

_____
Signature (of alien spouse)

Subscribed and sworn before me on_____ at_____

_____
Signature (of INS officer)

Witnessed by:_____ _____
Signature
CLERK

_____ _____
Title

Chapter 22

Entering The United States: The Process Of Getting Actually "Admitted" Into The Country After You've Got Your Visa In Hand

Alright. So you've gone through all those lengthy formalities and hassles customarily involved in applying or petitioning for a visa to enter the United States. And, at long last, let's say you have been granted the visa; and shortly thereafter, you left your home country and are now at a U.S. border port of entry with your "almighty" U.S. entry permit in your hands seeking to physically enter the United States! Are you automatically guaranteed or entitled to admission just because you have a valid visa in hand?

The answer, is a resounding: No! GET THIS POINT VERY CLEAR: think of the process of your admission into the U.S. as a TWO-step process; in this two-step process, the issuance of a visa to you is only the FIRST of the two steps! All that your possession of the visa does for you, in practical terms, is entitle you – accord you the right – to come to a border port of entry to the United States. And then, while you are at such a border or port of entry, you may then "apply" for actual admission into the country; and, what is more important, you will have to demonstrate your qualification and eligibility for admission into the U.S. all over again for a SECOND time, to the satisfaction of the U.S. immigration officers there at the border. And only then may you finally gain entry into the United States!

A. EVIDENCE OF YOUR VISA ISSUANCE

Upon the approval of your visa petition or application in a foreign country by a U.S. Consul there, if the visa granted you is a NONIMMIGRANT type, the consul shall have typically stamped your passport with a notation indicating for how long the visa is valid, the approved visa classification to which you belong, the number of entries you are permitted into the United States. And if the visa granted you is an IMMIGRANT type, the Consul shall have typically stamped your visa, as well, with a notation thereon about the type of visa granted you. At the issuance of your immigrant visa, the visa is valid for 6 months – that is, it allows you to arrive in the U.S. within those 6 months. And, technically, it is only at the moment when you make an entry into the U.S. with your visa in hand, that you actually acquire the status of being a green card (an immigrant visa) holder.

B. GOING THROUGH INSPECTION AT THE PORT OF ENTRY

In all the time the alien visa-seeker is in his home country, or is in any country whatsoever so long as it is outside the United States, the agency of the U.S. Government with the sole jurisdiction or authority over matters concerning the processing of the alien's visa application in the foreign country in question, is the Consular office, an arm of the U.S. Department of State. However, once the alien sets his or her foot on a port of entry in the United States (at a land border, an airport, or a seaport), from that moment on it is the Immigration and Naturalization Service

(INS), an arm of a different agency of the U.S. Government, namely, the Department of Justice, that now takes over and automatically assumes the decision-making powers on all matters concerning your admission or admissibility, and which decides whether you may be admitted or excluded from entry. *The key point to remember here, is that though you have your visa in hand at a port of entry quite properly issued you by a consulate official abroad, that fact, nevertheless, is NOT A GUARANTEE that you will necessarily be found acceptable for admission by the immigration officials at the port of entry, or that you will necessarily be allowed entry into the United States!*

Here's The way the Admission Process Works, in brief:

• Upon your (the alien's) arrival at the U.S. port of entry, you will have to undergo a "secondary inspection," meaning that you will have to be examined one more time, this time to determine your entitlement to enter the U.S. This time, though, this inspection is done by INS, as opposed to the Consular inspectors or examiners. You report for the "inspection and admission" procedures before the INS inspector; you surrender your passport and your visa (and any other relevant or applicable documents, e.g., information on school admission or report of medical examination) to the INS inspector, and, upon the inspector reviewing your documents, he'll probably ask you a number of questions regarding your eligibility and purpose for coming to the United States.

• Your name is checked against a "lookout book" (a list of names) the INS maintains for aliens who may be excludable and for other dangerous or criminal persons for whom government agencies have requested a "lookout". You may possibly (though not commonly) be required to take a complete medical and physical examination by a Public Health Service Officer, and may be subject to background investigations.

• In some cases, the immigration inspector may possibly decide that the alien is not eligible for admission. He may determine, for example, that the alien's background or record, in some way, is in violation of some requirements for which an "exclusion" from entry into the United States is called for under the immigration laws or regulations, or that some material documentation required from the alien has either not been provided or is incomplete or unsatisfactory.

Essentially, to be admitted into the United States, here is what you are required to satisfy the immigration inspector of: that you are "clearly and beyond doubt entitled to land in the United States" – in other words, that you basically meet the necessary qualifications as provided for under the law for the type of visa you hold, and that there truly are no legal barriers that would prevent you from being admitted into the United States.

C. ADMISSION OR DENIAL OF ADMISSION

In the end, assuming that the immigration inspector approves your being admitted, in that event if you are being admitted in one of the nonimmigrant *classifications, the immigration inspector will at that time grant you the specific length of time you will be authorized to stay in the U.S. in accordance with the particular type of visa you were issued. (This, and various other types of information designed to stand as evidence of the alien's lawful admission into the U.S., is either stamped in his passport or, more typically, entered on a FORM I-90 Departure Card and stapled to the inside of his passport). If, on the other hand, you are admitted as an* immigrant, *you may either be issued an Alien Registration Receipt Card (the "GREEN CARD") on the spot, or a rubber stamp will be placed in your passport to serve as your temporary Green Card; the actual card will then be manufactured and sent to you thereafter by mail at your designated address in the United States.*

D. IF DENIED ADMISSION, YOU COULD SEEK A REVIEW: AN "EXCLUSION" HEARING.

What happens if the immigration inspector conducting the initial port-of-entry examination were to determine that you are not admissible, and therefore "excludes" you – that is, denies you entry into the United States? Usually, you would probably be advised to appear for a *"secondary"* (i.e., a more formal) *examination* if the port of entry at which you arrived is a land border; or, if your place of arrival is at an INS office other than at an airport or seaport, you may be given a *"deferred inspection"*. Thereafter, if you are still found inadmissible, you are ordered "excluded" (i.e., barred from entry), at which point you are given a choice: either voluntarily return to your home country at your own expense, or your case is referred to an immigration judge for a hearing, the so-called *EXCLUSION HEARING PROCEEDINGS*

An "exclusion" hearing is the hearing that is of relevance to the alien who is refused entry at a port of entry, as opposed to a "deportation" hearing (Section F below). In a word, an EXCLUSION hearing is one held to determine an alien's right merely to <u>enter</u> the United States; it takes place <u>BEFORE</u> the right to enter is officially granted. It technically differs from a DEPORTATION hearing (Section F below), in that deportation has to do with determining the alien's right to remain in the U.S. <u>AFTER</u> he shall have already been admitted into the U.S. by an immigration officer and has probably lived in the country for a while.

E. RIGHTS OF DETAINED ALIENS & THE PROCEDURES IN EXCLUSION HEARINGS

To be sure, exclusion proceedings (and, in deed, the related subject of deportation proceedings) are clearly beyond the very limited scope of the present book, and an alien faced with such a circumstance may well be better advised, anyway, to seek the help of a competent immigration lawyer and immigration social services organizations. *Here, therefore, we can only present a brief outline of the alien's rights and the procedures involved:*

1. In exclusion hearings, it is the <u>alien</u> himself, and NOT the Immigration Service (INS), that has the big burden of proving that he or she is otherwise eligible for admission to the U.S. and that he has actually not violated any immigration laws. And he or she must make this proof by a "clear and convincing evidence".

2. Basically, under the premise that the alien in an exclusion hearing is a person merely "at the door" but who is not yet in, aliens in exclusion hearings are viewed as a group not entitled to the usual constitutional guarantees; hence, the normal constitutional rights and protections do not apply in exclusion hearings, inasmuch as admitting foreigners to the U.S. is said to be a "privilege" granted only at the pleasure of, and on the terms and conditions set by, the U.S. government.

3. *The INS District Director has a right to, if he so chooses, and may in his discretion, either hold you in an immigration detention facility pending the conclusion of the hearing, or release you on a bond or on your own personal recognizance.*

4. *The hearing takes place before a U.S. immigration judge; and you may (you have a right to, if you wish)* represent yourself in the case, or be represented by a friend or a lawyer of your choice, providing you can pay such a lawyer out of your own resources.

5. You are entitled to be told the charges made against you, and to be given the opportunity to present evidence in defense of yourself, and to confront and question any evidence presented or any witnesses who appear or testify against you.

6. Aside from other remedies you may consider, one thing you may do at this hearing is to make an *application for political asylum. (Political asylum procedures are outlined in Chapter 18.)*

7. *In the end, whatever the decision arrived at by the hearing judge such must be based SOLELY on the* evidence presented at the hearing and must be adequately supported by such evidence, and be supported in such a way that it can be rationally inferred that you (the alien) are not entitled to admission.

8. If the decision of the judge is that you be excluded from admission, he will issue an ORDER FOR EXCLU-SION (ORDER OF DEPORTATION, if a deportation case) against you to that effect.

9. You have a right (except if you are a crewman, stowaway or a person excluded on security or *medical disqualification grounds) to appeal the decision of the immigration judge to the next level,* namely, to the *Board of Immigration Appeals in Washington D. C.(To appeal, you must do so* immediately, at the conclusion of the hearing, if the decision is oral, or within 10 days of the decision, if the decision is a written one. Initiate the process by serving a written *NOTICE OF APPEAL* upon the INS promptly.)

10. If you fail to appeal the immigration judge's ORDER FOR EXCLUSION (or DEPORTATION), or fail to do so on time, you will immediately be deported - returned, in this instance, to the country from which you came to the U.S.

11. The judge may, at his "discretion", either decide to allow you to post a bail bond, or to release you on parole with or without a bond.

12. On appeal, the following are few grounds on which you can base your claim that the decision of the immigration judge deserves to be reversed or set aside: (i) that there were "improper procedures" at the hearing (i.e., that you had an unfair hearing or that it did not follow the legal and agency requirements set for such hearings); (ii) that the judge's ORDER OF EXCLUSION (or Deportation) was based on "mistake of fact" or "errors of law" (i.e., that the judge applied an incorrect meaning or interpretation of the relevant laws and regulations); (iii) that the decision did not have "adequate support in the evidence" or was rendered with "unwarranted disregard of the evidence" or was not based on "proper standard of evidence" (i.e., not having a substantial and reasonable basis in the evidence); and (iv) that there was, on the part of the judge an "arbitrary exercise of discretion" or "failure to exercise discretion" (i.e., that either no reason is given for the decision rendered, or the reason given is irrational or out of keeping with established policy, or discriminatory or based on improper grounds).

13. In exclusion hearings, if you appeal an immigration judge's decision to the Board of Immigration Appeals and the Board's decision still remains unfavorable to you, you have only one final right of appeal: the right to petition a court of law for a judicial review. This petition, called a *WRIT OF HABEAS CORPUS,* is filed with the U.S. District Court in the hearing area, the object being for the court to review the administrative action taken in the exclusion hearings and to establish that the Order of Exclusion is valid.

F. IF DENIED THE RIGHT TO REMAIN IN THE U.S., YOU COULD SEEK A REVIEW: DEPORTATION PROCEEDINGS

A "deportation" proceeding, as previously explained in Section D above, is primarily concerned with determining the alien's right (or lack of it) to remain in the United States AFTER he shall have already been duly admitted into the U.S. by the immigration officials. In short, whereas you'll seek an exclusion hearing if you have a valid visa but are denied entry into the U.S., a deportation hearing is what you seek to have when you are denied or threatened with denial of the right to remain in the U. S. at any time AFTER you have gained formal admission into the country. Usually, a deportation proceeding comes about because the immigration service, probably contending that an alien who had been duly admitted to the country has committed some acts which violate certain immigration laws or the terms upon which the alien had been granted his visa, has initiated a move to send the alien back to his home country.

G. RIGHTS OF ALIENS & PROCEDURES IN DEPORTATION HEARINGS
The following is a brief outline summarizing the alien's rights and the procedures involved in deportation hearings:

1. *An important preface is appropriate here: aside from a few important areas of differences,* by and large the rights of aliens involved in deportation hearings and the procedures thereof, are essentially the same as those of aliens involved in exclusion hearings and the procedures thereof. In the interest of brevity and to avoid unnecessary repetition, here's what you do: simply read all the rights and hearing procedures outlined in Section E above for the alien facing an "exclusion" hearing, and treat the said facts therein as equally applicable with respect to the alien facing deportation hearings, except for just a few differences as specified below.

2. The significant points of departure regarding the alien involved in deportation proceedings, are as follows:

i) Contrary to the situation prevailing in exclusion proceedings (see paragraph 2 of Section E above), the alien involved in deportation hearings is entitled to, and is accorded, all constitutional rights, protections and privileges that a U.S. citizen has, such as the right not to self-incriminate oneself. *In deed, this is probably the overriding distinguishing factor between the two types of hearings.*

ii) One manifest way by which the deportation-bound alien enjoys superior constitutional privileges not extended to the exclusion-bound alien, is this: in deportation hearings, it is the immigration service, and NOT the alien, as in the case of aliens facing exclusion, that has the burden of proving, by a "clear and convincing evidence", that the alien is deportable and/or has actually violated specific immigration laws.

iii) Among the remedies open for consideration to the alien in a deportation preceding, are the following "discretionary relief": aside from being able to apply for political asylum in the U.S., you may apply for a "stay (suspension) of deportation" (file immigration FORM 1-256); and you may apply to have your status adjusted from nonimmigrant to immigrant status, if qualified. (See Chapter 20 on the adjustment of status procedures).

iv) Just as in exclusion hearings, you can appeal a decision by a U.S. immigration judge in a deportation hearing to the *Board of Immigration Appeals* in Washington D.C. under basically the same grounds and ground rules (paragraphs 9 thru. 12 of Section E above). However, the final appeal in deportation proceedings is not from the Board's decision to the area's U. S. District Court, but to the area's *U.S. Court of Appeals*. You file for such review of the Board's decision by filing within 6 months after the Board's ruling a *"PETITION TO REVIEW DEPORTATION ORDER"*

NOTE: The Court of Appeals, in this instance, will look only at the previously assembled record of the appealed proceedings, with no new evidence submitted or considered. To apply for suspension of deportation, you need to be able to show: that you were continuously present in the U.S. for the previous 7 years or that you performed honorable service in the U.S. armed forces for at least 24 months; that you are of good moral character; how and why your deportation would result in "exceptional and extremely unusual hardship" to yourself or to a U.S. citizen or permanent resident to whom you are closely related by blood or marriage. As usual, massive documentations of sorts would have to be assembled and be presented to the judge at the hearing to prove such contentions: police records, affidavits of good character from respectable U.S. citizens, and of employment from an employer, records of permanent entry into the U.S, birth and/or marriage certificate, bank books, rent receipts, lease, licenses, church and school records, tax receipts, etc, showing continuous residence in the U.S.

v) If you should fail to appeal the INS Board's FINAL ORDER OF DEPORTATION (or, before that, the INS judge's Order), or fail to appeal on time, you have a right in deportation hearings to, upon application during the proceedings, be deported to any country of your choice (this contrasts with an alien's right in an exclusion case), or you may be granted a right to depart voluntarily (an *ORDER OF VOLUNTARY DEPARTURE) at your own expense, and thus avoid being deported. This is a very important right, the difference being that an alien who is deported requires a special permission by the INS to return to the U.S. in the future, but an alien who leaves voluntarily does not.*

vi) *If all else fails, there's still one ultimate relief that a person facing deportation may seek: you may contact your area's Congressman or Senator and request him or her to introduce a "private immigration bill"* in Congress to relieve you from deportation or to "stay" the deportation or otherwise permit you to stay in the U.S. Upon the introduction of such a bill in Congress for an alien, as a rule, the INS will usually stay the deportation of the alien, and, if the bill is neither voted down nor tabled nor withdrawn, and is acted upon favorably at the close of Congress and signed by the president, the alien beneficiary of the bill is rendered eligible to remain in the United States.

H. A WORD OF ADVICE FOR PERSONS SEEKING ENTRY OR FACING EXCLUSION OR DEPORTATION

To conclude this chapter, certain words of caution seem fitting as a guide for aliens in dealing with the immigration officials at the port of entry for purposes of admission, or in going through an exclusion or deportation proceedings, if need be. Much is often made about the supposed "imperial" powers said to be possessed by immigration officers (and even more so, by the consular officers) over decisions as to whether a visa application is to be granted, or about whether a visa-holding alien gets admitted into the country. True, the fact that the powers granted the immigration officers to exclusively decide on such matters are officially sweeping, cannot at all be disputed. Nevertheless, that aside, it is still most important that an alien facing an official encounter with the immigration officer in any of the above treated contexts should have the proper attitude and the right psychological mind-set for productively dealing with the immigration personnel.

To begin with, it is most important that the alien bears in mind that most immigration officials they encounter at the port of entry (or at exclusion or deportation proceedings or elsewhere) are generally fair-minded; that they are simply workers with no special axe to grind who are employed to do a job, and are honestly attempting to do just that the best way they can.

Sure, the decision as to whether to admit or to exclude a particular alien may often be "discretionary", even "subjective", and is for the most part based on the immigration official's past experiences which are necessarily limited. Nevertheless, in practice, the factual reality has been that by and large in those instances where aliens appear to have been granted special discretionary relief or favorable rulings by immigration officials, certain common denominators appear to have been present. Typically, to approve an admission, the INS officials would look for a showing of certain objective attributes[1] - such as a good moral character, close bona fide family ties in the United States, the existence of certain humanitarian reasons for which admission could be allowed, such as probability of hardship resulting to the alien or close relatives in the event of the alien being excluded or deported, and the like. On the other hand, ***most denials of entry into the U.S. have by and large been based on objective reasons, the most common among them being the following:*** violation of immigration requirements (such as engaging in unauthorized work in the U.S.), being previously excluded or deported from the U.S., entering the U.S. as a visitor but with the seeming intention to remain permanently, making false or contradictory statements and misrepresentations to consular and immigration officers or in connection with present or previous applications for visa, failure to make full disclosure of information regarding political or other associations with those having an ideology deemed unacceptable by the U.S. (e.g., past membership in, say, the Communist or Nazi Party), likelihood of an alien becoming a "public charge" and not being able to financially support himself, physical or mental disease, alcoholism, drug convictions, a record or history of immorality or of unacceptable criminal convic-

---

[1] In deed, the long-standing policy of the INS has been to grant an alien's application for the relief requested, except where there are specific reasons for it to be rejected. And such policy has been reinforced by a widely influential decision by the Board of Immigration Appeals. (See In Matter of Aral, 13 I & N Dec. 49)

tions (or conduct), especially if involving "moral turpitude" (defined as "a crime of baseness, vileness or depravity in the private or social duties" of a person), and so on.

THE POINT OF ALL THIS, SIMPLY, IS THAT aliens facing the port-of-entry admission process should have the psychological mind-set, and project the attitude, that in the final analysis, the decision of the border immigration officer regarding one's admission to (or exclusion from) the United State, will by and large be based on the objective qualities possessed by the alien himself and on the image and background the alien projects to the officer. It is most important that you be absolutely open and truthful with the immigration inspectors (or interviewers); that you be patient, polite, positive and cooperative with them, and be forthcoming in answering their questions. And, though it cannot be said that such attitude will necessarily guarantee that admission will materialize, it will nevertheless guarantee that you will enhance your case and minimize your potential losses and frustrations with the immigration officials.

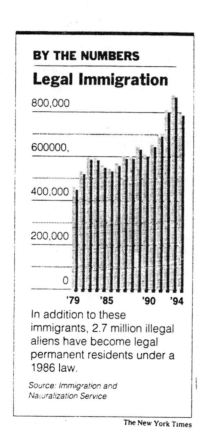

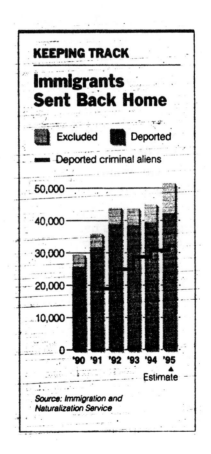

Chapter 23

Alien Labour Certification: The Procedures For Obtaining A Certificate

As has been repeatedly discussed in various parts of this book (see, for example, pp. 79, 88, and "Explanatory Note" on p. 89), a key prerequisite often needed by many aliens who seek admission to the United States, especially those who do so on the basis of employment offers or of labor or skills-related grounds, is what is known as an *approved LABOUR CERTIFICATION*. To put it simply, this is a document obtainable from a U.S. Department of Labor administrator, whereby the administrator states that upon his Department's study of the labor market in the given U.S. area, the Department determines ('certifies') that there are no U.S. citizens or Permanent Resident aliens who are able, willing, available and qualified to do the work the alien seeks, and that the alien's acceptance of the job will not displace a U.S. worker or adversely affect his wages or working conditions.

A. "SCHEDULE A" JOBS: THE JOB CATEGORIES FOR WHICH LABOUR CERTIFICATION MAY NOT BE APPLIED FOR

As structured by the U. S. Government, there are certain specified occupations about which the U.S. Department of Labor (DOL) has determined that qualified U.S. workers are chronically in short supply – that is, that there are NO sufficient U.S. workers (citizens or permanent resident aliens) who are able, willing, qualified and available to do them. Such occupations are listed under what is called **"SCHEDULE A"** of the Department of Labor's *"Pre-certification"* list of occupations. HERE IS THE CENTRAL POINT OF RELEVANCE HERE: for those occupations which fall under schedule A, the alien visa applicant or his U.S. employer does NOT have to file a separate application for labor certification for them. For such occupations (i.e., Schedule A occupations), aliens qualified for them are said to have a **"blanket" labor certification**, that is, an automatic labor certification, and hence the qualified aliens need not themselves personally apply for a labor certification for such occupations, nor do they have to show that they have a U.S. offer of employment. (Another term for such jobs needing no separate certification application, is "pre-certified" jobs).

The reader should be very clear, however, of what is being said here: occupations listed on SCHEDULE A are considered 'pre-certified' in one special sense – in the sense that an alien visa applicant who can establish to the satisfaction of the immigration authorities that he (she) is qualified for such an occupation, is viewed as having been granted automatic ('blanket') labor certification, and so needs not separately or personally apply for a labor certification (nor to show the existence of an offer of employment) before he may proceed to petition for a visa. *The point here is that, while the alien claiming qualification for a Schedule A occupation needs not make a separate, specific independent application for a labor certification issuance, he nevertheless will still have to make an application for the particular Schedule A job in question, and, more importantly, he'll still need to demonstrate to the satisfaction of the immigration officials that he fully meets the qualifications for the particular schedule A job.* Hence, it should be noted, a particular alien's 'pre-certification', or his entitlement to a 'blanket' certification under the Schedule A' occupation, is not necessarily 'automatic' in the ordinary sense as the alien must first prove his qualification for a Schedule A job to the immigration service (or consular officer) on a case-by-case basis.

Occupations and professions designated and listed as Schedule A jobs shift and change frequently from time to time. As of this writing in late 2001, the principal occupations on the current Schedule A list, are as listed in Table 23-A below:

TABLE 23-A
SCHEDULE "A" JOB CLASSIFICATIONS
(No Labor Certification needed)

(a) Physical therapists — people who have the equivalent of an American Bachelor's degree and have been licensed by the U.S. State where they will be working.

(b) Professional nurses who have passed the appropriate licensing examination and are considered to be registered nurses.

B. HOW TO APPLY FOR "PRE-CERTIFICATION" APPROVAL IN SCHEDULE A OCCUPATIONS

The following is a brief summary of the procedure for assuring labor pre-certification (also called 'automatic' or 'blanket' labor certification) in Schedule A occupation situations:

• The alien must (usually) have first applied for a job with his (her) potential U.S. employer and secured a job offer, or a pre-arrangement or some proof thereof that the employer has a "Schedule A" type position available. (Note that the normal formalities involved in the recruiting of U.S. workers (see Section E of this Chapter) do not apply with respect to Schedule A occupations).

• The U.S. employer completes only Part A of the application form, FORM ETA 750; and the alien completes Part B of the form. (See pp. 167-170 for an illustrative sample of this form. Note that when such Schedule A applications are filed, they are often accompanied by a petition for an immigrant employment-based Second or Third PREFERENCE classifications Chapters 14 & 15) and, in some cases, by an application for ADJUSTMENT of status (Chapter 20). When that is the case, then attach the applicable application forms and their supporting documents. See "Explanatory Note" on p. 141).

• All required documentations (most are specified in the instructions on the application Form) are attached to the form listing the job descriptions, working conditions, the alien's qualifications for the particular job sought, etc. To be attached, also, is proof that the employer has a position of "Schedule A" type available.

• The application forms, and all supporting documents, are forwarded to the Immigration and Naturalization Service (INS) office covering the area where the job is located in the U.S., or, in some very limited cases, to the U.S. consul in the alien's home country. NOTE that this particular application is not filed, in this instance, with the local Employment Service Office or the U.S. Department of Labor, as is the case in the regular labor certification cases (Section E below).

• The INS, upon determining that the alien is fully qualified and able to perform the duties for the Schedule A job, will approve the application, or delay it.

• If approved, then the next step for the alien would be for him to now commence the normal procedures for applying for an immigrant visa; if denied, the alien may do one of three things: either seek another route or basis by which to gain eligibility for an immigrant visa other than a job-related basis, or, alternatively, request an APPEAL with the Immigration Service (none could be filed whenever the U.S. consul abroad is the party to whom the application is submitted) for a review or reconsideration of the alien's case, or, thirdly, simply have the employer make, at once, a regular labor certification application for the job to the local Employment Service in the U.S. (see Section E below) without having to wait for the regular 6-month waiting period.

(The detailed procedures by which the overwhelming majority of Labor Certification applications are made by or for aliens, are outlined in Section E of this Chapter).

C. SCHEDULE "B" JOBS: THE JOB CATEGORIES FOR WHICH NO LABOR CERTIFICATE MAYBE ISSUED

To put it simply, "SCHEDULE B" occupations are exactly the opposite of the "Schedule A" occupations just discussed in Sections A & B above. In other words, this schedule contains occupations about which the U.S. Department of Labor has determined that there are generally sufficient U.S. workers who are able, willing, qualified and available to do them, and for which the DOL will therefore not entertain any application for its issuance. Schedule B normally covers the skilled, semiskilled and unskilled worker, as can be seen from the listing below. *HERE'S WHAT IS IMPORTANT ABOUT IT, THOUGH: ordinarily, an alien labor certification CANNOT be applied for or granted for Schedule B occupations.*

That is the general rule – the "theory" of it all. But wait a minute. Is that the end of the story? Not at all! In practice, you (basically your employer) still may be able to apply and to get labor certification for a Schedule B job – if you have the "right" conditions. **HERE'S THE KEY RULE:** If your prospective U.S. employer can show that he or she has tried exhaustively to obtain a worker for the Section B job·involved but without success in finding one, then, in that event, he is permitted to apply for a "waiver" that, in effect, frees him to go ahead and apply for an "affirmative" labor certification for the job. To put it in a different way, *the central key is to be able to make a credible case (or, more accurately, a documented case) that a prospective employer has not been able to find, at the prevailing wages and working conditions, a United States worker for the occupation he seeks to fill!* A prospective U.S. employer able to present such a situation, may apply for a waiver of the general rule regarding Schedule B jobs and, with that, the door is wide open for him to apply for the "affirmative" labor certification for the Schedule B job in question.

What follows below are the jobs currently designated under SCHEDULE B, and their descriptions.

TABLE 23-B
SCHEDULE "B" JOB CLASSIFICATIONS
(LIST AND DESCRIPTION OF THE JOBS ON SCHEDULE "B")

(1) *"Assemblers"* perform one or more repetitive tasks to assemble components and subassemblies using hand or power tools to mass produce a variety of components, products or equipment. They perform such activities as riveting, drilling, filing, bolting, soldering, spot welding, cementing, gluing, cutting and fitting. They may use clamps or other work aids to hold parts during assembly, inspect or test components, or tend previously set-up or automatic machines.

(2) *"Attendants, Parking Lot."* Park automobiles for customers in parking lots or garages and may collect fees based on time span of parking.

(3) *"Attendants (Service Workers such as Personal Service Attendants, Amusement and Recreation Service At-*

tendants)" perform a variety of routine tasks attending to the personal needs of customers at such places as amusement parks, bath houses, clothing checkrooms, and dressing rooms, including such tasks as taking and issuing tickets, checking and issuing clothing and supplies, cleaning premises and equipment, answering inquiries, checking lists, and maintaining simple records.

(4) *"Automobile Service Station Attendants"* service automotive vehicles with fuel, lubricants, and automotive accessories at drive-in service facilities; may also compute charges and collect fees from customers.

(5) *"Bartenders"* prepare, mix, and dispense alcoholic beverages for consumption by bar customers, and compute and collect charges for drinks.

(6) *"Bookkeepers"* keep records of one facet of an establishment's financial transactions by maintaining one set of books; specialize in such areas as accounts payable, accounts receivable, or interest accrued, rather than a complete set of records.

(7) *"Caretakers"* perform a combination of duties to keep a private home clean and in good condition, such as cleaning and dusting furniture and furnishings, hallways and lavatories; beating, vacuuming, and scrubbing rugs; washing windows, waxing and polishing floors; removing and hanging draperies; cleaning and oiling furnaces and other equipment; repairing mechanical and electrical appliances; and painting.

(8) *"Cashiers"* receive payments made by customers for goods or services, make change, give receipts, operate cash registers, balance cash accounts, prepare bank deposits and perform other related duties.

(9) *"Charworkers and Cleaners"* keep the premises of commercial establishments, office buildings, or apartment houses in clean and orderly condition by performing, according to a set routine, such tasks as mopping and sweeping floors, dusting and polishing furniture and fixtures, and vacuuming rugs.

(10) *"Chauffeurs and Taxicab Drivers"* drive automobiles to convey passengers according to the passengers' instructions.

(11) *"Cleaners, Hotel and Motel"* clean hotel rooms and halls, sweep and mop floors, dust furniture, empty wastebaskets, and make beds.

(12) *"Clerks, General"* perform a variety of routine clerical tasks not requiring knowledge of systems or procedures such as copying and posting data, proofreading records or forms, counting, weighing, or measuring material, routing correspondence, answering telephones, conveying messages, and running errands.

(13) *"Clerks, Hotel"* perform a variety of routine tasks to serve hotel guests, such as registering guests, dispensing keys, distributing mail, collecting payments, and adjusting complaints.

(14) *"Clerks and Checkers, Grocery Stores"* itemize, total, and receive payments for purchases in grocery stores, usually using cash registers; often assist customers in locating items, stock shelves, and keep stock control and sales transaction records.

(15) *"Clerk Typists"* perform general clerical work which, for the majority of duties, requires the use of typewriters; perform such activities as typing reports, bills, application forms, shipping tickets, and other matters from clerical records, filing records and reports, posting information to records, sorting and distributing mail, answering phones and similar duties.

(16) *"Cooks-Short Order"* prepare and cook to order all kinds of short-preparation-time foods; may perform such activities as carving meats, filling orders from a steam-table, preparing sandwiches, salads and beverages, and serving meals over a counter.

(17) *"Counter and Fountain Workers"* serve food to patrons at lunchroom counters, cafeterias, soda fountains, or similar public eating places; take orders from customers and frequently prepare simple items, such as dessert dishes; itemize and total checks; receive payment and make change; clean work areas and equipment.

(18) *"Dining Room Attendants"* facilitate food service in eating places by performing such tasks as removing dirty dishes, replenishing linen and silver supplies, serving water and butter to patrons, and cleaning and polishing equipment.

(19) *"Electric Truck Operators"* drive gasoline-or electric-powered industrial trucks or tractors equipped with forklift, elevating platform, or trailer hitch to move and stack equipment and materials in a warehouse, storage yard, or factory.

(20) *"Elevator Operators"* operate elevators to transport passengers and freight between building floors.

(21) *"Floorworkers "* perform a variety of routine tasks in support of other workers in and around such work sites as factory floors and service areas, frequently at the beck and call of others; perform such tasks as cleaning floors, materials and equipment, distributing materials and tools to workers, running errands, delivering messages, emptying containers, and removing materials from work areas to storage or shipping areas.

(22) *"Groundskeepers"* maintain grounds of industrial, commercial, or public property in good condition by performing such tasks as cutting lawns, trimming hedges, pruning trees, repairing fences, planting flowers, and shoveling snow.

(23) *"Guards"* guard and patrol premises of industrial or business establishments or similar types of property to prevent theft and other crimes and prevent possible injury to others.

(24) *"Helpers (any industry)"* perform a variety of duties to assist other workers who are usually of a higher level of competency or expertness by furnishing such workers with materials, tools, and supplies, cleaning work areas, machines and equipment, feeding or offbearing machines, and/or holding materials or tools.

(25) *"Hotel Cleaners"* perform routine tasks to keep hotel premises neat and clean such as cleaning rugs, washing walls, ceilings and windows, moving furniture, mopping and waxing floors and polishing metalware.

(26) *"Household Domestic Service Workers"* perform a variety of tasks in private households, such as cleaning, dusting, washing, ironing, making beds, maintaining clothes, marketing, cooking, serving food, and caring for children or disabled persons. This definition, however, applies only to workers who have had less than one year of documented full-time paid experience in the tasks to be performed, working on a live-in or live-out basis in private households or in public or private institutions or establishments where the worker has performed tasks equivalent to tasks normally associated with the maintenance of a private household. This definition does not include household workers who primarily provide health or instructional services.

(27) *"Housekeepers"* supervise workers engaged in maintaining interiors of commercial or residential buildings in a clean and orderly fashion, assign duties to cleaners (hotel and motel), charworkers, and hotel cleaners, inspect finished work, and maintain supplies of equipment and materials.

(28) *"Janitors"* keep hotels, office buildings, apartment houses, or similar buildings in clean and orderly condition, and tend furnaces and boilers to provide heat and hot water; perform such tasks as sweeping and mopping floors, emptying trash containers, and doing minor painting and plumbing repairs; often maintain their residence at their places of work.

(29) *"Keypunch Operators"*, using machines similar in action to typewriters, punch holes in cards in such a position that each hole can be identified as representing a specific item of information. These punched cards may be used with electronic computers or tabulating machines.

(30) *"Kitchen Workers"* perform routine tasks in the kitchens of restaurants. Their primary responsibility is to maintain work areas and equipment in a clean and orderly fashion by performing such tasks as mopping floors, removing trash, washing pots and pans, transferring supplies and equipment, and washing and peeling vegetables.

(31) *"Laborers, Common"* perform routine tasks, upon instructions and according to set routine, in an industrial, construction or manufacturing environment such as loading and moving equipment and supplies, cleaning work areas, and distributing tools.

(32) *"Laborers, Farm"* plant, cultivate, and harvest farm products, following the instructions of supervisors, often working as members of a team. Their typical tasks are watering and feeding livestock, picking fruit and vegetables, and cleaning storage areas and equipment.

(33) *"Laborers, Mine"* perform routine tasks in underground or surface mines, pits, or quarries, or at tipples, mills,

or preparation plants such as cleaning work areas, shoveling coal onto conveyors, pushing mine cars from working faces to haulage roads, and loading or sorting materials onto wheelbarrows.

(34) *"Loopers and Toppers"* (i) tend machines that shear nap, loose threads, and knots from cloth surfaces to give uniform finish and texture, (ii) operate looping machines to close openings in the toes of seamless hose or join knitted garment parts, (iii) loop stitches or ribbed garment parts on the points of transfer bars to facilitate the transfer of garment parts to the needles of knitting machines.

(35) *"Material Handlers"* load, unload, and convey materials within or near plants, yards, or worksites under specific instructions.

(36) *"Nurses' Aides and Orderlies"* assist in the care of hospital patients by performing such activities as bathing, dressing and undressing patients and giving alcohol rubs, serving and collecting food trays, cleaning and shaving hair from the skin areas of operative cases, lifting patients onto and from beds, transporting patients to treatment units, changing bed linens, running errands, and directing visitors.

(37) *"Packers, Markers, Bottlers, and Related"* pack products into containers, such as cartons or crates, mark identifying information on articles, insure that filled bottles are properly sealed and marked, often working in teams on or at end of assembly lines.

(38) *"Porters"* (i) carry baggage by hand or handtruck for airline, railroad or bus passengers, and perform related personal services in and around public transportation environments.
(ii) Keep building premises, working areas in production departments of industrial organizations, or similar sites in clean and orderly condition.

(39) *"Receptionists"* receive clients or customers coming into establishments, ascertain their wants, and direct them accordingly; perform such activities as arranging appointments, directing callers to their destinations, recording names, times, nature of business and persons seen and answering phones.

(40) *"Sailors and Deck Hands"* stand deck watches and perform a variety of tasks to preserve painted surfaces of ships and to maintain lines, running gear, and cargo handling gear in safe operating condition; perform such tasks as mopping decks, chipping rust, painting chipped areas, and splicing rope.

(41) *"Sales Clerks, General"* receive payment for merchandise in retail establishments, wrap or bag merchandise, and keep shelves stocked.

(42) *"Sewing Machine Operators and Hand-Stitchers"* (i) operate single- or multiple-needle sewing machines to join parts in the manufacture of such products as awnings, carpets, and gloves; specialize in one type of sewing machine limited to joining operations; (ii) join and reinforce parts of articles such as garments and curtains, sew button-holes and attach fasteners to such articles, or sew decorative trimmings on such articles, using needles and threads.

(43) *"Stock Room and Warehouse Workers"* receive, store, ship, and distribute materials, tools, equipment, and products within establishments as directed by others.

(44) *"Streetcar and Bus Conductors"* collect fares or tickets from passengers, issue transfers, open and close doors, announce stops, answer questions, and signal operators to start or stop.

(45) *"Telephone Operators"* operate telephone switchboards to relay incoming and internal calls to phones in an establishment, and make connections with external lines for outgoing calls; often take messages, supply information and keep records of calls and charges; often are involved primarily in establishing, or aiding telephone users in establishing, local or long distance telephone connections.

(46) *"Truck Drivers and Tractor Drivers"* (i) drive trucks to transport materials, merchandise, equipment or people to and from specified destinations, such as plants, railroad stations, and offices; (ii) Drive tractors to move materials, draw implements, pull out objects imbedded in the ground, or pull cables of winches to raise, lower, or load heavy materials or equipment.

(47) *"Typists, Lesser Skilled"* type straight-copy material, such as letters, reports, stencils, and addresses, from drafts or corrected copies. They are not required to prepare materials involving the understanding of complicated technical terminology, the arrangement and setting of complex tabular detail or similar items. Their typing speed in English does not exceed 52 words per minute on a manual typewriter and/or 60 words per minute on an electric typewriter and their error rate is 12 or more errors per 5 minute typing period on representative business correspondence.

(48) *"Ushers (Recreation and Amusement)"* assist patrons at entertainment events to find seats, search for lost articles, and locate facilities.

(49) *"Yard Workers"* maintain the grounds of private residences in good order by performing such tasks as mowing and watering lawns, planting flowers and shrubs, and repairing and painting fences. They work on the instructions of private employers.

D. CLASSES OF IMMIGRANTS WHO NEED TO HAVE LABOUR CERTIFICATION

In the first instance, a central point to remember is this: that with perhaps one exception, namely with respect to the H-2 temporary worker labor visa classification, certification does not apply to any alien or visa category of nonimmigrant classification. It applies only to aliens seeking to become Permanent Residents of the United States – that is, to IMMIGRANT or "GREEN CARD" applicants. (See Chapter 2; Procedures for obtaining the *Nonimmigrant* type of visas is the subject matter of Volume One of this manual).

The second point of relevance to remember in this regard, is that, by and large, the alien who needs a Labor Certification shall have probably lacked the other bases that are provided under the law for immigrant visa eligibility other than the work-related basis-namely, he shall have probably lacked the family-oriented, or "special immigrant" or refugee grounds for eligibility (see, for example, the bases for green card eligibility provided under Chapters 6 thru. 12, 16 thru. 19).

Thirdly, the labor certification process essentially applies mostly to the SECOND and THIRD preference categories within the employment-based immigrant visa preference classes (see Chapter 14 & 15).

To summarize, the following are the classes of aliens needing a labor certification in qualifying for an immigrant visa:

i) Aliens failing under the SECOND PREFERENCE category outlined in Chapter 14 (members of the professions or persons of exceptional ability in the sciences and the arts); and

ii) Aliens failing under the THIRD PREFERENCE category outlined in Chapter 15 (skilled and unskilled workers including Scheduled B workers, for which there's shortage in the U.S.)

E. STEP-BY-STEP PROCEDURES FOR APPLYING FOR AN AFFIRMATIVE LABOUR CERTIFICATION

The following is a summary of the applicable procedures for obtaining an "affirmative" labor certification:

FIRST: The employer-to-be in the U.S. fills out in duplicate the Department of Labor's (DOL's) FORM ETA 750, Part A, while the alien job applicant fills out Part B of the form. (Pick up this Form free of charge at your state's local Employment Service Office, for which the main offices are listed in appendix C, or at U.S. consular offices abroad. Illustrative sample of the form is reproduced at pp. 167 & 169).

SECOND: The U.S. employer (actual or prospective) submits ("files") the form at no charge, with all necessary supporting documentary evidence fully attached, to the local State Employment Service Office covering the area wherein the job is located. Include also among the submissions (except if Schedule A or Household domestic jobs are involved) a copy of signed statement by the employer, the POSTED NOTICE (see sample copy on p.171).

THIRD: The local State Employment Service Office reviews the application and the supporting documents, with particular attention paid to verifying the minimum requirements and wages. If the job appears to the reviewer to be a "Schedule B" type job (this is not applicable to "Schedule A" jobs), the Employment Service will notify the employer that he must advertise the job and try to find a U.S. worker for the position.

Assuming that the application is alright, the Employment Service will write up a job order for the position, assign a "JOB ORDER NUMBER" to it, and list the job with the Service's Job bank" for 30 days, during which period the Service will try to find a qualified U.S. worker to fill the job. However, if the application is found unacceptable, the Employment Service may return the application to the employer for correction, or for additional documentation or information.

FOURTH: It is possible for an employer to get a "reduction" or a "waiver" permitting him to suspend further recruitment efforts early on in the process. If, for example, you (i.e. the employer) have made sufficient recruitment efforts before you filed the labor application, you can request (by including a letter of request to that effect with the application) that additional recruiting by the Employment Service be reduced. [You will have to supply extensive documentation and other proof (copies of the advertisements, letters of previous experience at recruiting posted notices, etc.) showing that you made sufficient test of the labor market and had no luck in filling the job opening, and showing that further recruiting effort on your part is unlikely to locate a qualified U.S. worker. Note that no "reduction" can be made for any job on Schedule B, however].

NOTE: The employer often has an option to try to find a U.S. worker before he files the application with the Employment Service. Nevertheless, he runs the risk that the Employment Service may not accept the recruitment effort as satisfactory, or that he may later be required to advertise the job. This will prolong the processing time.

FIFTH: Should the Employment Service be unsatisfied with the adequacy of the recruitment effort already made by the employer at finding a U.S. worker, it may require further advertising of the job. The employer may be required to advertise in a local newspaper, professional journal, or whatever other medium that is most used for the particular occupation, all within 30 days of the labor application filing date. (To save yourself the expense of possibly having to re-run a job advertisement, it is often advisable to first cheek with the Employment Service for the requirements).

SIXTH: Upon satisfaction that sufficient U.S. recruitment effort have been made by the employer (recruitment efforts do not apply in Schedule A jobs), the Employment Service forwards the labor application, including the employer's report of his recruiting efforts and the supporting documentations thereof, to the Regional Office of the U.S. Department of Labor (DOL) for the area where the job is to be performed.

SEVENTH: The DOL certifying officer reviews the labor application. It may issue a NOTICE OF APPROVAL (if the certifying officer is satisfied from the facts of the case that sufficient recruitment efforts had been made, and that no qualified U.S. applicants either did apply or met the minimum qualifications), thereby granting the labor certification. (See samples on pp. 172 & 174)

Alternatively, the DOL's certifying officer may issue a notice that the application is unsatisfactory and spell out the basis on which it is so determined, and allow the said employer a specified amount of time within which to correct the deficiencies named by the certifying officer. The employer may attempt to make such correction of the specified deficiencies by sending a letter and supplying additional documents (a "rebuttal" response) to show why he nevertheless deems it deserving that the labor certification be issued. Now, if the employer's rebuttal response adequately corrects or addresses the deficiencies to the certifying officer's satisfaction, a Labor Certification will be issued. If not, the certifying officer will at this point issue a **FINAL DETERMINATION** denying the granting of labor certificate.

EIGHT: If certification is denied, the employer has the right, if he so chooses (and if he had sent in a rebuttal response on time), to make an **APPEAL** of the "Final Determination" to an Administrative Law Judge of the Department of Labor in Washington D.C. To do this, it will be sufficient if the employer makes a request in writing for a review of the denial detailing his grounds, and sends it by certified mail to the address listed on the Final Determination notice <u>within</u> the time allowed for such an appeal. Be forewarned, however, that such appeals rarely succeed, if ever!

F. POINTERS FOR SUCCESSFULLY APPLYING FOR A LABOR CERTIFICATION

Certain "practice pointers" (some call it 'trade secrets') that are often better known to lawyers and immigration consultants and other practitioners in the field, may be helpful in enabling the intending U.S. employer or the alien to file a more successful or smoother-running Labor Certificate application.

Among the major ones are the following:

• It cannot be emphasized enough: the crucial key for success in any labor certification filing, is *presentation of adequate supporting documentations.* Most applications fail or succeed based on this factor. Documentation is required showing that the alien has the necessary training and previous experience to qualify for the job in question: letters and affidavits from former tutors or employers or recognized experts in the field all testifying to the alien's technical training or specialized experience; copies of licenses held; copies of school diplomas and other records received; published materials by or about the alien; copies of advertisements and proof of other recruiting efforts for the job, if any, etc. *In a word, the more massive the documentation you can supply, the better!*

• It's helpful to include in the labor certification application (except for Schedule A or Household Domestic jobs), the following additional documents: a copy of the POSTED NOTICE (see a sample on p. 171), and a copy of the alien's PROOF OF PRIOR EXPERIENCE signed by the employer (see a sample on pp. 176 & 177)

• *Give a lot of advance thought and advance planning to each and every step and requirement involved* in the labor application. For example, think through what the term "job description" should entail in your particular case. As no two jobs or aliens are ever exactly alike, you (and/or the alien) should endeavor to prepare a set of papers, personality profiles, educational, training and job experience, that will be unique for the job being offered. Think of any special attributes possessed or equipment operated by the alien – some skills or knowledge not usually found among U.S. workers, e.g. knowledge of a foreign language, a foreign dance or culture, or the ability to prepare foreign dishes.

• Preferably, seek to fill occupations for which U.S. workers are traditionally not readily available at the "prevailing wages"- live-in domestic workers, welders, or auto mechanics, for example. (The local Employment Service could help with information about a job's "prevailing wages" for your area).

• In working up the requirements, the descriptions and duties of particular jobs or the description for the position the alien seeks to fill, consider consulting the **DICTIONARY OF OCCUPATIONAL TITLES (DOT)** – a widely accepted guide published by the U.S. Department of Labor and generally available in public libraries and at local Employment Service Offices.

• If the job being offered involves a "combination of duties" – that is, if it either calls for two separate job titles in the DOT (e.g. chauffeur/mechanic), or calls for duties from two jobs (say, an accountant's position whose duties includes answering the phone and serving as a receptionist) – then, papers must be attached to the application showing why such an arrangement is necessary, a so-called 'BUSINESS NECESSITY' letter of justification. A 'Business Necessity' letter of explanation should also be attached when the job being offered has a description or requirement significantly different from that found in the DOT. (See illustrative sample copy of a "combination of duties" letter on p.171, and of a business necessity letter on p. 179).

• When the position involved is a Household Domestic Worker title: note that, as a rule, virtually all present-day labor certification applications for such workers now contain a "live-in" requirement in the employer's job description, for it has become common knowledge that U.S. workers would usually be available to fill such a position when no live-in condition is required.

• The employer's recruitment effort should include whatever normal and usual methods that are used to find workers for the position involved: advertisement in professional, trade or ethnic publication, depending on the nature of the job involved; listing among associates and employment agencies, newspaper advertising (required in almost all cases), and if such job is unionized and the union is a customary source of jobs for workers, then an arrangement may have to be made with the union for it to refer applicants.

• A very wise practice idea is to consult with and discuss the job description, wage offer, and your plans for recruiting with the local Employment Service – *even BEFORE you ever start anything*. This way, you will be able to get an official guidance on what would constitute an approvable recruiting effort or methods, the methods by which to advertise, and so on. It could possibly save you a lot of unnecessary expenses or wasted efforts down the road!

• Finally, if you should receive the DOL's NOTICE OF FINDING and it appears to you (from the seriousness or weight of the evidence outlined thereof) that your application simply has no chance of being approved, then seriously consider withdrawing the whole application immediately. Submit a letter of its withdrawal at once – that is, BEFORE you can get the Final Determination notice. The significance of this has to do with *a rule that every one should be aware of, namely, that once a Final Determination is issued denying an application, and the reason is for anything other than that the wage offered was below the prevailing wage, then the employer is prohibited from filing another labor certification application for the same job opening for 6 months as from the date of the denial*. Hence, by withdrawing the application in advance, you will be able to avoid the 6 months waiting period to re-file. (A sample NOTICE OF FINDING is reproduced on p. 173).

G. THE SIGNIFICANCE OF HAVING A LABOR CERTIFICATION IN HAND:
   IT ONLY PUTS YOU IN A POSITION TO BEGIN THE PETITION FOR A VISA.

The process involved in merely trying to obtain an alien labor certification could often be so tedious, complex and prolonged for the average applicant. Consequently, it is no wonder, then, that many aliens and U.S. employers who have gone through the grueling certification process, often have the tendency to instinctively view the labor certification application as the actual petition for the visa itself.

The true reality needs to be borne in mind, however. *All that the issuance of a labor certification document means or represents is this: an official confirmation to the Immigration and Naturalization Service – the only agency having the responsibility to decide on your eligibility for issuance of a visa – that, in the judgment of the Department of Labor Officials, there is truly no American worker readily willing or available to fill a particular job opening for which you, an alien, indicated an interest in or qualification for.*

THAT'S ALL THAT THE LABOR CERTIFICATION MEANS, IN ESSENCE! In fact, certification does not even touch upon or address the issue of whether or not you are or will be ultimately found to be, eligible for issuance of a visa itself. For, the fact is that when you eventually get to "petition" for an immigrant visa, it will be to a different agency altogether that you will apply to, namely to the Immigration and Naturalization Service (INS), and not to the Department of Labor (DOL).

In deed, one other additional point of relevance ought to be borne in mind in this connection, and that is that, according to the courts' interpretations in many legal decisions* while the DOL's certification may carry a great deal of influence with the INS, *such certification is nevertheless not binding on the INS, and the INS may (and does), if and when it pleases, re-evaluate the basis of such labor certification and may invalidate a certification for a number of grounds* — fraud or willful misrepresentation of facts made in an underlying application, or a holding that the prospective employer will be unable to pay the prevailing wage, or simply that the alien is judged unqualified for the position in question.*

The central point of all these, then, is simple. It is simply to say that we should remind ourselves always that, even at best, the fundamental task of hopefully securing a Second or Third preference immigrant visa to the U.S. is only just begun, even with the securing of an approved LABOUR CERTIFICATION. With the Labor Certificate obtained, the alien and/or the U.S. employer, is only then in a position to BEGIN to file his petition for the real thing – the visa itself. And, now it's time you get on with it!

NOTE: It's most important that you be reminded that the law was changed as recently as June 20, 1986. Thus, effective thereafter, the new rule is that anyone who files for and receives labor certification from the 'Department of Labor, must file the visa petition (Form 1-140) within 60 days of receiving certification even if a visa number is not available. And if this is not done, the person will lose his "priority date" for a visa number which was established when the certification application was filed with the DOL.

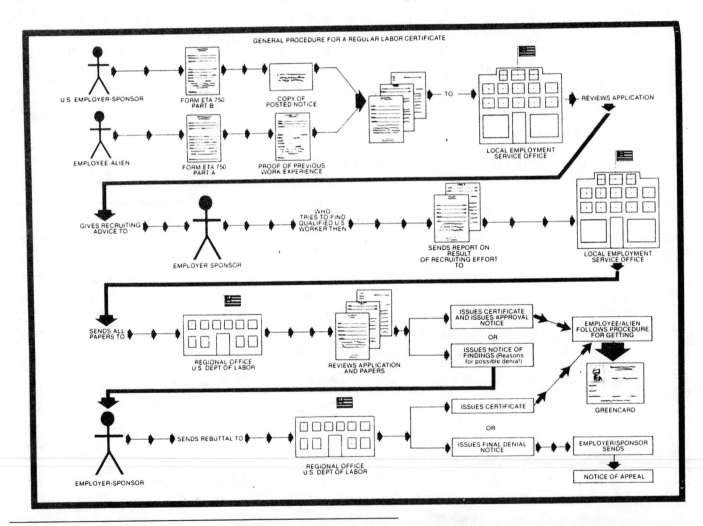

*In Madany v. Smith. 696 F.2d 1008 (D.C. Cir. 1983), the court. addressing the issue of INS authority to review an alien's qualification following an approved labour certification. held that the INS is not statutorily bound by the conclusions of the Dept. of Labor. and reasons that the DOL looks solely to the position offered when issuing a labour certification. while the INS looks to the individual seeking to fill the position when granting. at the time. a Third or Sixth preference petition.

167

ETA 750A (Part A)

p.1

U.S. DEPARTMENT OF LABOR
Employment and Training Administration

SAMPLE

FORM ETA 750A

APPLICATION FOR ALIEN EMPLOYMENT CERTIFICATION

IMPORTANT: READ CAREFULLY BEFORE COMPLETING THIS FORM

PRINT legibly in ink or use a typewriter. If you need more space to answer questions on this form, use a separate sheet. Identify each answer with the number of the corresponding question. SIGN AND DATE each sheet in original signature.

To knowingly furnish any false information in the preparation of this form and any supplement thereto or to aid, abet, or counsel another to do so is a felony punishable by $10,000 fine or 5 years in the penitentiary, or (18 U.S.C. 1001).

PART A. OFFER OF EMPLOYMENT

1. Name of Alien *(Family name in capital letter, First, Middle, Maiden)*	Arun

2. Present Address of Alien *(Number, Street, City and Town, State ZIP Code or Province, Country)*	3. Type of Visa *(If in U.S.)*
▓▓ Shields ▓▓, Fort Collins, Colorado, ▓▓, USA	F-1 (practical training)

The following information is submitted as evidence of an offer of employment.

4. Name of Employer *(Full name of organization)*	5. Telephone *(Area Code and Number)*
▓▓▓▓., Colorado ▓▓▓▓ Operation	303- ▓▓

6. Address *(Number, Street, City or Town, Country, State, ZIP Code)*
▓▓ Harmony Road, Fort Collins, Colorado,

NOTE: Refer to "Explanatory Note" on p. 89, esp. paragraph 3

7. Address Where Alien Will Work *(if different from Item 6)*
N/A

8. Nature of Employer's Business Activity	9. Name of Job Title	10. Total Hours Per Week		11. Work Schedule *(Hourly)*	12. Rate of Pay	
		a. Basic	b. Overtime		a. Basic	b. Overtime
Manufacturer of computers, peripherals & software, electronic equip, etc.	Development Engineer (Software)	40	--	8:00 a.m. 5:00 p.m.	$ 30,240 per year	$ -- per hour

13. Describe Fully the Job to be Performed *(Duties)*

Architect, design and develop advanced networking and operating system software on UNIX-based technical workstations, using C language; apply strong academic background in operating systems, networking, UNIX and C language to 2K NCSS (2,000 Non-Commented Source Statement) operating system and networking-related software products.

D.O.T. 003.167-062

14. State in detail the MINIMUM education, training, and experience for a worker to perform satisfactorily the job duties described in Item 13 above.					15. Other Special Requirements
EDU-CATION *(Enter number of years)*	Grade School	High School	College	College Degree Required *(specify)* Bachelor and Master	
	6	6	6	Major Field of Study Computer Science	
TRAINING	No. Yrs.	No. Mos.		Type of Training	
EXPERIENCE	Job Offered	Related Occupation		Related Occupation *(specify)*	
	Number				
	Yrs.	Mos.	Yrs.	Mos.	
	0				

16. Occupational Title of Person Who Will Be Alien's Immediate Supervisor	➤ Project Manager	17. Number of Employees Alien will Supervise	➤ 0

◄ **ENDORSEMENTS** *(Make no entry in section - for government use only)*

Date Forms Received	
L.O. MAY 0 2 1985	S.O.
R.O. 6/19/85	N.O.
Ind. Code 35	Occ. Code 003167062
Occ. Title Development Engineer	

CERTIFICATION

PURSUANT TO THE PROVISIONS OF SECTION 212 (A) (14) OF THE IMMIGRATION AND NATIONALITY ACT AS AMENDED I HEREBY CERTIFY THAT THERE ARE NOT SUFFICIENT U.S. WORKERS AVAILABLE AND THE EMPLOYMENT OF THE ABOVE WILL NOT ADVERSELY AFFECT THE WAGES AND WORKING CONDITIONS OF WORKERS IN THE U.S. SIMILARLY EMPLOYED.

10/8/85   Charles G. Vigil

Replaces MA 7-50A, B and C (Apr. 1970 edition) which is obsolete.

ETA 750 (Oct. 1979)

—OVER— ➤

FORM ETA 750-A

168 P.2

18. COMPLETE ITEMS ONLY IF JOB IS TEMPORARY			19. IF JOB IS UNIONIZED (Complete)	
a. No. of Openings To Be Filled By Aliens Under Job Offer	b. Exact Dates You Expect To Employ Alien		a. Number of Local	b. Name of Local
	From	To		
N/A				c. City and State

20. STATEMENT FOR LIVE-AT-WORK JOB OFFERS (Complete for Private Household Job ONLY)						
a. Description of Residence		b. No. Persons Residing at Place of Employment				c. Will free board and private room not shared with anyone be provided? ("X" one)
("X" one)	Number of Rooms	Adults	Children		Ages	☐ YES ☐ NO
☐ House			BOYS			
☐ Apartment	N/A		GIRLS			

21. DESCRIBE EFFORTS TO RECRUIT U.S. WORKERS AND THE RESULTS. *(Specify Sources of Recruitment by Name)*

Employer has and will conduct such recruitment efforts as are appropriate and normal to the industry and customary for this company.

22. Applications require various types of documentation. Please read PART II of the instructions to assure that appropriate supporting documentation is included with your application.

23. EMPLOYER CERTIFICATIONS

By virtue of my signature below, I HEREBY CERTIFY the following conditions of employment.

a. I have enough funds available to pay the wage or salary offered the alien.

b. The wage offered equals or exceeds the prevailing wage and I guarantee that, if a labor certification is granted, the wage paid to the alien when the alien begins work will equal or exceed the prevailing wage which is applicable at the time the alien begins work.

c. The wage offered is not based on commissions, bonuses, or other incentives, unless I guarantee a wage paid on a weekly, bi-weekly or monthly basis.

d. I will be able to place the alien on the payroll on or before the date of the alien's proposed entrance into the United States.

e. The job opportunity does not involve unlawful discrimination by race, creed, color, national origin, age, sex, religion, handicap, or citizenship.

f. The job opportunity is not:

(1) Vacant because the former occupant is on strike or is being locked out in the course of a labor dispute involving a work stoppage.

(2) At issue in a labor dispute involving a work stoppage.

g. The job opportunity's terms, conditions and occupational environment are not contrary to Federal, State or local law.

h. The job opportunity has been and is clearly open to any qualified U.S. worker.

24. DECLARATIONS

DECLARATION OF EMPLOYER ▶ Pursuant to 28 U.S.C. 1746, I declare under penalty of perjury the foregoing is true and correct.	
SIGNATURE	DATE 4-22-85
NAME (Type or Print) ████ Company By Marlene ████	TITLE Personnel Representative

AUTHORIZATION OF AGENT OF EMPLOYER ▶ I HEREBY DESIGNATE the agent below to represent me for the purposes of labor certification and I TAKE FULL RESPONSIBILITY for accuracy of any representations made by my agent.	
SIGNATURE OF EMPLOYER	DATE 4-22-85
NAME OF AGENT (Type or Print) C. James Cooper, Jr.	ADDRESS OF AGENT (Number, Street, City, State, ZIP Code) 999 Eighteenth Street, Suite 3220 Denver, Colorado 80202

-OVER- ➡

ETA 750B (Part B)

P.3

| PART B. | STATEMENT OF QUALIFICATIONS OF ALIEN |

FOR ADVICE CONCERNING REQUIREMENTS FOR ALIEN EMPLOYMENT CERTIFICATION: *If alien is in the U.S., contact nearest office of Immigration and Naturalization Service. If alien is outside U.S., contact nearest U.S. Consulate.*

IMPORTANT: READ ATTACHED INSTRUCTIONS BEFORE COMPLETING THIS FORM.

...int legibly in ink or use a typewriter. If you need more space to fully answer any questions on this form, use a separate sheet. Identify each answer with the number of the corresponding question. Sign and date each sheet.

1. Name of Alien (Family name in capital letters) — First name: Arun — Middle name: NMN — Maiden name: N/A

2. Present Address (No., Street, City or Town, State or Province and ZIP Code): ___. Shields, ___, Fort Collins, Colorado, ___ USA — Country — **3. Type of Visa (If in U.S.)** F-1 (prac. training)

4. Alien's Birthdate (Month, Day, Year): 9/17/61 — **5. Birthplace** (City or Town, State or Province): Southampton — Country: United Kingdom — **6. Present Nationality or Citizenship (Country):** Indian

7. Address In United States Where Alien Will Reside: ___. Shields, Rd, Fort collins, Colorado, ___, USA

8. Name and Address of Prospective Employer If Alien has job offer in U.S.: ___., Colorado ___ Operation — **9. Occupation in which Alien is Seeking Work:** Development Engineer (Software)

10. "X" the appropriate box below and furnish the information required for the box marked

a. ☐ Alien will apply for a visa abroad at the American Consulate in — City in Foreign Country — Foreign Country

b. ☒ Alien is in the United States and will apply for adjustment of status to that of a lawful permanent resident in the office of the Immigration and Naturalization Service at — City: Denver — State: Colorado

11. Names and Addresses of Schools, Colleges and Universities Attended

Schools	Field of Study	FROM Month/Year	TO Month/Year	Degrees or Certificate Received
Ohio State University Columbus, Ohio	Computer Science	Sept. 1983	Dec. 1984	M.S.
Indian Inst. of Tech. Kanpur, India	Computer Science	Aug. 1978	May 1983	B.Tech.
Colvin Talugdars Coll. Lucknow, India	Maths, Science	July 1975	July 1977	Graduated

SPECIAL QUALIFICATIONS AND SKILLS

12. Additional Qualifications and Skills Alien Possesses and Proficiency in the use of Tools, Machines or Equipment Which Would Help Establish if Alien Meets Requirements for Occupation in Item 9.

N/A

13. List Licenses (Professional, Journeyman, etc.)

N/A

14. List Documents Attached Which are Submitted as Evidence that Alien Possesses the Education, Training, Experience, and Abilities Represented

Diploma - school transcript

Endorsements — DATE REC. DOL — O.T. & C.

(Make no entry in this section — FOR Government Agency USE ONLY)

(Items continued on next page)

-OVER-→

FORM ETA 750-B

15. WORK EXPERIENCE. List all jobs held during past three (3) years. Also, list any other jobs related to the occupation, seeking certification as indicated in Item 9.   P.4

a. NAME AND ADDRESS OF EMPLOYER

██████████ ████ co., Colorado ████████ Operation
████. Harmony Road, Fort Collins, Colorado, ██████

£ OF JOB	DATE STARTED Month Year	DATE LEFT Month Year	KIND OF BUSINESS
Development Engineer (Software)	Jan. 1985	to present	Design & Mfg. of computers, etc.

DESCRIBE IN DETAILS THE DUTIES PERFORMED, INCLUDING THE USE OF TOOLS, MACHINES, OR EQUIPMENT	NO. OF HOURS PER WEEK
Creates software; responsible for assignments involving research, development, or design of new products or maintaining existing products, which includes development of standards, algorithms, architectures, specifications, languages, networking, as well as problem analysis, planning, scheduling, establishing operating data, and conducting tests.	40

b. NAME AND ADDRESS OF EMPLOYER

NAME OF JOB	DATE STARTED Month Year	DATE LEFT Month Year	KIND OF BUSINESS

DESCRIBE IN DETAIL THE DUTIES PERFORMED, INCLUDING THE USE OF TOOLS, MACHINES, OR EQUIPMENT	NO. OF HOURS PER WEEK

ME AND ADDRESS OF EMPLOYER

NAME OF JOB	DATE STARTED Month Year	DATE LEFT Month Year	KIND OF BUSINESS

DESCRIBE IN DETAIL THE DUTIES PERFORMED, INCLUDING THE USE OF TOOLS, MACHINES, OR EQUIPMENT	NO. OF HOURS PER WEEK

16. DECLARATIONS

DECLARATION OF ALIEN ► ► Pursuant to 28 U.S.C. 1746, I declare under penalty of perjury the foregoing is true and correct.

SIGNATURE OF ALIEN	DATE
██████████████████	3/19/85

AUTHORIZATION OF AGENT OF ALIEN ► ► I hereby designate the agent below to represent me for the purposes of labor certification and I take full responsibility for accuracy of any representations made by my agent.

SIGNATURE OF ALIEN	DATE
██████████████	3/19/85

OF AGENT (Type or print)	ADDRESS OF AGENT (No., Street, City, State, ZIP Code)
C. James Cooper, Jr.	999 Eighteenth Street, Suite 3220 Denver, Colorado 80202

(End of Form)

"BUSINESS NECESSITY" LETTER   (A SAMPLE)
(On the Employer's Letterhead)

Date:_____

Local Employment Service
Address:_____
City_____ State _____
Zip._____

Re: Business Necessity
Employee: Jozef Braun
Employer: Castle Export Corp.
Job: Supervisor, Export Department

Gentlemen:

We have required that the person who is in the position of Supervisor in the Export Department be able to speak French fluently.

This requirement is necessary for us since about 70% of our business is to buyers in France. The buyers do not speak English very well and always prefer to deal in French, their native language.

We have two other people in the Export Department who will be supervised by Mr. Braun. Both of these people speak some French but are not fluent. Our business has suffered in the past because of the language problem.

In addition to his supervisory duties, you will also note that his job includes receiving and processing orders, shipping documents, and other papers related to the export function. Many of these documents are in French. We have attached samples of documents we have received in the past. Sometimes we have had the documents translated by outside personnel at great cost of time and money.

Unless the Supervisor can speak and write French fluently, it will hurt our business very much and make it not possible for us to continue to compete.

Very truly yours,

Roger Perter
President

NOTE: This sample letter is cited, with permission for which we are most grateful to the Publisher, from the "Green Card Book".

NOTICE OF JOB OFFERING

COOK, GREEK STYLE FOOD. A job is open for a cook of Greek style food. Prepare Greek dishes such as spanakopita, keftedakia, stuffed grape leaves, and others. Requires two years experience in a similar job. Uses commercial cooking equipment including ovens, mixers, food processors, and other restaurant kitchen equipment. 40 hours per week at $250.00 per week. Call Mr_____ at phone No:_____, if interested. Phone between the hours of _____ and _____

To the Labour Department: this notice was posted on the Bulletin Board of the Greek Spoon Restaurant from _____ to _____ There were no responses.

Signed: _____
Name Signed & Your Title:_____

CERTIFICATE OF APPROVED LABOUR CERTIFICATION
(OR, OF DENIED LABOUR CERTIFICATION)

U.S. DEPARTMENT OF LABOR
EMPLOYMENT AND TRAINING ADMINISTRATION
1515 Broadway
New York, N.Y. 10036

Date: _____   In reply refer
to:DD/CB

TO: ABC Restaurant, Inc   John Doe , SPECIALTY COOK FRENCH/THAI
Address: _____   Alien's name and occupation
                                              DEC 15, 1980
         _____   Date of acceptance for processing

The Department of Labor has made a determination on your application for alien employment pursuant to Title 20, Code of Federal Regulations, Section 656.21 and as required by the Immigration and Nationality Act, as amended. Final action has been taken as follows:

☑ 1. Form ETA 7-50 has been certified and is enclosed with the supporting documents. All enclosures should be submitted to the Immigration and Naturalization Service District Office for consideration of alien's application for adjustment of status (I-485) or with your petition (Form I-140).

☐ 2. Form ETA 7-50 has been certified and forwarded to the _____
Consulate at which the alien has indicated he will file a visa application. The Consular Officer will inform the alien of any additional documents to be submitted and steps to be taken in order to apply for an immigrant visa.

☐ 3. Form ETA 7-50 has not been certified and is being returned. A certification cannot be issued as required by Section 212(a)(14) of the Immigration and Nationality Act, as amended, on the basis of information available for the following reasons:

☐ a. There are U.S. workers available who are able, willing, and qualified for the job.

☐ b. The employment of aliens would have an adverse effect on wages and/or working conditions of U.S. workers similarly employed.

The wage offer of .... is below the prevailing rate of ....
for this occupation in the proposed area of employment.

Prevailing wage was determined by ....

....

Sincerely,

Bette F. Roy

BETTE F. ROY
Certifying Officer

cc: State ES Agency   CC: John Doe

Request for a review of a denial of certification may be made. A request for review of a denial may only be made in writing addressed to the Chief Administrative Law Judge, Department of Labor, and submitted by certified mail to the Certifying Officer who denied certification within 35 days of date of this denial for transmittal and shall: (1) Clearly identify the particular certification determination for which review is sought; (2) set forth the particular grounds on which the request is based; and (3) include all documents which accompanied the denial of certification.

ETA 7-145 (Dec. 1976)

Form ETA 7-145

SAMPLES

NOTE: The above document, set forth herein for illustrative
purposes, is reproduced here by courtesy of and from
"The Greencard Book," by Richard Madison (Visa Publishing
Co., New York N.Y.), p.73. A few minor modifications have
been made herein by the present publisher.

NOTICE OF FINDINGS

U.S. DEPARTMENT OF LABOR
EMPLOYMENT AND TRAINING ADMINISTRATION
1515 Broadway
New York, N.Y. 10036

Date: _____

In reply refer
to: DD/CB

John Doe _____ /Spec. Cook French/Thai

Alien's name and occupation   12/15/80

Date of acceptance for processing

TO: ABC Restaurant, Inc.
     Address: _____

The Department of Labor has considered your application. In accordance with Title 20, Code of Federal Regulations, Section 656.25(C)(3), we hereby issue our Notice of Findings. You have until September 20, 1981..... to submit documentary evidence to rebut the finding outlined below by certified mail on or before the date specified above. If the rebuttal evidence is not received by certified mail on or before, this Notice of Findings automatically becomes the final decision to deny labor certification.

(1) Pursuant to 20 CFR 656.21(b)(7) the Revised Federal Requirements employer must document that if labor certification is granted, the wage rate paid will equal or exceed the prevailing wage applicable at that time. The statement will equal or exceed. The said prevailing wage at the time "is not satisfactory,

(2) Pursuant to 20 CFR 656.21(b)(15) employer has documented that he will be able to place the alien on the payroll on or before his date of proposed entry into U.S. It is noted that alien has been employed since March 1, 1978, therefore employer should document that alien is presently on the payroll.

(3) Pursuant to 20 CFR 656.21(b)(9) employer has documented "subsequent to filing with M my local employment service office. I placed a further advertisement in a newspaper of general circulation directing applicants to report to the local office of the employment service." This documentation was signed on 10/4/80 the job order was not placed until 11/30,/80 and the additional ad on May 23, 1981, therefore this is not a bonafide statement.

(4) Pursuant to 20 CFR 656.21(b)(10) employer has stated he posted a notice. A copy of this notice and the results of its posting must be submitted.

(5) Item 31, Form MA 7-50B, pertaining to education and training requirements, have not been answered. If none required so state.

(6) Items 5 and 6 of Form MA 7-50A, pertaining to names of schools attended or special qualifications and skills has not been answered.

(7) Should employer choose to comply with the above and/or rebut these findings he may address his letter to this office.

Sincerely,

BETTE F. ROY
Certifying Officer
cc: State E.S. Agency

ETA 7-145A

ETA 7-145A (Dec. 1976)

NOTE: The above document, set forth herein for illustrative purposes, is reproduced here by courtesy of and from "The Greencard Book," by Richard Madison (Visa Publishing Co.), p.72 . A few minor modifications have been made by the present Publisher herein.

FROM:

U.S. Department of Labor

Employment and Training Administration
1961 Stout Street
Denver, Colorado 80294

(DOL'S LETTER APPROVING CERTIFICATION)

NOTE: Refer to "Explanatory Note"
on P. 89, especially Item 3

Date: October 18, 1985

TO: Mr. C. James Cooper, Jr.
Attorney at Law for the Alien
999 - 18th Street, Suite #3220
Denver, Colorado 80202

Employer: ▆▆▆▆▆ Co.
Fort Collins, Colorado

NAME OF THE ALIEN
▆▆▆, ARUN
OCCUPATION OF THE ALIEN
Development Engineer (Software)
DATE APPLICATION SUBMITTED FOR PROCESSING
5/2/85

The U. S. Department of Labor has made a determination on your Application for Alien Employment Certification pursuant to Title 20, Code of Federal Regulations, Section 656.21, and as required by the Immigration and Nationality Act, as amended.

Form ETA 7-50A has been certified, and it is enclosed with the supporting documents.

All enclosures should be submitted to the Immigration and Naturalization Service District Office for consideration of the alien's application for adjustment of status (I-485), or with your petition (Form I-140).

Sincerely,

Becky Stuart

for CHARLES C. VIGIL
Certifying Officer

Attachments

cc: State Agency for State of Colorado;
Alien - Mr. Arun ▆▆▆, ▆▆▆ Shields, ▆▆, Ft. Collins, CO ▆▆

EXPLANATORY NOTE

This is Certification from the Department of Labor which is used by the Department of Labor office in Denver. Although the form is dated October 18, 1985, the alien's priority date for a visa number was May 2, 1985, which was the date the Application for Labor Certification was received by the State agency.

CONTRACT OF EMPLOYMENT (A SAMPLE)

This is a contract of Employment between Mr/Ms _____, who resides at _ (address?)__, City of_____, State of_____, (hereinafter called "EMPLOYER"), and Mr/Ms_____who resides at_____, city/town of_____, State of_____ Zip____(hereinafter called "EMPLOYER").

The Employer hereby agrees to employ the Employee as a live-in domestic worker in the Employer's home at the above address, at a salary of $_____ per hour for the first forty (40) hours worked, and $_____per hour, for the next four (4) hours worked, if any, up to the required forty-four (44) hours per week. The Employer also agrees to pay the Employee at the same "overtime" rate of $_____per hour for all time worked over forty-four (44) hours per week. The regular weekly wage (i.e., without overtime) is $_____ The Employee will be given private room and board at no expense to the Employee.

The duties of the Employee will consist of the following: general household work, cleaning, laundry, shopping, cooking and serving meals, child care, answering the door and phone, and running general errands, lawn tending.

Household equipment, which the Employee will operate, are: dishwasher, vacuum cleaner, washing machine and dryer, lawn mower.

The hours of employment will be forty-four (44) per week, from_____A.M. to_____P.M.; daily, 5 days per week, with a 2 hour rest period and 2 hours for meals each day. The Employee will work a guaranteed minimum of four (4) hours overtime per week at an hourly rate of $_____. The Employee agrees to live on the premises of the Employer. Employee is totally free to leave the premises at all times which are not working hours.

The Employer and the Employee, each agrees to give the other a two-week notice of intent to terminate the employment herein.

The Employer and the Employee, each acknowledges the receipt of a duplicate of this Contract, and each asserts that he/she entered into and signed this document freely, willingly, and voluntarily, after having first read, considered, and understood the contents thereof.

SIGNED: SIGNED:

_____   _____
(Employer)   (Employee)
Dated:_____200___ .   Dated:_____200___ .

EMPLOYER'S OFFER OF EMPLOYMENT LETTER

(Name of Employing company)

December 31, 1985

NOTE: See "Explanatory Note" on pp. 09 & 141

COLORADO ▮▮▮▮▮ OPERATION
3404 East Harmony Road, Fort Collins, Colorado 80525, Telephone 303 226-3800

TO: U.S. Immigration and Naturalization Service

RE: Mr. Arun ▮▮▮▮▮

Dear Sirs:

We write this letter in support of our application for permanent residency on behalf of Mr. Arun ▮▮▮▮▮.

▮▮▮▮▮ Company is one of the largest U.S. electronics companies, employing 84,000 employees worldwide in research, development, manufacture, and sales of a broad line of electronic test equipment used in commercial and industrial application. ▮▮▮▮▮ ranks in the top 20 of all U.S. corporations in terms of export dollars.

The United States and ▮ are in great need of computer scientists highly trained in the areas of computer networking and operating systems. The lack of sufficient networking has been claimed by many in our industry as being the primary reason for the current slump in the computer industry. From our market research, we have found the lack of sufficient networking to be the biggest limiter to the success of our computer products.

For the past two years we have conducted aggressive recruiting and training programs aimed at filling our needs for computer scientists highly trained in networking and operating systems. We have not been successful; in 1984 we fell ten people short of our target and in 1985 we have fallen 5 short of our target. Considering this, we obtained labor certification from the Department of Labor for this position.

In December of 1984 we found Mr. Arun ▮▮▮▮▮. Mr. ▮▮▮▮▮ met our qualifications extremely well. He obtained his masters degree in Computer Science from Ohio State University where he studied and researched networking and operating systems. Since that time he has become a key contributor on a very important networking product which will allow multi-vendor computer communication. His continued involvement in this project if required in order to avoid significant delays.

Upon approval by the Immigration Service, the company intends to hire Mr. Chandra permanently at a yearly salary of $32,640.00.

Thank you for your time and consideration for this petition.

Sincerely,

▮▮▮▮▮ COMPANY

Thomas J. ▮▮▮▮▮
Personnel Section Manager

TJL/1b

FROM:

 , INC.

EMPLOYER OFFER OF EMPLOYMENT
LETTER

TO:

Miss Dawning ████
Flat B, 10th Flr.
████████████
Gheung Shing St.
████████Hong Kong

April 3, 1984

Dear Dawning:

As we have discussed, I have offered you the position of Apparel Account
Executive with our company on a temporary basis, until we are able to locate,
hire and train an individual to fill this position on a permanent basis.

This letter is to confirm this offer and your acceptance of this position
at an annual salary of $42,000.00. This position's responsibilities
include the handling of all our clothing orders with each of the factories
in Hong Kong and Taiwan, coordinating all piece goods with each factory,
setting up production schedules that can be met, and setting up a file and
production system in our office that will correlate with those factories.

I became quite impressed with your experience and abilities in handling our
account with your employer in Hong Kong, and feel that you will add greatly
to the efficient organization of the development and production areas of our
business which will help increase our productivity.

As you are aware, the offer of the position of Apparel Account Executive is
subject to approval of our petition by the Immigration and Naturalization
Service.

Sincerely,

Bill ████████
Bill

BG:jcb

NOTE: See "Explanatory Note" on P. 89
especially the No. 2 paragraph thereof.

████████ Parkway████████████████████Englewood, Colorado 80111
Cable: ████████ ● TWX ████████ ● FAX (303) ████████

EMPLOYER LETTER IN SUPPORT OF H-1 PETITION

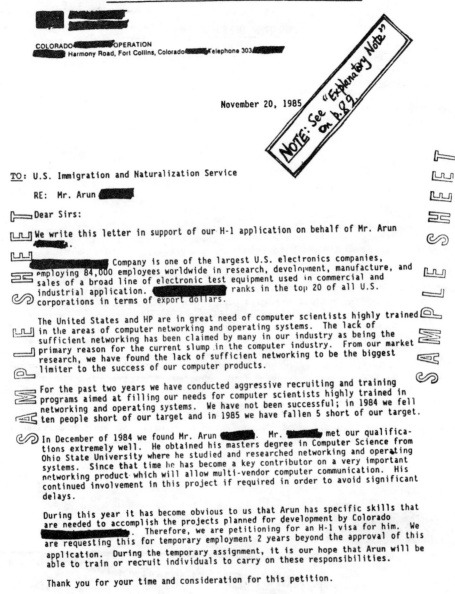

COLORADO ██████ OPERATION
████ Harmony Road, Fort Collins, Colorado ████ Telephone 303 ████

November 20, 1985

NOTE: See "Explanatory Note" on p. 89.

TO: U.S. Immigration and Naturalization Service

RE: Mr. Arun ████

Dear Sirs:

We write this letter in support of our H-1 application on behalf of Mr. Arun ████.

████ Company is one of the largest U.S. electronics companies, employing 84,000 employees worldwide in research, development, manufacture, and sales of a broad line of electronic test equipment used in commercial and industrial application. ████ ranks in the top 20 of all U.S. corporations in terms of export dollars.

The United States and HP are in great need of computer scientists highly trained in the areas of computer networking and operating systems. The lack of sufficient networking has been claimed by many in our industry as being the primary reason for the current slump in the computer industry. From our market research, we have found the lack of sufficient networking to be the biggest limiter to the success of our computer products.

For the past two years we have conducted aggressive recruiting and training programs aimed at filling our needs for computer scientists highly trained in networking and operating systems. We have not been successful; in 1984 we fell ten people short of our target and in 1985 we have fallen 5 short of our target.

In December of 1984 we found Mr. Arun ████. Mr. ████ met our qualifications extremely well. He obtained his masters degree in Computer Science from Ohio State University where he studied and researched networking and operating systems. Since that time he has become a key contributor on a very important networking product which will allow multi-vendor computer communication. His continued involvement in this project if required in order to avoid significant delays.

During this year it has become obvious to us that Arun has specific skills that are needed to accomplish the projects planned for development by Colorado ████. Therefore, we are petitioning for an H-1 visa for him. We are requesting this for temporary employment 2 years beyond the approval of this application. During the temporary assignment, it is our hope that Arun will be able to train or recruit individuals to carry on these responsibilities.

Thank you for your time and consideration for this petition.

Sincerely,

Sandy L. ████
R&D Section Manager

179

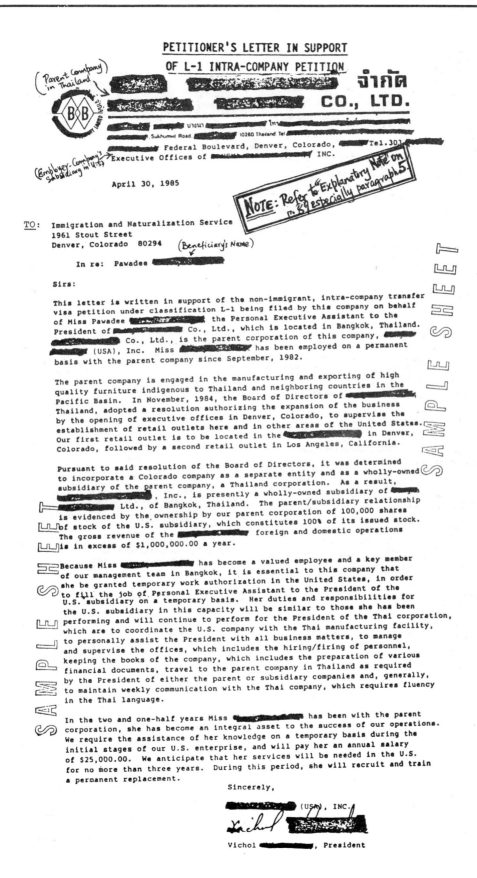

PETITIONER'S LETTER IN SUPPORT
OF L-1 INTRA-COMPANY PETITION

(Parent Company in Thailand)

CO., LTD.

จำกัด

Sukhumvi Road. ████ 10260 Thailand. Tel ████

████ Federal Boulevard, Denver, Colorado, ████ Tel.30█
Executive Offices of ████████ INC.

(Employing - Company's subsidiary in U.S.)

April 30, 1985

NOTE: Refer to Explanatory Note on p. 89 especially paragraph 5

TO: Immigration and Naturalization Service
1961 Stout Street
Denver, Colorado 80294

(Beneficiary's Name)

In re: Pawadee ████

Sirs:

This letter is written in support of the non-immigrant, intra-company transfer visa petition under classification L-1 being filed by this company on behalf of Miss Pawadee ████, the Personal Executive Assistant to the President of ████ Co., Ltd., which is located in Bangkok, Thailand. ████ Co., Ltd., is the parent corporation of this company, ████ (USA), Inc. Miss ████ has been employed on a permanent basis with the parent company since September, 1982.

The parent company is engaged in the manufacturing and exporting of high quality furniture indigenous to Thailand and neighboring countries in the Pacific Basin. In November, 1984, the Board of Directors of ████ Thailand, adopted a resolution authorizing the expansion of the business by the opening of executive offices in Denver, Colorado, to supervise the establishment of retail outlets here and in other areas of the United States. Our first retail outlet is to be located in the ████ in Denver, Colorado, followed by a second retail outlet in Los Angeles, California.

Pursuant to said resolution of the Board of Directors, it was determined to incorporate a Colorado company as a separate entity and as a wholly-owned subsidiary of the parent company, a Thailand corporation. As a result, ████, Inc., is presently a wholly-owned subsidiary of ████ Ltd., of Bangkok, Thailand. The parent/subsidiary relationship is evidenced by the ownership by our parent corporation of 100,000 shares of stock of the U.S. subsidiary, which constitutes 100% of its issued stock. The gross revenue of the ████ foreign and domestic operations is in excess of $1,000,000.00 a year.

Because Miss ████ has become a valued employee and a key member of our management team in Bangkok, it is essential to this company that she be granted temporary work authorization in the United States, in order to fill the job of Personal Executive Assistant to the President of the U.S. subsidiary on a temporary basis. Her duties and responsibilities for the U.S. subsidiary in this capacity will be similar to those she has been performing and will continue to perform for the President of the Thai corporation, which are to coordinate the U.S. company with the Thai manufacturing facility, to personally assist the President with all business matters, to manage and supervise the offices, which includes the hiring/firing of personnel, keeping the books of the company, which includes the preparation of various financial documents, travel to the parent company in Thailand as required by the President of either the parent or subsidiary companies and, generally, to maintain weekly communication with the Thai company, which requires fluency in the Thai language.

In the two and one-half years Miss ████ has been with the parent corporation, she has become an integral asset to the success of our operations. We require the assistance of her knowledge on a temporary basis during the initial stages of our U.S. enterprise, and will pay her an annual salary of $25,000.00. We anticipate that her services will be needed in the U.S. for no more than three years. During this period, she will recruit and train a permanent replacement.

Sincerely,

████ (USA), INC.

Vichol ████, President

FORM I-140

(Good till June 1986; after that date, you must use new Form sampled pp.123-5)

PETITION TO CLASSIFY PREFERENCE STATUS OF ALIEN ON BASIS OF PROFESSION OR OCCUPATION

Form I-140

UNITED STATES DEPARTMENT OF JUSTICE

IMMIGRATION AND NATURALIZATION SERVICE

OMB No. 1115-0061
Approval expires 4-86

P.1 of 2 pgs.

DATE RECEIVED	FEE STAMP

NOTE: Refer to "Explanatory Note" on p.144; P.39 especially paragraphs No.3 & 4

TO THE SECRETARY OF STATE	REMARKS

Petition was filed on _____

Beneficiary's file number: A _____

Petition is approved for status under section   ☐ 203(a)(3).   ☐ 203(a)(6)

☐ Sec. 212(a)(14) certification attached.

☐ Blanket Sec. 212(a)(14) certification issued.

DATE OF ACTION
DD
DISTRICT

PETITIONER IS NOT TO WRITE ABOVE THIS LINE

Read this form and the attached instructions carefully before filling in petition

Petition is hereby made to classify the status of the alien beneficiary named herein for issuance of an immigrant visa as ("X" one)

☒ A THIRD PREFERENCE IMMIGRANT — An alien who is a member of the professions, or who because of his exceptional ability in the sciences or arts will substantially benefit prospectively the national economy, cultural interests or welfare of the United States, and whose services are sought by an employer. (Sec. 203(a)(3), Immigration and Nationality Act, as amended.)

☐ A SIXTH PREFERENCE IMMIGRANT — An alien who is capable of performing skilled or unskilled labor, not of a temporary or seasonal nature, for which a shortage of employable and willing persons exists in the United States. (Sec. 203 (a) (6), Immigration and Nationality Act, as amended.)

(If you need more space to answer fully any questions on this form, use a separate sheet, identify each answer with the number of the corresponding question and sign and date each sheet.)

PART I— INFORMATION CONCERNING ALIEN BENEFICIARY

1. NAME (Last, in CAPS) ▓▓▓▓ (First) Arun (Middle) NMN	2. ALIEN REGISTRATION NO. (If any)	3. PROFESSION OR OCCUPATION Development Engineer
4. OTHER NAMES USED (Married woman give maiden name) None	5. DO NOT WRITE IN THIS SPACE	6. DOES BENEFICIARY INTEND TO ENGAGE IN HIS/HER PROFESSION OR OCCUPATION IN THE UNITED STATES ☒ YES ☐ NO. IF "NO," EXPLAIN
7. PLACE OF BIRTH (Country) United Kingdom	8. DATE OF BIRTH (Month, day, year) 9/17/61	

9. NAME OF PETITIONER (Full name of organization; if petitioner is an individual give full name with last in capital letters ▓▓▓▓▓▓ Co., Colorado Operation

10. NUMBER OF YEARS OF BENEFICIARY'S EXPERIENCE   (If none explain why.)

11. CITY AND STATE IN THE UNITED STATES WHERE ALIEN INTENDS TO RESIDE

Ft. Collins, Colorado

    (City)   (State)

Approx. 1 year

12. BENEFICIARY'S PRESENT ADDRESS (Number and street) (City or town) (State or province) (Country) (ZIP Code, if in U.S.)

▓▓▓▓.Shields Street, ▓▓▓, Ft.Collins,Colorado ▓▓▓▓

13. TO YOUR KNOWLEDGE, HAS A VISA PETITION EVER BEEN FILED BY OR ON BEHALF OF THIS BENEFICIARY BASED ON HIS/HER PROFESSION OR OCCUPATION? ☐ Yes ☒ No. If "Yes," give name of each petitioner and date and place of filing.

14. IF BENEFICIARY IS NOW IN THE U.S. (a) HE/SHE LAST ARRIVED ON ___8/20/83___
                                                  (Month) (Day) (Year)

AS A ___F-1___   (b) SHOW DATE BENEFICIARY'S STAY EXPIRED OR WILL EXPIRE AS
    (Visitor, student, exchange alien, temporary worker, crewman, stowaway, etc.)

SHOWN ON FORM I-94 OR I-95 (Show latest date) ___12-2-87___ H-1

15. BENEFICIARY'S SPOUSE (If Unmarried, State Unmarried)	NAME (Last name) (First name) Not married	(Middle name)	(Maiden name, if married woman)
	COUNTRY OF BIRTH	DATE OF BIRTH	PRESENT ADDRESS (No. and Street) (City or town) (State or Province) (Country)
16. BENEFICIARY'S CHILDREN (If None, State None)	NAME(Show M or S for married or single) None	M.S.	BIRTHDATE	COUNTRY OF BIRTH	ADDRESS

RECEIVED	TRANS. IN	RET'D. TRANS OUT	COMPLETED

Form I-140 (Rev. 5-5-83)N

—OVER— ➝

FORM I-140 (Expired June 1986)

p. 2 of 2 pgs.

17. "X" THE APPROPRIATE BOX BELOW AND FURNISH THE INFORMATION REQUIRED FOR THE BOX MARKED.

☐ Alien will apply for a visa abroad at the American Consulate in _____ _____
        (City in foreign country)   (Foreign country)

☒ Alien is in the United States and will apply for adjustment of status to that of a lawful permanent resident in the office of the Immigration and

Naturalization Service at   Denver   Colorado   If the application for adjustment of status is denied
      (City)   (State)

                                    Calgary, Alberta, Canada

the alien will apply for a visa abroad at the American Consulate in _____ _____
        (City in foreign country)   (Foreign country)

PART II—INFORMATION CONCERNING EMPLOYER AND POSITION

18. NAME OF PETITIONER (Full name of organization, if petitioner is an individual give full name with last in capital letters) | TELEPHONE NUMBER

████████████ Co., Colorado ████████ Operation   303-█████

19. ADDRESS   (Number and street)   (Town or city)   (State)   (ZIP code)

████ Harmony Road, Ft. Collins, Colorado ████

20. PETITIONER IS (X one)

☐ U S CITIZEN   ☐ PERMANENT RESIDENT ALIEN ("A" NUMBER _____)   ☐ NONIMMIGRANT   ☒ ORGANIZATION

21. NET ANNUAL INCOME   22 WILL BENEFICIARY BE EMPLOYED AT THE ABOVE ADDRESS? ☒ YES ☐ NO. IF "NO." GIVE ADDRESS
Excess of $6 Billion   WHERE THE ALIEN WILL WORK.

23. DO YOU DESIRE AND INTEND TO EMPLOY THE BENEFICIARY   ☒ YES ☐ NO.

24. HAVE YOU EVER FILED A VISA PETITION FOR AN ALIEN BASED ON PROFESSION OR OCCUPATION?   ☐ YES ☐ NO. IF "YES," HOW
MANY SUCH PETITIONS HAVE YOU FILED?

25. ARE SEPARATE PETITIONS BEING SUBMITTED AT THIS TIME FOR OTHER ALIENS?   ☐ YES ☒ NO. IF "YES," GIVE NAME OF EACH ALIEN.

26. THE FOLLOWING DOCUMENTS ARE SUBMITTED WITH THIS PETITION AND ARE MADE A PART THEREOF.

Labor Certification and attached documents showing alien's qualifications for
third preference status,
Employer's offer of employment letter;
Employer's latest annual report

PART III—CERTIFICATION OF PETITIONER OR AUTHORIZED REPRESENTATIVE

27. This petition was prepared by ("X" one) ☐ the petitioner ☐ another person

If petition was prepared by another person, Item 29 below must also be completed.

The petition may be completed and signed only by the following persons:

In third preference cases — by the beneficiary or by the person filing the petition on the beneficiary's behalf. If the petition is being filed by a person on behalf of the alien beneficiary, Item 28 below must be completed by that person.

In sixth preference cases — by the employer who desires and intends to employ the beneficiary. If the employer is an organization, the petition must be completed and signed by a high level officer or employee of the organization.

I certify, under penalty of perjury under the laws of the United States of America that the foregoing is true and corre ███████████

Executed on (date) __12/31/85__   Signature _Marlene_ ████████

If petitioner is an organization, print full name and title of authorized official who is signing petition in behalf of organization:

Name and Title __Marlene ████__   Personnel Representative _____ Date __12/31/85__

28. DECLARATION OF PERSON FILING PETITION FOR THIRD PREFERENCE ON BEHALF OF ALIEN BENEFICIARY

I declare that I have been reque ████████ by the alien beneficiary to file this petition on his (her) behalf.

Marlene ████████   ████ Harmony Road Ft.Collins   12/31/85
(Signature)   (Address – Number, Street, City, State and ZIP Code)   (Date)

29. SIGNATURE OF PERSON PREPARING FORM, IF OTHER THAN PETITIONER

I declare that this document was prepared by me at the request of the petitioner and is based on all information of which I have any knowledge

_____   999 Eighteenth St. Denver, CO   12/31/85
(Signature)   (Address – Number, Street, City, State and ZIP Code)   (Date)

TO PETITIONER: DO NOT FILL IN THIS BLOCK — FOR USE OF IMMIGRATION OFFICER

a Corrections numbered ( ) to ( ) were made by me or at my request.
                 (Date)   (City)

(Signature of petitioner or authorized member of petitioner's organization)   (Title)

b The person whose signature appears immediately above was interviewed under oath and affirmed all allegations contained herein

(Date)   (City)   (Signature and Title)

(End of Form)

FROM: , **INC.**

NOTE: See "Explanatory Note" on p. 141; p. 89, especially the No. 2 paragraph thereof.

April 9, 1984

(EMPLOYER'S JOB DESCRIPTION)

TO WHOM IT MAY CONCERN:

As our Account Executive, Miss Dawning ▒▒ will be responsible for the management and coordination of all areas related to the development and production of our product lines. At the current time, we have five lines of skiwear fashions for a total of approximately 300 styles. We work a year in advance in this industry, and for each season our development and production encompass the following sequence of activities:

1. Research the current market and trends.
2. Identify design concept, price point, and style catagories for each line.
3. Anticipate trends for the coming season by working with fabric, trim, and color resources. (To include: Arthur Kahn, Seatex, Toray, Gore-Tex, Y.K.K. zippers, Sumitomo, Schoeller Textil, Pottendorfer, and AuMan.)
4. Select fabrics and colors for the new season, and order greige goods and lab dips from each vendor.
5. Coordination of trim and hardware colors with these resources to complement fabric colors.
6. Design, sketch, and detail styles for each line.
7. Adopt styles from sketches to be made into prototype samples.
8. Select factory to make prototype based upon equipment necessary to produce this style of garment.
9. Send designer sketch with detailed specification sheet to factory.
10. Upon receipt of prototype from factory, each style is reviewed and comments are made on the fit, detail, construction, and design elements. These comments are sent back to the factory.
11. Each prototype style that is considered for adoption into the line is then priced from the factory.
12. All fabrics, knit, trim, hardware, and accessories are coordinated to be delivered to the factory for sample production.
13. Styles are selected for each line, and details regarding fabric, insulation, knit, hardware, etc. are sent to the factory. Sample colors are selected, labeling defined, sizing established, and prices are set for our catalog.
14. Sample production is coordinated to meet the scheduled selling shows for our industry.
15. Sales for each style are projected and greige goods are booked for each fabric for production. Production space with each factory is also booked in anticipation of our needs for the coming season.
16. Based on sales and early projections, all elements for production are coordinated for delivery to the factory so that the product ship dates meet the delivery requirements of our customers.

Miss ▒▒'s education, experience, and ability to communicate in Chinese make her a most desireable candidate for this position. Her knowledge of textiles and garment construction, as well as, her experience in working in the same factories we use in Hong Kong and Taiwan will provide us with the strong communication link we do not currently have. Since she has been managing our account in Hong Kong, we feel she can help us to more efficiently organize our development and production areas (as listed) to meet the needs of our factories. We expect that her contribution will help us to increase productivity and effect more timely delivery of samples and production for better business. Miss ▒▒ salary will be $42,000.

Sincerely,

Bill ▒▒

Suite 2000 ▒▒▒ Englewood, Colorado 80111
Cable: ▒▒▒ • TWX ▒▒▒ • FAX ▒▒▒

Chapter 24
Legal Grounds For Inadmissibility Of Aliens To The Unite States

A: WHAT IS INADMISSIBILITY?

The Illegal Immigration Reform And Immigrant Responsibility Act (IIRAIRA)* enacted by U.S. Congress in September 1996, enacted a broad and complex series of changes in the U.S. immigration law, and punitive measures against many typical visa violations, and created some new violations. Move particularly, it enacted major changes in the grounds for the removal of aliens from the U.S. and the rights and powers of the U.S. immigration authorities to bar aliens from admission into the U.S. The law of inadmissibility basically gives the ground and conditions for which the U.S. Consular and immigration authorities may consider an alien as being undesirable and unfit to be admissible into the United.

The basic restrictive element of the 1996 Immigration Reform Law, is what is called the *"summary exclusion"* provision of the law. This provision, which is widely viewed as the one element with probably the most profound and far-reaching impact on aliens planning or seeking to emigrate or gain entry to the U.S., basically empowers an INS inspector at the border to "summarily" exclude and deport an alien requesting admission to the U.S. – that is, the inspector may do so without being subject to a judicial review or an appeal from the inspector's decision – if certain conditions exist. The INS inspector may do so if, in the judgement of the inspector, either <u>one</u> of these conditions are true:

- if the INS inspector is of the opinion that you (the alien) have been untruthful or have made a misrepresentation of the facts about almost anything connected to your application for an immigrant or nonimmigrant visa to the U.S., such as your purpose for going, or your intent to return or to stay in the U.S., or your prior personal history or immigration history, or the use or suspected use of false documents, etc; or
- if the INS inspector is of the view that even if you are qualified for another type of visa, you do not have the proper documentation to support your entry to the U.S. in the specific visa category that you are requesting.

An alien who is excluded (for the first time) from entry by border inspector for whatever reason, is barred from making another application for entry for the next 5 years, unless a special waiver is granted. And if an alien has made his entry into the U.S. and subsequently had to be removed from the country, he is barred from entering the U.S. again for a period of 10 years from the date of the departure or removal (or for a period of 20 years in the case of a second or subsequent removal, or in the case of an alien convicted of an aggravate felony).

---

*It's often referred to as the Immigration Reform Law of 1996, for short.

B. THE NEW "SUMMARY EXCLUSION" LAW AGAINST ALIENS WHO ARE UNLAWFULLY PRESENT IN THE U.S.

A major new ground of inadmissibility which gives the INS officers and inspectors a sweeping administrative tool, is one provided under the 1996 Immigration Reform Law which subjects aliens who are "unlawfully present" in the United States for 6 months after April 1, 1997, who subsequently left the U.S. voluntarily before there was any removal proceedings and who now seek to be admitted into the U.S. (whether by Adjustment of Status, or by applying for an immigrant or nonimmigrant visa), to a stringent restriction: they are barred from re-entering the U.S. for 3 years; and if the unlawful presence has lasted for one year or move, the waiting period for which the alien is barred from reentering the U.S. is 10 years from the date of the alien's departure from the U.S. For purposes of counting the period of an alien's unlawful presence or overstay, the INS will only consider relevant or applicable a continuous, uninterrupted block of time which <u>continuously</u> runs up to 6 months or 1 year; it will not count or add up a few months (or weeks) during one stay, and few months during another, to be able to come up your "unlawful presence" period.

Who is an "unlawfully present" alien? As interpreted under the immigration regulations, the term "unlawfully present" has a complex definition, but it generally means the overstay by an alien of the time authorized him by the INS, as usually noted on the alien's Arrival-Departure Record (Form 1-94), for him or her to person to remain in the U.S. As interpreted by the INS, such time is defined to include also the time after the INS or the immigration court has determined that an alien has violated the conditions of his admission, as well as the time the alien is required to remain in the U.S. while in formal removal proceedings.

In addition, an alien will not be deemed to be unlawfully present for the purposes of the 3 and 10-year bars to re-entry, for any period of time in which the alien:
- was under the age of 18 years
- had a 'bona-fide' asylum application pending, or any related administrative or judicial review, unless the alien had been employed without authorization
- was the beneficiary of a family unity protection application
- was a 'battered woman or child' who demonstrates a reasonable connection between the status violation or unlawfully entry and the abuse claimed
- undertook a change or extension of status for a maximum period of 120 days, providing the alien had been lawfully admitted and had filed a bona-fide change or extension application and had not been employed without authorization.

For an alien who entered the U.S. after inspector who is admitted to the U.S. for "duration of status" (such as those holding the nonimmigrant A, F, G, or J visas), an unlawful presence will begin to be counted only if an immigration judge determines that the alien is unlawfully present and is deportable, or the INS, in the course of adjudicating on a visa application determines that the alien has violated his status. For an alien admitted until a specified date, unlawful presence will begin to be counted only as from the date designated on his Form 1-94 (or any extensions), or, when applicable, as from the date determined by the INS or an immigration judge to be when the status violation by the alien began. When an alien is granted a voluntary departure, unlawful presence for the purposes of overstay bar begins to be counted as from the date specified for departure in the voluntary departure order, if the alien fails to depart.

C. NATURE OF GROUNDS OF INADMISSIBILITY

Typically, an alien would encounter the issue of exclusion or removal (i.e., inadmissibility) into the U.S. on two primary occasions – first, when he (or she) appears at the U.S. Consulate in his home country to apply for a visa, and, then, when he arrives at the U.S. port of entry attempting to enter the United States. Thus, at the U.S. Consulate office in a foreign country, an alien might have his visa petition denied if the consular officer believes that this particular alien falls under one or more of the grounds of inadmissibility (chart on p. 188). And then, at the U.S. border or port of entry, an alien who already has been granted a visa in his home country and has a valid U.S. visa in his hands, may still be denied entry into the United States by the border Immigration and Naturalization inspectors on the basis that the alien falls under one or more of the grounds of inadmissibility.

The grounds of inadmissibility fall into various categories. They range from health related grounds (e.g. persons found to have a communicable disease of public health significance, such as HIV, tuberculosis, or those who failed to be vaccinated against certain diseases, or who are serious drug abusers or drug addicts etc.); to grounds related to past criminal activities and convictions by an alien; and grounds related to national security interests of the U.S. or to protection of the U.S. labor market, or aliens who have previously entered the U.S. without being properly admitted or paroled, and so on.

The following is a chart summarizing the legal grounds for exclusion ("inadmissibility") of an alien into the United States, and the related conditions under which a WAIVER may be available or unavailable for a given ground.

D. BASIS FOR POSSIBLY REVERSING AN INADMISSIBILITY FINDING

As a practical matter, most decisions made by the U.S. Consular officers on the exclusion or admission of an alien are very difficult, if not virtually impracticable, to reverse since such officers have broad discretion under the immigration rules in interpreting the factual circumstances surrounding any particular alien visa petitioner. As explained in Sections, A and B above, the 1996 law, IIRAIRA, made many profound changes in the areas of effecting the removal of an alien from the United States, and, among other things, it gave the border immigration inspector at the port of entry the power of expedited removal – coupled with the elimination of any appeals from any decision made by the border inspector.

Nevertheless, the immigration laws provide for some situations when certain of the grounds of inadmissibility may still be legally excused or waived, or a finding or inadmissibility by an INS officer reversed.

Ways By Which An Inadmissibility Decision May Be Reversed

If you are found inadmissible by a U.S. Consul officer or an INS inspector at the border, there are four basic ways by which you can get the decision of inadmissibility reversed:

1. In a case involving physical or mental illness only, where you have been cured of the condition by the time of your application for a visa, you can seek a reversal of the prior decision on the grounds that the condition has been corrected. Or, the same thing could also apply where you can show, in the case of certain criminal grounds of inadmissibility, that the underlying criminal conviction was unlawfully obtained, or has been "vacated" (i.e., erased or expunged) by the courts.

2. Where you can prove that the category of inadmissibility the INS had attributed to you is really erroneous and actually don't apply to you, you can get a reversal of the inadmissibility decision against you by the immigration authorities. This may, perhaps, be quite complicated, perhaps even downright impossible to do, quite alright. And you may very well need an experienced immigration lawyer to be able to do this, especially

when you have a criminal record in your past. This basis of winning a reversal is used mainly with respect to overcoming criminal and ideological grounds of inadmissibility. Different factors will determine whether your past criminal activity will really constitute an applicable ground of inadmissibility or not:

- The type of the crime committed and the nature of the punishment meted out
- Committing an act that is considered a crime of "moral turpitude" – those crimes that are indicative of bad moral character and extreme dishonesty and moral depravity, such as crimes of theft, assault and battery, murder, rape, and the like – is particularly damaging as a factor for consideration in establishing inadmissibility and can make you inadmissible even if you have not been convicted; if the criminal activities with which you were associated have no element of moral turpitude, however, they may not generally be considered legitimate grounds of inadmissibility.

Factors such as the following may be helpful to your case:
- Crimes and charges with which you have been charged but are dropped
- Expungement laws that remove the crime from your record
- Conviction later erased or vacated based on a showing that it was unlawfully obtained
- The length of the prison term
- How long ago the crime was committed, and the nature and character of your conduct and criminal record since then
- The number of convictions in your background
- Evidence, if any, that you (the alien) may have been rehabilitated
- Available pardons

3. In a situation where the situation is such that you can clearly show, through documentation and otherwise, that the facts or basis upon which the immigration officer rendered his determination of inadmissibility is simply incorrect, what you can do to reverse that decision is simple: merely present your documentation and credible evidence showing that the officer's finding of inadmissibility is incorrect. For example, lets say you were found inadmissible on the grounds of your having certain medical conditions, you simply would present medical reports from your doctor or medical experts demonstrating that the first diagnosis of your medical condition was wrong and that you do not have the medical problem which had been attributed to you. Or, lets' say, for another example, that the immigration office had charged that you lied or misrepresented the facts on your visa application. You can simply present some verifiable and credible evidence proving that you actually told the truth, or that any false statements you made were reasonable, honest mistakes unintentionally made.

4. WAIVERS* An important way specifically provided for under the 1996 Immigration Reform Law by which an alien may reverse or overcome a finding of inadmissibility by the immigration authorities, is the use of a "waiver" or exemptions. By obtaining a waiver, you are, in effect, obtaining an exception or a pardon of the grounds of inadmissibility used. You don't reverse, or eliminate or disprove the grounds of inadmissibility or its finding by the INS against you. Rather, you are merely asking the INS to overlook and discount the problem with which you are charged and grant you the visa, anyway, in spite of that.

The waiver remedy applies only with respect to some of the grounds for inadmissibility. You may apply for a waiver of inadmissibility only AFTER the U.S. Consulate or the INS office has made its decision on your visa

---

*Note that only the INS office, and no court of law, has jurisdiction to review a decision of the INS to grant or deny a waiver.

application or admission effort and rendered a decision that you are, in fact, inadmissible.

A waiver applies to grounds of inadmissibility involving circumstances such as the following, among others:
- For an alien adjudged a drug abuser or addict, if the alien has some vital family ties and can otherwise prove some mitigating circumstances wherein granting him a waiver is likely to keep his family together and to prevent a hardship, and that having a proper family environment on his part would mitigate any danger to the public; or where a bond is provided .
- Persons convicted even of crimes of moral turpitude where the crimes are of "minor offenses" (offences for which the sentence imposed is less than 6 months); where the crime was committed when the alien was under the age of 18 at the time of the crime, and was committed more than 5 years before the date of the application for the visa.
- Crimes for which the maximum possible penalty does not exceed one year, and, if the alien was actually convicted of the crime, where the alien was not in fact sentenced to a term of imprisonment in excess of 6 months.
- Non-drug-related crimes, or offence. of prostitution or for conviction of a single offence for possession of 30 grams of marijuana or less, providing the following basic conditions are met: there has been a passage either of 15 years from the disqualifying event coupled with proof of the alien's rehabilitation, or there is an extreme hardship to designated U.S. citizens or permanent resident relatives, such as a spouse, parent, or child.
- For persons charged with fraud or material misrepresentation of a material fact in a visa petition or other document relating to a visa, there is a waiver for those persons who are immediate relatives of U.S. citizens or of permanent resident aliens, or for cases where the fraud occurred at least 10 years before the entry to the U.S. (Applies only to aliens seeking to enter the U.S. as immigrants).
- Aliens guilty of smuggling their immediate family members into the United States, providing the alien is not engaged in the smuggling of any person into the U.S. for profit.
- Aliens who do not have a valid visa or entry document or who do not have the required documents in support of their immigration status at the time of their entry.
- An alien who, in the sole discretion of the INS, is able to establish that the imposition of a bar to re-entry into the U.S. against him for being unlawfully present in the U.S. or for overstaying the time authorized by the INS (a bar for a period of 3 years for overstaying for 180 days to 1 year, and 10 years for overstaying for 1 year or more) would create an extreme hardship on a U.S. citizen or permanent resident spouse or child.

Filing For A Waiver

You may apply for a waiver of inadmissibility only if and AFTER the U.S. Consulate or INS office shall have made a decision on your visa or entry application and has determined that you are, in fact, inadmissible.

In some cases, promptly upon the determination by the consulate or INS office that your answers to the questions on your visa application forms clearly show that you are inadmissible, the office would authority you to begin applying for a waiver immediately as soon as you file your application. But in most cases, however, the consulate or INS office will usually conduct its final interview with the alien before ruling that the alien is inadmissible. In any event, however, once the office makes the determination that the alien is inadmissible and that a waiver is necessary, the alien will be notified by mail. You (the alien) will be given Form 1-601, *Application For Waiver on Ground of Excludability Inadmissibility,* to complete and to file it with the appropriate INS office. The filing fee for this as of this writing is $195 (see sample of Form 1-601 on p. 235).

Waivers to Inadmissibility

GROUNDS TO INADMISSIBILITY	WAIVERS AVAILABLE	CONDITIONS OF WAIVER
Health Problems		
People with communicable diseases. The most common diseases are tuberculosis and HIV (AIDS).	Yes	A waiver is available to an individual who is the spouse or the unmarried son or daughter or the unmarried minor lawfully-adopted child of a U.S. citizen or permanent resident, or of an alien who has been issued an immigrant visa; or to an individual who has a son or daughter who is a U.S. citizen, or a permanent resident, or an alien issued an immigrant visa, upon compliance with INS' terms and regulations.
People with physical or mental disorders which threaten the safety of others.	Yes	Special conditions required by INS, at its discretion.
Drug abusers or addicts.	No	
People who fail to show that they have been vaccinated against certain vaccine-preventable diseases.	Yes	The applicant must show that he or she subsequently received the vaccine; that the vaccine is medically inappropriate as certified by a civil surgeon; or that having the vaccine administered is contrary to the applicant's religious beliefs or moral convictions.
Criminal and Related Violations		
People who have committed crimes involving moral turpitude.	Yes	Waivers are not available for commission of crimes such as attempted murder or conspiracy to commit murder or murder, torture or drug crimes, except for simple possession of less than 30 grams of marijuana, or for people previously admitted as permanent residents, if they have been convicted of aggravated felony since such admission or if they have less than seven years of lawful continuous residence before deportation proceedings are initiated aginst them. Waivers for all other offenses are available only if the applicant is a spouse, parent or child of a U.S. citizen or green card holder; or the only criminal activity was prostitution or the actions occurred more than 15 years before the application for a visa or green card is filed and the alien shows that he or she is rehabilitated and is not a threat to U.S. security.
People with multiple criminal convictions.	Yes	
Prostitutes.	Yes	
Criminals involved in serious criminal activity who have received immunity from prosecution.	Yes	
Drug offenders.	No	However, there may be an acception for a first and only offense or for juvenile offenders.
Drug traffickers.	No	
National Security and Related Violations		
Spies or governmental saboteurs.	No	
People intending to overthrow the U.S. government.	No	
Terrorists and representatives of foreign terrorist organizations.	No	

WAIVERS TO INADMISSIBILITY

GROUNDS TO INADMISSIBILITY	WAIVERS AVAILABLE	CONDITIONS OF WAIVER
People whose entry would endanger U.S. foreign policy, unless the applicant is an official of a foreign government, or the applicant's activities or beliefs would normally be lawful in the U.S., under the constitution.	No	
Voluntary members of totalitarian parties.	Yes	Waiver is available if the membership was involuntary, or is or was when the applicant was under 16 years old, by operation of law, or for purposes of obtaining employment, food rations or other "essentials" of living. Waiver is also possible for past membership if the membership ended at least two years prior to the application (five years if the party in control of a foreign state is considered a totalitarian dictatorship). If neither applies, a waiver is available only for an immigrant who is the parent, spouse, son, daughter, brother or sister of a U.S. citizen, or a spouse, son or daughter of a permanent resident.
Nazis	No	
People Likely to Become Dependent on Public Welfare	No	
Family-sponsored immigrants and employment-sponsored immigrants where a family member is the employment sponsor (or such a family member owns 5% of the petitioning business) whose sponsor has not executed an Affidavit of Support (Form I-864).	No	But an applicant may cure the ground of inadmissibility by subsequently satisfying affidavit of support requirements.
Nonimmigrant public benefit recipients (where the individual came as nonimmigrant and applied for benefits when he or she was not eligible or through fraud). Five-year bar to admissibility.	No	But ground of inadmissibility expires after five years.
Labor Certifications& Employment Qualifications	No	
People without approved labor certifications, if one is required in the category under which the green card application is made.	No	
Graduates of unaccredited medical schools, whether inside or outside of the U.S.; immigrating to the U.S. in a category based on their profession, who have not both passed the foreign medical graduates exam and shown proficiency in English. (Physicians qualifying as special immigrants who have been practicing medicine in the U.S. with a license since January 9, 1978 are not subject to this exclusion.)	No	
Uncertified foreign healthcare workers (not including physicians).	No	But applicant may show qualifications by submitting a certificate from the Commission on Graduates of Foreign Nursing Schools or the equivalent.

WAIVERS TO INADMISSIBILITY

GROUNDS TO INADMISSIBILITY	WAIVERS AVAILABLE	CONDITIONS OF WAIVER
Immigration Violators		
People who are present in the U.S. without proper paperwork ("Admission or parole").	Yes	Available for certain battered women and children who came to the U.S. escaping such battery or who qualify as self-petitioners. Also available for individuals who had visa petitions or labor certifications on file before January 14, 1998 ($1,000 penalty required for latter waiver). Does **not** apply to applicants outside of the U.S.
People who were previously deported.	Yes	Discretionary with INS.
People who have failed to attend removal (deportation) proceedings (unless they had reasonable cause for doing so). Five-year bar to inadmissibility.	Yes	Advance permission to apply for readmission. Discretionary with INS.
People who made misrepresentations during the immigration process.	Yes	The applicant must be the spouse or child of a U.S. citizen or green card holder. A waiver will be granted if the refusal of admission would cause extreme hardship to that relative.
People who made a false claim to U.S. citizenship.	No	
Individuals subject to a final removal (deportation) order under the Immigration and Naturalization Act §274C (Civil Document Fraud Proceedings).	Yes	Available to permanent residents who voluntarily left the U.S., and for those applying for permanent residence as immediate relatives or other family-based petitions if the fraud was committed solely to assist the person's spouse or child and provided that no fine was imposed as part of the previous civil proceeding.
Student visa abusers (person who improperly obtains F-1 status to attend a public elementary school or adult education program, or transfers from a private to a public program except as permitted.) Five-year bar to admissibility.	No	
Certain individuals previously removed (deported). Twenty-year bar to admissibility. Five-year bar to admissibility for aggravated felons and for second and subsequent removal.	Yes	Discretionary with INS (advance permission to apply for readmission).
Individuals unlawfully present (time counted only after April 1, 1997). Presence for 180-364 days, results in three-year bar to admissibility. Presence for 365 or more days creates ten-year bar to admissibility. Bars kick in only if the individual departs the U.S. and seeks reentry after a period of unlawful presence.	Yes	One is not considered "unlawfully present" for up to 120 days if, after a lawful admission, an individual filed a valid change or extension of status before the end of the authorized stay (but then subsequently fell out of status) as long as the individual did not work without authorization. Similarly, time spent as a minor, as an asylum applicant (provided the person had a bona fide asylum claim and did not work without authorization), beneficiaries of family unity legislation and claimants under the battered spouse/child provisions do not accrue time in unlawful presence. Individuals admitted for "duration of status" are not unlawfully present until INS or an immigration judge makes such a determination. A waiver is provided for an immigrant who has a U.S. citizen or permanent resident spouse or parent to whom refusal of the application would cause extreme hardship.

WAIVERS TO INADMISSIBILITY

GROUNDS TO INADMISSIBILITY	WAIVERS AVAILABLE	CONDITIONS OF WAIVER
Individuals unlawfully present after previous immigration violations. (Applies to individuals present unlawfully for an aggregate period over one year, who subsequently reenter without being properly admitted. Also applies to anyone ordered removed who subsequently attempts entry without admission.)	No	A permanent ground of inadmissibility. However, after being gone for ten years an applicant can apply for advance permission to reapply for admission.
Stowaways.	No	
Smugglers of illegal aliens.	Yes	Waivable if the applicant was smuggling in people who were immediate family members at the time, and either is a permanent resident or is immigrating under a family or employment-based visa petition.

Document Violations

People without required current passports or visas.	Yes	Discretionary with INS. Under new "summary removal" procedures, INS may quickly deport people for five years who arrive without proper documents or make misrepresentations during the inspection process.

Draft Evasion and Ineligibility for Citizenship

People who are permanently ineligible for citizenship.	No	
People who are draft evaders, unless they were U.S. citizens at the time of evasion or desertion.	No	

Miscellaneous Grounds

Practicing polygamists.	No	
Guardians accompanying excludable aliens.	No	
International child abductors. (The exclusion does not apply if the applicant is a national of a country that signed the Hague Convention on International Child Abduction.)	No	
Unlawful voters (voting in violation of any federal, state or local law or regulation).	No	
Former U.S. citizens who renounced citizenship to avoid taxation.	No	

Chapter 25

Inside The Immigration Offices: How They Work, How To Get The Best Results In Your Visa Processing

To be sure, the U.S. government agencies that process your immigration applications – principally the Embassies or Consulates abroad, and the Immigration and Naturalization Service - and the workers and bureaucrats who work in those agencies in the processing of the visa application, have a reputation for being a bunch of tough-minded, unfeeling, no-nonsense bureaucrats whose primary concern and interest is often in merely laying down the immigration law and enforcing the rules, and not in delivering services. Nevertheless, *there are a number of things you can do as a visa applicant in order to insure that your dealings with those agencies that process your immigration application move as smoothly and problem-free as possible.*

In this chapter, we provide a general idea of some of such measures.

A. FINDING OUT ABOUT YOUR LOCAL IMMIGRATION OFFICE'S PROCEDURES

As a practical matter, the factual reality is that the nature and extent of the documentation which will be required to support an alien's visa application often vary, even significantly, from one U. S. consulate (or INS) office to another. Hence, even before you begin your application, it is best to contact your local US Consulate or INS office, as the case may be, to inquire about and get the basic information about its office procedures – its work hours, whether it accepts personal inquiries, personal filing of petitions and applications, information on where specifically to file or mail the forms, and inquiry about any special forms or procedures that the office may utilize and about what type of supporting documents are required. For example, some immigration offices may only allow you to file by mail, while others insist may insist that the papers be filed personally in case of questions about the information given or documents submitted.

Unless these questions can be adequately answered for you by the office's recordings on the telephone answering machine, you would probably have to get such answers by making a personal visit to the office, or perhaps possibly by phone or letter. Contact or seek to speak with the person in charge of the processing of immigration application and be sure you get and note the officer's name.

B. IMMIGRATION FORMS PROCEDURES

A few pointers about the proper immigration forms procedures:

● Never give false answers! *This is the most fundamental, governing rule to bear in mind in filling out and answering any and all questions whatsoever on the immigration forms: HONESTY IS THE VERY BEST POLICY!!* Answer any questions asked on the forms truthfully as well as fully – your previous (or present) marital situation and children by present or previous marriage or relationship, list of any brothers and sisters (list then all, including full and half siblings or step siblings, but be fully prepared, as in all other matters with the immigration, to present good documentation for any claims).

This is the time to be absolutely certain that you are accurate and truthful; once you submit these forms, its' too late to try to change your answers after that!

• Check with your local INS office or the American Consulate in your country of residence, whichever is applicable, before submitting the immigration forms, about the most recent or current forms, and counter-check the filing fee amount.

• Whenever you file your papers by mail with the consulate or INS office, always do so by _certified_ or _registered_ mail with return receipt requested. This way, you will have a written confirmation that your papers were received. Keep both the receipt of mailing from the post office, and copies of other papers you submit, in your files for future reference and confirmation. For papers submitted in person, always obtain a written proof of receipt from the office recipient. (See Appendix A for the U.S. Embassy/Consulate contact offices around the world, and Appendix B for a complete list of the INS offices).

C. HERE'S THE BASIC KEY IN CORRECTLY FILLING OUT THE FORMS

A few general rules in regard to completing the immigration forms. A truly important aid to anyone preparing all such forms, are the "blocks" provided on the forms; such blocks are generally self-explanatory and would explicitly indicate the exact information required to be entered for a particular question, and the order in which such information is to be entered in the spaces provided. Secondly, almost every immigration form has a set of "INSTRUCTIONS" on the body of the form, clearly telling the reader the purpose(s) for which the form is appropriate, and giving some pointers on how to complete or file them, and guidelines on the information and supporting documents required to be furnished.

Hence, the first rule in completing the forms is this: in all instances, always be absolutely sure first, to read the forms and to thoroughly understand the information required of you before filling them out. BE DELIBERATELY CAREFUL. Remember this: that the initial batch of forms you complete and submit are what is known as the "primary" documents, meaning that this is the documentary source which the consular and immigration authorities will probably go back to and refer to again and again, and against which they will cross-check any future documents and information from you for consistency.

D. DO NOT SEND THE ORIGINALS OF YOUR DOCUMENTS

When sending or submitting any documents to the consulate or the INS, never send your originals. Rather, simply make a photocopy of the documents and send them. Originals of documents, often irreplaceable, sent to such offices have been known to be lost or misplaced in the crowded offices and massive paperwork of the vast immigration bureaucracy. Hence, always retain the originals, and take them in person to the immigration or consular officers for their own personal inspection and verification on the spot at the proper time.

E. KEEP A COMPLETE FILE OF YOUR OWN

Always make photocopies of each and every form and document you submit to the consular and immigration authorities (quite apart and separate from your originals). The same with every receipt (or cancelled check) the consulate or INS issues you for any fees you pay. Make a separate file and retain such papers in this file for your own records.

As a rule, the same set of papers that are submitted in the filing of the original "petition" (plus more), may have to be submitted for the filing of the visa "application," proper, in the American Consulate abroad, or when you attend the visa interview. And, quite important, these immigration offices do sometimes misplace or lose documents!

F. THE PROPER VISA PHOTO SPECIFICATIONS TO OBTAIN

The INS imposes a number of strict specifications for the photographs and the poses it will accept from applicants for immigration purposes. See sample FORM M-378 on p. 195 for information on the kind of photograph that meets the proper INS specifications.

NOTE: There are professional photographers who specialize in doing INS photos that comply with the INS strict requirements for size, lighting and clarity. They are usually located near and around the INS offices.

G. EVALUATION CENTERS FOR THE ALIEN'S FOREIGN DIPLOMAS

There are many immigrant visa preferences (as well as nonimmigrant visa classifications) that require some United States advanced degrees and academic qualification or its foreign equivalent.

Generally, for the American Consulate or INS to accept a diploma earned in a foreign country, it requires that the university transcripts of the schooling be sent to an accredited academic evaluator for the agency's assessment. Their fees for the evaluation service range from $90 to $170. Here are some of such INS–recognized academic evaluators you may send your school transcripts to in the United States:

World Education Services
P. O. Box 745 Old Chelsea Station
New York, N.Y. 10113-0745
Phone: 212-966-6311

Cultural House, Inc.
29 John St., Suite 503
New York, N.Y. 10038
Phone: 212-285-1022
Fax: 212-285-1366

Educational Credential Evaluators Inc
P. O. Box 17499
Milwaukee, WI 53217
Phone: 414-964-0477

Credentials Evaluation Service
International Education Research Foundation
P. O. Box 66940
Los Angeles, CA 90066
Phone: 310-390-6276

Sample Form M-378

U. S. IMMIGRATION & NATURALIZATION SERVICE

COLOR PHOTOGRAPH
SPECIFICATIONS

IDEAL PHOTOGRAPH
◄

IMAGE MUST FIT INSIDE THIS
BOX ►

THE PICTURE AT LEFT IS IDEAL SIZE, COLOR,
BACKGROUND, AND POSE. THE IMAGE SHOULD
BE 30MM (1 3/16IN) FROM THE HAIR TO
JUST BELOW THE CHIN, AND 26MM (1 IN)
FROM LEFT CHEEK TO RIGHT EAR. THE IMAGE
MUST FIT IN THE BOX AT RIGHT.

THE PHOTOGRAPH
• THE OVERALL SIZE OF THE PICTURE, INCLUDING THE
BACKGROUND, MUST BE AT LEAST 40MM (1 9/16 INCHES)
IN HEIGHT BY 35MM (1 3/8IN) IN WIDTH.

• PHOTOS MUST BE FREE OF SHADOWS AND CONTAIN NO MARKS,
SPLOTCHES, OR DISCOLORATIONS.

• PHOTOS SHOULD BE HIGH QUALITY, WITH GOOD BACK
LIGHTING OR WRAP AROUND LIGHTING, AND MUST HAVE
A WHITE OR OFF-WHITE BACKGROUND.

• PHOTOS MUST BE A GLOSSY OR MATTE FINISH AND
UN-RETOUCHED.

• POLAROID FILM HYBRID #5 IS ACCEPTABLE; HOWEVER SX-70
TYPE FILM OR ANY OTHER INSTANT PROCESSING TYPE FILM IS
UNACCEPTABLE. NON-PEEL APART FILMS ARE EASILY RECOGNIZED
BECAUSE THE BACK OF THE FILM IS BLACK. ACCEPTABLE INSTANT
COLOR FILM HAS A GRAY-TONED BACKING.

THE IMAGE OF THE PERSON
• THE DIMENSIONS OF THE IMAGE SHOULD BE 30MM (1 3/16
INCHES) FROM THE HAIR TO THE NECK, JUST BELOW THE CHIN,
AND 26MM (1 INCH) FROM THE RIGHT EAR TO THE LEFT CHEEK.
IMAGE CANNOT EXCEED 32MM BY 28MM (1 1/4IN X 1 1/16IN).

• IF THE IMAGE AREA ON THE PHOTOGRAPH IS TOO LARGE
OR TOO SMALL, THE PHOTO CANNOT BE USED.

• PHOTOGRAPHS MUST SHOW THE ENTIRE FACE OF THE PERSON
IN A 3/4 VIEW SHOWING THE RIGHT EAR AND LEFT EYE.

• FACIAL FEATURES **MUST BE IDENTIFIABLE.**

• CONTRAST BETWEEN THE IMAGE AND BACKGROUND IS
ESSENTIAL. PHOTOS FOR VERY LIGHT SKINNED PEOPLE
SHOULD BE SLIGHTLY UNDER-EXPOSED. PHOTOS FOR VERY
DARK SKINNED PEOPLE SHOULD BE SLIGHTLY OVER-EXPOSED.

SAMPLES OF UNACCEPTABLE PHOTOGRAPHS

INCORRECT POSE

IMAGE TOO LARGE

IMAGE TOO SMALL

IMAGE TOO DARK
UNDER-EXPOSED

IMAGE TOO LIGHT

DARK BACKGROUND

OVER-EXPOSED

SHADOWS ON PIC

Immigration & Naturalization Service
Form M-378 (6-92)

Appendix A
U.S. Embassies and Consulates

Albania
U.S. Embassy
Ruga E. Labinoti 103
PSC 59 Box 100 (A)
APO AE 09624
Tirana
Telephone: 355-42-32875
Fax: 355-42-32222

Algeria
U.S. Embassy
4 Chemin Cheich Bachir Brahimi
Algiers
Telephone: 691255
Fax: 693979

Angola
U.S. Embassy
Rua Houari Boumedienne No. 32
Miramar, Luanda
Telephone: 244-2-346-418/
244-2-345-481
Fax: 244-2-346-924

Argentina
U.S. Embassy
4300 Colombia, 1425
Buenos Aires
Telephone: 777-4533
Fax: 777-0197

Armenia
U.S. Embassy
18 Gen Bagramian
Yerevan
Telephone: 3742-151-144
Fax: 3742-151-550

Australia
U.S. Embassy
Moonah Pl.
Canberra ACT 2600
Telephone: 270-5000
Fax: 270-5970

U.S. Consulate
553 St. Kilda Road
South Melbourne, Victoria 3004
Telephone: 03-9526-5900
Fax: 03-9529-6774

U.S. Consulate
59th Floor
MLC Centre
19-29 Martin Place
Sydney, NSW 2000
Telephone: 61-2-373-9200
Fax: 61-2-373-9125

U.S. Consulate
246 St. George's Terrace
Perth, WA 6000
Telephone: 61-9-231-9400
Fax: 61-9-231-9444

Austria
U.S. Embassy
Boltzmanngasse 16
A-1091
Vienna
Telephone: 43-1-313-39
Fax: 43-1-310-0682

Azerbaijan
U.S. Embassy
Azadliq Prospekti 83
Baku
Telephone: 9-9412-98-03-35
Fax: 9-9412-98-37-55

Bahamas
U.S. Embassy
Mosmar Building
Queen Street
Nassau
Telephone: 809-322-1181
Fax: 809-356-0222

Bahrain
U.S. Embassy
Shaikh Isa Road
Manama
Telephone: 973-273-300
Fax: 973-275-418

Bangladesh
U.S. Embassy
Diplomatic Enclave
Madani Avenue
Baridhara Model Town
Dhaka
Telephone: 880-2-884700-22
Fax: 880-2-883744-22

Barbados
U.S. Embassy
P.O. Box 302
Bridgetown
Telephone: 246-436-4950
Fax: 246-429-5246

Belarus
U.S. Embassy
Starovilenskaya #46-220002
Minsk
Telephone: 375-172-31-50-00
Fax: 375-172-34-78-53

Belgium
U.S. Embassy
27 Boulevard du Regent
Brussels
Telephone: 32-2-508-2111
Fax: 32-2-511-2725

Belize
U.S. Embassy
Gabourel Lane & Hutson Streets
Belize City
Telephone: 501-2-77161
Fax: 501-2-30802

Benin
U.S. Embassy
Rue Caporal Anani Bernard
Cotonou
Telephone: 30-06-50
Fax: 30-14-39

Bermuda
U.S. Consulate
Crown Hill 16
Middle Road
Devonshire
Hamilton
Telephone: 441-295-1342
Fax: 441-295-1592

Bolivia
U.S. Embassy
Ave. Arce No. 2780
La Paz
Telephone: 591-2-430251
Fax: 591-2-433900

Bosnia
Herzegovina
43 Ul. Dure Dakovica
Sarajevo
Telephone: 387-71-445-700
or 387-71-667-391
Fax: 387-71-659-722

Botswana
U.S. Embassy
P.O. Box 90
Gaborone
Telephone: 267-353-982
Fax: 267-356-947

Brazil
U.S. Embassy
Avenida das Nocoes
Lote 3
Brasilia
Telephone: 55-61-321-7272
Fax: 55-61-321-2833

U.S. Consulate
Avenida Presidente Wilson, 147
Rio de Janeiro
Telephone: 55-21-292-7117
Fax: 55-21-220-0439

U.S. Consulate
Rua Padre Joao Manoel, 933
Sao Paulo
Telephone: 55-11-881-6511
Fax: 55-11-852-1395

U.S. Consulate
Rua Coronel Genuino, 421
9th Floor
Porto Alegre
Telephone: 55-51-226-4288
Fax: 55-51-221-2213

U.S. Consulate
Rua Goncalves Maia, 163
Recife
Telephone: 55-81-421-2441
Fax: 55-81-231-1906

Brunei
U.S. Embassy
P.O. Box B
Bandar Seri Begawan
Telephone: 29670
Fax: 225-293

Bulgaria
U.S. Embassy
1 Sabrona St.
Sofia
Telephone: 980-5241
Fax: 981-8977

Burkina Faso
U.S. Embassy
B.P. 35
Ouagadougou
Telephone: 30-67-23
Fax: 30-38-90

Burma
U.S. Embassy
581 Merchant Street
Rangoon
Telephone: 282055
Fax: 280409

Burundi
U.S. Embassy
B.P. 1720
Avenue du Zaire
Bujumbura
Telephone: 22-29-86
Fax: 22-29-26

Cambodia
U.S. Embassy
27 EO Street 240
Phnom Penh
Telephone: 885-23-426-436
Fax: 885-23-426-437

Cameroon
U.S. Embassy
Rue Nachtigal
Yaounde
Telephone: 237-23-05-12
Fax: 237-23-07-53

Canada
U.S. Embassy
100 Wellington St
Ottawa K1P 5T1
Telephone: 613-238-5335
Fax: 613-238-5720

U.S. Consulate
615 Macleod Trail S.E.
Calgary, Alberta T2G 4T8
Telephone: 403-266-8962
Fax: 403-264-6630

U.S. Consulate
Suite 910, Cogswell Tower
Scotia Square
Halifax, NS B3J 3K1
Telephone: 902-429-2480
Fax: 902-423-6861

U.S. Consulate
1155 St. Alexandre St.
Montreal, Quebec H2Z 1Z2
Telephone: 514-398-9695
Fax: 514-398-0973

U.S. Consulate
P.O. Box 939
Quebec City, Quebec G1R 4T9
Telephone: 418-692-2095
Fax: 418-692-4640

U.S. Consulate
360 University Ave
Toronto, Ontario M5G 1S4
Telephone: 416-595-1700
Fax: 416-595-0051

U.S. Consulate
1095 West Pender St.
Vancouver, B.C. V6E 2M6
Telephone: 604-685-4311
Fax: 604-685-5285

Cape Verde
U.S. Embassy
Rua Abilio Macedo 81
Praia
Telephone: 238-61-56-16
Fax: 238-61-13-55

Central African Republic
U.S. Embassy
Avenue President Dacko
Bangui
Telephone: 236-61-02-00
Fax: 236-61-44-94

Chad
U.S. Embassy
Ave. Felix Eboue
N'Djamena
Telephone: 235-51-70-09
Fax: 235-51-56-54

Chile
U.S. Embassy
Ave. Andres Bello 2800
Santiago
Telephone: 56-2-232-2600
Fax: 56-2-330-3710

China, Mainland
U.S. Embassy
Xiu Shui Bei Jie 3
Beijing
Telephone: 86-10-6532-3831
Fax: 86-10-6532-6422

U.S. Consulate
No. 1 Shamian St. South
Guangzhou
Telephone: 86-20-8188-8911
Fax: 86-20-8186-2341

U.S. Consulate
1469 Huai Hai Middle Road
Shanghai
Telephone: 86-21-6433-6880
Fax: 86-21-6433-4122

U.S. Consulate
52 14th Wei Road
Heping District, 110003
Shenyang
Telephone: 86-24-322-1198
Fax: 86-24-322-2374

U.S. Consulate
4 Lingshiguan Road
Chengdu 610041, Sichuan
Telephone: 86-28-558-3992
Fax: 86-28-558-3520

China, Taiwan
American Institute in Taiwan
7 Lane 134
Hsin Yi Road
Section 3
Taipei
Telephone: 886-2-709-2000
Fax: 886-2-702-7675

Colombia
U.S. Embassy
Calle 22D-BIS No. 47-51
Apartado Aero 3831
Bogota
Telephone: 57-1-315-0811
Fax: 57-1-315-2197

U.S. Consulate
Calle 77 Carrera 68
Centro Comercial Mayorista
Barranquilla
Telephone: 95-353-0970
Fax: 95-353-5216

Comoro Islands
(See Mauritius)

Congo, Democratic Republic of the
(Formerly Zaire)
U.S. Embassy
310 Avenue Des Aviateurs
Kinshasa
Telephone: 243-12-21533
Fax: 243-88-43805

Congo, Republic of
U.S. Embassy
Avenue Amilcar Cabral
Brazzaville
Telephone: 242-83-20-70
Fax: 243-88-43805

Costa Rica
U.S. Embassy
Pavas Road
San Jose
Telephone: 506-220-3939
Fax: 506-220-2305

Cote D'Ivoire
(Formerly Ivory Coast)
U.S. Embassy
5 Rue Jesse Owens
Abidjan
Telephone: 225-21-09-79
Fax: 225-22-32-59

Croatia
U.S. Embassy
Andrije Hebranga 2
Zagreb
Telephone: 385-1-455-55-00
Fax: 385-1-455-85-85

Cuba
U.S. Interest, Swiss Embassy
Calzada entre L & M
Vedado Seccion
Havana
Telephone: 53-7-33-3551/9
Fax: 53-7-33-3700

Cyprus
U.S. Embassy
Metochiou and Ploutarchou
Streets
Engomi, Nicosia
Telephone: 357-2-476100
Fax: 357-2-465944

Czech Republic
U.S. Embassy
Trziste 15-12548 Praha
Prague
Telephone: 420-2-5732-0663
Fax: 420-2-5732-0614

Denmark
U.S. Embassy
Dag Hammarskjolds Alie 24
Copenhagen
Telephone: 45-31-42-31-44
Fax: 45-35-43-02-23

Djibouti
U.S. Embassy
Plateau de Serpent
Blvd. Marechal Joffre
Djibouti
Telephone: 35-3995
Fax: 35-3940

Dominican Republic
U.S. Embassy
Calle Cesar Nicolas Penson &
  Calle Leopoldo Navarro
Santo Domingo
Telephone: 809-221-2171
Fax: 809-686-7437

Ecuador
U.S. Embassy
Avenida 12 de Octubre y
  Avenida Patria
Quito
Telephone: 593-2-562-890
Fax: 593-2-502-052

U.S. Consulate
9 de Octubre y Garcia Moreno
Guayaquil
Telephone: 593-4-323-570
Fax: 593-4-324-558

Egypt
U.S. Embassy
8, Kamal El-Din Salah St.
Garden City
Cairo
Telephone: 20-2-355-7371
Fax: 20-2-357-3200

U.S. Consulate
3 El Fardaha Street
Alexandria
Telephone: 20-3-472-1009
Fax: 20-3-483-3811

El Salvador
U.S. Embassy
Final Blvd. Santa Elena
Antiguo Cuscatlan
San Salvador
Telephone: 503-278-4444
Fax: 503-278-6011

Eritrea
U.S. Embassy
Franklin D. Roosevelt St.
Asmara
Telephone: 291-1-120004
Fax: 291-1-127584

Estonia
U.S. Embassy
Kentmanni 20, EE 0001
Tallinn
Telephone: 372-6-312-021
Fax: 372-6-312-025

Ethiopia
U.S. Embassy
Entoton Street
Addis Ababa
Telephone: 251-1-550-666
Fax: 251-1-552-191

Fiji
U.S. Embassy
31 Loftus Street
Suva, Fiji
Telephone: 679-314-466
Fax: 679-303-872

Finland
U.S. Embassy
Itainen Puistotie 14A
Helsinki
Telephone: 358-9-171931
Fax: 358-9-635332

France
U.S. Embassy
2 Avenue Gabriel
75382 Paris Cedex 08
Telephone: 33-1-4312-2222
Fax: 33-1-4312-2172

U.S. Consulate
Boulevard Paul Peytral 12
13286 Marseille
Telephone: 33-91-549-200
Fax: 33-91-550-947

U.S. Consulate
15 Avenue d'Alsace
67082 Strasbourg
Telephone: 33-88-35-31-04
Fax: 33-88-24-06-95

Gabon
U.S. Embassy
Blvd. de la Mer
Libreville
Telephone: 241-762-003 or
  241-762-004
Fax: 241 745-507

The Gambia
U.S. Embassy
Fajara East-
Kairaba Ave.
Banjul
Telephone: 220-392-856
Fax: 220-392-475

Georgia
U.S. Embassy
25 Atoneli
Tbilisi
Telephone:
  SWBD 995-32-989-67 or
  995-32-933-803
Fax: 995-32-933-759 or
  995-32-938-951

Germany
U.S. Embassy (Branch Office)
108 Berlin
Neustaedtischee Kirchstrasse 4-5
Berlin
Telephone: 49-30-238-5174
Fax: 49-30-238-6290

U.S. Embassy
Deichmanns Ave
53170 Bonn
Telephone: 49-228-3391
Fax: 49-339-2663

U.S. Consulate
Kennedydamm 15-17
40476 Dusseldorf
Telephone: 49-211-47061-0
Fax: 49-211-43-14-48

U.S. Consulate
Siesmayerstrasse 21
60323 Frankfurt
Telephone: 49-69-7535-0
Fax: 49-69-748-204

U.S. Consulate
Alsterufer 27/28
20354 Hamburg
Telephone: 49-171-351269
Fax: 49-40-443004

U.S. Consulate
Wilhelm-Seyfferth-Strasse 4
04107 Leipzig
Telephone: 49-341-213-840
Fax: 49-341-213-8417

U.S. Consulate
Koeniginstrasse 5
80539 Muenchen
Telephone: 49-171-815-4805
Fax: 49-171-283-047

Ghana
U.S. Embassy
Ring Road East
Accra
Telephone: 233-21-775348
Fax: 233-21-776008

Greece
U.S. Embassy
91 Vasilissis Sophias Blvd.
10160 Athens
Telephone: 30-1-721-2951
Fax: 30-1-721-8660

U.S. Consulate
59 Leoforos Nikis
GR-546-22 Thessaloniki
Telephone: 30-31-242905 or
30-31-720-2400
Fax: 30-31-242927 or
30-31242915

Grenada
U.S. Embassy
Box 54
St. Georges
Telephone: 809-444-1173
Fax: 809-444-4820

Guatemala
U.S. Embassy
7-01 Avenida de la Reforma
Zone 10
Guatemala City
Telephone: 502-2-31-15-41
Fax: 502-2-32-04-95

Guinea
U.S. Embassy
Rue KA 038 B.P. 603
Conakry
Telephone: 224-41-15-20 or
224-41-15-21 or
224-41-15-23
Fax: 224-41-15-22

Guinea-Bissau
U.S. Embassy
1 Rua Ulysses S. Grant
Bairro de Penha
Bissau
Telephone: 245-25-2273
Fax: 245-25-2282

Guyana
U.S. Embassy
99-100 Young and Duke Sts.
Kingston, Georgetown
Telephone: 592-2-54900-9
Fax: 592-2-58497

Haiti
U.S. Embassy
5 Harry Truman Blvd.
Port-au-Prince
Telephone: 509-22-0354
Fax: 509-23-1641

The Holy See
U.S. Embassy
Villa Domiziana
Via Delle Terme Deciane 26
00153 Rome, Italy
Telephone: 396-46741
Fax: 396-575-8346 or
396-573-0682

Honduras
U.S. Embassy
Avenido La Paz
Tegucigalpa
Telephone: 504-36-9320
Fax: 504-36-9037

Hong Kong
U.S. Consulate
26 Garden Road
Hong Kong
Telephone: 852-2523-9011
Fax: 852-2845-4845

Hungary
U.S. Embassy
V. Szabadsag Ter 12
Budapest
Telephone: 36-1-267-4400
Fax: 36-1-269-9326

Iceland
U.S. Embassy
Laufasvegur 21
Reykjavik
Telephone: 354-5629100
Fax: 354-5629118

India
U.S. Embassy
Shanti Path
Chanakyapuri 110021
New Delhi
Telephone: 91-11-688-9033
Fax: 91-11-687-2391

U.S. Consulate
Lincoln House
78 Bhulabhai Desai Rd.
Mumbai 400026
Telephone: 91-22-363-3611
Fax: 91-22-363-0350

U.S. Consulate
5/1 Ho Chi Minh Sarani
Calcutta 700071
Telephone: 91-33-282-3611
Fax: 91-33-282-2335

U.S. Consulate
220 Mount Road 600006
Madras
Telephone: 91-44-827-3040
Fax: 91-44-826-2538

Indonesia
U.S. Embassy
Merdeka Selatan 5
Jakarta
Telephone: 62-21-344-2211
Fax: 62-21-386-2259

U.S. Consular Agency
Jalan Segara Ayu No. 5
Sanur 00228
Bali
Telephone: 62-361-88478
Fax: 62-361-87760

U.S. Consulate
Jalan Raya Dr. Sutomo 33
Surabaya
Telephone: 62-31-582287
Fax: 62-31-574492

Iraq
U.S. Embassy
Opp. For. Ministry Club
Masbah Quarter
Baghdad
Telephone: 964-1-719-6138/9
Fax: 964-1-718-9297

Ireland
U.S. Embassy
42 Elgin Road
Ballsbridge
Dublin
Telephone: 353-1-6688777
Fax: 353-1-6670056

Israel
U.S. Consulate
18 Agron Road
Jerusalem 94190
Telephone: 9726-2-253288
Fax: 9726-2-59270

U.S. Embassy
71 Hayarkon St.
Tel Aviv
Telephone: 973-3-519-7575
Fax: 973-3-510-7215

Italy
U.S. Embassy
Via Veneto 119/A
00187 Rome
Telephone: 39-6-46741
Fax: 39-488-2672

U.S. Consulate
Banca d'America e
d'Italia Bldg.
Piazza Poheilo 6
Genoa
Telephone: 39-10-282-741
Fax: 39-10-543-877

U.S. Consulate
Via Principe Amedeo 2
20121 Milano
Telephone: 39-2-290-351
Fax: 39-2-2900-1165

U.S. Consulate
Piazza della Repubblica
80122 Naples
Telephone: 39-81-583-8111
Fax: 39-81-761-1869

U.S. Consulate
Via Re Federico
No. 18 BIS
Palermo
Telephone: 39-091-611-00-20

U.S. Consulate
Lungarno Amerigo Vespucci 38
Florence 50123
Telephone: 39-55-239-8276
Fax: 39-55-216-531

U.S. Consulate
Via Roma 15
Trieste 34132
Telephone: 39-0-040-660-177
Fax: 39-0-040-631-240

Ivory Coast
(See Cote d'Ivoire)

Jamaica
U.S. Embassy
Jamaica Mutual Life Center
2 Oxford Road, 3rd Floor
Kingston
Telephone: 809-929-4850
Fax: 809-926-6743

U.S. Consulate
St. James Place, 2nd Floor
Gloucester Ave.
Montego Bay
Telephone: 809-952-0160/5050

Japan
U.S. Embassy
10-5 Akasaka 1-chome
Minato-ku 107-
Tokyo
Telephone: 81-3-3224-5000
Fax: 81-3-3505-1862

U.S. Consulate
2564 Nishihara
Urasoe City, Okinawa 90121
Telephone: 81-98-876-4211
Fax: 81-98-876-4243

U.S. Consulate
11-5 Nishitenma 2-chome
Kita-Ku
Osaka 530
Telephone: 81-6-315-5900
Fax: 81-6-315-5930

U.S. Consulate
5-26 Ohori 2-chome, Chuo-ku
Fukuoka 810
Telephone: 81-92-751-9331
Fax: 81-92-713-9222

U.S. Consulate
Nishiki SIS Building 6F 10-33
Nishiki 3-chome
Nagoya 460
Telephone: 81-52-203-4011
Fax: 81-52-201-4612

U.S. Consulate
Kita I-Jo
Nisi 28-chome
Chuo-ku
Sapporo 061
Telephone: 81-11-641-1115/7
Fax: 81-11-643-1283

Jordan
U.S. Embassy
Box 354
Amman 11118
Telephone: 962-6-820-101
Fax: 962-820-163

Kazakstan
U.S. Embassy
99/97 Furmanova St.
Almaty
Republic of Kazakstan 4800 12
Telephone: 7-3272-63-39-05
Fax: 7-3272-63-38-83

Kenya
U.S. Embassy
Moi/Haile Selassie Ave
Nairobi
Telephone: 254-2-334141
Fax: 254-2-340838

Korea
U.S. Embassy
82 Sejong-Ro
Chongro-Ku
Seoul
Telephone: 82-2-397-4111
Fax: 82-2-738-8845

Kuwait
U.S. Embassy
P.O. Box 77 SAFAT
Kuwait
Telephone: 965-539-5307
Fax: 965-538-0282

Kyrgyzstan
U.S. Embassy
Erkindik Prospect #66
Bishkek 720002
Telephone: 7-3312-22-29-20
Fax: 7-3312-22-35-51

Laos
U.S. Embassy
Rue Bartholonie
B.P. 114
Vientiane
Telephone: 856-21-212-581
Fax: 856-21-212-584

Latvia
U.S. Embassy
Raina Boulevard 7, LV-1510
Riga
Telephone: 371-2-721-0005
Fax: 371-2-782-0047

Lebanon
U.S. Embassy
P.O. Box 70-840
Antelias
Beirut
Telephone: 961-1-402-200
Fax: 961-1-403-313

Lesotho
U.S. Embassy
P.O. Box 333
Maseru
Telephone: 266-312-666
Fax: 266-310-116

Liberia
U.S. Embassy
1111 United Nations Drive
Monrovia
Telephone: 231-226-370
Fax: 231-226-148

Lithuania
U.S. Embassy
Akmenu
Vilnius 2600
Telephone: 370-2-223-031
Fax: 370-670-6084

Luxembourg
U.S. Embassy
22 Blvd Emmanuel-Servais
2535 Luxembourg
Telephone: 352-460123
Fax: 352-461401

Macedonia
(The former Yugoslav Republic of)
U.S. Embassy
Bul. Ilinden bb
9100 Skopje
Telephone 389-91-116-180
Fax: 389-91-117-103

Madagascar
U.S. Embassy
14 and 16 Rue Raintovo
Antsahavola
Antannanarivo
Telephone: 2612-212-57
Fax: 2612-345-39

Malawi
U.S. Embassy
P.O. Box 30016
Lilongwe
Telephone: 265-783-166
Fax: 265-780-471

Malaysia
U.S. Embassy
376 Jalan Tun Razak
50400 Kuala Lumpur
Telephone: 603-248-9011
Fax: 603-242-2207

Mali
U.S. Embassy
Rue Rochester NY and Rue
Mohamed V, B.P.34
Bamako
Telephone: 223-225-470
Fax: 223-223-712

Malta
U.S. Embassy
2d Floor, Development House
St. Anne Street
Floriana, Valletta
Telephone: 356-235-960
Fax: 356-246-917

Marshall Islands
U.S. Embassy
Oceanside Mejen Loeto
Long Island
Majuro, Republic of the
   Marshall Islands
Telephone: 692-247-4011
Fax: 692-247-4012

Mauritania
U.S. Embassy
B.P. 222
Nouakchott
Telephone: 222-2-526-60
Fax: 222-2-515-92

Mauritius
U.S. Embassy
Rogers Building, 4th Floor
John Kennedy Street
Port Louis
Telephone: 230-208-2347
Fax: 230-208-9534

Mexico
U.S. Embassy
Paseo de la Reforma 305
Mexico City
Telephone: 525-211-0042
Fax: 525-208-3373

U.S. Consulate
924 Avenue Lopez Mateos
Ciudad Juarez
Telephone: 52-16-11300
Fax: 52-16-169056

U.S. Consulate
Progreso 175
Guadalajara, Jalisco
Telephone: 52-3-825-2998
Fax: 52-3-826-6549

U.S. Consulate
Monterrey 141 Pre;
Hermosillo 83260, Sonora
Telephone: 52-62-17-2375
Fax: 52-62-17-2578

U.S. Consulate
Tapachula 96
Tijuana, B.C.
Telephone: 52-66-81-7400
Fax: 52-66-81-8016

U.S. Consulate
Paseo Montejo 453
Merida, Yucatan
Telephone: 52-99-25-5011
Fax: 52-99-25-6219

U.S. Consulate
Avenide Constitucion
411 Poniente
Monterrey, N.L.
Telephone: 52-8-345-2120
Fax: 52-8-342-0177

U.S. Consulate
Calle Allende 3330
Col. Jardin
88260 Nuevo Laredo, Tamps.
Telephone: 52-87-14-0152
Fax: 52-87-14-7984

U.S. Consulate
Ave. Primera 2002
87330 Matamoros, Tamps.
Telephone: 52-88-12-44-02
Fax: 52-88-12-21-71

Micronesia
U.S. Embassy
P.O. Box 1286
Kolonia
Telephone: 691-320-2187
Fax: 691-320-2186

Moldova
U.S. Embassy
Strada Alexei Mateevicie #103
277014 Chisinau
Telephone: 373-2-23-37-72
Fax: 373-223-30-44

Mongolia
U.S. Embassy
Ulaanbaatar
Telephone: 976-1-329-095
Fax: 976-1-320-776

Morocco
U.S. Embassy
2 Ave de Marrakech
Rabat
Telephone: 212-7-76-2265
Fax: 212-7-76-5621

U.S. Consulate
8 Blvd. Moulay Youssef
Casablanca
Telephone: 212-2-264-550
Fax: 212-2-204-127

Mozambique
U.S. Embassy
Avenida Kenneth Kaunda
Maputo
Telephone: 258-1-49-27-97
Fax: 258-1-49-01-14

Namibia
U.S. Embassy
Ausplan Building
14 Lossen St.
Private Bag 12029 Ausspannplatz
Windhoek
Telephone: 264-61-221-601
Fax: 264-61-229-792

Nepal
U.S. Embassy
Pani Pokhari
Kathmandu
Telephone: 977-1-411179
Fax: 977-1-419963

Netherlands
U.S. Embassy
Lange Voohout 102
2514 EJ, Den
The Hague
Telephone: 31-70-310-9209
Fax: 31-70-361-4688

U.S. Consulate
Museumplein 19
Amsterdam
Telephone: 31-20-5755-309
Fax: 31-20-5755-310

Netherlands Antilles
U.S. Consulate
J.B. Gorsiraweg #1
Curacao
Telephone: 599-9-613066
Fax: 599-9-616489

New Zealand
U.S. Embassy
29 Fitzherbert Ter.
Thorndon
Wellington
Telephone: 64-4-472-2068
Fax: 64-4-471-2380

U.S. Consulate
4th Floor Yorkshire
 General Bldg.
Shortland and O'Connel Sts.
Auckland
Telephone: 64-9-303-2724
Fax: 64-9-366-0870

Nicaragua
U.S. Embassy
Km. 4-1/2 Carretera Sur
Managua
Telephone: 505-2-666010
Fax: 505-2-669074

Niger
U.S. Embassy
B.P. 11201
Niamey
Telephone: 227-72-26-61
Fax: 227-73-31-67

Nigeria
U.S. Embassy
2 Eleke Crescent
Lagos
Telephone: 234-1-261-0097
Fax: 234-1-261-0257

Norway
U.S. Embassy
Drammensveien 18
Oslo 2
Telephone: 47-22-44-85-50
Fax: 47-22-44-33-63

Oman
U.S. Embassy
P.O. Box 50202
Muscat
Telephone: 968-698-989
Fax: 968-699-779

Pakistan
U.S. Embassy
Diplomatic Enclave
Ramna 5
Islamabad
Telephone: 92-51-826-161
Fax: 92-51-214-222

U.S. Consulate
8 Abdullah Haroon Rd
Karachi
Telephone: 92-21-568-5170
Fax: 92-21-568-0496

U.S. Consulate
50 Shahrah-E Bin Badees
Lahore
Telephone: 92-42-636-5530
Fax: 92-42-636-5177

U.S. Consulate
11 Hospital Road
Peshawar
Telephone: 92-521-279801
Fax: 92-521-276712

Palau
P.O. Box 6028
Koror
Telephone: 680-488-2920
Fax: 680-488-2911

Panama
U.S. Embassy
Apartado
6959 Panama City
Telephone: 507-227-1777
Fax: 507-227-1964

Papua New Guinea
U.S. Embassy
Douglas St.
Port Moresby
Telephone: 675-321-1455
Fax: 675-321-3423

Paraguay
U.S. Embassy
1776 Mariscal Lopez Ave.
Asuncion
Telephone: 595-21-213-715
Fax: 595-21-213-728

Peru
U.S. Embassy
Avenida Encalada
Cuadra 17
Monterrico, Lima
Telephone: 51-1-434-3000
Fax: 51-1-434-3037

Philippines
U.S. Embassy
1201 Roxas Blvd.
Manila
Telephone: 63-2-523-1001
Fax: 63-2-522-4361

U.S. Consulate
3rd Floor
Philippine American Life
Ins. Bldg.
Jones Ave.
Cebu
Telephone: 63-32-310-261/2
Fax: 63-32-310-174

Poland
U.S. Embassy
Aleje Ujazdowskle 29/31
Warsaw
Telephone: 48-22-628-3041
Fax: 48-22-628-8298

U.S. Consulate
Ulica Stolarska 9
31043 Krakow
Telephone: 48-12-229764
Fax: 48-12-218292

Portugal
U.S. Embassy
Avenida das Forcas Armadas
1600 Lisbon
Telephone: 351-1-727-3300
Fax: 351-1-726-9109

U.S. Consulate
Avenida D. Henrique
Ponta Delgada, Sao Miguel
Azores
Telephone: 351-96-22216
Fax: 351-96-27216

Qatar
U.S. Embassy
Fariq Bin Omran
Doha
Telephone: 974-864701
Fax: 974-861669

Romania
U.S. Embassy
Strada Tudor Argheze 7-9
Bucharest
Telephone: 40-1-210-4042
Fax: 40-1-210-0395

Russia
*(New embassies for former Soviet
states will be opening soon)*
U.S. Embassy
Novinskiy Bul'var 19/23
Moscow
Telephone: 7-095-252-2451
Fax 7-095-956-4261

U.S. Consulate
Ulitsa
Petra Lavrova St. 15
St. Petersburg
Telephone: 7-812-275-1701
Fax: 7-812-110-7022

Rwanda
U.S. Embassy
Blvd de la Revolution
B.P. 28
Kigali
Telephone: 301-985-9339
Fax: 301-250-72128

Saudi Arabia
U.S. Embassy
Collector Road M
Riyadh Diplomatic Quarter
Riyadh
Telephone: 966-1-488-3800
Fax: 966-1-488-3989

U.S. Consulate
Between Aramco Hqrs &
  Dhahran Int'l Airport
Dharhran
Telephone: 966-3-891-3200
Fax: 933-3-891-6816

U.S. Consulate
Palestine Rd.
Ruwais
Jeddah
Telephone: 966-2-667-0080
Fax: 966-2-669-2991

Senegal
U.S. Embassy
B.P. 49
Avenue Jean XXIII
Dakar
Telephone: 221-23-42-96
Fax: 221-22-29-91

Serbia–Montenegro
U.S. Embassy
Belgrade
Telephone: 381-11-645-655
Fax: 381-11-645-332

Seychelles
(See Mauritius)

Sierra Leone
U.S. Embassy
Walpole & Siaka Stevens Sts.
Freetown
Telephone: 232-22-226-481
Fax: 232-22-225-471

Singapore
U.S. Embassy
30 Hill Street
Singapore 0617
Telephone: 65-338-0251
Fax: 65-338-4550

Slovak Republic
U.S. Embassy
Hviezdoslavovo Namestie 4
81102 Bratislava
Telephone: 421-7-533-3338
Fax: 421-7-533-5439

Slovenia
U.S. Embassy
Box 254
Prazakova 4
1000 Ljubljana
Telephone: 386-61-301-427
Fax: 386-61-301-401

South Africa
U.S. Consulate
Broadway Industries Center
Heerengracht, Foreshore
Cape Town
Telephone: 27-21-21-4280
Fax: 27-21-25-3014

U.S. Consulate
Durban Bay House, 29th Floor
333 Smith Street
Durban 4001
Telephone: 27-31-304-4737
Fax: 27-31-301-8206

U.S. Consulate
11th Floor, Kine Center
Commissioner & Krulis Streets
Johannesburg
Telephone: 27-11-331-1681
Fax: 27-11-331-6178

U.S. Consulate
877 Pretorius St.
Arcadia 0083
Pretoria
Telephone: 27-12-342-1048
Fax: 27-12-342-2244

South Korea
(See Korea)

Spain
U.S.Embassy
Serrano 75
Madrid
Telephone: 34-1-587-2200
Fax: 34-1-587-2303

U.S. Consulate
Reina Elisenda 23
Barcelona 08034
Telephone: 34-3-280-2227
Fax: 34-3-205-7764

Sri Lanka
U.S. Embassy
210 Galle Rd.
Colombo 3
Telephone: 94-1-448007
Fax: 94-1-437-345

Sudan
U.S. Embassy
Sharia Ali Abdul Latif
Khartoum
Telephone: 249-11-774461
Fax: 249-11-873-151-6770

Suriname
U.S. Embassy
Dr. Sophie Redmondstraat 129
Paramaribo
Telephone: 472900
Fax: 42800

Swaziland
U.S. Embassy
Central Bank Buiding
P.O. Box 199, Warner Street
Mbabane
Telephone: 268-46441
Fax: 268-45959

Sweden
U.S. Embassy
Strandvagen101
Stockholm
Telephone: 46-8-783-5300
Fax: 46-8-661-1964

Switzerland
U.S. Embassy
Jubilaeumstrasse 93
3005 Bern
Telephone: 41-31-357-7011
Fax: 41-31-357-7344

U.S. Consulate
11, Route de Pregny
1292 Chambesy
Geneva
Telephone: 41-22-749-4111
Fax: 41-22-749-4880

Syria
U.S. Embassy
Abu Rumaneh
Al Mansur St. No. 2
Damascus
Telephone: 963-11-333-2814
Fax: 963-11-224-7938

Tajikistan
U.S. Embassy
Octyabrskaya Hotel
105A Prospect Rudaki
Dushanbe, Tajikistan 734001
Telephone: 7-3772-21-03-56
Fax: 7-3772-20-03-62

Tanzania
U.S. Embassy
36 Laibon Rd.
Dar es Salaam
Telephone: 255-51-666010
Fax: 255-51-666701

Thailand
U.S. Embassy
95 Wireless Rd.
Bangkok
Telephone: 66-2-205-4000
Fax: 66-2-255-2915

U.S. Consulate
Vidhayanond Rd.
Chiang Mai
Telephone: 66-53-252-629
Fax: 66-53-252-633

Togo
U.S. Embassy
Rue Pelletier Caventou &
 Rue Vouban
Lome
Telephone: 228-21-77-17
Fax: 228-21-79-52

Trinidad and Tobago
U.S. Embassy
15 Queens Park West
Port of Spain
Telephone: 809-622-6372
Fax: 809-628-5462

Tunisia
U.S. Embassy
144 Ave. de la Liberte
Tunis
Telephone: 216-1-782-566
Fax: 216-1-789-719

Turkey
U.S. Embassy
110 Ataturk Blvd.
Ankara
Telephone: 90-312-468-6110
Fax: 90-312-467-0019

U.S. Consulate
Ataturk Caddesi
Adana
Telephone: 90-322-454-2145
Fax: 90-322-457-6591

U.S. Consulate
104-108 Mesrutiyet Cadesi
Tepebasi
Istanbul
Telephone: 90-212-251-3602
Fax: 90-212-251-2554

Turkmenistan
U.S. Embassy
9 Pushkin Street
Ashgabat
Telephone: 9-9312-35-00-45
Fax: 9-9312-51-13-05

Uganda
U.S. Embassy
Parliament Avenue
Kampala
Telephone: 256-41-259792
Fax: 256-41-259794

Ukraine
U.S. Embassy
10 Yuria Kotsubynskoho
254053 Kiev
Telephone: 380-44-244-7345
Fax: 380-44-244-7350

United Arab Emirates
U.S. Embassy
Al-Sudan St.
Abu Dhabi
Telephone: 971-2-436-691
Fax: 971-2-434-771

U.S.Consulate
Dubai International Trade Ctr
Dubai
Telephone: 971-2-314-043
Fax: 971-2-434-771

United Kingdom
U.S. Embassy
24/31 Grosvenor Square
London, W1A 1AE
Telephone: 44-171-499-9000
Fax: 44-171-409-1637

U.S. Consulate
Queen's House
14 Queen Street
Belfast, Northern Ireland
Telephone: 44-1232-241279
Fax: 44-1232-248482

Uruguay
U.S. Embassy
Lauro Muller 1776
Montevideo
Telephone: 598-2-23-60-61
Fax: 592-2-48-86-11

Uzbekistan
U.S. Embassy
82 Chilanzarskaya
Tashkent
Telephone: 7-3712-77-14-07
Fax: 7-3712-40-63-35

Venezuela
U.S. Embassy
Colle F con Calle Suapure
Colinas de Valle Arriba
Caracas
Telephone: 58-2-977-2011
Fax: 58-2-977-3253

Vietnam
U.S. Embassy
7 Lang Ha Road
Ba Dinh District
Hanoi
Telephone: 84-4-843-1500
Fax: 84-4-835-0484

Western Samoa
U.S. Embassy
P.O. Box 3430
Apia
Telephone: 685-21-631
Fax: 685-22-030

Yemen–Republic of
U.S. Embassy
Dhahr Himyar Zone
Sheraton Hotel District
Sanaa
Telephone: 967-1-238-843
Fax:967-1- 251-563

Zaire
(See Congo, Democratic
Republic of the)

Zambia
U.S. Embassy
Independence & United
 Nations Avenues
Lusaka
Telephone: 260-1-250-955
Fax: 260-1-252-225

Zimbabwe
U.S. Embassy
172 Herbert Chitepo Ave.
Harare
Telephone: 263-4-794-521
Fax: 263-4-796-488

Appendix B

Directory of INS Offices

INS Central Office

Immigration & Naturalization Service
Justice Department
425 Eye St. N.W.
Washington, D.C. 20536
Information: 202-514-2648
Form Requests: 800-870-3676
Fax: 202-514-3296

INS Regional Offices

California Service Center
Immigration & Naturalization Service
24000 Avila Road
P.O. Box 30080
Laguna Niguel, CA 92677-8080
Telephone: 714-306-2995
Fax: 714-306-3081

Nebraska Service Center
Immigration & Naturalization Service
850 S Street
Lincoln, NE 68508
Telephone: 402-437-5218

Texas Service Center
Immigration & Naturalization Service
Room 2300
7701 N. Stemmons Freeway
Dallas, TX 75247
Telephone: 214-767-7020
Fax: 214-767-7477

Vermont Service Center
Immigration & Naturalization Service
70 Kimball Ave.
South Burlington, VT 05403-6813
Telephone: 802-660-5000
Fax: 802-660-5114

INS DISTRICT OFFICES

Anchorage, Alaska
620 E. 10th Avenue
Suite 102
Anchorage, AK
907-271-3524

Atlanta, Georgia
77 Forsythe Street, SW
Room G-85
Atlanta, GA 30303
404-331-0253

Baltimore, Maryland
100 S. Charles St.
Baltimore, MD 21201
410-962-2010

Boston, Massachusetts
John F. Kennedy Federal Bldg.
Government Center, Room 700
Boston, MA 02203
617-565-4214

Buffalo, New York
130 Federal Center
Buffalo, NY 14202
716-651-4741

Chicago, Illinois
10 W. Jackson Blvd.
Chicago, IL 60604
312-886-6770

Cleveland, Ohio
1240 E. 9th St., Room 1917
Cleveland, OH 44199
216-522-4766

Dallas, Texas
8101 N. Stemmons Freeway
Dallas, TX 75247
214-655-3011

Denver, Colorado
4730 Paris Street
Denver, CO 80209
303-371-0986

Detroit, Michigan
333 Mount Elliott St.
Detroit, MI 48207
313-586-6000

El Paso, Texas
1545 Hawkins Blvd., Suite 167
El Paso, TX 79901
915-540-7341

Harlingen, Texas
2102 Teege Road
Harlingen, TX 78550
210-427-8592

Helena, Montana
2800 Skyway Drive
Helena, MT 59601
406-449-5220

Honolulu, Hawaii
595 Ala Moana Blvd.
Honolulu, HI 96813
808-449-5220

Houston, Texas
509 N. Belt Drive
Houston, TX 77060
713-847-7950

Kansas City, Missouri
9747 North Conant Ave.
Kansas City, MO 64153
816-891-0684

Los Angeles, California
300 N. Los Angeles Street
Los Angeles, CA 90012
213-894-2780

Miami, Florida
7880 Biscayne Blvd.
Miami, FL 33138
305-530-7657

New Orleans, Louisiana
701 Loyola Avenue
Room T-8005
New Orleans, LA 70113
504-589-6521

New York, New York
Jacob K. Javits Federal Building
26 Federal Plaza
New York, NY 10278
212-206-6500

Newark, New Jersey
Federal Building
970 Broad Street
Newark, NJ 07102
201-645-2269

Omaha, Nebraska
3736 S. 132nd Street
Omaha, NE 68144
402-697-9155

Philadelphia, Pennsylvania
1600 Caldwell St.
Philadelphia, PA 19130
215-656-7150

Phoenix, Arizona
2035 N. Central Ave.
Phoenix, AZ 85004
602-379-3114

Portland, Maine
739 Warren Avenue
Portland, ME 04103
207-780-3399

Portland, Oregon
Federal Building
511 N.W. Broadway
Portland, OR 97209
503-326-3962

St. Paul, Minnesota
2901 Metro Drive
Bloomington, MN 55425
612-335-2211

San Antonio, Texas
727 E. Durango
San Antonio, TX 78206
210-871-7000

San Diego, California
880 Front Street
San Diego, CA 92188
619-557-5645

San Francisco, California
Appraisers Building
630 Sansome Street
San Francisco, CA 94111
415-705-4411

San Juan, Puerto Rico
Carlos E. Chardon Street
Room 359
Hato Rey, PR 00918
809-766-5380

Seattle, Washington
815 Airport Way South
Seattle, WA 98134
206-553-0070

Washington, D.C.
4420 N. Fairfax Drive
Arlington, VA 22003
203-307-1642

Appendix C

REGIONAL DEPARTMENT OF LABOR Offices

REGION	STATES
Atlanta 100 Alabama St. SW Suite 6M12 Atlanta, GA 30367 Tel: 404-562-2092 Fax: 404-562-2149	Alabama, Florida, Georgia, Kentucky, Mississippi, North Carolina, South Carolina, Tennessee
Boston JFK Federal Building Room E-350 Boston, MA 02203 Tel: 617-565-3630 Fax: 617-565-2229	Connecticut, Maine, Massachusetts, New Hampshire, Rhode Island, Vermont
Chicago 230 South Dearborn St. 6th Floor Chicago, IL 60604 Tel: 312-353-1053 Fax: 312-353-4474	Ilinois, Indiana, Michigan, Minnesota, Ohio, Wisconsin
Dallas 525 Griffin Street Room 317 Dallas, TX 75202 Tel: 214-767-8263 Fax: 214-767-5113	Arkansas, Louisiana, New Mexico, Oklahoma, Texas
Denver 1999 Broadway Suite 1780 Denver, CO 80202 Tel: 303-844-1650 Fax: 303-844-1685	Colorado, Montana, North Dakota, South Dakota, Utah, Wyoming

REGION	STATES
Kansas City 1100 Main St., Suite 1050 City Center Square Kansas City, MO 64106 Tel 816-426-3796 Fax: 816-426-2929	Iowa, Kansas, Missouri, Nebraska
New York 201 Varick Street Room 755 New York, NY 10014 Tel: 212-337-2185 Fax: 212-337-2144	New York, New Jersey, Puerto Rico, Virgin Islands

Philadelphia
3535 Market St.
Philadelphia, PA 19101
Tel: 215-596-6363
Alien Certification
  Fax: 215-596-0480
Administrator Fax:
  215-596-0329
	Delaware, District of Columbia, Maryland, Pennsylvania, Virginia, West Virginia

San Francisco P.O. Box 193767 San Francisco, CA 94119-3767 Tel: 415-975-4610 Fax: 415-975-4612	Arizona, California, Guam, Hawaii, Nevada
Seattle 1111 Third Avenue Suite 900 Seattle, WA 98101 Tel: 206-553-7700 Fax: 206-553-0098	Alaska, Idaho, Oregon, Washington

APPENDIX D
Glossary Of Terms & Some Relevant Definitions

ACCOMPANYING OR FOLLOWING TO JOIN: Immediate family members who travel to the U.S. with the principal alien, or who arrive in the U.S. after the principal alien. Does not include those who come to the U.S. before the principal alien.

ADMITTED: An alien who has been inspected and allowed to enter the U.S. in an Immigrant or non-Immigrant status.

ADJUSTMENT OF STATUS: The procedure for changing an alien's non-Immigrant status to an Immigrant status while in the U.S. (see Chapter 20 of text)

ADVISORY OPINION: A procedure which allows the Visa Office in Washington, D.C. (part of the U.S. State Department) to review the decision of a U.S. Consul. A Consul is generally not obligated to change the decision even after an Advisory Opinion is issued.

ALIEN: A person who is NOT a citizen or national of the U.S. (Chapter 2, Section A the text).

APPEAL: A procedure allowed in certain cases for a superior person or board to review the decision and papers in a case. After review, the person or board can return the papers for further action, allow the original decision to stand, change the decision in whole or in part.

ATTORNEY: A lawyer admitted to practice law in any jurisdiction in the United States.

BOARD OF IMMIGRATION APPEALS: The part of the U.S. Justice Department responsible for review of decisions on Preference Petitions and for certain other appeals from decisions or actions of the Immigration and Naturalization Service.

BRIEF. The paper or letter accompanying an appeal or motion which contains the facts or rebuttal.

BUSINESS NECESSITY: A justification for requiring a Combination of Duties, foreign language requirement, or other special requirement not found in the Dictionary of Occupational Titles. Business Necessity arises when the absence of the requirement would tend to undermine the business. Business Necessity can also refer to a situation in a private household when a Live-in requirement for a domestic worker is essential to the household.

CERTIFYING OFFICER: The employee of the U.S. Labor Department responsible for issuing the Labor Certificate and for affixing the Certification Stamp to the Application Form.)

DICTIONARY OF OCCUPATIONAL TITLES: A publication of the U.S. Government listing job titles and descriptions. It is used as a guide by the local Employment Service offices and the U.S. Department of Labor. It is available for examination in many public libraries and government agencies. The Dictionary is for sale by the Superintendent of Documents in Washington, D.C., and in U.S. Government Book Stores in larger U.S. cities.

EXCEPTIONAL ABILITY: (See discussion in text at Chapter 14)

EXCLUDABLE: An excludable alien is barred from entering the U.S. Some excludable aliens are barred permanently; others may enter after receiving a waiver. (See discussion in Chap. 22 and 24 of text)

GREEN CARD: A card identifying the holder as being registered as a Permanent Resident of the U.S. The color of the card is no longer green, but the name has remained. The Green Card is officially a Form 1-551 "Alien Registration Receipt."

IMMEDIATE FAMILY: An alien's spouse and children. The spouse must be the legal spouse. The children must be under 21 years of age, unmarried, and be considered legitimate by the Immigration Service or U.S Consul.

IMMIGRANT: An alien who intends to remain in the U.S. permanently or for an indefinite time.

IMMIGRANT VISA: The type of Visa issued to persons who are qualified for U.S. Permanent Residence.

IMMIGRATION AND NATURALIZATION SERVICE (INS): A part of the U.S. Department of Justice responsible for implementing and enforcing most of the immigration laws.

IMMIGRATION SERVICE: See Immigration and Naturalization Service.

INS: See Immigration and Naturalization Service.

INSPECTION: The procedure which occurs when an alien is questioned (or allowed to pass without questioning) by an Officer of the U.S. Immigration Service at a port of entry. No "Inspection" occurs if the alien falsely claims to be a U.S. Citizen or evades a proper examination.

LABOR CERTIFICATE: Issued by the U.S. Department of Labor after it finds that U.S. workers will not be adversely affected if an alien fills a particular job. The finding is shown by the placement of a special stamp upon the application form. The stamp contains the words of the Certificate and the Signature of the Certifying Officer. (See Chap. 23 of text)

LIVE-IN JOB: A job which requires the employee to live on the employer's premises as a condition of employment.

LOCAL EMPLOYMENT SERVICE OFFICE: The unit responsible for the initial receipt and processing of applications for Labor Certificates except for Schedule A Occupations. These offices are part of a State or other non-Federal employment service (except in Washington, D.C.). It is distinct (separate) from the U.S. Department of Labor but acts as a preprocessor of Labor Certificate applications on behalf of the U.S. Department of Labor. (See Chapter 23 of text)

MOTION: A written request made to a government agency as part of an application procedure.

NON-IMMIGRANT: An alien on a temporary visit or stay who intends to depart from the U.S. after completing the purpose of his trip of limited duration.

NOTICE OF FINDING: (See discussion in text at p.   ).

NUMERICAL LIMITATION: (See Chap. 5 of text)

PAROLE: A status granted by the Immigration Service to an alien who has been inspected and who is allowed to enter the U.S. for a particular purpose even though the alien lacks required documents or visa. For an example, parole status may be granted by the Immigration Service at the port of entry to allow an alien to apply for political asylum, or to testify at a judicial proceeding, or receive necessary medical treatment. It may also be granted to allow an alien to complete a pending Adjustment of Status application upon his return to the U.S. if the alien had been given Advance Parole before departing.

PETITION: A form used to apply for a preference under the immigration law. Refers to the Form 1-140, Petition for First, Second and Third Preferences, or Form 1-130 for family-based petitions.

PREFERENCE: One of the categories in which an alien may qualify for an immigrant Visa (Permanent Residence).

PREFERENCE DATE: The date which determines an alien's place on the list for a Preference. (See discussion in Chapter 5 of text).

PRINCIPAL ALIEN: An alien who has qualified for U.S. Permanent Residence directly and not derivatively. As an example, the alien who has an approved Labor Certificate and an approved Preference Petition is the "principal alien," while his or her spouse and minor unmarried children are not principal aliens but obtain their right to the Immigrant (Resident) Visa only derivatively. The derivative aliens are usually those who will accompany, or follow to join, the Principal Alien.

PRIORITY DATE: See Preference Date.

REBUTTAL: The written response to a Notice of Finding by the U.S. Labor Department. (See discussion in

Chapter 23, Section E of text)

RECONSIDERATION: The procedure for having the papers in a case re-examined by the appropriate government agency so that a more favorable decision will be made.

REOPENING: The procedure which allows additional facts or papers to be added to the record of a case.

REGIONAL OFFICE: An office of the Employment and Training Administration of the U.S. Department of Labor responsible for final processing and issuing regular Labor Certificates. The Certifying Officer is an employee in the Regional Office. There are several Regional Offices in the U.S.

REGULAR LABOR CERTIFICATE: A Labor Certificate for a job not on Schedule A (see Chapter 23 of text)

SCHEDULE A: A list of occupations for which an alien employee need not receive a Labor Certificate. (See Section A of Chapter 23)

SCHEDULE B: A list of occupations for which an alien employee cannot receive a Labor Certificate unless with a waiver.

TRWOV or TWOV: *TRansit WithOut Visa*. Refers to an alien who is allowed to enter the U.S. without a visa while in transit between airplane flights or between ships.

U.S.: United States.

U.S. CONSUL: An employee of the U.S. State Department posted at a Consulate or Embassy of the U.S. abroad, responsible for approving and issuing Immigrant or non-Immigrant Visas.

U.S. DEPARTMENT OF LABOR: Refers to the section of the U.S. Labor Department responsible for processing and issuing Labor Certificates. It is part of the Labor Department's Employment and Training Administration.

U.S. EMPLOYER: Any person with a U.S. location authorized to offer a job to an alien for Labor Certificate purposes. Can be an individual, corporation, or other legal person. Does not include an alien temporarily in the U.S. even though authorized to work.

U.S. WORKER: A person who is authorized to work in the U.S. including U.S. citizens and U.S. permanent residents. Does not include an alien temporarily in the U.S. even though authorized to work.

VISA APPOINTMENT: The procedure which occurs when an applicant for U.S. immigrant (residence) status appears before a U.S. Consul abroad to allow the Consul to determine if the alien is qualified for an Immigrant Visa.

VISA BULLETIN: A publication issued by the U.S. State Department which gives the status of the Immigrant Visa priority dates. (See Chap. 5 of text)

WAIVER: Special permission issued by a U.S. government agency to allow an alien to receive a privilege or benefit that the alien could not otherwise have received. For example, a Labor Certificate cannot be issued for a job on Schedule B without special permission (a waiver) from the Labor Department. Some excludable aliens can be admitted to the U.S. but only if they receive a waiver.

APPENDIX E
SAMPLE IMMIGRATION FORMS LISTED IN THE MANUAL
(Where To Find Them)

(Forms are Listed in their numerical order)

Other Forms or Special Documents Listed In Manual

U.S. Department of Justice
Immigration and Naturalization Service (INS)

Form I-129F   OMB #1115-0054

Petition for Alien Fiancé(e)

DO NOT WRITE IN THIS BLOCK

Case ID#	Action Stamp	Fee Stamp
A#		
G-28 or Volag #		

The petition is approved for status under Section 101(a)(15)(k). It is valid for four months from date of action.

AMCON: _____
☐ Personal Interview   ☐ Previously Forwarded
☐ Document Check
☐ Field Investigations

Remarks:

A. Information about you

1. Name (Family name in CAPS)   (First)   (Middle)

2. Address (Number and Street)   (Apartment Number)

    (Town or City)   (State/Country)   (ZIP/Postal Code)

3. Place of Birth (Town or City)   (State/Country)

4. Date of Birth (Mo/Day/Yr)   5. Sex   6. Marital Status
    ☐ Male   ☐ Married   ☐ Single
    ☐ Female   ☐ Widowed   ☐ Divorced

7. Other Names Used (including maiden name)

8. Social Security Number   9. Alien Registration Number (if any)

10. Names of Prior Husbands/Wives   11. Date(s) Marriages(s) Ended

12. If you are a U.S. citizen, complete the following:
    My citizenship was acquired through (check one)
    ☐ Birth in the U.S.
    ☐ Naturalization
        Give number of certificate, date and place it was issued

    ☐ Parents
        Have you obtained a certificate of citizenship in your own name?
        ☐ Yes   ☐ No
    If "Yes", give number of certificate, date and place it was issued

13. Have you ever filed for this or any other alien fiancé(e) or husband/wife before?   ☐ Yes   ☐ No   ,
    If you checked "yes," give name of alien, place and date of filing, and result

B. Information about your alien fiancé(e)

1. Name (Family name in CAPS)   (First)   (Middle)

2. Address (Number and Street)   (Apartment Number)

    (Town or City)   (State/Country)   (ZIP/Postal Code)

3. Place of Birth (Town or City)   (State/Country)

4. Date of Birth (Mo/Day/Yr)   5. Sex   6. Marital Status
    ☐ Male   ☐ Married   ☐ Single
    ☐ Female   ☐ Widowed   ☐ Divorced

7. Other Names Used (including maiden name)

8. Social Security Number   9. Alien Registration Number (if any)

10. Names of Prior Husbands/Wives   11. Date(s) Marriages(s) Ended

12. Has your fiancé(e) ever been in the U.S.?
    ☐ Yes   ☐ No

13. If your fiancé(e) is currently in the U.S., complete the following:
    He or she last arrived as a (visitor, student, exchange alien, crewman, stowaway, temporary worker, witout inspection, etc.)

    Arrival/Departure Record (I-94) Number   Date arrived (Month/Day/Year)

    | | | | |■| | | | | | | |

    Date authorized stay expired, or will expire, as shown on Form I-94 or I-95

INITIAL RECEIPT	RESUBMITTED	RELOCATED		COMPLETED		
		Rec'd	Sent	Approved	Denied	Returned

Form I-129F (Rev. 4/11/91) Y

B. (continued) Information about your alien fiancé (e)

14. List all children of your alien fiancé(e) (if any)

(Name)	(Date of Birth)	(Country of Birth)	(Present Address)

15. Address in the United States where your fiancé(e) intends to live

(Number and Street)	(Town or City)	(State)

16. Your fiancé (e)'s address abroad

(Number and Street)	(Town or City)	(Province)	(Country)	(Phone Number)

17. If your fiancé (e)'s native alphabet is other than Roman letters, write his or her name and address abroad in the native alphabet:

(Name)	(Number and Street)	(Town or City)	(Province)	(Country)

18. Your fiancé (e) is related to you. ☐ Yes ☐ No

If you are related, state the nature and degree of relationship, e.g., third cousin or maternal uncle, etc.

19. Your fiancé (e) has met and seen you. ☐ Yes ☐ No

Describe the circumstances under which you met. If you have not personally met each other, explain how the relationship was established, and explain in detail any reasons you may have for requesting that the requirement that you and your fiancé (e) must have met should not apply to you.

20. Your fiancé (e) will apply for a visa abroad at the American Consulate in _____

      (City)   (Country)

(Designation of a consulate outside the country of your fiancé(e)'s last residence does not guarantee acceptance for processing by that consulate. Acceptance is at the discretion of the designated consulate.)

C. Other Information

If you are serving overseas in the armed forces of the United States, please answer the following:

I presently reside or am stationed overseas and my current mailing address is _____

I plan to return to the United States on or about _____

Penalties: You may, by law be imprisoned for not more than five years, or fined $250,000, or both, for entering into a marriage contract for the purpose of evading any provision of the immigration laws and you may be fined up to $10,000 or imprisoned up to five years or both, for knowingly and willfully falsifying or concealing a material fact or using any false document in submitting this petition.

Your Certification

I am legally able to and intend to marry my alien fiancé(e) within 90 days of his or her arrival in the United States. I certify, under penalty of perjury under the laws of the United States of America, that the foregoing is true and correct. Furthermore, I authorize the release of any information from my records which the Immigration and Naturalizaton Service needs to determine eligibility for the benefit that I am seeking.

Signature _____ Date _____ Phone Number _____

Signature of Person Preparing Form if Other than Above

I declare that I prepared this document at the request of the person above and that it is based on all information of which I have any knowledge.

Print Name _____ (Address) _____ (Signature) _____ (Date) _____

G-28 ID Number _____

Volag Number _____

For sale by the Superintendent of Documents, U.S. Government Printing Office Washington, D.C. 20402

*U.S.GPO:1996-405-024/34021

U.S. Department of Justice
Immigration and Naturalization Service (INS)

Form I-130 OMB #1115-0054
Petition for Alien Relative

DO NOT WRITE IN THIS BLOCK - FOR EXAMINING OFFICE ONLY

Case ID#	Action Stamp	Fee Stamp
A#		
G-28 or Volag #		

Section of Law:
□ 201 (b) spouse   □ 203 (a)(1)
□ 201 (b) child   □ 203 (a)(2)
□ 201 (b) parent   □ 203 (a)(4)
   □ 203 (a)(5)
AM CON: _____

Petition was filed on: _____ (priority date)
□ Personal Interview   □ Previously Forwarded
□ Pet. Ben. "A" File Reviewed   □ Stateside Criteria
□ Field Investigations   □ I-485 Simultaneously
□ 204 (a)(2)(A) Resolved   □ 204 (h) Resolved

Remarks:

A. Relationship

1. The alien relative is my
□ Husband/Wife   □ Parent   □ Brother/Sister   □ Child

2. Are you related by adoption?
□ Yes   □ No

3. Did you gain permanent residence through adoption?
□ Yes   □ No

B. Information about you

1. **Name** (Family name in CAPS)   (First)   (Middle)

2. **Address** (Number and Street)   (Apartment Number)

(Town or City)   (State/Country)   (ZIP/Postal Code)

3. **Place of Birth** (Town or City)   (State/Country)

4. **Date of Birth** (Mo/Day/Yr)

5. **Sex**
□ Male   □ Female

6. **Marital Status**
□ Married   □ Single
□ Widowed   □ Divorced

7. **Other Names Used** (including maiden name)

8. **Date and Place of Present Marriage** (if married)

9. **Social Security Number**

10. **Alien Registration Number** (if any)

11. **Names of Prior Husbands/Wives**

12. **Date(s) Marriages(s) Ended**

13. If you are a U.S. citizen, complete the following:
My citizenship was acquired through (check one)
□ Birth in the U.S.
□ Naturalization (Give number of certificate, date and place it was issued)

Parents
Have you obtained a certificate of citizenship in your own name?
□ Yes   □ No
If "Yes", give number of certificate, date and place it was issued

14a. If you are a lawful permanent resident alien, complete the following:
Date and place of admission for, or adjustment to, lawful permanent residence, and class of admission:

14b. Did you gain permanent resident status through marriage to a United States citizen or lawful permanent resident?   □ Yes   □ No

C. Information about your alien relative

1. **Name** (Family name in CAPS)   (First)   (Middle)

2. **Address** (Number and Street)   (Apartment Number)

(Town or City)   (State/Country)   (ZIP/Postal Code)

3. **Place of Birth** (Town or City)   (State/Country)

4. **Date of Birth** (Mo/Day/Yr)

5. **Sex**
□ Male   □ Female

6. **Marital Status**
□ Married   □ Single
□ Widowed   □ Divorced

7. **Other Names Used** (including maiden name)

8. **Date and Place of Present Marriage** (if married)

9. **Social Security Number**

10. **Alien Registration Number** (if any)

11. **Names of Prior Husbands/Wives**

12. **Date(s) Marriages(s) Ended**

13. Has your relative ever been in the U.S.?
□ Yes   □ No

14. If your relative is currently in the U.S., complete the following: He or she last arrived as a (visitor, student, stowaway, without inspection, etc.)

Arrival/Departure Record (I-94) Number   Date arrived (Month/Day/Year)

Date authorized stay expired, or will expire, as shown on Form I-94 or I-95

15. Name and address of present employer (if any)

Date this employment began (Month/Day/Year)

16. Has you relative ever been under immigration proceedings?
□ Yes   □ No   Where _____ When _____
□ Exclusion   □ Deportation   □ Recission   □ Judicial Proceedings

INITIAL RECEIPT	RESUBMITTED	RELOCATED		COMPLETED		
		Rec'd	Sent	Approved	Denied	Returned

C. (continued) Information about your alien relative

16. **List husband/wife and all children of your relative** (if your relative is your husband/wife, list only his or her children).

(Name)	(Relationship)	(Date of Birth)	(Country of Birth)

17. **Address in the United States where your relative intends to live**

(Number and Street)   (Town or City)   (State)

18. **Your relative's address abroad**

(Number and Street)   (Town or City)   (Province)   (Country)   (Phone Number)

19. **If your relative's native alphabet is other than Roman letters, write his or her name and address abroad in the native alphabet:**

(Name)   (Number and Street)   (Town or City)   (Province)   (Country)

20. **If filing for your husband/wife, give last address at which you both lived together:** | **From** | **To**

(Name)   (Number and Street)   (Town or City)   (Province)   (Country)   (Month) (Year)   (Month) (Year)

21. **Check the appropriate box below and give the information required for the box you checked:**

☐ Your relative will apply for a visa abroad at the American Consulate in _____

(City)   (Country)

☐ Your relative is in the United States and will apply for adjustment of status to that of a lawful permanent resident in the office of the Immigration and Naturalization Service at _____. If your relative is not eligible for adjustment of status, he or she will

(City)   (State)

apply for a visa abroad at the American Consulate in _____.

(City)   (Country)

(Designation of a consulate outside the country of your relative's last residence does not guarantee acceptance for processing by that consulate. Acceptance is at the discretion of the designated consulate.)

D. Other Information

1. **If separate petitions are also being submitted for other relatives, give names of each and relationship.**

2. **Have you ever filed a petition for this or any other alien before?**   ☐ Yes   ☐ No
   If "Yes," give name, place and date of filing, and result.

Warning: The INS investigates claimed relationships and verifies the validity of documents. The INS seeks criminal prosecutions when family relationships are falsified to obtain visas.

Penalties: You may, by law be imprisoned for not more than five years, or fined $250,000, or both, for entering into a marriage contract for the purpose of evading any provision of the immigration laws and you may be fined up to $10,000 or imprisoned up to five years or both, for knowingly and willfully falsifying or concealing a material fact or using any false document in submitting this petition.

Your Certification: I certify, under penalty of perjury under the laws of the United States of America, that the foregoing is true and correct. Furthermore, I authorize the release of any information from my records which the Immigration and Naturalization Service needs to determine eligibility for the benefit that I am seeking.

Signature _____ Date _____ Phone Number _____

Signature of Person Preparing Form if Other than Above

I declare that I prepared this document at the request of the person above and that it is based on all information of which I have any knowledge.

Print Name _____ (Address) _____ (Signature) _____ (Date) _____

G-28 ID Number _____

Volag Number _____

U. S. Department of Justice
Immigration and Naturalization Service

Form I-134 Affidavit of Support

(ANSWER ALL ITEMS: FILL IN WITH TYPEWRITER OR PRINT IN BLOCK LETTERS IN INK.)

I, _____, *residing at* _____
　　　　　(Name)　　　　　　　　　　　　　　　　　(Street and Number)

_____
　(City)　　　　　(State)　　　(ZIP Code if in U.S.)　　(Country)

BEING DULY SWORN DEPOSE AND SAY:

1. I was born on _____ at _____
　　　　　　　　　(Date)　　　　　　　　　(City)　　　　　　　(Country)

　If you are **not** a native born United States citizen, answer the following as appropriate:

　　a. If a United States citizen through naturalization, give certificate of naturalization number _____

　　b. If a United States citizen through parent(s) or marriage, give citizenship certificate number _____

　　c. If United States citizenship was derived by some other method, attach a statement of explanation.

　　d. If a lawfully admitted permanent resident of the United States, give "A" number _____

2. That I am _____ years of age and have resided in the United States since (date) _____

3. That this affidavit is executed in behalf of the following person:

Name			Sex	Age
Citizen of—(Country)		Marital Status	Relationship to Deponent	
Presently resides at—(Street and Number)	(City)	(State)	(Country)	

Name of spouse and children accompanying or following to join person:

Spouse	Sex	Age	Child		Sex	Age
Child	Sex	Age	Child		Sex	Age
Child	Sex	Age	Child		Sex	Age

4. That this affidavit is made by me for the purpose of assuring the United States Government that the person(s) named in item 3 will not become a public charge in the United States.

5. That I am willing and able to receive, maintain and support the person(s) named in item 3. That I am ready and willing to deposit a bond, if necessary, to guarantee that such person(s) will not become a public charge during his or her stay in the United States, or to guarantee that the above named will maintain his or her nonimmigrant status if admitted temporarily and will depart prior to the expiration of his or her authorized stay in the United States.

6. That I understand this affidavit will be binding upon me for a period of three (3) years after entry of the person(s) named in item 3 and that the information and documentation provided by me may be made available to the Secretary of Health and Human Services and the Secretary of Agriculture, who may make it available to a public assistance agency.

7. That I am employed as, or engaged in the business of _____ with _____
　　　　　　　　　　　　　　　　　　　　　　　(Type of Business)　　　　　　(Name of concern)

　at _____
　　　(Street and Number)　　　　(City)　　　　(State)　　　(Zip Code)

　I derive an annual income of *(if self-employed, I have attached a copy of my last income tax return or report of commercial rating concern which I certify to be true and correct to the best of my knowledge and belief. See instruction for nature of evidence of net worth to be submitted.)*　　　　$_____

　I have on deposit in savings banks in the United States　　　$_____

　I have other personal property, the reasonable value of which is　　　$_____

Form I-134 (Rev. 12-1-84) Y　　　　　　　　　　　OVER

I have stocks and bonds with the following market value, as indicated on the attached list
which I certify to be true and correct to the best of my knowledge and belief. $ _____
I have life insurance in the sum of $ _____
With a cash surrender value of $ _____
I own real estate valued at $ _____
With mortgages or other encumbrances thereon amounting to $ _____

Which is located at _____
(Street and Number)   (City)   (State)   (Zip Code)

8. That the following persons are dependent upon me for support: *(Place an "X" in the appropriate column to indicate whether the person named is **wholly or partially** dependent upon you for support.)*

Name of Person	Wholly Dependent	Partially Dependent	Age	Relationship to Me

9. That I have previously submitted affidavit(s) of support for the following person(s). If none, state *"None"*

Name _____   Date submitted _____

_____

_____

10. That I have submitted visa petition(s) to the Immigration and Naturalization Service on behalf of the following person(s). If none, state none.

Name _____   Relationship _____   Date submitted _____

_____

_____

11. *(Complete this block only if the person named in item 3 will be in the United States temporarily.)*
That I ☐ do intend ☐ do not intend, to make specific contributions to the support of the person named in item 3. *(If you check "do intend", indicate the exact nature and duration of the contributions. For example, if you intend to furnish room and board, state for how long and, if money, state the amount in United States dollars and state whether it is to be given in a lump sum, weekly, or monthly, or for how long.)*

_____

_____

OATH OR AFFIRMATION OF DEPONENT

I acknowledge at that I have read Part III of the Instructions, Sponsor and Alien Liability, and am aware of my responsibilities as an immigrant sponsor under the Social Security Act, as amended, and the Food Stamp Act, as amended.

I swear (affirm) that I know the contents of this affidavit signed by me and the statements are true and correct.

Signature of deponent _____

Subscribed and sworn to (affirmed) before me this _____ *day of* _____, 19 _____

at _____ *.My commission expires on* _____

Signature of Officer Administering Oath _____ *Title* _____
If affidavit prepared by other than deponent, please complete the following: I declare that this document was prepared by me at the request of the deponent and is based on all information of which I have knowledge.

_____
(Signature)   *(Address)*   *(Date)*

U.S. Department of Justice
Immigration and Naturalization Service

Form I-140 OMB #1115-0061
Immigrant Petition for Alien Worker

START HERE - Please Type or Print

Part 1. Information about the person or organization filing this petition.

If an individual is filing, use the top Name line. Organizations should use the second line.

Family Name	Given Name	Middle Initial

Company or Organization

Address - Attn:

Street Number and Name	Room #

City	State or Province

Country	ZIP/Postal Code

IRS Tax #	Social Security #

Part 2. Petition Type. This petition is being filed for: (check one)

a. ☐ An alien of extraordinary ability
b. ☐ An outstanding professor or researcher
c. ☐ A multinational executive or manager
d. ☐ A member of the professions holding an advanced degree or an alien of exceptional ability
e. ☐ A skilled worker (requiring at least two years of specialized training or experience) or professional
f. ☐ An employee of a U.S. business operating in Hong Kong
g. ☐ Any other worker (requiring less than two years training or experience)

Part 3. Information about the person you are filing for.

Family Name	Given Name	Middle Initial

Address - C/O

Street # and Name	Apt. #

City	State or Province

Country	Zip or Postal Code

Date of Birth (month/day/year)	Country of Birth

Social Security # (if any)	A # (if any)

If in the U.S.	Date of Arrival (month/day/year)	I-94#
	Current Nonimmigrant Status	Expires on (month/day/year)

Part 4. Processing Information.

Below give the U.S. Consulate you want notified if this petition is approved and if any requested adjustment of status cannot be granted.

U.S Consulate: City   Country

Form I-140 (Rev. 12-2-91)   *Continued on back.*

FOR INS USE ONLY

Returned / Receipt

Resubmitted

Reloc Sent

Reloc Rec'd

☐ Petitioner Interviewed
☐ Beneficiary Interviewed

Classification
☐ 203(b)(1)(A) Alien Of Extraordinary Ability
☐ 203(b)(1)(B) Outstanding Professor or Researcher
☐ 203(b)(1)(C) Multi-national executive or manager
☐ 203(b)(2) Member of professions w/adv. degree or of exceptional ability
☐ 203(b)(3) (A) (i) Skilled worker
☐ 203(b)(3) (A) (ii) Professional
☐ 203(b)(3) (A) (iii) Other worker
☐ Sec. 124 IMMACT-Employee of U.S. business in Hong Kong

Priority Date	Consulate

Remarks

Action Block

To Be Completed by Attorney or Representative, If any
☐ Fill in box if G-28 is attached to represent the petitioner
VOLAG#
ATTY State License #

Part 4. Processing Information. *(continued)*

If you gave a U. S. address in Part 3, print the person's foreign address below. If his/her native alphabet does not use Roman letters, print his/her name and foreign address in the native alphabet.

Name

Address

Are you filing any other petitions or applications with this one?	☐ No	☐ yes attach an explanation
Is the person you are filing for in exclusion or deportation proceedings?	☐ No	☐ yes attach an explanation
Has an immigrant visa petition ever been filed by or in behalf of this person?	☐ No	☐ yes attach an explanation

Part 5. Additional Information about the employer.

Type of petitioner
(check one)

☐ Self   ☐ Individual U.S. Citizen   ☐ Company or organization

☐ Permanent Resident   ☐ Other explain_____

If a company, give the following:
Type of business

Date Established	Current # of employees	Gross Annual Income	Net Annual Income

If an individual, give the following:
Occupation   Annual Income

Part 6. Basic information about the proposed employment.

Job Title   Nontechnical description of job

Address where the person will work if different from address in Part 1.

Is this a full-time position?   ☐ yes   ☐ No (hours per week _____)   Wages per week

Is this a permanent position?:   ☐ yes   ☐ No   Is this a new position? ☐ yes ☐ No

Part 7. Information on spouse and all children of the person you are filing for.

Provide an attachment listing the family members of the person you are filing for. Be sure to include their full name, relationship, date and country of birth, and present address.

Part 8. Signature. *Read the information on penalties in the instructions before completing this section.*

I certify under penalty of perjury under the laws of the United States of America that this petition, and the evidence submitted with it, is all true and correct. I authorize the release of any information from my records which the Immigration and Naturalization Service needs to determine eligibility for the benefit I am seeking.

Signature   Date

Please Note: If you do not completely fill out this form, or fail to submit required documents listed in the instructions, you cannot be found eligible for the requested document and this application may to be denied.

Part 9. Signature of person preparing form if other than above. *(Sign below)*

I declare that I prepared this application at the request of the above person and it is based on all information of which I have knowledge.

Signature   Print Your Name   Date

Firm Name and Address

Form OF-169

INSTRUCTIONS FOR IMMIGRANT VISA APPLICANTS

This office has received evidence entitling you to immigrant visa status. While no assurance can be given regarding the date of your visa interview appointment, you should now prepare for that appointment by taking the following three steps:

FIRST: Complete and send immediately to the consular office processing your case the enclosed Form OF-230 I, APPLICATION FOR IMMIGRANT VISA AND ALIEN REGISTRATION, PART I, BIOGRAPHIC DATA. The consular office cannot process your case until this form is received.

SECOND: Obtain the following documents on this checklist which pertain to you. Do **NOT** send them to the consular office.

☐ 1. PASSPORTS: A Passport must be valid for travel to the United States and must have at least six months validity beyond the issuance date of the visa. Children may be included in a parent's passport, but, if over the age of 16, they must have their photographs attached to the passport.

☐ 2. BIRTH CERTIFICATES: One certified copy of the birth certificate of each person named in the application is required. Birth records must be presented for all unmarried children under age 21, even if they do not wish to immigrate at this time. (If children are deceased, so state giving year of death.) The certificate must state the date and place of birth and the names of both parents. The certificate must also indicate that it is an extract from official records. If you, or any children were adopted, you must submit a certified copy of the final adoption decree. Photostatic copies are acceptable provided the original is offered for inspection by the consular officer.

UNOBTAINABLE BIRTH CERTIFICATE: In rare cases, it may be impossible to obtain a birth certificate because records have been destroyed or the government will not issue one. In such cases, you should obtain a statement to that effect from the civil registrar's office and proceed to obtain secondary evidence of birth. A baptismal certificate may be submitted for consideration provided it contains the date and place of the applicant's birth and information concerning parentage and provided the baptism took place shortly after birth. Should a baptismal certificate be unobtainable, a close relative, preferably the applicant's mother, should prepare a notarized statement giving the place and date of the applicant's birth, the names of both parents, and the maiden name of the mother. The statement must be executed before an official authorized to administer oaths or affirmations. In such cases, please bring any secondary evidence you might have concerning your birth.

☐ 3. POLICE CERTIFICATES: Each visa applicant aged 16 years or over is required to submit a police certificate from the police authorities of each locality of the country of the applicant's nationality or current residence where the applicant has resided for at least six months since attaining the age of sixteen. Police certificates are also required from all other countries where the applicant has resided for at least one year. A police certificate must also be obtained from the police authorities of any place where the applicant has been arrested for any reason, regardless of how long he or she lived there. Police certificates must cover the entire period of the applicant's residence in any area. A certificate issued by the police authorities where you now reside must be of recent date when presented to the consular officer. The term "police certificate" as used in this paragraph means a certification by appropriate police authorities stating what their records show concerning each applicant, including all arrests, the reasons for the arrests, and the disposition of each case of which there is a record.

Police certificates from certain countries are considered unobtainable. See the attached list on form DSL-1078. If specific questions arise regarding police certificates, please consult the consular office.

☐ 4. COURT AND PRISON RECORDS: Persons who have been convicted of a crime must obtain a certified copy of each court record and of any prison record, regardless of the fact that they may have benefited subsequently from an amnesty, pardon, or other act of clemency.

☐ 5. MILITARY RECORDS: A certified copy of any military record, if applicable and obtainable, is required.

☐ 6. PHOTOGRAPHS: Two (2) color photographs with white background on glossy paper, unretouched, and unmounted are required. The photograph must be a three-quarter frontal portrait with the right side of the face and right ear visible. The dimensions of the facial image must measure about one inch (25mm) from chin to top of hair. No head covering or dark glasses should be worn. Color Polaroid photos are acceptable. Photos are required of all applicants, regardless of age.

☐ 7. EVIDENCE OF SUPPORT: Any evidence which will show that you and members of your family who will accompany you are not likely to become public charges while in the United States. The enclosed information sheet, Optional Form 167, lists evidence which may be presented to meet this requirement of the law. Form I-134 should be used when an affidavit of support is to be submitted.

OPTIONAL FORM 169(CPC) 3-92
DEPT. OF STATE

☐ 8. MARRIAGE CERTIFICATES: Married persons are required to present a certified copy of their marriage certificate. Proof of the termination of any previous marriage must also be submitted (e.g. death certificate of spouse; final decree of divorce or annulment).

☐ 9. ORIGINAL DOCUMENTS: If you are the beneficiary of a family–based immigrant visa petition, you must be prepared to present the originals of all civil documents which establish your claimed relationship to the petitioner.

☐ 10. TRANSLATIONS: All documents not in English, or in the official language of the country in which application for a visa is being made, must be accompanied by certified English translations. Translations must be certified by a competent translator and sworn to before a Notary Public. (All documents in Japanese must be translated.)

ONLY ONE COPY OF EACH DOCUMENT, EXCEPT PHOTOGRAPHS, MUST BE SUBMITTED WITH THE VISA APPLICATION. YOU ARE ADVISED, HOWEVER, TO OBTAIN THE NECESSARY DOCUMENTS IN DUPLICATE, AS THIS WILL ENABLE YOU TO PROVIDE IDENTICAL COPIES IN THE EVENT THE FIRST SET IS LOST OR DAMAGED.

PLEASE READ THE FOLLOWING CAREFULLY

THIRD: As soon as you have obtained all of documents that apply to your case, carefully read the statement at the bottom of this page, sign and date it, and send the form to the consular office processing your case. You will **not** be scheduled for an appointment until you sign and return this checklist.

After this form has been sent to the consular office, you will be scheduled for a visa interview at the earliest possible date. It is not possible to predict when this will be since it depends upon when the priority date for your visa category and country becomes current. You will receive an appointment letter along with instructions for a medical examination approximately one month before your scheduled interview with a consular officer. You will not normally receive any further correspondence from the consular office until the appointment is scheduled.

The total fee for an immigrant visa is U.S. $200, or the local currency equivalent. Each applicant must be prepared to pay this fee on the appointment date.

You need not check with the consular office unless you have to report a CHANGE OF ADDRESS or change in your situation such as marriage, death of petitioner, or birth of children. Please do not send any documents to the consular office unless you are specifically requested to do so.

Enclosures:
1. Optional Form 230 I, Immigrant Visa Application, Part I, Biographic Data
2 Optional Form 167, Evidence Which May be Presented to Meet the Public Charge Provision of the Law
3 Form DSL–1083, Immigrant Visa Supplemental Information Sheet
4 Form I–134, Affidavit of Support

I have in my possession and am prepared to present all the documents listed in items 1 through 10 which apply to my case, as indicated by the check mark I have placed in the appropriate boxes. I fully realize that no advance assurance can be given when or whether a visa will actually be issued to me and I also understand that I should NOT give up my job, dispose of property, or make any final travel arrangements until a visa is actually issued to me. At such time as it is possible for me to receive an appointment to make formal visa application, I intended to apply: *(check appropriate box)*

☐ 1. Alone
☐ 2. Together with my spouse *(Print first name: _____)*
☐ 3. Together with my spouse and the following minor children: *(Print first names of each child who will accompany you)*

_____
Date

_____
Case Number (If available)

_____
Signature

_____
Print Name

_____
Current Address

_____

_____

YOU WILL NOT BE SCHEDULED FOR AN APPOINTMENT UNTIL YOU SUBMIT THIS FORM.

PLEASE DO NOT SEND ANY DOCUMENTS TO THIS OFFICE.

UR RESPONSIBILITY TO KEEP THE CONSULAR OFFICE INFORMED OF YOUR CURRENT ADDRESS AT ALL TIMES. 'URE TO DO SO MAY RESULT IN TERMINATION OF YOUR REGISTRATION AS AN INTENDING IMMIGRANT.

Form OF-230 –1

OMB APPROVAL NO. 1405-0015
EXPIRES 8-31-92
*ESTIMATED BURDEN: 1 HOUR

APPLICATION FOR IMMIGRANT VISA AND ALIEN REGISTRATION

PART I - BIOGRAPHIC DATA

INSTRUCTIONS: Complete one copy of this form for yourself and each member of your family, regardless of age, who will immigrate with you. Please print or type your answer to all questions. Questions that are Not Applicable should be so marked. If there is insufficient room on the form, answer on a separate sheet using the same numbers as appear on the form. Attach the sheet to this form.

WARNING: Any false statement or concealment of a material fact may result in your permanent expulsion from the United States.

This form is Part I of two parts which, together with Optional Form OF-230 PART II, constitute the complete Application for Immigrant Visa and Alien Registration.

1. FAMILY NAME	FIRST NAME	MIDDLE NAME

2. OTHER NAMES USED OR BY WHICH KNOWN *(If married woman, give maiden name)*

3. FULL NAME IN NATIVE ALPHABET *(If Roman letters not used)*

4. DATE OF BIRTH *(Day) (Month) (Year)*	5. AGE	6. PLACE OF BIRTH *(City or town) (Province) (Country)*

7. NATIONALITY *(If dual national, give both)*	8. SEX ☐ Male ☐ Female	9. MARITAL STATUS ☐ Single *(Never married)* ☐ Married ☐ Widowed ☐ Divorced ☐ Separated Including my present marriage, I have been married _____ times.

10. PERSONAL DESCRIPTION a. Color of hair _____ c. Height _____ b. Color of eyes _____ d. Complexion _____	11. OCCUPATION

12. MARKS OF IDENTIFICATION	13. PRESENT ADDRESS Telephone number: Home Office

14. NAME OF SPOUSE *(Maiden or family name)*   *(First name)*   *(Middle name)*

Date and place of birth of spouse:

Address of spouse *(If different from your own)*:

15. LIST NAME, DATE AND PLACE OF BIRTH, AND ADDRESSES OF ALL CHILDREN

NAME	DATE AND PLACE OF BIRTH	ADDRESS *(If different from your own)*
_____	_____	_____
_____	_____	_____
_____	_____	_____
_____	_____	_____
_____	_____	_____
_____	_____	_____

THIS FORM MAY BE OBTAINED GRATIS AT CONSULAR OFFICES OF THE UNITED STATES OF AMERICA
NSN 7540-00-149-0919
50230-106   Previous editions obsolete

OPTIONAL FORM 230 I (ENGLISH)
REVISED 4-91
DEPT. OF STATE

16. PERSON(S) NAMED IN 14 AND 15 WHO WILL ACCOMPANY OR FOLLOW ME TO THE UNITED STATES.

17. NAME OF FATHER, DATE AND PLACE OF BIRTH, AND ADDRESS (If deceased, so state, giving year of death)

18. MAIDEN NAME OF MOTHER, DATE AND PLACE OF BIRTH, AND ADDRESS (If deceased, so state, giving year of death)

19. IF NEITHER PARENT IS LIVING PROVIDE NAME AND ADDRESS OF NEXT OF KIN (nearest relative) IN YOUR HOME COUNTRY.

20. LIST ALL LANGUAGES YOU CAN SPEAK, READ, AND WRITE

LANGUAGE	SPEAK	READ	WRITE

21. LIST BELOW ALL PLACES YOU HAVE LIVED FOR SIX MONTHS OR LONGER SINCE REACHING THE AGE OF 16. BEGIN WITH YOUR PRESENT RESIDENCE.

CITY OR TOWN	PROVINCE	COUNTRY	OCCUPATION	DATES (FROM - TO)

22. LIST ANY POLITICAL, PROFESSIONAL, OR SOCIAL ORGANIZATIONS AFFILIATED WITH COMMUNIST, TOTALITARIAN, TERRORIST OR NAZI ORGANIZATIONS WHICH YOU ARE NOW OR HAVE BEEN A MEMBER OF OR AFFILIATED WITH SINCE YOUR 16TH BIRTHDAY.

NAME AND ADDRESS	FROM/TO	TYPE OF MEMBERSHIP

23. LIST DATES OF ALL PREVIOUS RESIDENCE IN OR VISITS TO THE UNITED STATES. (If never, so state) GIVE TYPE OF VISA STATUS IF ANY. GIVE I.N.S. "A" NUMBER IF ANY.

LOCATION	FROM/TO	VISA	I.N.S. FILE NO. (If known)

SIGNATURE OF APPLICANT	DATE

NOTE: Return this completed form immediately to the consular office address on the covering letter. This form will become part of your immigrant visa and your visa application cannot be processed until this form is complete.

*Public reporting burden for this collection of information is estimated to average 24 hours per response, including time required for searching existing data sources, gathering the necessary data, providing the information required, and reviewing the final collection. Send comments on the accuracy of this estimate of the burden and recommendations for reducing it to: Department of State (OIS/RA/DR) Washington, D.C. 20520-0264, and to the Office of Information and Regulatory Affairs, Office of Management and Budget, Paperwork Reduction Project (1405-0015), Washington, D.C. 20503.

Form OF230-11

OMB APPROVAL NO.: 1405-0015
EXPIRES: 8-31-92
ESTIMATED BURDEN: 23 HOURS

 APPLICATION FOR IMMIGRANT VISA AND ALIEN REGISTRATION

PART II – SWORN STATEMENT

INSTRUCTIONS: Complete one copy of this form for yourself and each member of your family, regardless of age, who will immigrate with you. Please print or type your answer to all questions. Questions that are **Not Applicable** should be so marked. If there is insufficient room on the form, answer on a separate sheet using the same numbers as appear on the form. Attach the sheet to this form. DO NOT SIGN this form until instructed to do so by the consular officer. The fee for filing this application is listed under tariff item No. 20. The fee should be paid in United States dollars or local currency equivalent, or by bank draft, when you appear before the consular officer.

WARNING: Any false statement or concealment of a material fact may result in your permanent exclusion from the United States. Even though you should be admitted to the United States, a fraudulent entry could be grounds for your prosecution and/or deportation.

This form is a continuation of Form OF-230 PART I, which together, constitute the complete Application for Immigrant Visa and Alien Registration.

24. FAMILY NAME | FIRST NAME | MIDDLE NAME

25. ADDRESS *(Local)*

Telephone No.

26. FINAL ADDRESS TO WHICH YOU WILL TRAVEL IN THE UNITED STATES *(Street address including ZIP code)*

Telephone No.

27. PERSON YOU INTEND TO JOIN *(Name, address, and relationship)*

28. NAME AND ADDRESS OF SPONSORING PERSON OR EMPLOYER

29. PURPOSE IN GOING TO THE UNITED STATES

30. LENGTH OF INTENDED STAY *(If permanently, so state)*

31. INTENDED PORT OF ENTRY

32. DO YOU HAVE A TICKET TO FINAL DESTINATION?
☐ Yes   ☐ No

33. United States laws governing the issuance of visas require each applicant to state whether or not he or she is a member of any class of individuals excluded from admission into the United States. The excludable classes are described below in general terms. You should read carefully the following list and answer YES or NO to each category. The answers you give will assist the consular officer to reach a decision on your eligibility to receive a visa.

EXCEPT AS OTHERWISE PROVIDED BY LAW, ALIENS WITHIN THE FOLLOWING CLASSIFICATIONS ARE INELIGIBLE TO RECEIVE A VISA.
DO ANY OF THE FOLLOWING CLASSES APPLY TO YOU?

a. An alien who has a communicable disease of public health significance, or has had a physical or mental disorder that poses, or is likely to pose a threat to the safety or welfare of the alien or others; an alien who is a drug abuser or addict. [212(a)(1)]   YES ☐ NO ☐

b. An alien convicted of, or who admits committing a crime involving moral turpitude, or violation of any law relating to a controlled substance; an alien convicted of 2 or more offenses for which the aggregate sentences were 5 years or more; an alien coming to the United States to engage in prostitution or commercialized vice, or who has engaged in prostitution or procuring within the past 10 years; an alien who is or has been an illicit trafficker in any controlled substance; an alien who has committed a serious criminal offense in the United States and who has asserted immunity from prosecution [212(a)(2)]   YES ☐ NO ☐

c. Alien who seeks to enter the United States to engage in espionage, sabotage, export control violations, overthrow of the Government of the United States, or other unlawful activity; an alien who seeks to enter the United States to engage in terrorist activities; an alien who has been a member of or affiliated with the Communist or any other totalitarian party; an alien who under the direction of the Nazi government of Germany, or any area occupied by, or allied with the Nazi Government of Germany, ordered, incited, assisted, or otherwise participated in the persecution of any person because of race, religion, national origin, or political opinion; an alien who has engaged in genocide. [212(a)(3)]   YES ☐ NO ☐

d. An alien who is likely to become a public charge. [212(a)(4)]   YES ☐ NO ☐

e. An alien who seeks to enter for the purpose of performing skilled or unskilled labor who has not been certified by the Secretary of Labor; an alien graduate of a foreign medical school seeking to perform medical services who has not passed the NBME exam or its equivalent. [212(a)(5)]   YES ☐ NO ☐ Not Applicable ☐

f. An alien previously deported within one year, or arrested and deported within 5 years; an alien who seeks or has sought a visa, entry into the United States, or any U.S. immigration benefit by fraud or misrepresentation; an alien who knowingly assisted any other alien to enter or try to enter the United States in violation of the law; an alien who is in violation of Section 274C of the Immigration Act. [212(a)(6)]   YES ☐ NO ☐

g. An alien who is permanently ineligible to U.S. citizenship; a person who has departed the United States to evade military service in time of war. [212(a)(8)]   YES ☐   NO ☐

h. An alien who is coming to the United States to practice polygamy; an alien who is a guardian required to accompany an excluded alien; an alien who withholds custody of a child outside the United States from a United States citizen granted legal custody. [212(a)(9)]   YES ☐   NO ☐

i. An alien who is a former exchange visitor who has not fulfilled the 2-year foreign residence requirement. [212(e)]   YES ☐   NO ☐

If the answer to any of the foregoing questions is YES or if unsure, explain in the following space or on a separate sheet of paper.

---

34. Have you ever been arrested, convicted or ever been in a prison or almshouse; have you ever been the beneficiary of a pardon or an amnesty; have you ever been treated in an institution or hospital or other place for insanity or other mental disease. [222(a)]   YES ☐   NO ☐

---

35. I am unlikely to become a public charge because of the following:
☐ Personal financial resources *(describe)*   ☐ Employment *(attach)*   ☐ Affidavit of Support *(attach)*

---

36. Have you ever applied for a visa to enter the United States?   YES ☐   NO ☐
(If answer is Yes, state where and when, whether you applied for a nonimmigrant or an immigrant visa, and whether the visa was issued or refused.)

---

37. Have you been refused admission to the United States?   YES ☐   NO ☐
(If answer is Yes, explain)

---

38. Were you assisted in completing this application?   YES ☐   NO ☐
(If answer is Yes, give name and address of person assisting you, indicating whether relative, travel agent, attorney, or other)
NAME   **ADDRESS**   **RELATIONSHIP**

---

39. The following documents are submitted in support of this application:

☐ Passport   ☐ Military Record   ☐ Evidence of own assets
☐ Birth certificate   ☐ Police certificate   ☐ Affidavit of support
☐ Marriage certificate   ☐ Medical records   ☐ Offer of employment
☐ Death certificate   ☐ Photographs   ☐ Other *(describe)*
☐ Divorce decree   ☐ Birth certificates of all children who will not
                                be immigrating at this time. (List those for
                                whom birth certificates are not available.)

DO NOT WRITE BELOW THE FOLLOWING LINE
The consular officer will assist you in answering items 40 and 41.

---

40. I claim to be exempt from ineligibility to receive a visa and exclusion under item _____ in Part 33 for the following reasons:
212(a) (5)   Beneficiary of a Waiver under:
☐ Not Applicable   ☐ 212(a) (3) (D) (ii)   ☐ 212(e)   ☐ 212(h)
☐ Not Required   ☐ 212(a) (3) (D) (iii)   ☐ 212(g) (1)   ☐ 212(i)
☐ Attached   ☐ 212(a) (3) (D) (iv)   ☐ 212(g) (2)

---

41. I claim to be: I am subject to the following:

☐ A Family-Sponsored Immigrant   ☐ I derive foreign state chargeability   ☐ Preference: _____
☐ An Employment Based-Immigrant   under Sec. 202(b) through my _____   ☐ Numerical limitation: _____
☐ A Diversity Immigrant   *(foreign state)*
☐ A Special Category (Specify) _____
   (Returning resident, Hong Kong, Tibetan, Private Legislation, etc.)

I understand that I am required to surrender my visa to the United States Immigration Officer at the place where I apply to enter the United States, and that the possession of a visa does not entitle me to enter the United States if at that time I am found to be inadmissable under the immigration laws.
   I understand that any wilfully false or misleading statement or willfull concealment of a material fact made by me herein may subject me to permanent exclusion from the United States and, if I am admitted to the United States, may subject me to criminal prosecution and/or deportation.
   I, the undersigned applicant for a United States immigrant visa, do solemnly swear (or affirm) that all statements which appear in this application, consisting of Optional Forms 230 PART I and 230 PART II combined, have been made by me, including the answers to items 1 through 41 inclusive, and that they are true and complete to the best of my knowledge and belief. I do further swear (or affirm) that, if admitted into the United States, I will not engage in activities which would be prejudicial to the public interest, or endanger the welfare, safety, or security of the United States; in activities which would be prohibited by the laws of the United States relating to espionage, sabotage, public disorder, or in other activities subversive to the national security; in any activity a purpose of which is the opposition to or the control, or overthrow of, the Government of the United States, by force, violence, or other unconstitutional means.
   I understand all the foregoing statements, having asked for and obtained an explanation on every point which was not clear to me.

_____
(Signature of Applicant)

The relationship claimed in items 14 and 15 verified by
documentation submitted to consular officer except as noted:

   Subscribed and sworn to before me this _____ day of _____, 19____ at _____

TARIFF ITEM NO. 20.
                                                     _____
                                                     (Consular Officer)

FINGERPRINTS

Form FD-258

LEAVE BLANK

APPLICANT

TYPE OR PRINT ALL INFORMATION IN BLACK

FBI   LEAVE BLANK

LAST NAME NAM	FIRST NAME	MIDDLE NAME
▓▓▓▓	Sang	Kil

SIGNATURE OF PERSON FINGERPRINTED

X ▓▓▓▓▓▓▓▓ (S....) ▓▓▓▓

ALIASES AKA

Sung ▓▓▓▓

ORI COINSDNOO
USINS
DENVER, CO

DATE OF BIRTH DOB		
Month	Day	Year
3	3	45

RESIDENCE OF PERSON FINGERPRINTED

▓▓▓ Clinton Street
▓▓▓, Colorado, 80010

CITIZENSHIP CTZ
Korea

SEX	RACE	HGT.	WGT.	EYES	HAIR	PLACE OF BIRTH POB
M	-	5'7"	160	Brn	Blk	Korea

DATE   SIGNATURE OF OFFICIAL TAKING FINGERPRINTS

1/24 ▓▓ L. Creutzburg 2/95

TOUR NO. OCA

LEAVE BLANK

EMPLOYER AND ADDRESS   of Fingerprinter
Aurora Police Department
Alameda Avenue
Aurora, Colorado

FBI NO. FBI

CLASS _____

ARMED FORCES NO. MNU

REP. _____

SOCIAL SECURITY NO. SOC

REASON FINGERPRINTED

Permanent Resident Applicant

MISCELLANEOUS NO. MNU

SAMPLE SHEET

1. R. THUMB	2. R. INDEX	3. R. MIDDLE	4. R. RING	5. R. LITTLE

6. L. THUMB	7. L. INDEX	8. L. MIDDLE	9. L. RING	10. L. LITTLE

LEFT FOUR FINGERS TAKEN SIMULTANEOUSLY   L. THUMB   R. THUMB   RIGHT FOUR FINGERS TAKEN SIMULTANEOUSLY

NOTE: Upon filling in the applicable information in the upper part of this form, the actual "fingerprinting" is to be done by an appropriate official (e.g. a police officer or other law enforcement personnel). See instructions on the back side of this form.

225

U.S. Department of Justice

Immigration and Naturalization Service

For G-325A
BIOGRAPHIC INFORMATION

OMB No. 1115-0066

(Family name)	(First name)	(Middle name)	☐ MALE ☐ FEMALE	BIRTHDATE (Mo.-Day-Yr.)	NATIONALITY	FILE NUMBER A-
ALL OTHER NAMES USED (Including names by previous marriages)			CITY AND COUNTRY OF BIRTH			SOCIAL SECURITY NO. (If any)

	FAMILY NAME	FIRST NAME	DATE. CITY AND COUNTRY OF BIRTH (If known)	CITY AND COUNTRY OF RESIDENCE
FATHER				
MOTHER (Maiden name)				

HUSBAND (If none, so state) OR WIFE	FAMILY NAME (For wife, give maiden name)	FIRST NAME	BIRTHDATE	CITY & COUNTRY OF BIRTH	DATE OF MARRIAGE	PLACE OF MARRIAGE

FORMER HUSBANDS OR WIVES (if none, so state)

FAMILY NAME (For wife, give maiden name)	FIRST NAME	BIRTHDATE	DATE & PLACE OF MARRIAGE	DATE AND PLACE OF TERMINATION OF MARRIAGE

APPLICANT'S RESIDENCE LAST FIVE YEARS. LIST PRESENT ADDRESS FIRST.

STREET AND NUMBER	CITY	PROVINCE OR STATE	COUNTRY	FROM MONTH	FROM YEAR	TO MONTH	TO YEAR
						PRESENT TIME	

APPLICANT'S LAST ADDRESS OUTSIDE THE UNITED STATES OF MORE THAN ONE YEAR

STREET AND NUMBER	CITY	PROVINCE OR STATE	COUNTRY	FROM MONTH	FROM YEAR	TO MONTH	TO YEAR

APPLICANT'S EMPLOYMENT LAST FIVE YEARS. (IF NONE, SO STATE.) LIST PRESENT EMPLOYMENT FIRST

FULL NAME AND ADDRESS OF EMPLOYER	OCCUPATION (SPECIFY)	FROM MONTH	FROM YEAR	TO MONTH	TO YEAR
				PRESENT TIME	

Show below last occupation abroad if not shown above. (Include all information requested above.)

THIS FORM IS SUBMITTED IN CONNECTION WITH APPLICATION FOR: ☐ NATURALIZATION ☐ STATUS AS PERMANENT RESIDENT ☐ OTHER (SPECIFY):	SIGNATURE OF APPLICANT	DATE
Are all copies legible? ☐ Yes	IF YOUR NATIVE ALPHABET IS IN OTHER THAN ROMAN LETTERS. WRITE YOUR NAME IN YOUR NATIVE ALPHABET IN THIS SPACE	

PENALTIES: SEVERE PENALTIES ARE PROVIDED BY LAW FOR KNOWINGLY AND WILLFULLY FALSIFYING OR CONCEALING A MATERIAL FACT.

APPLICANT: BE SURE TO PUT YOUR NAME AND ALIEN REGISTRATION NUMBER IN THE BOX OUTLINED BY HEAVY BORDER BELOW.

COMPLETE THIS BOX (Family name) (Given name) (Middle name) (Alien registration number)

Form G-325 A (Rev. 10-1-82)   **(1) Ident.**

U.S. Department of Justice
Immigration and Naturalization Service

Form I-360

OMB #1115-0117

Petition for Amerasian, Widow or Special Immigrant

START HERE - Please Type or Print

FOR INS USE ONLY

Part 1. Information about person or organization filing this petition. (Individuals should use top name line; organizations should use the second line.) *If you are filing for yourself, skip to Part 2. A widow(er) must file for him/her self.*

Family Name	Given Name	Middle Initial

Company or Organization Name

Address - C/O

Street Number and Name		Apt. #
City	State or Province	
Country	ZIP/Postal Code	

U.S. Social Security #	A #	IRS Tax # (if any)

Part 2. Classification Requested (check one):

a. ☐ Amerasian
b. ☐ Widow(er) of a U.S. citizen who died within the past 2 years
c. ☐ Special Immigrant Juvenile
d. ☐ Special Immigrant Religious Worker
e. ☐ Special Immigrant based on employment with the Panama Canal Company, Canal Zone Government or U.S. Government in the Canal Zone
f. ☐ Special Immigrant Physician
g. ☐ Special Immigrant International Organization Employee or family member

Part 3. Information about the person this petition is for.

Family Name	Given Name	Middle Initial

Address - C/O

Street Number and Name		Apt. #
City	State or Province	
Country	ZIP/Postal Code	

Date of Birth (Month/Day/Year)	Country of Birth
U.S. Social Security # (if any)	A # (if any)

Complete the items below if this person is in the United States:

Date of Arrival (Month/Day/Year)	I-94 #
Current Nonimmigrant Status	Expires on (Month/Day/Year)

FOR INS USE ONLY (right column)

Returned

_____

_____

Resubmitted

_____

_____

Reloc Sent

_____

_____

Reloc Rec'd

_____

_____

☐ Petitioner/ Applicant Interviewed

☐ Beneficiary Interviewed

☐ I-485 Filed Concurrently
☐ Bene "A" File Reviewed

Classification

Consulate

Priority Date

Remarks:

Receipt

Action Block

To Be Completed by Attorney or Representative, if any

☐ Fill in box if G-28 is attached to represent the applicant

VOLAG#

ATTY State License #

Form I-360 (Rev. 09/19/91) N

Continued on back.

Part 4. Processing Information.

Below give the United States Consulate you want notified if this petition is approved and if any requested adjustment of status cannot be granted.

American Consulate: City	Country

If you gave a United States address in Part 3, print the person's foreign address below. If his/her native alphabet does not use Roman letters, print his/her name and foreign address in the native alphabet.

Name	Address

Sex of the person this petition is for.	☐ Male	☐ Female
Are you filing any other petitions or applications with this one?	☐ No	☐ Yes (How many? _____)
Is the person this petition is for in exclusion or deportation proceedings?	☐ No	☐ Yes (Explain on a separate sheet of paper)
Has the person this petition is for ever worked in the U.S. without permission?	☐ No	☐ Yes (Explain on a separate sheet of paper)
Is an application for adjustment of status attached to this petition?	☐ No	☐ Yes

Part 5. Complete only if filing for an Amerasian.

Section A. Information about the mother of the Amerasian

Family Name	Given Name	Middle Initial

Living? ☐ No (Give date of death _____) ☐ Yes (complete address line below) ☐ Unknown (attach a full explanation)

Address

Section B. Information about the father of the Amerasian: If possible, attach a notarized statement from the father regarding parentage. Explain on separate paper any question you cannot fully answer in the space provided on this form.

Family Name	Given Name	Middle Initial

Date of Birth (Month/Day/Year)	Country of Birth

Living? ☐ No (give date of death _____) ☐ Yes (complete address line below) ☐ Unknown (attach a full explanation)

Home Address

Home Phone #	Work Phone #

At the time the Amerasian was conceived:

☐ The father was in the military (indicate branch of service below - and give service number here): _____

    ☐ Army   ☐ Air Force   ☐ Navy   ☐ Marine Corps   ☐ Coast Guard

☐ The father was a civilian employed abroad. Attach a list of names and addresses of organizations which employed him at that time.

☐ If the father was not in the military, and was not a civilian employed abroad. (Attach a full explanation of the circumstances.)

Part 6. Complete only if filing for a Juvenile.

Section A. Information about the Juvenile

List any other names used.

Marital Status:	☐ Single	☐ Married	☐ Divorced	☐ Widowed

Answer the following questions regarding the person this petition is for. If you answer "no" explain on a separate sheet of paper.

Is he/she still a juvenile under the laws of the state in which the juvenile

court upon which the alien has been declared dependent is located?	☐ No	☐ Yes
Does he/she continue to be dependent upon the juvenile court?	☐ No	☐ Yes
Does he/she continue to be eligible for long term foster care?	☐ No	☐ Yes

Continued on next page.

Part 7. Complete only if filing for a Widow or Widower.

Section A. Information about the U.S. citizen husband or wife who died.

Family Name		Given Name	Middle Initial

Date of Birth (Month/Day/Year)	Country of Birth	Date of Death (Month/Day/Year)

His/her U.S. citizenship was based on (check one)

☐ Birth in the U.S.   ☐ Birth abroad to U.S. citizen parent(s)   ☐ Naturalization

Section B. Additional information about you.

How many times have you been married?	How many times was the person in Section A married?

Give the date and place you and the person in Section A were married.

Did you live with this U.S. citizen spouse from the date you were married until he/she died?
☐ Yes   ☐ No (attach explanation)

Were you legally separated at the time of the United States citizen's death?
☐ Yes (attach explanation)   ☐ No

Give your address at the time of the United States citizen's death.

Part 8. Information about the children and spouse of the person this petition is for.
For a widow or widower, include any children of your deceased spouse.

A.
Family Name	Given Name	Middle Initial	Date of Birth (Month/Day/Year)
Country of Birth	Relationship ☐ Spouse ☐ Child		A #

B.
Family Name	Given Name	Middle Initial	Date of Birth (Month/Day/Year)
Country of Birth	Relationship ☐ Spouse ☐ Child		A #

C.
Family Name	Given Name	Middle Initial	Date of Birth (Month/Day/Year)
Country of Birth	Relationship ☐ Spouse ☐ Child		A #

D.
Family Name	Given Name	Middle Initial	Date of Birth (Month/Day/Year)
Country of Birth	Relationship ☐ Spouse ☐ Child		A #

E.
Family Name	Given Name	Middle Initial	Date of Birth (Month/Day/Year)
Country of Birth	Relationship ☐ Spouse ☐ Child		A #

F.
Family Name	Given Name	Middle Initial	Date of Birth (Month/Day/Year)
Country of Birth	Relationship ☐ Spouse ☐ Child		A #

G.
Family Name	Given Name	Middle Initial	Date of Birth (Month/Day/Year)
Country of Birth	Relationship ☐ Spouse ☐ Child		A #

H.
Family Name	Given Name	Middle Initial	Date of Birth (Month/Day/Year)
Country of Birth	Relationship ☐ Spouse ☐ Child		A #

Continued on back.

Part 9. Signature.
Read the information on penalties in the instructions before completing this part. If you are going to file this petition at an INS office in the United States, sign below. If you are going to file it at a U.S. consulate or INS office overseas, sign in front of a U.S. INS or consular official.

I certify, or, if outside the United States, I swear or affirm, under penalty of perjury under the laws of the United States of America, that this petition, and the evidence submitted with it, is all true and correct. If filing this on behalf of an organization, I certify that I am empowered to do so by that organization. I authorize the release of any information from my records, or from the petitioning organization's records, which the Immigration and Naturalization Service needs to determine eligibility for the benefit being sought.

Signature	Date

Signature of INS or Consular Official	Print Name	Date

Please Note: If you do not completely fill out this form, or fail to submit required documents listed in the instructions, then the person(s) filed for may not be found eligible for a requested benefit, and it may have to be denied.

Part 10. Signature of person preparing form if other than above. (sign below)

I declare that I prepared this application at the request of the above person and it is based on all information of which I have knowledge.

Signature	Print Your Name	Date

Firm Name and Address

U.S. Department of Justice
Immigration and Naturalization Service

Form I-485
Application to Register Permanent Residence or Adjust Status
OMB No. 1115-0053

START HERE - Please Type or Print

FOR INS USE ONLY

Part 1. Information about you.

Family Name	Given Name	Middle Initial

Address - C/O

Street Number and Name	Apt. #

City

State	Zip Code

Date of Birth (month/day/year)	Country of Birth

Social Security #	A # (if any)

Date of Last Arrival (month/day/year)	I-94 #

Current INS Status	Expires on (month/day/year)

FOR INS USE ONLY

Returned
_____
_____

Receipt

Resubmitted
_____
_____

Reloc Sent
_____
_____

Reloc Rec'd
_____
_____

☐ Applicant Interviewed

Part 2. Application Type. *(check one)*

I am applying for adjustment to permanent resident status because:

a. ☐ an immigrant petition giving me an immediately available immigrant visa number has been approved (attach a copy of the approval notice), or a relative, special immigrant juvenile, or special immigrant military visa petition filed with this application will give me an immediately available visa number if approved.

b. ☐ My spouse or parent applied for adjustment of status or was granted lawful permanent residence in an immigrant visa category which allows derivative status for spouses and children.

c. ☐ I entered as a K-1 fiance(e) of a U.S. citizen whom I married within 90 days of entry, or I am the K-2 child of such a fiance(e) (attach a copy of the fiance(e) petition approval notice and the marriage certificate).

d. ☐ I was granted asylum or derivative asylum status as the spouse or child of a person granted asylum and am eligible for adjustment.

e. ☐ I am a native or citizen of Cuba admitted or paroled into the U.S. after January 1, 1959, and thereafter have been physically present in the U.S. for at least 1 year.

f. ☐ I am the husband, wife, or minor unmarried child of a Cuban described in (e) and am residing with that person, and was admitted or paroled into the U.S. after January 1, 1959, and thereafter have been physically present in the U.S. for at least 1 year.

g. ☐ I have continuously resided in the U.S. since before January 1, 1972.

h. ☐ Other-explain_____

I am already a permanent resident and am applying to have the date I was granted permanent residence adjusted to the date I originally arrived in the U.S. as a nonimmigrant or parolee, or as of May 2, 1964, whichever is later, and: *(Check one)*

i. ☐ I am a native or citizen of Cuba and meet the description in (e), above.

j. ☐ I am the husband, wife or minor unmarried child of a Cuban, and meet the description in (f), above.

Section of Law
Sec. 209(b), INA
Sec. 13, Act of 9/11/57
Sec. 245, INA
Sec. 249, INA
Sec. 1 Act of 11/2/66
Sec. 2 Act of 11/2/66
Other_____

Country Chargeable

Eligibility Under Sec. 245
Approved Visa Petition
Dependent of Principal Alien
Special Immigrant
Other_____

Preference

Action Block

To Be Completed by
***Attorney* or *Representative*, if any**
Fill in box if G-28 is attached to represent the applicant

VOLAG#

ATTY State License #

Continued on back.

Part 3. Processing Information.

A. City/Town/Village of birth	Current occupation
Your mother's first name	Your father's first name

Give your name exactly how it appears on your Arrival /Departure Record (Form I-94)

Place of last entry into the U.S. (City/State)	In what status did you last enter? *(Visitor, Student, exchange alien, crewman, temporary worker, without inspection, etc.)*
Were you inspected by a U.S. Immigration Officer? □ Yes □ No	
Nonimmigrant Visa Number	Consulate where Visa was issued

Date Visa was Issued (month/day/year)	Sex: □ Male □ Female	Marital Status: □ Married □ Single □ Divorced □ Widowed

Have you ever before applied for permanent resident status in the U.S?   □ No   □ Yes (give date and place of filing and final disposition):

B. List your present husband/wife, all of your sons and daughters (if you have none, write "none". If additional space is needed, use separate paper).

Family Name	Given Name	Middle Initial	Date of Birth (month/day/year)
Country of birth	Relationship	A #	Applying with you? □ Yes □ No
Family Name	Given Name	Middle Initial	Date of Birth (month/day/year)
Country of birth	Relationship	A #	Applying with you? □ Yes □ No
Family Name	Given Name	Middle Initial	Date of Birth (month/day/year)
Country of birth	Relationship	A #	Applying with you? □ Yes □ No
Family Name	Given Name	Middle Initial	Date of Birth (month/day/year)
Country of birth	Relationship	A #	Applying with you? □ Yes □ No
Family Name	Given Name	Middle Initial	Date of Birth (month/day/year)
Country of birth	Relationship	A #	Applying with you? □ Yes □ No

C. List your present and past membership in or affiliation with every political organization, association, fund, foundation, party, club, society, or similar group in the United States or in any other place since your 16th birthday. Include any foreign military service in this part. If none, write "none". Include the name of organization, location, dates of membership from and to, and the nature of the organization. If additional space is needed, use separate paper.

_____
_____
_____
_____
_____
_____
_____

Form I-485 (Rev. 09-09-92) N   Continued On Next Page

Part 4.   Signature.   *(Read the information on penalties in the instructions before completing this section.   You must file this application while in the United States.)*

I certify under penalty of perjury under the laws of the United States of America that this application, and the evidence submitted with it, is all true and correct. I authorize the release of any information from my records which the Immigration and Naturalization Service needs to determine eligibility for the benefit I am seeking.

Signature	Print Your Name	Date	Daytime Phone Number

Please Note: *If you do not completely fill out this form, or fail to submit required documents listed in the instructions, you may not be found eligible for the requested document and this application may be denied.*

Part 5.   Signature of person preparing form if other than above. *(Sign Below)*

I declare that I prepared this application at the request of the above person and it is based on all information of which I have knowledge.

Signature	Print Your Name	Date	Day time Phone Number

Firm Name
and Address

START HERE - Please Type or Print

Part 1.   Information about you.

Family Name	Given Name	Middle Initial

Address - In
Care of:

Street # and Name		Apt. #

City or town	State or Province

Country	Zip or Postal Code

Date of Birth (month/day/year)	Country of Birth

Social Security #	A#

If in the U.S.	Date of Arrival (month/day/year)	I-94#
	Current Nonimmigrant Status	Expires on (month/day/year)

Part 2.   Application Type (check one).

a. ☐ This petition is based on an investment in a commercial enterprise in a targeted employment area for which the required amount of capital invested has been adjusted downward.

b. ☐ This petition is based on an investment in a commercial enterprise in an area for which the required amount of capital invested has been adjusted upward.

b. ☐ This petition is based on an investment in a commercial enterprise which is not in either a targeted area or in an upward adjustment area.

Part 3.   Information about your Investment.

Name of Commercial
Enterprise Invested In

Street Address

Phone #	Business Organized as (Corporation, partnership, etc...)

Kind of Business
(Example: Furniture Manufacturer)

Date established (month/day/year)	IRS Tax #

Date of your initial Investment(month/day/year)	Amount of your Initial Investment $

Your total Capital Investment in Enterprise to date $	% of Enterprise you own

If you are not the sole investor in the new commercial enterprise, list on separate paper the names of all other parties (natural and non-natural) who hold a percentage share of ownership of the new enterprise and indicate whether any of these parties is seeking classifications as an alien entrepreneur. Include the name, percentage of ownership and whether or not the person is seeking classification under section 203(b)(5).

If you indicated in Part 2 that the enterprise was in a targeted employment area or in an upward adjustment area, give the location at right.

County   State

——————   ——————

Form I-526 (Rev. 12-2-91)   *Continued on back.*

FOR INS USE ONLY

Returned	Receipt

Resubmitted

Reloc Sent

Reloc Rec'd

☐ Applicant Interviewed

Action Block

To Be Completed by
Attorney or Representative, if any
☐ Fill in box if G-28 is attached to represent the applicant

VOLAG#

ATTY State License #

Part 4.   Additional Information about the enterprise.

Type of enterprise (check one):
- ☐ new commercial enterprise resulting from the creation of a new business
- ☐ new commercial enterprise resulting from the reorganization of an existing business.
- ☐ new commercial enterprise resulting from a captial investment in an existing business.

Assets:

Total amount in U.S. bank account		$ _____
Total value of all assets purchased for use in the enterprise		$ _____
Total value of all property transferred from abroad to the new enterprise		$ _____
Total of all debt financing		$ _____
Total stock purchases		$ _____
Other (explain on separate paper)		$ _____
Total		$ _____

Income:

When you made investment	Gross	$ _____	Net	$ _____
Now	Gross	$ _____	Net	$ _____

Net worth When you made investment $ _____   Now $ _____

Part 5.   Employment creation information.

# of full-time employees in Enterprise In U.S. (excluding you, spouse, sons & daughters)

When you made your initial investment _____   Now _____   Difference _____

How many of these new jobs were created by your investment? _____

How many additional new jobs will be created by your additional investment? _____

What is your position, office or title with the new commercial enterprise?
_____

Briefly describe your duties, activities and responsibilities.
_____
_____
_____

Your Salary _____   Cost of Benefits _____

Part 6.   Processing information.

Below give the U.S. Consulate you want notified if this petition is approved and if any requested adjustment of status cannot be granted.

American Consulate: City _____   Country _____

If you gave a U.S. address in Part 1, print your foreign address below. If your native alphabet does not use Roman letters, print your name and foreign address in the native alphabet.

Name _____   **Foreign Address** _____

Is an application for adjustment of status attached to this petition?	☐ yes		☐ no
Are you in exclusion or deportation proceedings?	☐ yes (If yes, explain on separate paper)		☐ no
Have you ever worked in the U.S. without permission?	☐ yes (explain on separate paper)		☐ no

Part 7.   Signature. *Read the information on penalties in the instructions before completing this section.*

I certify under penalty of perjury under the laws of the United States of America that this petition, and the evidence submitted with it, is all true and correct.   I authorize the release of any information from my records which the Immigration and Naturalization Service needs to determine eligibility for the benefit I am seeking.

Signature _____   **Date** _____

Please Note: If you do not completely fill out this form, or fail to submit required documents listed in the instructions, you may not be found eligible for the requested document and this application may be denied.

Part 8.   Signature of person preparing form if other than above. *(Sign below)*

I declare that I prepared this application at the request of the above person and it is based on all information of which I have knowledge.

Signature _____   Print Your Name _____   **Date** _____

Firm Name
and Address _____

Form I-526 (Rev. 12-2-91)

U.S. Department of Justice
Immigration and Naturalization Service

Form I-600A

OMB No. 1115-0049
Application for Advance Processing
of Orphan Petition [8CFR 204.1(b)(3)]

Please do not write in this block.

It has been determined that the
☐ Married   ☐ Unmarried
prospective petitioner will furnish proper care to a
beneficiary orphan if admitted to the United States.

There
☐ are   ☐ are not
preadoptive requirements in the state of the child's
proposed residence.

The following is a description of the preadoption requirements,
if any, of the state of the child's proposed residence:

The preadoption requirements, if any,
☐ have been met.   ☐ have not been met.

Fee Stamp

DATE OF FAVORABLE
DETERMINATION

DD

DISTRICT

File number of petitioner, if applicable

Please type or print legibly in ink.

Application is made by the named prospective petitioner for advance processing of an orphan petition.

BLOCK I - Information About Prospective Petitioner

1. My name is: (Last)   (First)   (Middle)

2. Other names used (including maiden name if appropriate):

3. I reside in the U.S. at: (C/O if appropriate)   (Apt. No.)

   (Number and street)   (Town or city)   (State)   (ZIP Code)

4. Address abroad (if any): (Number and street)   (Apt. No.)

   (Town or city)   (Province)   (Country)

5. I was born on: (Month)   (Day)   (Year)

   In: (Town or City)   (State or Province)   (Country)

6. My phone number is: (Include Area Code)

7. My marital status is:
   ☐ Married
   ☐ Widowed
   ☐ Divorced
   ☐ Single
       ☐ I have never been married.
       ☐ I have been previously married _____ time(s).

8. If you are now married, give the following information:

   Date and place of present marriage

   Name of present spouse (include maiden name of wife)

   Date of birth of spouse   Place of birth of spouse

   Number of prior marriages of spouse

   My spouse resides ☐ With me   ☐ Apart from me
                                       (provide address below)

   (Apt. No.) (No. and street) (City) (State) (Country)

9. I am a citizen of the United States through:
   ☐ Birth   ☐ Parents   ☐ Naturalization   ☐ Marriage
   If acquired through naturalization, give name under which naturalized,
   number of naturalization certificate, and date and place of naturalization:

   If not, submit evidence of citizenship. See Instruction 2.a(2).

   If acquired through parentage or marriage, have you obtained a
   certificate in your own name based on that acquisition?
   ☐ No   ☐ Yes

   Have you or any person through whom you claimed citizenship ever lost
   United States citizenship?
   ☐ No   ☐ Yes (If yes, attach detailed explanation.)

Continue on reverse.

Received	Trans. In	Ret'd Trans. Out	Completed

Form I-600A (Rev. 4/11/91) Y

234

BLOCK II - General Information

10. Name and address of organization or individual assisting you in locating or identifying an orphan

    (Name)

    _____

    (Address)

11. Do you plan to travel abroad to locate or adopt a child?

    ☐ Yes   ☐ No

12. Does your spouse, if any, plan to travel abroad to locate or adopt a child?

    ☐ Yes   ☐ No

13. If the answer to question 11 or 12 is "yes", give the following information:

    a. Your date of intended departure _____

    b. Your spouse's date of intended departure _____

    c. City, province _____

4.. Will the child come to the United States for adoption after compliance with the preadoption requirements, if any, of the state of proposed residence?

    ☐ Yes   ☐ No

15. If the answer to question 14 is "no", will the child be adopted abroad after having been personally seen and observed by you and your spouse, if married?

    ☐ Yes   ☐ No

16. Where do you wish to file your orphan petition?

    The service office located at

    _____

    The American Consulate or Embassy at _____

17. Do you plan to adopt more than one child?

    ☐ Yes   ☐ No

    If "Yes", how many children do you plan to adopt? _____

Certification of Prospective Petitioner

I certify under penalty of perjury under the laws of the United States of America that the foregoing is true and correct and that I will care for an orphan/orphans properly if admitted to the United States.

(Signature of Prospective Petitioner)

Executed on (Date)

Certification of Married Prospective Petitioner's Spouse

I certify under penalty of perjury under the laws of the United States of America that the foregoing is true and correct and that my spouse and I will care for an orphan/orphans properly if admitted to the United States.

(Signature of Prospective Petitioner)

Executed on (Date)

Signature of Person Preparing Form if Other Than Petitioner

I declare that this document was prepared by me at the request of the prospective petitioner and is based on all information of which I have any knowledge.

(Signature)

Address

Executed on (Date)

Form I-601

U.S. Department of Justice
Immigration and Naturalization Service

Application for Waiver of Ground of Excludability

OMB No. 1115-0048

DO NOT WRITE IN THIS BLOCK

☐ 212 (a) (1)   ☐ 212 (a) (10)   Fee Stamp
☐ 212 (a) (3)   ☐ 212 (a) (12)
☐ 212 (a) (6)   ☐ 212 (a) (19)
☐ 212 (a) (9)   ☐ 212 (a) (23)

A. Information about applicant -

1. Family Name (Surname in CAPS)   (First)   (Middle)

2. Address (Number and Street)   (Apartment Number)

3. (Town or City)   (State/Country)   (ZIP/Postal Code)

4. Date of Birth *(Month/Day/Year)*   5. I&N File Number
    A-

6. City of Birth   7. Country of Birth

8. Date of visa application   9. Visa applied for at:

10. Applicant was declared inadmissible to the United States for the following reasons: (List acts, convictions, or physical or mental conditions. If applicant has active or suspected tuberculosis, the reverse of this page must be fully completed.)

_____

_____

_____

_____

_____

11. Applicant was previously in the United States, as follows:
  City & State   From (Date)   To (Date)   I&NS Status

_____

_____

_____

_____

_____

_____

12. Social Security Number

_____

B. Information about relative, through whom applicant claims eligibility for a waiver -

1. Family Name (Surname in CAPS)   (First)   (Middle)

2. Address (Number and Street)   (Apartment Number)

3. (Town or City)   (State/Country)   (ZIP/Postal Code)

4. Relationship to applicant   5. I&NS Status

C. Information about applicant's other relatives in the U.S.
(List only U.S. citizens and permanent residents)

1. Family Name (Surname in CAPS)   (First)   (Middle)

2. Address (Number and Street)   (Apartment Number)

3. (Town or City)   (State/Country)   (ZIP/Postal Code)

4. Relationship to applicant   5. I&NS Status

1. Family Name (Surname in CAPS)   (First)   (Middle)

2. Address (Number and Street)   (Apartment Number)

3. (Town or City)   (State/Country)   (ZIP/Postal Code)

4. Relationship to applicant   5. I&NS Status

1. Family Name (Surname in CAPS)   (First)   (Middle)

2. Address (Number and Street)   (Apartment Number)

3. (Town or City)   (State/Country)   (ZIP/Postal Code)

4. Relationship to applicant   5. I&NS Status

Signature (of applicant or petitioning relative)

Relationship to applicant   *Date*

Signature (of person preparing application, if not the applicant or petitioning relative) I declare that this document was prepared by me at the request of the applicant, or petitioning relative, and is based on all information of which I have any knowledge.
Signature

Address   *Date*

		Relocated		Completed		
Initial receipt	**Resubmitted**	Received	Sent	Approved	Denied	Returned

Form I-601 (Rev. 04-11-91) Y
Page 1

To be completed for applicants with
active tuberculosis or suspected tuberculosis

A. Statement by Applicant

Upon admission to the United States I will:

1. Go directly to the physician or health facility named in Section B;

2. Present all X-rays used in the visa medical examination to substantiate diagnosis;

3. Submit to such examinations, treatment, isolation, and medical regimen as may be required; and

4. Remain under the prescribed treatment or observation whether on inpatient or outpatient basis, until discharged.

_____
Signature of Applicant

_____
Date

_____

B. Statement by Physician or Health Facility

(May be executed by a private physician, health department, other public or private health facility, or military hospital.)

I agree to supply any treatment or observation necessary for the proper management of the alien's tuberculous condition.

I agree to submit Form CDC 75.18 "Report on Alien with Tuberculosis Waiver" to the health officer named in Section D:

1. Within 30 days of the alien's reporting for care, indicating presumptive diagnosis, test results, and plans for future care of the alien; or

2. 30 days after receiving Form CDC 75.18 if the alien has not reported.

Satisfactory financial arrangements have been made. (This statement does not relieve the alien from submitting evidence, as required by consul, to establish that the alien is not likely to become a public charge.)

I represent (enter an "X" in the appropriate box and give the complete name and address of the facility below.)

☐ 1. Local Health Department
☐ 2. Other Public or Private Facility
☐ 3. Private Practice
☐ 4. Military Hospital

_____
Name of Facility (please type or print)

_____
Address (Number & Street)   (Apartment Number)

_____
City, State & ZIP Code

_____
Signature of Physician   Date

_____

C. Applicant's Sponsor in the U.S.

Arrange for medical care of the applicant and have the physician complete Section B.

If medical care will be provided by a physician who checked box 2 or 3, in Section B., have Section D. completed by the local or State Health Officer who has jurisdiction in the area where the applicant plans to reside in the U.S.

If medical care will be provided by a physician who checked box 4., in Section B., forward this form directly to the military facility at the address provided in Section B.

Address where the alien plans to reside in the U.S.

_____
Address (Number & Street)   (Apartment Number)

_____
City, State & ZIP Code

_____

D. Endorsement of Local or State Health Officer

Endorsement signifies recognition of the physician or facility for the purpose of providing care for tuberculosis. If the facility or physician who signed in Section B is not in your health jurisdiction and is not familiar to you, you may wish to contact the health officer responsible for the jurisdiction of the facility or physician prior to endorsing.

_____
Endorsed by: *Signature of Health Officer*

_____
Date

_____

Enter below the name and address of the Local Health Department to which the "Notice of Arrival of Alien with Tuberculosis Waiver" should be sent when the alien arrives in the U. S.

_____
Official Name of Department

_____
Address (Number & Street)   (Apartment Number)

_____
City, State & ZIP Code

_____

Please read instructions with care.

If further assistance is needed, contact the office of the Immigration and Naturalization Service with jurisdiction over the intended place of U.S. residence of the applicant.

OMB No. 1115-0145

U.S. Department of Justice
Immigration and Naturalization Service

Form I-751

Petition to Remove the Conditions on Residence

START HERE - Please Type or Print

	FOR INS USE ONLY	
Returned		Receipt

Part 1. Information about you.

Family Name	Given Name	Middle Initial

Address - C/O:

Street Number and Name		Apt. #
City	State or Province	
Country	ZIP/Postal Code	

Date of Birth (month/day/year)	Country of Birth
Social Security #	A #

Conditional residence expires on (month/day/year)

Mailing address if different from residence in C/O:

Street Number and Name		Apt #
City	State or Province	
Country	ZIP/Postal Code	

FOR INS USE ONLY

Returned _____

Resubmitted _____

Reloc Sent _____

Reloc Rec.,d _____

☐ Applicant Interviewed

Remarks

Action

Part 2. Basis for petition *(check one).*

a. ☐ My conditional residence is based on my marriage to a U.S. citizen or permanent resident, and we are filing this petition together.

b. ☐ I am a child who entered as a conditional permanent resident and I am unable to be included in a Joint Petition to Remove the Conditional Basis of Alien's Permanent Residence (Form I-751) filed by my parent(s).

My conditional residence is based on my marriage to a U.S. citizen or permanent resident, but I am unable to file a joint petition and I request a waiver because: (check one)

c. ☐ My spouse is deceased.

d. ☐ I entered into the marriage in good faith, but the marriage was terminated though divorce/annulment.

e. ☐ I am a conditional resident spouse who entered in to the marriage in good faith, or I am a conditional resident child, who has been battered or subjected to extreme mental cruelty by my citizen or permanent resident spouse or parent.

f. ☐ The termination of my status and deportation from the United States would result in an extreme hardship.

Part 3. Additional information about you.

Other names used *(including maiden name)*:	Telephone #
Date of Marriage	Place of Marriage

If your spouse is deceased, give the date of death (month/day/year)

Are you in deportation or exclusion proceedings?	☐ Yes ☐ No
Was a fee paid to anyone other than an attorney in connection with this petition?	☐ Yes ☐ No

To Be Completed by Attorney or Representative, if any

☐ Fill in box if G-28 is attached to represent the applicant

VOLAG#

ATTY State License #

Form I-751 (Rev. 12-4-91)   Continued on back.

238

Part 3. Additional Information about you. (con't)

Since becoming a conditional resident, have you ever been arrested, cited, charged, indicted, convicted, fined or imprisoned for breaking or violating any law or ordinace (excluding traffic regulations), or committed any crime for which you were not arrested? ☐ Yes ☐ No

If you are married, is this a different marriage than the one through which conditional residence status was obtained? ☐ Yes ☐ No

Have you resided at any other address since you became a permanent resident? ☐ Yes ☐ No *(If yes, attach a list of all addresses and dates.)*

Is your spouse currently serving employed by the U. S. government and serving outside the U.S.? ☐ Yes ☐ No

Part 4. Information about the spouse or parent through whom you gained your conditional residence

Family Name	Given Name	Middle Initial	Phone Number ( )

Address

Date of Birth *(month/day/year)*	Social Security #	A#

Part 5. Information about your children. *List all your children. Attach another sheet if necessary*

	Name	Date of Birth *(month/day/year)*	If in U.S., give A#, current immigration status and U.S. Address	Living with you?
1				☐ Yes ☐ No
2				☐ Yes ☐ No
3				☐ Yes ☐ No
4				☐ Yes ☐ No

Part 6. Complete if you are requesting a waiver of the joint filing petition requirement based on extreme mental cruelty.

Evaluator's ID Number: State: ☐☐ Number: ☐☐☐☐☐☐☐	Expires on *(month/day/year)*	Occupation

Last Name	First Name	Address

Part 7. Signature. *Read the information on penalties in the instructions before completing this section. If you checked block "a" in Part 2 your spouse must also sign below.*

I certify, under penalty of perjury under the laws of the United States of America, that this petition, and the evidence submitted with it, is all true and correct. If conditional residence was based on a marriage, I further certify that the marriage was entered into in accordance with the laws of the place where the marriage took place, and was not for the purpose of procuring an immigration benefit. I also authorize the release of any information from my records which the Immigration and Naturalization Service needs to determine eligibility for the benefit being sought.

Signature	Print Name	Date
Signature of Spouse	Print Name	Date

Please note: If you do not completely fill out this form, or fail to submit any required documents listed in the instructions, then you cannot be found eligible for the requested benefit, and this petition may be denied.

Part 8. Signature of person preparing form if other than above.

I declare that I prepared this petition at the request of the above person and it is based on all information of which I have knowledge.

Signature	Print Name	Date

Firm Name and Address

Form I-751 (Rev. 12-4-91)

U.S. Department of Justice
Immigration and Naturalization Service

Form I-829

239

OMB No. 1115-0190

Petition by Entrepreneur to Remove the Conditions

START HERE - Please Type or Print

Part 1. Information about you.

Family Name	Given Name	Middle Initial

Address - C/O:

Street Number and Name		Apt. #

City	State or Province

Country	ZIP/Postal Code

Date of Birth (Mo/Day/Yr)	Country of Birth

Social Security #	A #

Conditional residence expires on (Mo/Day/Yr)

Mailing address if different from residence in C/O:

Street Number and Name		Apt #

City	State or Province

Country	ZIP/Postal Code

Since becoming a conditional permanent resident, have you ever been arrested, cited, charged, indicted, convicted, fined or imprisoned for breaking or violating any law or ordinance (excluding traffic regulations), or committed any crime for which you were not arrested? ☐ Yes ☐ No

Part 2. Basis for petition. (Check one)

a. ☐ My conditional permanent residence is based on an investment in a commercial enterprise in a targeted employment area for which the required amount of capital invested has been adjusted downward.

b. ☐ My conditional permanent residence is based on an investment in a commercial enterprise in an area for which the required amount of capital invested has been adjusted upward.

c. ☐ My conditional permanent residence is based on an investment in a commercial enterprise which is not in either a targeted area or in an upward adjustment area.

d. ☐ I am a conditional permanent resident spouse or child of an entrepreneur, and I am unable to be included in a Petition by Entrepreneur to Remove Conditions (Form I-829) filed by my conditional resident spouse or parent.

e. ☐ I am a conditional permanent resident spouse or child of an entrepreneur who is deceased.

Part 3. Information about your spouse or children. (List all your children. Attach another sheet if necessary.)

Name	Date of Birth (Mo/Day/Yr)	If in U.S., give A#, current immigration status and U.S. Address

Part 4. Information about your commercial enterprise.

Name of commercial enterprise in which you have invested:

Street Address		City or Town

State	ZIP/Postal Code	Business Telephone #	IRS Tax #

Form I-829 (1-7-94)

Part 4.   Continued.

Type of Enterprise *(Check one)*:

☐   New commercial enterprise resulting from the creation of a new business.
☐   New commercial enterprise resulting from the reorganization of an existing business.
☐   New commercial enterprise resulting from a capital investment in an existing business.

Kind of Business *(Be as specific as possible.)*

Date Business Established (Mo/Day/Yr)	Amount of Initial Investment	Date of Initial Investment (Mo/Day/Yr)	% of Enterprise you Own

List number of full-time employees in enterprise in U.S. (excluding you, spouse, sons and daughters):

At the time of your initial investment _____   Presently _____   Difference _____

How many of these new jobs were created by your investment?   _____

Subsequent Investment in the Enterprise

Date of Investment	Amount of Investment	Type of Investment

Please provide the gross and net income generated annually by the commercial enterprise since your initial investment. Include all income generated up to date during the present year.

Year	Gross Income	Net Income

Has your commercial enterprise filed for bankruptcy, ceased business operations, or have any changes in its business organization or ownership occurred since the date of your initial investment?   ☐ Yes (Explain on separate sheet)   ☐ No

Has your commercial enterprise sold any corporate assets, shares, property, or had any capital withdrawn since the date of your initial investment?   ☐ Yes (Explain on separate sheet)   ☐ No

Part 5.   Signature. *(Read the information on penalties in the instructions before completing this section.)*

I certify, under penalty of perjury under the laws of the United States of America, that this petition and the evidence submitted with it, is all true and correct. I further certify that the investment was made in accordance with the laws of the United States and was not for the purpose of evading United States immigration laws. I also authorize the release of any information from my records which the Immigration and Naturalization Service needs to determine eligibility for the benefit being sought.

Signature of Applicant	Print Name	Date

Please note: If you do not completely fill out this form, or fail to submit any required documents listed in the instructions, you cannot be found eligible for the requested benefit, and this petition may be denied.

Part 6.   Signature of person preparing form if other than above.

I declare that I prepared this petition at the request of the above person and it is based on all information of which I have knowledge.

Signature	Print Name	Date

Firm Name and Address

Form I-829 (1-7-94)

Form I-864   Affidavit of Support Under Section 213A of the Act

241

OMB #1115-0214

START HERE - Please Type or Print

Part 1.   Information on Sponsor (You)

Last Name	First Name	Middle Name

Mailing Address *(Street Number and Name)* | Apt/Suite Number

City | State or Province

Country | ZIP/Postal Code | Telephone Number ( )

Place of Residence if different from above *(Street Number and Name)* | Apt/Suite Number

City | State or Province

Country | ZIP Postal Code | Telephone Number ( )

Date of Birth   *(Month, Day, Year)* | Place of Birth   *(City, State, Country)* | Are you a U.S. Citizen? ☐ Yes ☐ No

Social Security Number | A-Number *(If any)*

FOR AGENCY USE ONLY

This Affidavit | Receipt

[ ] Meets

[ ] Does not meet

Requirements of Section 213A

Part 2.   Basis for Filing Affidavit of Support

I am filing this affidavit of support because *(check one)*:

a. ☐ I filed/am filing the alien relative petition.

b. ☐ I filed/am filing an alien worker petition on behalf of the intending immigrant, who is related to me as my _____.
(relationship)

c. ☐ I have ownership interest of at least 5% of _____.
(name of entity which filed visa petition)
which filed an alien worker petition on behalf of the intending immigrant, who is related to me as my _____.
(relationship)

d. ☐ I am a joint sponsor willing to accept the legal obligations with any other sponsor(s).

Officer's Signature

Location

Date

Part 3.   Information on the Immigrant(s) You Are Sponsoring

Last Name	First Name	Middle Name

Date of Birth *(Month, Day, Year)* | Sex: ☐ Male ☐ Female | Social Security Number *(If any)*

Country of Citizenship | A-Number *(If any)*

Current Address   *(Street Number and Name)* | Apt/Suite Number | City

State/Province | Country | ZIP/Postal Code | Telephone Number ( )

List any spouse and or children immigrating with the immigrant named above in this Part: *(Use additional sheet of paper if necessary.)*

Name	Relationship to Sponsored Immigrant			Date of Birth			A-Number *(If any)*	Social Security Number *(If any)*
	Spouse	Son	Daughter	Mo.	Day	Yr.		

Part 4.   Eligibility to Sponsor

To be a sponsor you must be a U.S. citizen or national or a lawful permanent resident. If you are not the petitioning relative, you must provide proof of status. To prove status, U.S. citizens or nationals must attach a copy of a document proving status, such as a U.S. passport, birth certificate, or certificate of naturalization, and lawful permanent residents must attach a copy of both sides of their Alien Registration Card (Form I-551).

The determination of your eligibility to sponsor an immigrant will be based on an evaluation of your demonstrated ability to maintain an annual income at or above 125 percent of the Federal poverty line (100 percent if you are a petitioner sponsoring your spouse or child and you are on active duty in the U.S. Armed Forces). The assessment of your ability to maintain an adequate income will include your current employment, household size, and household income as shown on the Federal income tax returns for the 3 most recent tax years. Assets that are readily converted to cash and that can be made available for the support of sponsored immigrants if necessary, including any such assets of the immigrant(s) you are sponsoring, may also be considered.

The greatest weight in determining eligibility will be placed on current employment and household income. If a petitioner is unable to demonstrate ability to meet the stated income and asset requirements, a joint sponsor who *can* meet the income and asset requirements is needed. Failure to provide adequate evidence of income and or assets or an affidavit of support completed by a joint sponsor will result in denial of the immigrant's application for an immigrant visa or adjustment to permanent resident status.

A. Sponsor's Employment

I am: 1.   ☐ Employed by _____*(Provide evidence of employment)*

                  Annual salary $ _____ *or* hourly wage $ _____ *(for _____ hours per week)*

       2.   ☐ Self employed _____*(Name of business)*

                  Nature of employment or business _____

       3.   ☐ Unemployed or retired since _____

B. Use of Benefits

Have you or anyone related to you by birth, marriage, or adoption living in your household or listed as a dependent on your most recent income tax return received any type of means-tested public benefit in the past 3 years?

     ☐Yes   ☐   No *(If yes, provide details, including programs and dates, on a separate sheet of paper)*

C. Sponsor's Household Size   **Number**

1. Number of persons (related to you by birth, marriage, or adoption) living in your residence, including yourself. *(Do NOT include persons being sponsored in this affidavit.)*   _____
2. Number of immigrants being sponsored in this affidavit *(Include all persons in Part 3.)*   _____
3. Number of immigrants **NOT** living in your household whom you are still obligated to support under a previously signed affidavit of support using Form I-864.   _____
4. Number of persons who are otherwise dependent on you, as claimed in your tax return for the most recent tax year.   _____
5. Total household size. *(**Add lines 1 through 4.**)*   **Total** _____

List persons below who are included in lines 1 or 3 for whom you previously have submitted INS Form I-864, *if your support obligation has not terminated.*

(If additional space is needed, use additional paper)

Name	A-Number	Date Affidavit of Support Signed	Relationship

Part 4. Eligibility to Sponsor *(Continued)*

D. Sponsor's Annual Household Income

Enter total unadjusted income from your Federal income tax return for the most recent tax year below. If you last filed a joint income tax return but are using only your *own* income to qualify, list total earnings from your W-2 Forms, or, *if* necessary to reach the required income for your household size, include income from other sources listed on your tax return. If your *individual* income does not meet the income requirement for your household size, you may also list total income for anyone related to you by birth, marriage, or adoption currently living with you in your residence if they have lived in your residence for the previous 6 months, or any person shown as a dependent on your Federal income tax return for the most recent tax year, even if not living in the household. For their income to be considered, household members or dependents must be willing to make their income available for support of the sponsored immigrant(s) and to complete and sign Form I-864A, Contract Between Sponsor and Household Member. A sponsored immigrant/household member only need   complete Form I-864A if his or her income will be used to determine your ability to support a spouse and/or children immigrating with him or her.

You must attach evidence of current employment and copies of income tax returns as filed with the IRS for the most recent 3 tax years for yourself and all persons whose income is listed below. See "Required Evidence" in Instructions. Income from all 3 years will be considered in determining your ability to support the immigrant(s) you are sponsoring.

☐ I filed a single/separate tax return for the most recent tax year.
☐ I filed a joint return for the most recent tax year which includes only my own income.
☐ I filed a joint return for the most recent tax year which includes income for my spouse and myself.
    ☐ I am submitting documentation of my individual income (Forms W-2 and 1099).
    ☐ I am qualifying using my spouse's income; my spouse is submitting a Form I-864A.

Indicate most recent tax year   _____ *(tax year)*

Sponsor's individual income $_____

or

Sponsor and spouse's combined income $_____
(If joint tax return filed; spouse must submit Form I-864A.)

Income of other qualifying persons.
(List names; include spouse if applicable. Each person must complete Form I-864A.)

_____ $_____
_____ $_____
_____ $_____

Total Household Income $_____

Explain on separate sheet of paper if you or any of the above listed individuals are submitting Federal income tax returns for fewer than 3 years, or if other explanation of income, employment, or evidence is necessary.

E. Determination of Eligibility Based on Income

1. ☐ I am subject to the 125 percent of poverty line requirement for sponsors.
    ☐ I am subject to the 100 percent of poverty line requirement for sponsors on active duty in the U.S. Armed Forces sponsoring their spouse or child.
2. Sponsor's total household size, from Part 4.C., line 5 _____.
3. Minimum income requirement from the Poverty Guidelines chart for the year of _____ is $_____ for this household size. *(year)*

If you are currently employed and your household income for your household size is equal to or greater than the applicable poverty line requirement (from line E.3.), you do not need to list assets (Parts 4.F. and 5) or have a joint sponsor (Part 6) unless you are requested to do so by a Consular or Immigration Officer. You may skip to Part 7, Use of the Affidavit of Support to Overcome Public Charge Ground of Admissibility. Otherwise, you should continue with Part 4.F.

Part 4. Eligibility to Sponsor   *(Continued)*

F. Sponsor's Assets and Liabilities

Your assets and those of your qualifying household members and dependents may be used to demonstrate ability to maintain an income at or above 125 percent (or 100 percent, if applicable) of the poverty line *if* they are available for the support of the sponsored immigrant(s) and can readily be converted into cash within 1 year. The household member, other than the immigrant(s) you are sponsoring, must complete and sign Form I-864A, Contract Between Sponsor and Household Member. List the cash value of each asset *after* any debts or liens are subtracted. Supporting evidence must be attached to establish location, ownership, date of acquisition, and value of each asset listed, including any liens and liabilities related to each asset listed. See "Evidence of Assets" in Instructions.

Type of Asset	Cash Value of Assets *(Subtract any debts)*
Savings deposits	$
Stocks, bonds, certificates of deposit	$
Life insurance cash value	$
Real estate	$
Other *(specify)*	$
Total Cash Value of Assets	$_____

Part 5. Immigrant's Assets and Offsetting Liabilities

The sponsored immigrant's assets may also be used in support of your ability to maintain income at or above 125 percent of the poverty line *if* the assets are or will be available in the United States for the support of the sponsored immigrant(s) and can readily be converted into cash within 1 year.

The sponsored immigrant should provide information on his or her assets in a format similar to part 4.F. above. Supporting evidence must be attached to establish location, ownership, and value of each asset listed, including any liens and liabilities for each asset listed. See "Evidence of Assets" in Instructions.

Part 6. Joint Sponsors

If household income and assets do not meet the appropriate poverty line for your household size, a joint sponsor is required. There may be more than one joint sponsor, but each joint sponsor must individually meet the 125 percent of poverty line requirement based on his or her household income and/or assets, including any assets of the sponsored immigrant. By submitting a separate Affidavit of Support under Section 213A of the Act (Form I-864), a joint sponsor accepts joint responsibility with the petitioner for the sponsored immigrant(s) until they become U.S. citizens, can be credited with 40 quarters of work, leave the United States permanently, or die.

Part 7. Use of the Affidavit of Support to Overcome Public Charge Ground of Inadmissibility

Section 212(a)(4)(C) of the Immigration and Nationality Act provides that an alien seeking permanent residence as an immediate relative (including an orphan), as a family-sponsored immigrant, or as an alien who will accompany or follow to join another alien is considered to be likely to become a public charge and is inadmissible to the United States unless a sponsor submits a legally enforceable affidavit of support on behalf of the alien. Section 212(a)(4)(D) imposes the same requirement on an employment-based immigrant, and those aliens who accompany or follow to join the employment-based immigrant, if the employment-based immigrant will be employed by a relative, or by a firm in which a relative owns a significant interest. Separate affidavits of support are required for family members at the time they immigrate if they are not included on this affidavit of support or do not apply for an immigrant visa or adjustment of status within 6 months of the date this affidavit of support is originally signed. The sponsor must provide the sponsored immigrant(s) whatever support is necessary to maintain them at an income that is at least 125 percent of the Federal poverty guidelines.

I submit this affidavit of support in consideration of the sponsored immigrant(s) not being found inadmissible to the United States under section 212(a)(4)(C) (or 212(a)(4)(D) for an employment-based immigrant) and to enable the sponsored immigrant(s) to overcome this ground of inadmissibility. I agree to provide the sponsored immigrant(s) whatever support is necessary to maintain the sponsored immigrant(s) at an income that is at least 125 percent of the Federal poverty guidelines. I understand that my obligation will continue until my death or the sponsored immigrant(s) have become U.S. citizens, can be credited with 40 quarters of work, depart the United States permanently, or die.

Part 7.   Use of the Affidavit of Support to Overcome Public Charge Grounds   *(Continued)*

Notice of Change of Address.

Sponsors are required to provide written notice of any change of address within 30 days of the change in address until the sponsored immigrant(s) have become U.S. citizens, can be credited with 40 quarters of work, depart the United States permanently, or die. To comply with this requirement, the sponsor must complete INS Form I-865. Failure to give this notice may subject the sponsor to the civil penalty established under section 213A(d)(2) which ranges from $250 to $2,000, unless the failure to report occurred with the knowledge that the sponsored immigrant(s) had received means-tested public benefits, in which case the penalty ranges from $2,000 to $5,000.

> *If my address changes for any reason before my obligations under this affidavit of support terminate, I will complete and file INS Form I-865, Sponsor's Notice of Change of Address, within 30 days of the change of address. I understand that failure to give this notice may subject me to civil penalties.*

Means-tested Public Benefit Prohibitions and Exceptions.

Under section 403(a) of Public Law 104-193 (Welfare Reform Act), aliens lawfully admitted for permanent residence in the United States, with certain exceptions, are ineligible for most Federally-funded means-tested public benefits during their first 5 years in the United States. This provision does not apply to public benefits specified in section 403(c) of the Welfare Reform Act or to State public benefits, including emergency Medicaid; short-term, non-cash emergency relief; services provided under the National School Lunch and Child Nutrition Acts; immunizations and testing and treatment for communicable diseases; student assistance under the Higher Education Act and the Public Health Service Act; certain forms of foster-care or adoption assistance under the Social Security Act; Head Start programs; means-tested programs under the Elementary and Secondary Education Act; and Job Training Partnership Act programs.

Consideration of Sponsor's Income in Determining Eligibility for Benefits.

If a permanent resident alien is no longer statutorily barred from a Federally-funded means-tested public benefit program and applies for such a benefit, the income and resources of the sponsor and the sponsor's spouse will be considered (or deemed) to be the income and resources of the sponsored immigrant in determining the immigrant's eligibility for Federal means-tested public benefits. Any State or local government may also choose to consider (or deem) the income and resources of the sponsor and the sponsor's spouse to be the income and resources of the immigrant for the purposes of determining eligibility for their means-tested public benefits. The attribution of the income and resources of the sponsor and the sponsor's spouse to the immigrant will continue until the immigrant becomes a U.S. citizen or has worked or can be credited with 40 qualifying quarters of work, provided that the immigrant or the worker crediting the quarters to the immigrant has not received any Federal means-tested public benefit during any creditable quarter for any period after December 31, 1996.

> *I understand that, under section 213A of the Immigration and Nationality Act (the Act), as amended, this affidavit of support constitutes a contract between me and the U.S. Government. This contract is designed to protect the United States Government, and State and local government agencies or private entities that provide means-tested public benefits, from having to pay benefits to or on behalf of the sponsored immigrant(s), for as long as I am obligated to support them under this affidavit of support. I understand that the sponsored immigrants, or any Federal, State, local, or private entity that pays any means-tested benefit to or on behalf of the sponsored immigrant(s), are entitled to sue me if I fail to meet my obligations under this affidavit of support, as defined by section 213A and INS regulations.*

Civil Action to Enforce.

If the immigrant on whose behalf this affidavit of support is executed receives any Federal, State, or local means-tested public benefit before this obligation terminates, the Federal, State, or local agency or private entity may request reimbursement from the sponsor who signed this affidavit. If the sponsor fails to honor the request for reimbursement, the agency may sue the sponsor in any U.S. District Court or any State court with jurisdiction of civil actions for breach of contract. INS will provide names, addresses, and Social Security account numbers of sponsors to benefit-providing agencies for this purpose. Sponsors may also be liable for paying the costs of collection, including legal fees.

Part 7. Use of the Affidavit of Support to Overcome Public Charge Grounds *(Continued)*

I acknowledge that section 213A(a)(1)(B) of the Act grants the sponsored immigrant(s) and any Federal, State, local, or private agency that pays any means-tested public benefit to or on behalf of the sponsored immigrant(s) standing to sue me for failing to meet my obligations under this affidavit of support. I agree to submit to the personal jurisdiction of any court of the United States or of any State, territory, or possession of the United States if the court has subject matter jurisdiction of a civil lawsuit to enforce this affidavit of support. I agree that no lawsuit to enforce this affidavit of support shall be barred by any statute of limitations that might otherwise apply, so long as the plaintiff initiates the civil lawsuit no later than ten (10) years after the date on which a sponsored immigrant last received any means-tested public benefits.

Collection of Judgment.

I acknowledge that a plaintiff may seek specific performance of my support obligation. Furthermore, any money judgment against me based on this affidavit of support may be collected through the use of a judgment lien under 28 U.S.C. 3201, a writ of execution under 28 U.S.C. 3203, a judicial installment payment order under 28 U.S.C. 3204, garnishment under 28 U.S.C. 3205, or through the use of any corresponding remedy under State law. I may also be held liable for costs of collection, including attorney fees.

Concluding Provisions.

I, _____ , certify under penalty of perjury under the laws of the United States that:

    (a) *I know the contents of this affidavit of support signed by me;*
    (b) *All the statements in this affidavit of support are true and correct;*
    (c) *I make this affidavit of support for the consideration stated in Part 7, freely, and without any mental reservation or purpose of evasion;*
    (d) *Income tax returns submitted in support of this affidavit are true copies of the returns filed with the Internal Revenue Service; and*
    (e) *Any other evidence submitted is true and correct.*

_____   _____
(Sponsor's Signature)   *(Date)*

Subscribed and sworn to *(or affirmed)* before me this

_____ day of _____ , _____
           (Month)   *(Year)*

at _____ .

My commission expires on _____ .

_____
(Signature of Notary Public or Officer Administering Oath)

_____
(Title)

Part 8. If someone other than the sponsor prepared this affidavit of support, that person must complete the following:

I certify under penalty of perjury under the laws of the United States that I prepared this affidavit of support at the sponsor's request, and that this affidavit of support is based on all information of which I have knowledge.

Signature	Print Your Name	Date	Daytime Telephone Number ( )

Firm Name and Address

U.S. Department of Justice
Immigration and Naturalization Service

OMB #1115-0214
Attachment to Affidavit of Support

1997 Poverty Guidelines*
Minimum Income Requirement For Use in Completing Form I-864

For the 48 Contiguous States, the District of Columbia, Puerto Rico, the U.S. Virgin Islands, and Guam:

Sponsor's Household Size	100% of Poverty Line For sponsors on active duty in the U.S. Armed Forces who are petitioning for their spouse or child	125% of Poverty Line For all other sponsors
2	$10,610	$13,262
3	13,330	16,662
4	16,050	20,062
5	18,770	23,462
6	21,490	26,862
	Add $2,720 for each additional person.	Add $3,400 for each additional person.

Sponsor's Household Size	For Alaska		For Hawaii	
	100% of Poverty Line For sponsors on active duty in the U.S. Armed Forces who are petitioning for their spouse or child	125% of Poverty Line For all other sponsors	100% of Poverty Line For sponsors on active duty in the U.S. Armed Forces who are petitioning for their spouse or child	125% of Poverty Line For all other sponsors
2	$13,270	$16,587	$12,200	$15,250
3	16,670	20,837	15,330	19,162
4	20,070	25,087	18,460	23,075
5	23,470	29,337	21,590	26,987
6	26,870	33,587	24,720	30,900
	Add $3,400 for each additional person.	Add $4,250 for each additional person.	Add $3,130 for each additional person.	Add $3,912 for each additional person.

Means-tested Public Benefits

Federal Means-tested Public Benefits. To date, Federal agencies administering benefit programs have determined that Federal means-tested public benefits include, but are not limited to, Food Stamps, Medicaid, Supplemental Security Income (SSI), and Temporary Assistance for Needy Families (TANF).

State Means-tested Public Benefits. Each State will determine which, if any, of its public benefits are means-tested. If a State determines that it has programs which meet this definition, it is encouraged to provide notice to the public on which programs are included. Check with the State public assistance office to determine which, if any, State assistance programs have been determined to be State means-tested public benefits.

Programs Not Included: The following Federal and State programs are *not* included as means-tested benefits: emergency Medicaid; short-term, non-cash emergency relief; services provided under the National School Lunch and Child Nutrition Acts; immunizations and testing and treatment for communicable diseases; student assistance under the Higher Education Act and the Public Health Service Act; certain forms of foster-care or adoption assistance under the Social Security Act; Head Start programs; means-tested programs under the Elementary and Secondary Education Act; and Job Training Partnership Act programs.

*Published March 10, 1997

Form 9003

Form **9003** (January 1992)	Department of the Treasury—Internal Revenue Service **Additional Questions to be Completed by All Applicants for Permanent Residence in the United States**	OMB Clearance No. 1545-1065 Expires 8-31-94

This form must accompany your application for permanent residence in the United States

Privacy Act Notice: Your responses to the following questions will be provided to the Internal Revenue Service pursuant to Section 6039E of the Internal Revenue Code of 1986. Use of this information is limited to that needed for tax administration purposes. Failure to provide this information may result in a $500 penalty unless failure is due to reasonable cause.

On the date of issuance of the Alien Registration Receipt Card, the Immigration and Naturalization Service will send the following information to the Internal Revenue Service: your name, social security number, address, date of birth, alien identification number, occupation, class of admission, and answers to IRS Form 9003.

Name *(Last—Surname—Family)*   *(First—Given)*   *(Middle Initial)*

Taxpayer Identification Number . . . .

Enter your Social Security Number (SSN) if you have one. If you do not have an SSN but have used a Taxpayer Identification Number issued to you by the Internal Revenue Service, enter that number. Otherwise, write "NONE" in the space provided; i.e., "⌐ ⌐ ⌐ ⌐ N,O,N,E,".

	Mark appropriate column	
	Yes	**No**
1. Are you self-employed? Mark "yes" if you own and actively operate a business in which you share in the profits other than as an investor.		
2. Have you been in the United States for 183 days or more during any one of the three calendar years immediately preceding the current calendar year? Mark "yes" if you spent 183 days or more (not necessarily consecutive) in the United States during any one of the three prior calendar years whether or not you worked in the United States.		
3. During the last three years did you receive income from sources in the United States? Mark "yes" if you received income paid by individuals or institutions located in the United States. Income includes, but is not limited to, compensation for services provided by you, interest, dividends, rents, and royalties.		
4. Did you file a United States Individual Income Tax Return (Forms 1040, 1040A, 1040EZ or 1040NR) in any of the last three years?		

If you answered yes to question 4, for which tax year was the last return filed? . . . . 19 __ __

Paperwork Reduction Act Notice—We ask for the information on this form to carry out the Internal Revenue laws of the United States. You are required to give us the information. We need it to ensure that you are complying with these laws and to allow us to figure and collect the right amount of tax.

The time needed to complete and file this form will vary depending on individual circumstances. The estimated average time is 5 minutes.

If you have comments concerning the accuracy of this time estimate or suggestions for making this form more simple, we would be happy to hear from you. You can write to both the **Internal Revenue Service**, Washington, DC 20224. Attention: IRS Reports Clearance Officer, **T:FP**, and **Office of Management and Budget.** Paperwork Reduction Project (1545-1065) Washington, DC 20503. **DO NOT send this form to either of these offices. Instead, return it to the appropriate office of the Department of State or the Immigration and Naturalization Service.**

Remarks

Cat. No. 10126D

Form **9003** (Rev. 1-92)

Appendix

LIST OF OTHER PUBLICATIONS FROM DO-IT-YOURSELF LEGAL PUBLISHERS

Please **DO NOT** tear out this page. Consider others!

The following is a list of books obtainable from the Do-It-Yourself Publishers/Selfhelper Law Press of America.

(Customers: For your convenience, just make a photocopy of this page and send it along with your order. All prices quoted here are subject to change without notice.)

1. How To Draw Up Your Own Friendly Separation/Property Settlement Agreement With Your Spouse
2. Tenant Smart: How To Win Your Tenants' Legal Rights Without A Lawyer (New York Edition)
3. How To Probate & Settle An Estate Yourself Without The Lawyers' Fees ($35)
4. How To Adopt A Child Without A Lawyer
5. How To Form Your Own Profit/Non-Profit Corporation Without A Lawyer
6. How To Plan Your 'Total' Estate With A Will & Living Will, Without a Lawyer
7. How To Declare Your Personal Bankruptcy Without A Lawyer ($29)
8. How To Buy Or Sell Your Own Home Without A Lawyer or Broker ($29)
9. How To File For Chapter 11 Business Bankruptcy Without A Lawyer ($29)
10. How To Legally Beat The Traffic Ticket Without A Lawyer (forthcoming)
11. How To Settle Your Own Auto Accident Claims Without A Lawyer ($29)
12. How To Obtain Your U.S. Immigration Visa Without A Lawyer ($29) Volume 1 or 2
13. How To Do Your Own Divorce Without A Lawyer [10 Regional State-Specific Volumes] ($35)
14. How To Legally Change Your Name Without A Lawyer
15. How To Properly Plan Your 'Total' Estate With A Living Trust, Without The Lawyers' Fees ($35)
16. Legally Protect Yourself In A Gay/Lesbian Or Non-Marital Relationship With A Cohabitation Agreement
17. Before You Say 'I do' In Marriage Or Co-Habitation, Here's How To First Protect Yourself Legally
18. The National Home Mortgage reduction Kit (forthcoming) ($26.95)
19. The National Home Mortgage **Qualification** Kit ($28.95)

Prices: Each book, except for those specifically priced otherwise, costs $26, plus $4.00 per book for postage and handling. New Jersey residents please add 6% sales tax. **ALL PRICES ARE SUBJECT TO CHANGE WITHOUT NOTICE**

CUSTOMERS: Please make and send a zerox copy of this page with your orders)

ORDER FORM

TO: **Do-it-Yourself Legal Publishers**
60 Park Place # Suite **1013,** Newark, NJ 07102

Please send me the following:
1. _____ copies of _____
2. _____ copies of _____
3. _____ copies of _____
4. _____ copies of _____

Enclosed is the sum of $_____ to cover the order. *Mail my order to:*
Mr./Mrs.//Ms/Dr. _____
Address (include Zip Code please): _____
_____
Phone No. and area code: ( ) _____ Job: ( ) _____
*New Jersey residents enclose 6% sales tax.

IMPORTANT: Please do NOT rip out the page. Consider others! Just make a photocopy and send it.

INDEX